Blood-Dark Track

Also by Joseph O'Neill

The Breezes
This is the Life

Blood-Dark Track

A Family History

JOSEPH O'NEILL

Granta Books
London

Granta Publications, 2/3 Hanover Yard, London N1 8BE

First published in Great Britain by Granta Books 2000

A CIP catalogue record for this book
is available from the British Library.

3 5 7 9 10 8 6 4 2

ISBN 1 86207 288 4

Typeset by M Rules
Printed and bound in Great Britain by
Mackays of Chatham plc

Some day we shall get up before the dawn
And find our ancient hounds before the door,
And wide awake know that the hunt is on;
Stumbling upon the blood-dark track once more,
That stumbling to the kill beside the shore

      – W. B. Yeats, 'Hound Voice'

To the memory of Joseph Dakad (1899–1964) and James O'Neill (1909–1973); to my sons; and to Sally.

Acknowledgements

This book is largely the product of help I have received from my family, Turkish and Irish. As regards the latter, I am grateful, first and foremost, to my grandmother, Eileen O'Neill, who freely lent herself to a project that, by its nature, was troubling to her. I owe a similar debt of gratitude to Jim O'Neill, Terry O'Neill, Ann Pollock-O'Neill and Marian O'Sullivan-O'Neill, who shared thoughtful and sensitive insights into the character and life of my Irish grandfather, Jim O'Neill. My greatest debt, here, is to Brendan O'Neill. His generosity of spirit and willingness to reflect openly on sensitive historical issues made a huge contribution to this book. I also wish to thank, in relation to the Irish story, Acushla Bastible, Pat Buckley, Con and Orelia Conner, Dan Daly, Antony Farrell, Mick Fitzgibbon, Derry and Phyllis Kelleher, Paddy Lynch, Peig Lynch, Frank and Mary Morris, Barney McFadden, Angela McEvoy-O'Neill, Shammy O'Connell, Pat O'Neill, Seán O'Neill, Mary O'Sullivan, Billy Pollock, Mrs Salter-Townshend, Brendan Sealy, Christopher Somerville. John Bowyer Bell was an essential source of information about the shooting of Admiral Somerville and pre-Emergency republicanism generally. My heavy reliance on the work of Peter Hart and Uinseann MacEoin will be evident to readers.

Amy Dakad's translation of Joseph Dakad's testimony is the foundation of my inquiry into my Turkish grandfather's life, and I am enormously appreciative of her work. I am deeply grateful for the scholarship and friendly help of Sir Denis Wright, whose influence on this book has been vital. I also wish to thank, in relation to the Turkish story, Florent Arnaud, Henri Atat, Salvator Avigdor, Sara Bershtel, Oliver Dacade, Pierre Dakad, Giselle Daniel, Ugur Ersoy, Ginette Estève, Patrick Grigsby, Professor O.R. Gurney, Brother Guy of Latrun, the late Bill Henderson, Haidar Husseini, the Kurdish Human Rights Project, René Messageot, Paula and Yuki Nader, Tim Ottey, Georges Özgen, Denis Ryan, Rachel and Semir Salman, Tom Segev, Astrid Seime, Yitzhak Shamir, Fonda Tahintzi, Phédon Tahintzi, Philippe Tahintzi, Yves-Marie Villedieu, Lolo Zahlout. I wish to acknowledge the contribution of my late great-aunts, Alexandra and Isabelle Nader, and grandmother, Georgette Dakad.

A variety of institutions enabled my research, in particular the Middle East Centre at St Antony's College, Oxford; the New York Public Library; the British Library. While I wrote the book, my unlucrative presence was tolerated by the staff and proprietors of La Bergamote (thank you, Romain Lamaze); the Malibu Diner; and the Riss Restaurant. Bob and Nan Stewart were wonderfully hospitable to me in Ontario, Canada.

The following helped me in various ways: Tom Astor, Pete Ayrton, Matthew Batstone, David Bieda, Daniel Bobker, Susie Boyt, Will Buckley, Philippe Carré, Moniqe el-Faizy, Jean Fermin, Vanessa Friedman, Michael Gorchov, Adam Green, Philip Horne, Philip Hughes, Nico Israel, Damian Lanigan, Darian Leader, Simon Page, Oliver Phillips, Michael Rips, Colin Robinson, Leon Singer and family, Grub Smith, David Stewart, Arnold Weinstein, Jos Williams. Ann, David and Elizabeth O'Neill have been a great help to me, and I am deeply indebted to the chambers of Mark Strachan Q.C. for its good-humoured assent to my lengthy sabbaticals. I wish to thank Neil Belton for his important editorial contribution, and Gill Coleridge for her steadfast encouragement and guidance over many years. My parents, Kevin O'Neill and Caroline O'Neill-Dakad, have, more than ever, been a vital source of encouragement, inspiration and advice; and so, too, my wife, Sally Singer. This book was her idea.

The author and publisher thank the following: A. P. Watt Ltd and Michael B. Yeats for permission to quote from *Hound Voice* by W. B. Yeats, from the *Collected Poems* of W. B. Yeats published by Scribner Paperback Poetry, 1996; Anvil Books, Dublin for permission to quote from *Guerrilla Days in Ireland* by Tom Barry; Harcourt Brace & Company for permission to quote from their English translation of *Invisible Cities* by Italo Calvino © 1974 by Harcourt Brace & Company; Verso Ltd for permission to quote from their English translation of *Minima Moralia* by Theodor Adorno © NLB, 1974; Penguin UK for permission to quote from *The Rebel* by Albert Camus, translated by Anthony Bower (first published as *L'Homme Révolté*, 1951, Hamish Hamilton, 1953). Translation copyright © 1953 by Anthony Bower; S. Fischer Verlag, Frankfurt am Main for permission to quote from Thomas Mann's 'Letter to the Dean of the Philosophical Faculty of the University of Bonn, 1937'; Syracuse University Press for permission to quote from their 1997 edition of *An Only Child* by Frank O'Connor; Penguin UK to quote from *Essays and Aphorisms* by Arthur Schopenhauer, translated by R. J. Hollingdale (Penguin Classics, 1970). Translation copyright © R. J. Hollingdale, 1970; Christopher Somerville for permission to quote from an appendix of *Will Mariner* by Admiral Boyle Somerville, published and edited posthumously by Edith Somerville; Penguin UK for permission to quote from *The House of the Dead* by Fyodor Dostoevsky, translated by David McDuff (Penguin Classics, 1985). Translation copyright © David McDuff, 1985.

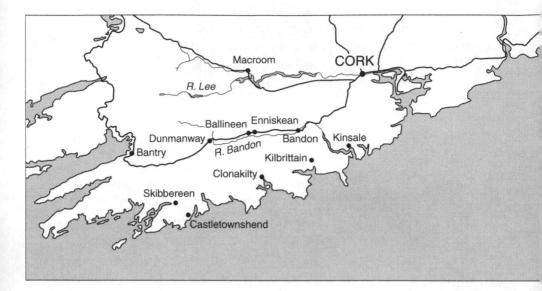

West Cork

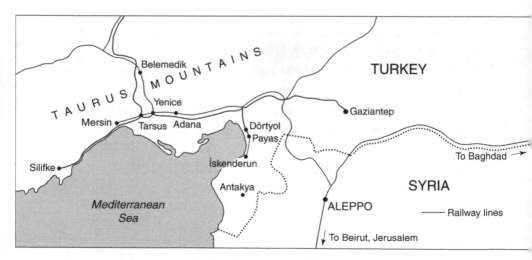

Turkey/Syrian border, Spring 1942

Prologue

For me it began in far-off Mesopotamia now called Iraq, that land of Biblical names and history, of vast deserts and date groves, scorching suns and hot winds, the land of Babylon, Baghdad and the Garden of Eden, where the rushing Euphrates and the mighty Tigris converge and flow down into the Persian Gulf.

It was there in that land of the Arabs, then a battle-ground for the contending Imperialistic armies of Britain and Turkey, that I awoke to the echoes of guns being fired in the capital of my own country, Ireland.

— Tom Barry, *Guerrilla Days in Ireland*

At some point in my childhood, perhaps when I was aged ten, or eleven, I became aware that during the Second World War my Turkish grandfather – my mother's father, Joseph Dakad – had been imprisoned by the British in Palestine, a place exotically absent from any atlas. A shiver of an explanation accompanied this information: the detention had something to do with spying for the Germans. At around the same age, I also learned that my Irish grandfather, James O'Neill, had been jailed by the authorities in Ireland in the course of the same war. Nobody explained precisely why, or where, or for how long, and I attributed his incarceration to the circumstances of a bygone Ireland and a bygone IRA. These matters went largely unmentioned, and certainly undiscussed, by my parents in the two decades that followed. Indeed, the subject of my late grandfathers was barely raised at all and, save for a wedding-day picture of Joseph and his wife, Georgette, there were no photographs of them displayed in our home. Dwelling in the jurisdiction of parental silence, my grandfathers remained mute and out of mind.

Partially as a consequence of this, it was not until I was thirty that the curious parallelism in my grandfathers' lives struck me with any force and that I was driven to explore it, to fiddle at doors that had remained unopened, perhaps even locked, for so many years; and not until then that I began to make out what connected these two men, who never met, and these two captivities – one in the Levant heat, the other in the rainy, sporadically incandescent plains of central Ireland.

As will soon become apparent, I wasn't bringing a reflective political mind to bear on my grandfathers' lives, or any expertise as a historian, or even any abnormal inclination to wonder about what might lie behind a closed door. In general, I'm as content as the next man to proceed on the footing that any information of importance – anything that has a bearing on my essential interests – will be brought to my attention by those entrusted with such things: families, schools, news agencies, subversives. This is so even though the information I have on most historical and political subjects could be written out on a luggage tag; is almost certainly wrong; and, at bottom, probably functions as a political soporific – which perhaps explains why the insights I gained into my grandfathers' lives often took the form of a slow, idiotic awakening. It took anomalous forces – a writer's professional curiosity turned into something like an obsession – to push me, reluctant and red-eyed and stumbling, into the past and, it turned out, its dream-bright horrors.

Two inklings set me on my way, one for each grandfather.

My Turkish grandmother, Mamie Dakad – *mamie* being French for granny – had an extreme attachment to a set of keys. She clung to them from morning till night and then, secreting them under her pillow, from night till morning. When she mislaid them, all hell broke loose, in multiple languages. She would shriek first at herself in Arabic ('*Yiii!*'), next at her family, in French ('*Où sont mes clefs?*'), and finally – with terrifying loudness and venom – at the nearest servant, in Turkish: '*ANAHTARLAR NERDE?*' The loss of keys was not the only thing that would set her off. My grandmother yelled frequently and for a whole variety of reasons at the waiters, maids, managers, cleaners and cooks whom she employed to staff her hotel and to attend to her personal needs and the needs of her family. All day they scurried in and out of her apartment in a sweat, delivering panniers of toast, bars of goat's cheese, lamb cutlets, fish, aubergines, meat pancakes, melons, watermelons, water, glasses of lemonade, bottles of Efes beer, sodas, Coca-Colas, Turkish coffees, Turkish teas. You could never have enough to drink. Mersin, the port in south-east Turkey where my grandmother lived, is as humid a spot as you'll find in the Mediterranean, and in August, when my parents and their four children arrived for their annual holiday, my grandmother's breezeless apartment on the top floor of the hotel was as hot as a hammam. Fans vainly circulated warm air, and the trickle of coolness produced by the grinding air-conditioning machine escaped ineffectually through the windows towards the harbour, where Turkish warships sat on the still water like cakes on a salver. When we were not immobilized on the divans, pooped out, stunned, minimizing our movements, we were opening one of the refrigerators – the doors, tall as ourselves, swung out with a gasping, rubbery suck – and taking long, burning slugs of the freezing water that filled the Johnnie Walker and Glenfiddich bottles jammed in the rack. My grandmother's outbursts were all the more terrible for their suddenness and unfairness, the minor domestic booboos, if any, from which they sprang (a fork misplaced in a drawer filled with Christofle silver, a floor-mopping delinquency) shockingly disproportionate to the condemnation that followed. I have never really understood why she was prone to these authoritarian rages. She was loving and unstinting with her friends and family and, it so happens, a loyal

employer. Perhaps the heat played a part, and racial and class con-
tempt. Either way, Mehmet Ali, Mehmet, Huseyin, Fatma and the
rest of them got it in the neck.

As I said, Mamie Dakad carried a bunch of keys about her
person at all times. She never jingled them or fixed them to a pretty
ring. She strung them around a bare loop of metal and gripped
them – even in her old age, when arthritis had curled her fists into
strengthless talons.

One morning, in a summer of the late 'eighties, when I was in my
mid-twenties, there occurred an episode which might have belonged
to a kids' mystery story. My cousin Phaedon (the son of my
mother's sister, Amy) and I decided to take a look around a storage
room in the hotel known as the depot. We knew that family stuff
was kept there and we were curious. So we asked our grandmother
for the key to the depot.

'Why?' she asked. She was getting her hair cut as she sat in the
hot dining room, a white towel over her shoulders, a spectacular
length of ash hanging crookedly from a butt in her mouth. Even
though she was nearing the end of her career as a smoker (forty
years of seeing off at least forty, preferably extra-strong Pall Mall,
non-filters a day), she was still able to suck back an entire cigarette
without touching it with her fingers.

I explained why. Mamie Dakad looked at me sceptically, then
wordlessly pointed at her keys, which lay on a nearby table. I
brought them to her. She plucked out a skeleton key. 'Bring it back,'
she said.

We walked down the long corridor outside Mamie Dakad's
apartment. Ashtrays filled with sand were fixed to the walls, and
dead, half-buried cigarettes protruded from the sand. The depot
was half way down the corridor, next to the staircase that led to the
roof of the hotel. From that scorching roof you saw, heaped on the
northern horizon, the cool Taurus Mountains, whose name, spelled
in phonetic Turkish, my grandfather Joseph gave to the hotel: the
Toros Otel.

The depot was a stale, hot space overlooking the hotel's oven-like
internal yard. We found neat piles of sea-stained old paperbacks

from the 'seventies; snorkels; junior-sized flippers; my mother's schoolbooks and school reports. Then I noticed, on top of a trunk, some papers held together by a large, rusting safety-pin – sixty or so pages extracted from a ledger book, with columns for debits and credits and totting up. But if this was an accounting, it wasn't of the financial kind. In place of figures, lines of elegant manuscript Turkish filled the pages.

Phaedon took a look while I peered over his shoulder. After a minute or so, he said that the writing had to be our grandfather's. It was an account, Phaedon said slowly, of his arrest, in 1942, and his subsequent imprisonment. We looked at each other. We knew we were entering, maybe trespassing on, a dark corner of the family history. Then we read on. Flicking quickly through the pages, Phaedon reported the main features of the story as best as he could; he had difficulty in understanding the old-fashioned, Arab-influenced Turkish.

What Phaedon said was this: in March 1942, my grandfather went to Palestine on a business trip. He spent some time in Jerusalem, where he associated with Palestinian Arabs and a female acquaintance. On his way home, he was arrested at the Turkish–Syrian border by the British. He was taken to Haifa and then to the British headquarters in Jerusalem, and then detained elsewhere for the rest of the war. Phaedon couldn't figure out what the exact nature of the document was. 'It seems to be addressed to the Turkish authorities,' he said with a shrug.

By the time we returned to Mamie Dakad's apartment, the hairdresser was clearing up and my mother was laying the table for lunch for twelve: chicken, stuffed peppers, tabbouleh, cucumber and watercress salad with a lemon dressing, beans, lentils with rice, yoghurt, bread. A rubble of watermelons, grapes and peaches was piled up in the kitchen. For my grandmother and the community she belonged to, nothing, not even cards, was of greater social importance than food.

When I broke the news of our scoop to my mother, she reacted in a curious way; that is, apart from a raising of her eyebrows, she did not react. Almost as if she hadn't heard me, she continued to set out

the forks and knives. Unabashed and excited, I turned to my grandmother and asked about the document. 'Don't speak about it,' my
mother said sharply to me in English, which was not one of Mamie
Dakad's languages, 'it'll upset her.' It was too late. My grandmother
was already in tears. '*Le pauvre,*' she said, her face wrinkling and her
hand raised in a distressed gesture of explanation, '*le pauvre, il a
beaucoup souffert.*'

'You see?' my mother said. 'You see what you've done?'

I returned the key to Mamie Dakad. Joseph Dakad's papers were
locked away once more, not to be seen again until years later.

My first moment of access to the life of my Irish grandfather,
Jim O'Neill – and my first clue as to what may have formed his
life's hard, insubstantial heart – was also fortuitous. It took place
in The Hague, the city where, in 1970, after series of migrations
that had bounced us like a skipping roulette ball through South
Africa, Mozambique, Syria, Turkey and Iran, my family came to
a permanent halt. In the top shelf of the bookcase in the dining
room was a hardback entitled *Letters of Fyodor Dostoevsky*.
Although as a teenager I'd read most of my parents' books, I'd
never been enthused by this one. It had an uncompromising black
cover and an unappetising introduction by one Avrahm
Yarmalinsky, and Dostoevsky himself, the balding, anxious man in
the jacket photograph, whose writing I had not read, did not look
like a lot of fun. The Hague, however, is an uneventful place, and
eventually I found myself idly leafing through the *Letters*; and I
encountered, trapped in the book's thick pages, two newspaper
clips.

The first read as follows:

O'NEILL (Cork and Ardkitt, Enniskean) – On September 6,
1973, at the South Infirmary, James, beloved husband of
Eileen (née Lynch), Dún Ard, Southlodge, Browningstown
Park (1st. Batt., First Cork Brigade, I.R.A.). Deeply
regretted by his loving wife and family. Funeral on today
(Saturday) after 2.30 o'clock Mass at our Lady of Lourdes
Church, Ballinlough, to St Michael's Cemetery, Blackrock.

The second cutting was an article headed *Around the G.A.A. Clubs.*

St Vincents. It was with the deepest regret that we learned of the passing away of our esteemed member, Mr. Jim O'Neill, during the past week. Beannacht De ar a anam.

For many years Jim had been a staunch worker in our club. He held many positions over the years, but for him no job was too big or menial where St. Vincents was concerned. He was behind much of our early plan making, nevertheless when those plans dictated the arduous work it took to fulfil them, Jim was oft times only too willing to undertake that work. Over a period of 22 years in which I knew him, he proved to be a true Gael. Ever mindful of our beautiful Gaelic culture, he had a life-time dedication to the cause of one united Ireland. In character he was straight and true. I remember 12 years ago being in employment with Jim. I happened one day to remark to him the briskness and dedication he put to his work. He replied that he was morally bound to give a just return for his pay. This was the honesty and directness I learned to expect always from him. Four of his sons, Brendan, Padraig, Kevin and Terry, have been stalwart members of our club down through the years. On behalf of St. Vincents I tender to his wife and family our sincere deepest sympathy.

The sudden palpability of my grandfather, of whom I knew and remembered next to nothing, caused in me a lurch of proud affiliation. *First Battalion, First Cork Brigade, IRA.* There was something appealing about this simple and assured assertion of his soldiership, and there was poetic force in the phrase *a true Gael.* To me these were glamorous texts, calls from a gritty world of hurling and revolution that was thrillingly distant from the bourgeois, entirely agreeable environment of The Hague. My vague imagining of my grandfather's rebel world was in terms of the jacket illustration for *Guerrilla Days in Ireland* by Tom Barry, a tatty paperback memoir that had always occupied an incongruous niche between my mother's multilingual dictionaries and volumes of French literature. The illustration is of an IRA ambush at dusk on a deserted country road in West Cork, the sky burgundy, the sunken day a low-lying mass of yellow. A convoy of trucks is turning into view, and waiting to jump them are a smart officer in a blue jacket and a tie, who is holding a pistol, and two sturdy, rifle-toting fellows in rough shirts. It is a colourful, quasi-fictional scene in the style of a boys' comic, and speaks of cold, adventurous nights and clean-cut valour.

Hurling, on the other hand, I knew something about. Hurling was the fastest field sport in the world and required great skill and guts from its players. It was a wild, precise game in which the ball was kicked and fisted and swiped with flattened hockey sticks, the object being to score in goals that combined rugby uprights and soccer nets. It was gorgeous mayhem. My father, Kevin O'Neill, had played top-class hurling for his club, St Vincents, and county, Cork, losing half a mouthful of teeth and gaining a network of forehead scars in the process. I had played the game myself in the field behind my grandmother's house, and knew the pleasure of juggling the ball on the hurley and skimming it through the air with a cack-handed thwack. The O'Neills were crazy about sports. They played Gaelic football – at which my father had also fleetingly represented Cork – golf, athletics and, in the case of my younger uncles, the English games of soccer and rugby. Grandma O'Neill's house, the detached house where she has lived since the 'sixties, was full of the prizes her seven sons had won; entering her dining room felt like entering the trophy room of Real Madrid or Manchester United, the walls densely hung with ribbons and medals, the fireplace loaded with pewter cups on which silvery hurlers and footballers teetered.

Their love of games apart, I knew little about the O'Neills. By contrast with Mersin, where I had spent practically every summer of my life, I had only visited Cork intermittently. My father had nine brothers and sisters (in order of seniority: Jim, Brendan, Padraig, Terry, Ann, Declan, Angela, Marian, Fergus) who between them had nine spouses and more than thirty children, and keeping track of them all from Holland was a tall order. I knew my uncle

Brendan and his family, but after that it became trickier. My aunts and uncles were warm but inevitably distant older figures, my cousins youngsters and elusive; at any rate, more elusive than my Turkish cousins, whom I saw most summers and whose itineraries as students of medicine, economics, dentistry and computer studies fitted easily into the professional grid with which I was brought up to view the world. And whereas Dakads were to be found in Paris, Nice, Lausanne, Istanbul, Lyon and San Francisco, the strewage of work and study and marriage, the O'Neills stayed put in Cork.

A decade or so later, I re-opened Dostoevsky's *Letters*. The death notices were still there. No doubt my father had received the cuttings from his mother, who snips out and files newspaper articles that catch her interest. Often, these have to do with her grandchildren – the musical exploits of Seán, who was briefly a rock star, the swimming results of Ciaran, the picture of Deirdre at the pony club, the mention of Clodagh in her school magazine – but just as often they have to do with politics. You'll find reports on the jailing of uncle Brendan for refusal to pay services charges imposed by Cork City Corporation ('Union Chief Jailed', *Cork Examiner*); on the welfare of the South Yorkshire miners during the year-long British miners' strike ('A Conquered People', *Irish Times*); on the decision of the Irish government to inform the British government of IRA plans to mount a military campaign in Northern Ireland ('A People Betrayed', *Irish Republican Bulletin*, 1957); on the life and death of Mairead Farrell, the IRA volunteer killed by British forces in Gibraltar ('From Teenage Recruit to Prison Leader', *Irish Times*).

There is a pronounced, almost comical, contrast between, on the one hand, Grandma's appearance and civilian goodness and, on the other hand, her militaristic political stance. To appreciate the contrariety, you have to understand that Grandma is five foot nothing and a wonder of friendliness. She has curly white hair, clear blue eyes and a girlish, irresistible chortle. Aside from occasional attacks of sciatica, she is a model of health and energy which, even in her late eighties, she devotes to organizing meals on wheels for the elderly, going to Mass, promoting raffles and lotteries in good causes, visiting the sick, and saying rosaries for friends and family in need. All day she receives a stream of visitors – neighbours, children, old pals – in her kitchen, fixing them up with snacks and cups of milky tea. She remembers every birthday of her ten children and thirty-six grandchildren and ever-multiplying great-grandchildren, and she remembers every person who has lived on her street and every disease that has afflicted them. She is unflinching in her love of her family and, remarkably, is somehow able to care for all of us deeply and appropriately. She follows all major international events at which Ireland is represented, from the Eurovision Song Festival to the soccer World Cup to the women's 5000 metres in the Olympic Games. She is an honorary member of British National Union of Miners, South Wales Area (in 1984, she put up striking miners in her home for months). She boycotts retailers such as Dunnes Stores for breaking the South African trade embargo and mistreating their employees. She is an unblinking supporter of the cause of a united Ireland. She is a veteran of Cumann na mBan, the women's republican organization. She has given shelter to the most wanted men in the country. She has stored guns under the floorboards.

By the time I went back to the newspaper cuttings about Jim O'Neill, I had already started to mull over my grandfathers' double troubles. This led me turn to the actual contents of the *Letters of Dostoevsky* and to read Mr Yarmolinsky's introduction: hadn't Dostoevsky himself been in a political jam of some kind? I still barely knew anything about Fyodor Dostoevsky. I certainly didn't know until Mr Yarmolinsky told me about it that, in April 1849, Dostoevsky was arrested and imprisoned in Petropaulovsky Fortress, accused of 'having taken part in conversations about the severity of the Censorship; of having read, at a meeting in March 1849, Bielinsky's revolutionary letter to Gogol; of having read it at Dourov's rooms, and of having given it to Monbelli to copy; of having listened at Dourov's to the reading of various articles'. In December 1849, when he was twenty-eight years old, Dostoevsky received the death sentence – which, luckily for him, was commuted moments before he was due to be shot; less luckily, the commutation was to four years' hard labour in Siberia.

I felt a tingle: there was synchrony in the cuttings being lodged in a book that touched on political radicalism and the loss of freedom. I turned to a letter Dostoevsky wrote to his brother Michael on 22 February 1854, when he had finally served his sentence and was able to write for the first time in years. In the letter – a lengthy and somewhat frazzled dispatch, voicing a jumble of anxieties and needs – Dostoevsky outlined the conditions of his imprisonment and the tribulations he had undergone. In its jittery and unstyled way, the outline was deeply affecting and for a moment plunged me into the cold pool of my grandfathers' imprisonment. For the first time, albeit for only an instant, I was alerted to how forsaken they must have felt; for the first time, and with a shock, I sympathized with them.

I am not sure why it took a stranger's letter, and one written in the middle of the last century, to stir my compassion (or, indeed, whether such a roundabout stirring is perverse or heartless); but a clue to this aloofness, may, I think, also be found in Dostoevsky's letter to his brother.

One midwinter night on the way to Siberia, the horses and sledges transporting Dostoevsky to his exile became stuck in the snow. This happened in the Urals, and as the prisoner waited in the snowstorm for the horses to struggle free, he was struck by the melancholy realization that ahead lay only Asia, and that Europe and his whole past – his whole existence, by implication – were now behind him. Dostoevsky never lost this feeling of disconnection and isolation, which engendered in him the particular fear that he had lost his brother's love. To combat this fear, he asserted the contrary in his letter ('I know that you love me, and keep me in kindly remembrance'); but a telling moment of uncertainty arrived when, having furiously criticized Michael for not writing to him in the prison camp, he begged for news:

Write and answer me as quickly as possible; write, without awaiting an opportunity, officially, and be as explicit and detailed as you possibly can. I am like a slice cut from a loaf nowadays; I long to grow back, but can't. *Les absents ont toujours tort.* Is that saying to come true of us two?

The lingering phrase, here, is the one in French: *'les absents ont toujours tort'*. As it happens, the use to which it is put is ambiguous: one cannot be sure whether Michael is the absent wrongdoer, or Fyodor. Either way, the saying resonates in the context of my grandfathers.

An element of the taut silences that enclosed Joseph and Jim – surrounded them almost completely, like seas around peninsulas – was that of condemnation. Normally, we may count on an afterlife as a mouthful of stories, but for Joseph and Jim it had not worked out that way. It could be said that there is nothing unusual or wrong about this. If we are lucky, we have better and more urgent things to do than indulge in the regressive business of dwelling on the dead – children to raise, homes to keep up, work problems to figure out, spouses to love. My parents, for example, have been this lucky. However, I had always felt, growing up, that there was more to their silence than distraction or coyness. Nor was it the case that my grandfathers' absence was due to my grandmothers' engulfing presences. No, the silence meant more than that. It meant, I sensed, that Joseph and Jim were each in some way in the wrong. *Les absents ont toujours tort.*

But I didn't know this for a fact. Actually, I knew just about nothing for a fact – nothing about these men, and very little about the historical circumstances of their lives.

Some might consider ignorance a virtuous trait in an inquirer, a clean slate on which evidence may impartially be inscribed. But it doesn't work like that, at least it did not in my case. I was, of course, prejudiced; and, like most prejudices, mine found an infantile manifestation. It was not simply that my grandfathers stood accused in my mind of offences that I had not even formulated: it was that I didn't like their faces. I didn't like Jim's face – there was something frightening about his handsome, tooth-baring smile – and I didn't like the face of Joseph either, in particular the black moustache that made me think of Adolf Hitler.

What had they done wrong, though? Was it connected to their imprisonment? What *were* the facts?

It so happens that I am, by my professional training, supposed to be equipped as anybody to answer these sorts of questions and set to one side the kind of prejudice I have mentioned. I am a lawyer; more precisely, since lawyers are varietal as butterflies, I am a barrister working mainly in business law. It is a charmless but profitable field. There are countless commercial transactions effected every day, and they give rise to countless disputes. Were the goods defective? Did the surveyor give the bank negligent advice as to the value of a property development? Was there a material non-disclosure entitling the insurer to avoid the policy? For much of my working life I have gone into my chambers, pulled out ring binders from my shelves and tried to get to the bottom of these sorts of hard-boiled questions. After I have gone through hundreds of pages of correspondence, pleadings, affidavits and attendance notes, and sifted the relevant from the discardable, there are further, more finicky sub-questions. What was said in the telephone conversation of 14 February 1998? When did the cracks first appear in the wall? Who is Mr MacDougal? Often, meetings with the client are required to fill in the gaps or to quiz him closely to make sure nothing of significance has been left out. What one learns, pretty quickly, is that frequently the truth remains anybody's guess – even after all the documents have been scrutinized, all the witnesses have been grilled, and all the solicitors, juniors, silks and experts, racking up fees of hundreds of thousands of pounds, have trained their searchlights into the factual darkness.

Sometimes, however, something is illumined that is strange and unlooked-for and that, although perhaps not decisive of the hard-boiled question, twists the case and gives it a new meaning. This is, in a sense, what transpired after I began to look into the unknown lives of Joseph and Jim, following the narrow beam of their coincidental imprisonment. It led to times and places in which politics might have dramatic and personal consequences; in which people might be impelled to act or acquiesce in the face of evil and embark on journeys of the body and spirit that to many of us, living in the democratic west at the beginning of the new century, may seem fantastical; and in which people might through political action or inaction discover boundaries in themselves – good and bad – that we, casting our vote twice a decade, or losing our temper at the dinner table, or shunning the wines and cheeses of France, maybe cannot hope to know. Maybe. It may be, in fact, that our lives are thrown into greater ethical relief than we suspect. We may be judged strenuously by our descendants, who will perceive distinct rights and wrongs, shadows and crests, that we failed to notice. In part, my grandfathers' predicaments stemmed from what they saw or did not see around them. To this extent, they stand as paradigms of political and moral visions of different sorts, the blind eye and the dazzled eye, each with its own compensations and each with its own price.

1

. . . the old post cards do not depict Maurilia as it was, but a different
city which, by chance, was called Maurilia, like this one.

— Italo Calvino, *Invisible Cities*

I was born on 23 February 1964 in the Bon Secours Hospital,
Cork. The following day my father flew into Cork and went
directly from the airport to the nursery ward, where to everybody's
amazement he unhesitatingly picked me out from the sixteen new-
born babies lying anonymously in their cots. Then he walked
quickly to the maternity ward to see my mother. She was in bed,
and my father sat down on the rim of the bed. He took her hand.
He had been abroad working, and it was their first meeting for over
a week. 'Your father has died,' he said. My mother began to weep,
and so did my father.

Born the day after his death, I was given my grandfather's name –
Joseph.

He died on a rain-blurred day in Istanbul. At some point in the
afternoon, Pierre, my mother's brother, sat grieving alone in an
Istanbul café. A concerned stranger approached the tearful young
man and gently asked him what his trouble was. 'My father has

died,' Oncle Pierre said. The stranger took hold of Pierre by the shoulders and looked him in the eyes. 'See to your mother,' he said.

Joseph had for years been troubled by a heart problem that necessitated trips to Istanbul for treatment; and in 1961, he suffered a heart attack that brought Oncle Pierre, who was in Lyon studying law and economics, back to Mersin to help his father with the completion of the new Toros Hotel building. Joseph's condition worsened. In January 1964, when Fonda Tahintzi went to ask for the hand of my aunt Amy, he found Joseph in bed, dressed in his bathrobe and too weak to rise. In February, X-rays of my grandfather's heart were taken; these were, according to the Mersin doctors, inconclusive. Joseph appealed for help to Muzaffer Ersoy, his former personal physician, in whom he had great faith. Dr Ersoy, who had moved his practice to Istanbul and was on his way to substantial professional fame, requested that the X-rays be sent to him. Once he'd seen them, he responded immediately. The Mersin doctors had misread the X-rays: far from being inconclusive, they showed that the patient's heart had suddenly enlarged; it was vital that he go to Istanbul immediately for further treatment and tests. Joseph's worst fears were confirmed: for days, now, he had been vomiting in the mornings, grimly muttering, '*J'aime pas ça.*' So, wearing a hat placed on his head by Amy, Joseph caught a flight at Adana. It was his first experience of aviation, the death of a friend in an air crash having previously scared him off. On this occasion, though, getting on board the aeroplane truly was a matter of living or dying. Dr Ersoy said that the next three days would be decisive; either the patient would perish or the crisis would pass. Joseph said to his wife, Georgette, 'I promise that if I survive I'll buy you a fur coat. I'll buy one for you and one for the wife of Muzaffer Ersoy.'

Nobody got a fur coat. On the third day of his hospitalization, Joseph died; but not before he had seduced my grandmother one last time. Lying on his bed, he asked her forgiveness for all the harm he'd caused her: '*Pardonne moi pour tout le mal que je t'ai fait.*' Mamie Dakad replied, 'I am very happy with what I have had.' My grandfather closed his eyes. For a long time he had worried terribly about dying, but now he was surprisingly and suddenly at peace.

'*Comme c'est bon,*' he said, and he squeezed his wife's hand; whereupon he died.

My grandmother attached great weight to these dramatic gestures and would occasionally tell the story of her husband's last moments to her daughters. It was, in her eyes, a kind of happy ending, and one which decisively vindicated the steadfast and exclusive love she had borne my grandfather for over thirty years. My mother said to me, 'Because of what he said in the hospital, Maman always kept a good memory of Papa.'

A van came down overnight from Istanbul with the body. The journey was not easy. Snow was falling as the van crossed the Anatolian plateau, a near-desert of desolate, immeasurable darkness. The van slowly made its way through the snowstorm, the flakes falling without cease and still falling hours later as the vehicle slowly climbed the Taurus mountains, where, at the village of Pozanti, Fonda and Amy escorted it for the remainder of the journey. The convoy proceeded through forests and along terrifying precipices towards a narrow chasm known as the Cilician Gate, through which the army of Alexander the Great and the crusaders of the Holy Roman Emperor, Frederick Barbarossa, once passed. Eventually the snow and the mountains gave way to heavy rain and foothills, and finally to drizzle and the maritime plain of Çukurova, which is still referred to by westerners as Cilicia, after the Roman province (briefly governed by Cicero) of which the plain formed part. My grandfather's body was driven through Tarsus, the birthplace of St Paul, where a still-visible hole in the ground is alleged to be the well in which the evangelist hid from his pursuers. Legend also sticks to Tarsus' river, the Cydnus, on whose then navigable waters Cleopatra sailed her barge to meet Mark Antony. The convoy continued south-westward for about thirty kilometres, coming to a place that according to one conjecture is the location of Eden, a theory that, however crazy, is consistent with the remarkable fertility of the local earth, in which superb fruits and vegetables grow, and also with archaeological evidence (produced by the excavations of an English Hittitologist, John Garstang) which suggests that the area – that is, the area now occupied by the city of

Mersin – is one of the oldest continuously inhabited spots on the planet.

The van followed Fonda's car along an avenue of eucalyptus trees. This was the eastern road into Mersin. On they went: past the railway line that reaches a charming terminus at Mersin's old railway station, past the courthouse, past the prison, past what used to be known as the Maronite quarter, past the Catholic church, past the old Greek quarter. They entered a town which I imagine I just about remember, a quiet port of white-stoned villas and lush gardens, of untidy shacks and donkeys loaded with panniers leaking peaches, of card-games and tittle-tattle in multiple languages – a town reeking, in the springtime, of orange blossom. There was practically no motorized traffic as the convoy proceeded up the main street, Atatürk Çaddesi, and drove by the Toros Hotel, whose transformation – two large old limestone houses knocked down and replaced by a single, brand-new, four-storey building with fifty-three rooms – Joseph Dakad had only recently completed. The only other vehicles of any size on the street were cabs, which is to say, red-spoked carriages drawn by two blinkered horses whipped into exhaustion.

As recently as the early 'seventies these squeaking, rocking contraptions were Mersin's main form of taxi transport, and I often boarded them with my tiny, hunchbacked great-aunt, Tante Isabelle, to go from the hotel to the little stone house she shared with her tiny, hunchbacked sister, Tante Alexandra. Shaded by the cab's tassel-fringed bonnet, mesmerized by the carriage's brassy curves and the horses' flying red pom-poms, surrounded by the odours of dung and Tante Isabelle's Turkish eau-de-Cologne, I settled back in the scarlet leather seat like a pocket pasha and waited for the jolt that signalled the start of a ride of heavenly unsteadiness. We took the route taken by the convoy six or so years earlier, past rows of splendid palm trees that seemed to stand to attention, the whitewashed bases of their trunks smart as the spats worn by the Turkish soldiers who, to my delight, seemed constantly to march and parade on the streets of Mersin, often with glorious rockets and artillery on display. '*Dooma, dooma, doom*,' I chanted from my great-aunts' balcony in imitation of the drums. I loved the invasion of Cyprus in the summer of 1974, when Mersin was filled with troops and there was a blackout in case the Greeks bombed the town.

Me, watching a military parade in Mersin

We clip-clopped past the official house of the Vali (the provincial governor), past the monumental Halkevi (the House of the People) and its seaward-gazing statue of Atatürk, and then past the Greek Orthodox Church. At the rear of the church was the priest's house. It overlooked an open-air cinema where shadows of bats flitted across the screen. I could not follow the films – usually tragic melo-dramas involving disastrous migrations from country to city – or why the paying public, massed amongst winking red cigarette tips, intermittently snapped into fierce, sudden applause, the men rising from blue wooden chairs to clap with frowning, emotional faces. Peering through the rear window with my great-aunt and the priest's family, I looked out on a world full of stories I did not understand.

After the Greek Orthodox Church, the carriage jingled past big merchants' houses, some semi-abandoned, most in disrepair. In the top corner of each, it seemed, lived an old lady whom one knew – Madame Dora, Madame Rita, Madame Fifi, Madame Juliette, Madame Virginie. It was a leafy street, and turtle doves purred in the trees. On we went, hoofbeats clacking, the gentle stink of horse-shit wafting up from the street, until we came to Camlibel (pronounced *Chumleybell*), a small oval park surrounded by villas with gardens that overran with fruit trees and bougainvillaea. At the far end of Camlibel was the Dakad residence, a large, cool, rented apartment on the first floor of a villa. Tante Isabelle's place was only a little further on, just before the military barracks at the edge of the town. That was the long and the short of Mersin in those days: a quarter-hour ride in a carriage, or a five minute drive for a slow-moving car such as the van transporting the body of Joseph Dakad to Camlibel.

If you drove out west of Mersin, you travelled along a beautiful coastline. Once you had passed through the avenue of palm trees by the barracks, crossed the dry riverbed and gone past the stadium of Mersin Idmanyurdu (the football team that has always yo-yoed between Turkey's first and second divisions), in a deafening roar of frogs you came upon mile after mile of orange groves and lemon groves planted, at their perimeters, with pomegranate, grapefruit, tangerine, lime and medlar trees. Then came the villages of Mezitli and Elvanli and Erdemli, the Taurus foothills meanwhile getting closer and closer until, after you'd motored for the best part of an hour, the farmland expired and the road was hemmed in by, on the left, the sea – which indented the land with bays that flared turquoise at their confluence with freshwater streams – and, on the right, rocks covered with wild olive trees, sarcophagi, basilica, aque-ducts, castles, arches, mosaics, ruined temples and ghost villages. You drove on until you came to Kizkalesi, an island fortress won-drously afloat three hundred yards offshore that is a relic of the medieval kingdom of Lesser Armenia, and you got out of the car and went swimming in hot, lucid waters. There was nobody else around except for the occasional camel or shy children hoping to be photographed.

In the last twenty years, the beach holiday has arrived in Turkey. Nowadays Kizkalesi is a swollen, chaotic resort crowded by tourists from Adana and the landlocked east. The roadside antiquities are dwarfed by advertising hoardings, *pansiyons* and summer homes, the inlets and creeks are covered by a mess of unplanned structures, the citrus groves have been razed to make way for holiday complexes and towering, gloomy suburbs. The belching frogs have gone (some, decades ago, packed in ice and shipped by Oncle Pierre to the tables of France), and an hour's drive will barely take you clear of Mersin's concrete outskirts and the moan of cement-mixers and the fog of building dust.

In Mersin itself, a huge boulevard now swings along the seafront. Countless young palm trees spring from the pavements, new stop-lights regulate the chaos at junctions, traffic islands are dense with flowering laurels, and block after block after block of bone-white apartments take shape from grey hulks. Hooting minibuses race through the streets three abreast, residential complexes multiply along the coast, the minarets of enormous new mosques make their way skywards in packs. In the final thirty years of the last century, the population, swollen by a massive influx from the east, much of it Kurdish, has multiplied sixfold to around six hundred thousand. It's a boomtown. The port, with its officially designated Free Trade Zone, ships' commodities worldwide in unprecedented quantities: pumice-stones from Nevşehir to Savannah and Casablanca; pulses from Gaziantep to Colombo, Karachi, Chittagong, Doha and Valencia; apple concentrate from Niğde to New York and Ravenna; TV parts from Izmir to Felixstowe and Rotterdam; insulation material from Tarsus to Alexandria and Abu Dhabi; dried apricots from Malatya to Antwerp (and thence Germany and France); Iranian pistachios to Haifa (in secret shipments, to save political embarrassment); Russian cotton to Djakarta and Keelung; citrus fruit from Mersin to Hamburg and Taganrog; synthetic yarn from Adana to Norfolk and Alexandria; carpets from Kayseri to Oslo and to Jeddah. Just along from the new marina, you'll find a Mersin Hilton and luxury seaside condominiums; and in the unremarkable interior of the city, the gigantic Mersin Metropol Tower (popularly known as the dick of Mersin) lays claim to the title of 'the tallest building between Frankfurt and Singapore'. On the streets, young women are turned out in European trends, teenagers smooch, and male students at the new Mersin University amble along Atatürk Çaddesi, Mersin's first pedestrianized street, with long hair and clean-shaven faces.

Of course, some things never change. Sailors still sport snowy flares. Men wear vests under their shirts in the clammy August heat, and moustaches, and old-fashioned trousers with a smart crease leading down to the inevitable dainty loafer. You'll still see vendors pushing carts loaded with pistachios, grapes, or prickly pears; corn on the cob (grilled or boiled) is sold at street corners; and shoeblacks grow old behind their brassy boxes. The old vegetable and meat and fish market has kept going, and the pleasant little Catholic Church of Mersin where my parents were married and which I have intermittently attended over the years is the same. As ever, a fountain spurts a loop of water in the church's small, leafy courtyard, and Sunday Mass attracts adherents to all six Catholic rites – Roman, Syrian, Chaldaean, Maronite, Armenian, and Greek. It's a varied congregation. You'll see ageing westernized Christians in drab urban clothes, enthusiastic children packed in scrums into the front pews (boys right of the aisle, girls left), and a big turn-out of worshippers vividly dressed in shawls and baggy pants; these last are Chaldaeans from the mountains in the extreme south-east of Turkey. Not all Mersin Christians are rich.

But old Mersin – the Mersin to which my grandfather's body returned, a town of verandas, gardens and large stone houses – has largely disappeared. One by one, the villas have been sold, knocked down and replaced by tower blocks. The last surviving villa of the Naders, my grandmother's family, is in Camlibel. The fate of this elegant building, which until only a few years ago was occupied by my mother's cousin Yuki Nader and his Alexandrian wife, Paula, is not atypical. Surrounded on all sides by tower blocks whose

My grandfather's childhood home

occupants bombard it with junk, it is boarded up and empty – awaiting the bulldozer or, I've heard it rumoured, conversion to a bank – its avocado trees, shutters, gates, even its footpath stones, ripped out by persons unknown. Nobody seems to notice or, more precisely, attach significance to this spectacle.

A few other places survive. An ancient Nader property is now a primary school, and in the old Maronite quarter, the house where Joseph Dakad grew up is in use as a police station.

For what it is worth, I like the new city and am excited by it. I know what fantasy and work and guts underpin its progress, I know that with its parks, shops and up-to-date facilities it is a pleasant, utilitarian and altogether desirable place to live – a model Turkish city, in many ways. But because of its modern, commercial character, Mersin has no place in western European narratives. British guide books, for example, are unanimously dismissive: 'Can serve as an emergency stop on your way through,' is the assessment of one book, 'none too attractive' and 'almost without interest' of others. One guide book asserts that the city was 'little more than a squalid fishing hamlet' at the beginning of the twentieth century, while another declares that the place did not even exist until fifty years ago.

Although Mersiners would probably find hurtful and wrong the notion that their city is nothing more than an ugly point of onward transit, it is likely that they would agree, without anxiety, with the suggestion that it has no past to speak of. Very few families have been rooted in the town for more than a generation or two, and most have histories connected to distant Anatolian villages or Kurdish mountainsides. No collective stock of stories or postcards of the old Mersin circulates, and no real interest exists in the handful of crumbling stone buildings that appear here and there, without explanation, between the apartment blocks. What matters overwhelmingly is the here and now, and so Mersin is unmythologized and ghostless, and contentedly so. Of course, it is not exempt from the generic Kemalist myth and, like every other urban settlement in the Turkish Republic, it is haunted by Atatürk, whose image, in a variety of get-ups, attitudes, silhouettes and situations, continues to adorn schools, shops, offices, homes, buses, stamps, bank notes and public spaces. (How many millions of times is a Turk fated to behold that wise, subtly pained visage?) If the past has any meaning, it is as a realm of Kemalist socio-economic progress: the only printed history of Mersin that exists, an illustrated book produced by a local lawyer, concentrates on municipal achievements like the reclamation of seaside land, the construction of the modern port, the creation of the waterfront park.

Atatürk famously visited the city in 1923. He stayed in an imposing mansion of white stone and red rooftiles that, with its ballroom, its huge mountain-facing balcony and its lush garden, was Mersin's best shot at a palazzo. In recent years the house has been meticulously restored. Decades of grime have been scraped from its walls, shutters have been replaced and metalwork renewed. It has been named Atatürk's House, and for a small fee visitors may stroll about its rooms to admire the enormous proportions of the building and the painted ceilings and the period furniture, and to try to envisage the great leader breakfasting here or consulting with his adjutants there or, as happened on 17 March 1923, stepping out on to the wrought-iron balcony at the front of the house and shouting at the crowd gathered below – for reasons it took me a long time to fathom – 'People of Mersin, take possession of your town!'

A tiny and dwindling number of Mersiners will never really think of the big house as Atatürk House. For them, it will always be the Tahintzi house, the house where my uncle Fonda and his fore-bears lived. Fonda himself says that the house used to be known as the Christmann house, after Xenophon Christmann. The Christmann family arrived in the Levant as part of the entourage of the German Prince Athon, who was summoned to Greece in the 1830s by prospectors for a Greek royal family. Xenophon Christmann wound up as the German consul in Mersin, married Fonda's great-aunt, and spent a chunk of his fortune on building the most magnificent building in the town. Years later, when Atatürk requisitioned the residence and the Tahintzi family stand-offishly withdrew into a wing of the house, the Gazi (warrior of Islam) took offence and demanded, 'Where is the lady of the house?'

My grandmother had a tale of this kind – a colourful jelly of small facts in which the family origins are suspended and conserved. She said that her patrilinear ancestors, the Naders, came to Turkey from Lebanon. The arrivals were two brothers from Tripoli – *les grandpères*, she called them both, although only one, Dimitri, was her grandfather – who were in the business of shipping timber cut from the fir and juniper forests of the Taurus Mountains to the Suez Canal. The buyers of the timber offered to pay with gold or, if the brothers preferred, shares in the Suez Canal Company. The Nader brothers chose gold, and with it they bought land in the burgeoning port of Mersin. They planted orchards and, in 1875,

built two large stone houses for themselves on Mersin's main drag.
The houses formed a single immense building two stories high and
a block wide, with the ground floor given over to commercial units;
sixty or so years later, these premises were transformed by my grandfather into the Toros Hotel.

Such fragments of lore aside, the Christian community is fully
implicated in Mersin's general lack of retrospection. I never grew
up with a clear sense of what these strange French-speaking Turks
were doing in Mersin, or who they – we – really were. I knew that
some families had connections with Lebanon, but I had little idea of
what that meant. We were in Mersin now, and there was very little
else to say.

In order to gain a picture of historic Mersin, I had to leave the
city – leave Turkey, in fact – and track down the writings of travellers kept in European libraries. I read that in 1818, when Captain
Beaufort went there, Mersin consisted of nothing more than a few
wretched huts raised on piles. Some years later, a long-term English
resident of Tarsus called William Burckhardt Barker noticed that
on the slightest appearance of bad weather, Arab lombards from
Syria would take shelter at a spot known as Zephyrium, or Mursina,
where the roadstead was excellent. Mursina was a name derived
from the Greek for myrtle, because immense bushes of that plant
were practically the only thing to characterize the site. In 1838,
there were only a few magazines and huts there, and bales of cotton
were left out in the rain until French vessels arrived to ship them to
Marseille. Barker saw an opportunity. He built large warehouses
capable of holding the cargoes of fifteen vessels at one time, and
soon these were filled with the produce of the hinterland for export:
cotton, wool, wheat, barley, wax, sesame-seed, linseed, madder-
roots, Persian yellow-berries, hides. Imports – sugar, coffee, indigo,
cochineal, soap, Persian tobacco – also brought traffic to the area,
and before long others had built magazines and settled there.

However, a Frenchman who visited Mersin in 1853, Victor
Langlois, saw only a damned, marsh-covered, fever-devastated land
with a population that decreased every year; the air was lethal, the
water insalubrious, the fruit harmful. (He was not exaggerating: in

the Adana plain, entire colonies of Circassian refugees, escaping from Russian anti-Muslim oppression, would be rubbed out by malarial fever.) By April 1875, things had noticeably improved. The Reverend E.J. Davis, arrived from Egypt, gained the impression of a bustling scala whose success he attributed to the active demand for cereals consequent upon the Crimean War. Mersina, as the port was known to westerners, struck the Reverend as a 'flourishing little place; its bazaars, thronged by the various races who have settled here, present a scene of great animation; some of its streets are paved with square blocks of limestone; and there are many really good stone houses'. Officials apart, the Reverend observed, very few Turks lived in Mersin: 'As usual in ports of these regions, Greeks and Christians of Syria are the principal inhabitants – the Greeks being energetic, enterprising, and many of them rich. The purely European residents are very few in number; an unhealthy climate and the lax commercial morality of the place, render it almost impossible for a European to thrive, or even live there.' He noted that nearly all the Syrians spoke French – 'it is remarkable how great an influence France has had upon the Roman Catholic population of Syria' – and was impressed by the Greek hospital and church and, especially, the Greek school (which, forty years later, my grand-mother would attend), where masters fluent in French taught ancient and modern Greek, sacred history, French, geography, arith-metic. Then, in July, when he returned to Mersin to catch a steamer home, Davis saw a dark side of the town that almost cost him his life. Descending from cool mountains, he was horrified by an intensely humid and enervating heat and the spectacle of sick people lying on mattresses at the door of their houses. To make things worse, cholera had appeared in Syria, and the service of the Russian steam-ers had been suspended due to a ten-day quarantine imposed by the Ottoman government on all arrivals from Syria. Davis was forced to sweat it out in Mersin. He almost didn't make it. With the whole town in the grip of fever, and funerals passing regularly under his windows, and sleep impossible during nights he compared to a 'damp, yet hot, oven,' Davis fled for the relative relief of Boluklu, a village in the foothills about an hour's ride away, where the air was marginally better. He stayed in the Mavromati house – the house, that is, of my uncle Fonda's great-grandfather. Eventually, after eight feverish days during which he lay tormented by horrid dreams and visions, he booked a passage on a French mail steamer to Marseille and escaped Mersin's 'entrancing beauty and deadly air and heat'.

There was one book, however, that I came across not in London libraries but in Mersin, at my grandmother's apartment in the Toros Hotel. A first edition with crumbling leather covers, *La Syrie D'Aujourd'hui,* by Dr Lortet of the Faculty of Medicine of Lyon University, was an account of the author's travels in the Near East in 1875, the year that saw the visit of the Reverend Davis and the acquisition of Mersin property by the Nader brothers. Dr Lortet observed that there wasn't much more to this port than thirty or so houses, and there was not even a proper harbour, vessels having to anchor in the roadstead some distance out at sea. His description was illustrated by an etching of Mersin and its 'miserable buildings': a strand, jetties, some beached rowing-boats, a huddle of two-storey buildings. Dr Lortet did say that the town had the most picturesque population you could wish to see, a commingling of Turks, Arabs, Syrians, negroes, Ansarians and others, all dressed in brilliant, variegated clothing. Behind the houses, orchards surrounded by verdant hedges grew vigorously; the pear and apricot trees were particularly fine, producing fruit much sought after in Beirut and Rhodes. Dr Lortet took a horseback trip to Tarsus. The countryside he passed through seems to have been paradisal. Ploughs drawn by buffaloes and camels and oxen churned up dark, fertile earth, clouds of aquatic birds rose from waters full of turtles, and storks pecked in the wake of the ploughs. The plain of Mersina, noted Dr Lortet, saw an abundance of boars, francolin, yellow-necked vultures, gazelles and a tigerishly striped deer. Beavers, black otters, jackals and hyenas were still in evidence, and the hunter in the pine forests might encounter the leopard. In the dark forests of the Cilician mountains were also bears, badgers, black squirrels and, at the highest summits, gigantically horned goats. 'The English,' Dr Lortet commented, 'have been inspired in their recent annexation of Cyprus. From that island, they are the absolute masters of the beautiful gulf of Alexandretta, which delivers to them, through Mersina, eastern Asia Minor, and, through Alexandretta, Aleppo and the upper valley of the Euphrates; thus they hold the key to the Mesopotamian railway line which is soon to be the great route between the Far East and Europe.'

The significance of this comment would only later become evident to me. My immediate attention was fixed on the next sentence: 'A great future evidently lies in store for the port of Mersina,' wrote Lortet, 'once [blank] is no longer an obstacle to the creation of lines of communication to the surrounding valleys.'

The blank was arresting. Three or four words had been removed from the text – scraped away so as to leave a vacancy. A few pages later, there was a second such intervention. The port of Alexandretta, Lortet wrote, was a dreadful settlement lost in swampland and half-invaded by green, pestilential pools. The majority of its houses were huts swarming with pale, emaciated wretches, the children particularly afflicted by typhoid fever and dysentery. 'And yet all it would take is a few channels and a few swings of a pick to make all of these stagnant waters run to the sea and save these pour souls condemned to an early death. But this work will never be done [blank].' Here, three whole lines were scraped away. What instrument the censor had used for this purpose, I couldn't be sure; perhaps a knife, or a specialized print-scraping instrument from a censor's tool-kit of effacers. I couldn't say who the censor was, when he did his work, or what (presumably anti-Turkish) sentiments he obliterated. Nor, for that matter, did I know how this book had come to be in the possession of Joseph Dakad's brother, Georges, from whom my grandmother had received it as a gift. I meant to ask Mamie Dakad about this, as I meant to ask her many other questions; but, a reluctant interrogator, preoccupied by swimming and eating, I never did. In January 1995, while I was in India on my honeymoon, my grandmother died and was buried next to her husband.

The funeral procession of Joseph Dakad is recorded in a photograph. My grandfather's coffin is being shouldered by six men of differing heights, a variation that is causing them a little discomfort. Employees from the hotel lead the way, holding small bunches of flowers. My grandmother, wearing dark glasses and a black head-scarf, is escorted by Pierre. Amy is also there, at her mother's shoulder; behind them, an assortment of family friends. The cortège is on Atatürk Çaddesi. It has come from the deceased's house and is heading for the Toros Hotel, still a few hundred metres away. Afterwards, at the Catholic Church, *le père* François will say prayers for my grandfather's departed soul. It is a cold day, and the mourn-ers are warmly clothed. As is often the case in Turkey when a private affair is being played out in the street, members of the public are making their presence felt, some simply looking on, others respect-fully issuing instructions and hand-signals to the coffin-bearers. The sorrowful, dramatic tableau might be a scene from a film I watched from the rear window of the priest's house.

The cemetery in which Joseph is buried lies between the north-ern edge of the city and the foothills of the mountains. The burial ground is bordered by enormous cypress trees, and inside, more evergreens throw cooling shadows, bestowing on the graveyard the tranquillity and amenity of woodland. Nearest the entrance are the Christian dead. They lie in the oldest and best plots with their un-Turkish names: Mavromati, Levante, Butros, Nader, Naccache, Chalfoun, Rickards, Saad, Del Conte. Among these mausoleums is a raised box-like structure of grey-white marble, about three feet high, ten feet wide and twelve feet long. It is enclosed by a specially planted thicket of twelve pine trees that shed needles on the surface of the tomb; young boys unobtrusively present in the cemetery hose these away in the hope of a tip. A pale marble cross rises from the tomb, and beneath the cross appears the Turkish phrase *Dakad Ailesi*: the Dakad Family.

The names of the individual dead are not inscribed on the tomb, but I am told that my grandmother lies there with two of her sisters, Isabelle and Alexandra; two brothers, Anton and Joseph; and, probably (no one is quite sure), her mother, Nezha Nader (*née* Dibo), commonly known as Teta (Arabic for grandma) and post-humously nicknamed Madame Promenade on account of her fondness for taking strolls. Amidst this crowd of Nader dead lies only one born Dakad: Joseph.

Actually, that is not strictly accurate. My grandfather was born Joseph *Dakak* (itself a transformation of a gargle of Arabic, *da'a*, which means 'smith'). He changed his name in around 1939, the year he married. He wanted to bear the same name as his younger brother, Georges, who'd emigrated to France and amended Dakak to the more French-sounding *Dacade*. Despite his name-change, Joseph would still refer to himself and be known as Dakak.

For the record, Joseph was first buried in an old Nader plot which dated back to 1892; then, when the preparation of the new plot – which he had acquired himself – was completed, he was reburied. It is doubtful that many more of his descendants will join him in the family tomb. Pierre is in Paris, Amy in Geneva, my mother in The Hague; and only two of these three's eleven children are still in Mersin. The city's other Christian families have splintered in the same way to the United States of America, Canada, Malaysia and (in the case of the Chaldaeans, who emigrate in great numbers) Germany. On top of these dispersions, religious and cultural migrations: the remaining young, my own generation, are now married to and loved by Muslims, and if they speak French, it is as a frail, diminished third language, after Turkish and English. Arabic, the oldest tongue of all, is vestigial, restricted to the food-stuffs that continue to appear at dinner tables: *muhshi, fassoulia, kibbe, tabbouleh, siyadiyeh*. Thus the distinctively Christian community is disappearing, disappearing together with the place that it built and found marvellous, the Ottoman port with its dolphins, its gambling, its Club, its contagions.

All of this matters because the life of my Turkish grandfather is mixed inextricably with the life of that evanescent city.

One night around the Christmas of 1960, my father, a responsible and dutiful twenty-one-year-old employee of Chicago Bridge & Iron Co., an American corporation devoted to the profitable worldwide erection of tanks, pipelines, towers and other petrochemical constructions, trashed his room at the Toros Hotel with the petulance and panache of a rock star. He was the worse for a considerable quantity of cheap whiskey when a friend from work, an American called Bill Purdey, called by his room to get him to come out. My father, lying on his bed, sullenly declined the invitation, and Purdey, sensing the need for decisive action, said, 'Come on, let's get going,' and abruptly slammed shut a window – and cracked the pane. My father perked up. 'That's typical of you, Purdey. You just can't do anything right.' He got out of bed, picked up the portable electric fire and threw it through the cracked pane of glass. 'You see? That's how you do it.' He paused to contemplate his deed; then he smashed each of the remaining windows of the room.

The next morning, my father went down to the *bureau* of Joseph Dakad to make amends. He felt like a boy going to see the principal. Monsieur Dakad, not a barrel of laughs at the best of times, used the grave and headmasterly English of Alec Guinness in *Lawrence of Arabia*. He sat behind a large desk equipped with inkwells, blotters and fountain pens. On the wall behind him hung a photograph of a grim-faced Atatürk.

He listened to my father's apology in unimpressed silence. Joseph Dakad was not a whiskey man himself, nor even a raki man. The only alcohol he touched was the very occasional beer. He had got drunk once in his life, as a youth, and had never allowed himself to forget the indelicate consequences. Joseph Dakad was a water man; indeed, he was something of a water connoisseur. 'This water is poor,' he would declare, pushing aside the tumbler filled with the offending liquid; or, sipping appreciatively, 'Now, *this* is water.' Soda – as carbonated mineral water is called in Turkey – was a particular favourite, since it went easy on his troublesome stomach. He also liked *ayran* – strained yoghurt, water and salt – which he enjoyed making and foisting on his family. 'Drink,' he would command his children. When my grandmother was unable to nurse my infant mother and the wet-nurse tested positive for tuberculosis, Joseph bought a cow to ensure a supply of fresh and hygienic milk for his daughter. He was discriminating and imperious about all food. He would stick a long knife vertically into a watermelon and listen for the long tearing sound – *craaatch* – that signalled a good fruit; if the melon was pale or watery or otherwise substandard, he would discard it, sometimes getting through ten before he was satisfied. He was a vigorous and fussy shopper at the market and bought meat from a personal *kebabçi* whose every motion of the cleaver he would supervise and direct. Joseph also enjoyed receiving imported goods – tinned ham and the like – that my father was able to procure at the American air base near Adana. On one occasion, my father offered him sardines. Monsieur Dakad reflected for a moment or two, weighing words. His use of English was very skilful, and he searched his mind until he found the expression that exactly reflected his sentiments. 'Fuck sardines,' he said.

Joseph's approach to food was one manifestation of a general authoritarianism. His children all described him as *très autoritaire*, and his niece, Ginette, affectionately recalled that her uncle was 'very commanding, like a Turk'. My grandmother (whom Joseph sometimes called *yamara*, Arabic for 'my wife'), about as forceful a woman as you could wish for, deferred to him in almost all things. Why? Perhaps (as her elderly friends suggested to me) it was out of love; or perhaps because she guessed that a sense of his supremacy lay at the centre of her husband's self-estimation, and indeed of her estimation of him. Either way, my grandfather didn't impose himself by shouting or physical violence. Only once did he spank my mother, after she and Amy had naughtily rearranged the furniture; and when it came to giving tiny Amy her *pan pan*, he let her off. Ten years later, when Amy plucked up the courage to ask for permission to ride with her friends on a *mobilette*, he said, 'How dare you even *think* of asking for my permission for such a thing?' Usually, in such a situation, Joseph would simply frown and darken his eyes, making a forbidding face: a face that said *Non*. And no meant no. 'Of course,' my mother told me lightly, 'we were all afraid of him.'

My mother, who all my life barely breathed a word about her father, at first only spoke about him if prompted, and then apparently spoke unemotionally, as if the subject were a distant country of moderate interest she had once visited. But then came a thaw, and a runnel of information began to flow my way. This may have been due to a sense that if her father's life was to be reduced to ink and paper, it was as well she had her say; but I think her openness really stemmed from an impulse to commemorate her recently deceased mother, with whom she had enjoyed very happy relations and whose finished life was inextricable from that of her husband and *grand amour*.

My mother disclosed small, pleasant things. For example: that Joseph would proudly instruct her – his eleven-year-old daughter finally returned from four years' schooling in France – '*Récite!*' and she would speak verses by Alphonse Daudet to gathered adults; that in the evenings he would take his daughters out on a rowboat in the sea (a boatman, and not Joseph himself, would man the oars); that he would take my mother for a spin in the car through the citrus groves or to the patisserie in Tarsus to buy baklava; that he bathed three times a day; that he read newspapers fanatically (often, wearing crisp pyjamas, in his bed: for an enterprising man, he was curiously idle), consuming six a day, morning and evening editions; and that Papa, whose suits were beautifully cut, always wore a clean white handkerchief in his breast pocket.

Amy also remembered little moments. When she was fifteen years old, her father saw her wearing a touch of mascara. He explained to her: 'Let me tell you something. Girls who wear make-up do so because they need to. You have big brown eyes, so you have no need to wear make-up.' Amy was very interested in my investigations into her father's life, and she sent me documents and photos and suggested lines of inquiry. It seemed that for her, too, Joseph – who died, after all, when she was only twenty-one, and whom for years she'd only seen during school holidays – was obscured in a dimness out of which she wished to haul him. There was, naturally enough, an iconolatrous element to this desire, but there was also plain curiosity. My mother became curious, too – she was only twenty-three when Joseph died and, like her sister, had been away from home for much of her life's short overlap with her father's – and after a time her long reticence about her father largely disappeared. That reticence, my siblings and I had always vaguely sensed, had been expressive of a some kind of injury. The only

paternal tort we could think of – apart from the unknown matter of
our grandfather's wartime activities – was Joseph's refusal to permit
my mother to pursue a university career. Equipped with a French
baccalaureate, she desperately wanted to study medicine or law at a
French university, but her father would not contemplate the
expense: a young woman had no real business acquiring professional qualifications of that kind. Crushingly, the matter was not
even debated. Although no Mersin women attended university at
that time, it was probably not until my mother had graduated *doc-
torandus* in French from Leiden University in her thirties that she
began to forgive her father his act of chauvinism.

In the event, Joseph did authorize Lina (Caroline) to go to
London and take a bilingual secretarial course at a college in
Dunraven Street, in Mayfair. My mother lived in The Boltons, a
splendid address in South Kensington, in a hostel overshadowed by
the mansion of Douglas Fairbanks Junior. In the mornings she
would walk across Hyde Park to her college. She found London,
with its stupendous fogs and polite, pin-striped pedestrians, strange
and wonderful. She made friends, among them the about-to-be-
famous model Jean Shrimpton, ate lunch at Selfridges, improved
her English. She was not homesick. To keep in touch with home,
she corresponded with her mother. 'Did your father write to you?'
I asked her. 'No,' she said, 'just my mother. Maman cared for the
children – visited us at school, looked after our day-to-day needs.
We were part of her domestic domain. My father's domain was
outside the house, at work, at the hotel. I had a very quiet childhood,' my mother said. 'I never recall my parents raising their
voices at each other.'

My mother's spell in England – which also included some
months spent teaching conversational French at Tolmer's, an
obscure boarding school for girls near St Albans – was the finishing
touch on an international upbringing. She attended Turkish primary school, and then, aged seven, went to boarding school in
Lyon, where she did not see her parents for the best part of four
years. For her secondary education, Lina was transferred to the
Ecole Franciscaine in Aleppo, a convent school for girls. Schooling

in Aleppo or Beirut was customary for the well-to-do Christian girls of Mersin. Its objective was to produce nice, *comme il faut* young women who would return home to excite the attentions of the resident young men – the Alberts and the Andrés and the Michels and the Henris – and fall sufficiently in love as to get married. They would speak French (with a distinctive Levantine accent) as their first language and Turkish (also with a distinctive Levantine accent) as their second. Their speech in both tongues would be unidiomatic and relatively unsupple, limitations reinforced by the spectrum of activities awaiting them: cooking expertly; supporting their husbands' business exploits; bearing and raising children; throwing and going to tea parties and cocktail parties; putting up with the heat in the summer and the boredom in the winter; periodically voyaging to Europe and, once there, shopping – for shoes in Italy, silk scarves in France, chocolates in Switzerland, raincoats in England. My mother was not enthusiastic, when the time came, about leaving London.

However, when she returned in 1960, Mersin, its population grown to sixty-something thousand, was livening up. A new port had been built and all kinds of projects were in progress at the new industrial complex, Ataş. It was at Ataş that my mother found work as a secretary with the American construction company, Foster Wheeler. She made a good living and, most importantly, she met her husband.

The improbability of my parents' union is of the kind usually associated with being whacked by a rock fallen from outer space. Even leaving geography out of it, Cork boys would appear to have little in common with Mersin girls; and Kevin O'Neill – monolingual, freckled from head to toe, teeth ravaged by blows received from hurling sticks and the negligent interventions of Cork dentists – was, on the surface, pure Cork. He had been sent to Turkey to lay the ground for a project which Chicago Bridge had undertaken, the building of a small oil refinery for Mobil Oil. It was a big job for a young man, particularly one whose only experience abroad was a short time spent in Germany. But my father was energetic and undaunted, and, sustained by the O'Neill trait of easiness and unfathomable confidence, he took to the task and to the town. For the first few months, he stayed at the best hotel in Mersin, the Toros, whose top floor was still under construction and whose owner, Monsieur Dakad, would pass days judicially supervising the works in a chair across the road, his *casque coloniale* firmly placed on his head. When the time came to adjudicate in the matter of the windows my father had smashed, Monsieur Dakad, although displeased, did not overreact. He heard out my father and then calmly, without reprimand, leaned across his desk and handed over an estimate for the repairs. He never spoke of the incident again – not even a year or so later, when my father again requested a private interview, this time to ask for permission to marry his eldest daughter, Lina.

Over the years there has been a seepage of stories about my parents' courting days. My father would borrow a car and pick up my mother from her home in Camlibel. Oncle Pierre, still a teenager, would come along to chaperone his older sister. As soon as the car had turned around the corner, Pierre would jump out of the car and my parents would be free to drive where they pleased – along the coast, or up to the blissfully cool *yayla* (mountain retreat) of Gözne. Overlooked by a ruined castle and laced with streams, Gözne was a gorge dotted with rickety wooden houses that were barely visible in the thick greenery of oak, hawthorn, honeysuckle, myrtle, arbutus, jujube and Judas trees. Other times, Kevin would take Lina for a walk to the beach or along Atatürk Çaddesi, where the pavement was shaded by awnings of vine leaves and bougainvillaea. They were in love. In November 1961, they got engaged.

Joseph Dakad was unhappy about the match. He did not like the idea of his daughter marrying a foreigner and going away overseas. 'She has only just returned from England,' he complained to my father. 'And besides, how do you propose to support her?' 'The same way that you've done,' my father said. 'By working.' Joseph Dakad was not satisfied. He knew for a fact that his daughter had good values; but how could he be sure this Irishman shared them? What sort of family was he from? 'I must have a reference,' he said finally. He wrote to my father's parish priest in Cork and obtained

a written assurance as to the suitor's good character and background. In February 1962, my parents were married at the Catholic
Church in Mersin, after a slight scare: the bride, detained at the
coiffeur by a bad hairstyle that required refixing, was one hour late
for the wedding. My mother was led up the aisle by her father. She,
of course, wore white; he wore an expression of happiness and – it
was chilly inside the church – a smart overcoat.

    Actually, Joseph's characteristic nattiness was one of the few
things I had always known about him – that, and the fact that he
spoke seven languages (five – French, Arabic, Turkish, English and
German – very well, and two – Italian and Spanish – well enough);
in the Levant, linguistic expertise has always been highly esteemed.
When I asked people about him, they mentioned his dapperness
straight away, by way of a headline, as though it led right down to
the bottom of things. He was very *chic* in an understated, entirely
appropriate way; sometimes he wore pure silk shirts made especially
for him in Istanbul. Another headline was that he was not a serious
card player. He played for small amounts – a *petit jeu*. Just about

anywhere else this would be a non-story, but in old Mersin so much turned on cards and the fortunes that were won and lost at the tables of the Merchants' Club. By contrast, Georgette – here, deference would enter the reporter's voice – played a *grand jeu*. Stud poker and *concain* (a kind of gin rummy) were the preferred games, and play went on in the Club until the early hours. The stakes were high. Someone told me that a night of gambling once cost my grandmother an apartment.

There was a final thing I knew about Joseph. He was, in my grandmother's phrase, a *coureur*. To be exact, she exclaimed: 'Was he interested in women? *Et comment! C'était un grand coureur!*' This pronouncement came a couple of years before her death, as she sat in her favourite armchair. Her voice had contained a clear note of amusement or pride and this, together with the use of *coureur*, threw me slightly. Literally, the word means 'runner', and its inno-cent athletic connotation planted the notion in my head that my grandfather's interest in women was a harmless pastime, somehow morally akin to pounding the track. The other expression I'd heard used about him, *ladies man*, also rang innocently in my ears, con-juring up an old-fashioned gallantry consistent with something Tante Amy later told me: 'Papa was very knowledgeable about law and property and was of great assistance to widows who required his help. Every night there would be a lady in his office, seeking his advice about some matter or other.' He enjoyed dropping in on women friends for tea, taking them for strolls and presenting them with gifts. He would promenade with Giselle Chalfoun's mother and aunt, mischievously suggesting to each that her cooking was better than the other's. He gave large gold rings to René Messageot's sister and wife, and doted on René's mother; when Madame Messageot died, Joseph was inconsolable. He was very good friends with his friend Riri Levante's wife, the attractive and socially powerful Rosie, and very often visited them with my grand-mother. All this suggested that perhaps he was not a man's man, that he found an unusual measure of social gratification in female company. Then I discovered that *coureur* was short for *coureur de jupons*, skirt-chaser, and when further inquiries revealed that Joseph was sometimes nicknamed Rasputin, my impression of him as an attentive gallant came under strain. My sister Elizabeth repeated a story which Mamie Dakad, again in a curiously triumphant tone, once told her: before the war, Joseph had a Muslim mistress staying at the hotel whom he was anxious to be shot of, so he asked Georgette to move into the hotel for a few days to make the woman's position impossible. '"Never!" I told him. "You got yourself into this position, now get yourself out of it!"' 'He loved me,' my grandmother once said, 'but he paid attention to other women.'

As often happens with the heartbreakers of yesteryear, my grandfather's dreamboat charms are not revealed by the photographs of him, which show a bespectacled fellow with smallish eyes and a dark concentration of hair beneath the nose. However, his famous spruceness does come through, not least in a picture that turned up in early 1995 in my grandmother's papers. The photo was copied and sent to various family members, almost as if it were an official portrait. Its seductive, iconic value was obvious. Joseph, thirty-something, sat atop a horse. (The animal's name was *Tayara*, Arabic for aeroplane. It lived in a makeshift stable in the hotel, where a full-time groom fed it and polished it up every day like a shoe. Occasionally, Tayara ran unsuccessfully at the Adana hippodrome.) He sported a smart wide-brimmed hat and round glasses, a sleeveless sweater, a white shirt with the sleeves rolled up into neat scrolls above the elbows, breeches, and superb riding boots. He carried a whip and he wore white gloves. It was hard for me, a non-equestrian, to say whether a certain horsemanship was captured by the photograph, but to my inexpert eyes he looked the part. The horse was prancing, and its heraldic posture lent the rider – straight-backed, impassive, assured – a chivalric air. *Le chevalier* Dakad: this was what the ensemble was calculated to impress upon the world.

What particularly interested me about this image was that Joseph lived in a dusty Turkish port populated by the families of shipping agents, cotton traders, commercial landlords, shopkeepers, stall-holders, tradesmen, importers, exporters. These people were not cavaliers, and to the best of my knowledge there hadn't been a local class of *chevaliers* to which Joseph might have belonged since Crusader times.

Of course, displays of class are, to an important degree, self-fulfilling and artificial, but it seemed that the aspirant and romantic elements in Joseph's brand of stylishness did not pass unnoticed. Into his thirties, he would be teased by girls chanting the rhyme

O Dakak-e
Tu nous fais tourner
La tête.

(Oh Dakak, you turn our heads.) The chant illustrated something else: contrary to the local custom of calling people by their first name (Monsieur Jean, Monsieur Theodore, etc.), for some reason Joseph's peers generally referred to him by his surname, *Dakak*.

But if Mersin was a one-horse town, and my grandfather owned that horse, it was to be noted that when Mersin was a one-fridge town, Joseph owned that fridge – a tall Frigidaire, expensive as a motorcar, bought in around 1950. He also owned the first car with automatic transmission in Mersin, a blue Pontiac bought in around 1956, and in the new hotel he installed Mersin's first central heating system and first elevator. When Mersin was a one-pedigree-dog town, Joseph owned the dog: Tarzan, a Great Dane acquired in Lyon in 1947, whose gargantuan appearance would send the people of Mersin diving for cover. (In those days there was so little traffic that Tarzan was allowed out on solo tours. His master rarely took him out for walks.) Back in 1939, Joseph employed a European architect to build the town's first decent cinema, the Günes Cinema, which was equipped with plush seats and loges. And, of course, Joseph at all times owned and ran the premier hotel in Mersin.

It was clear that these material firsts – many of which, in a backwater like Mersin, could only be achieved with a great deal of effort and expense – were more than social affectations. My grandfather's imagination was grabbed by technological progress. New things, modern things, brought into view cultural horizons which profoundly excited him. That said – and here was a rare trait in

Mersin – he also was interested in ancient forms of civilization. He had an antiquary's curiosity about relics and would ask local villagers whether they had come across any objects of interest. He wrote to Ankara to protest at the local habit of incorporating ancient blocks of limestone into the villagers' houses. He was proud of his friendship with Professor John Garstang, the English archaeologist, and also made friends, in the 'forties, with another English archaeologist, Michael Gough, whose wife Mary subsequently wrote of 'the good M. Dakad'. When the English travel-writer Freya Stark checked in at the Toros Hotel in April 1954, she wrote, 'Such a kind welcome because all here are friends of John Garstang's. They gave me one look and asked me what period I was studying – and are full of interest in Alexander the Great.' In *Alexander's Path* (1958), she described Joseph Dakad as 'overflow[ing] with kindness and a passion for cleanliness unique in my experience of Turkish inns'.

Joseph Dakad enjoyed reading history books and subscribed to the French journal *Historia*. He liked non-fiction. Novels did not interest him; neither, despite his interest in the Günes Cinema, did movies. Aided by his voracious newspaper reading habits, he was knowledgeable about a wide range of matters. When Julian Huxley came to the hotel, Joseph knew who he was. He took an interest in domestic and international affairs, which he viewed from a perspective that was 'not left-wing, that's for sure,' according to Oncle Pierre. My father was surprised to learn that his father-in-law knew all about Terence MacSwiney, the Lord Mayor of Cork who died on hunger strike in 1920, and Roger Casement, the Irish patriot hanged by the British in August 1916 for treasonably acting as Germany's 'willing agent'; Joseph even knew the name of the gun-filled trawler, the *Aud*, with which Casement's U-boat had a rendezvous off the coast of Ireland.

'Papa was a cultivated man,' my mother said quietly. 'There was no one like him in the whole of Mersin.'

On the subject of cultivation, it was Joseph's dream to own an orange garden. He bought books about the farming of citrus fruit and kept an eye open for land that might suit his purposes. He loved having oranges about the house, buying them in crates that he kept on top of a cupboard, out of the children's reach. It would seem that his love affair with citrus fruit endured even after, on one view, it had played a decisive part in the most disastrous episode of his life.

It is lunchtime, and hours of planning, shopping and cooking by my grandmother and her servants are about to pay off – or not. The lamb cutlets have been consumed approvingly, the correct acridity of the babaganoushe has been noted, the *böreks* have not been criticized. Now everything turns on the watermelon. That so much should hinge on this fruit is strange, since its quality will merely reflect on the choice made by the majordomo, Ahmet, at the market that morning; but that is the way it has always been: in the final analysis, the *pastèque* is the king of the table.

A rich red tranche is forked up from the serving dish and placed on Oncle Pierre's dessert plate. Pierre frowns, noting the consistency of the fruit's redness. A hush descends at the table as he brushes the dark pips from the flesh and inserts a morsel into his mouth. All the while, my grandmother watches anxiously. Oncle Pierre chews, then swallows. '*Pas mal*,' he concedes. '*Sept sur dix.*'

Mamie Dakad is happy and relieved, and general conversation resumes.

'*Everything* is marvellous, Georgette.' The speaker, in French, is Madame Olga Caton, an old friend of the family. Olga has a strong, gravelly accent in every language she speaks, her r's rolled with a regal finality; and indeed everything about her suggests a tsarina in exile. She takes out a cigarette and fixes it in her cigarette holder. My sister Ann, who knows the routine, offers a flame from a silver lighter. 'Here you are, Auntie Olga,' Ann says. 'Thank you, darling,' Olga says in English. Olga sucks on her cigarette holder, and her eyebrows – plucked into nothingness and replaced by a stroke of pencil – curve upwards appreciatively. 'You're so pretty, my dear, you really are.' She turns to Mamie Dakad and says in Arabic, 'She takes after her mother – the eyes, the hair, the chin.'

Mamie Dakad says, slightly begrudgingly, 'She has her mother's colouring, perhaps. But the bone structure is the father's.'

Pastries – *pains d'Espagne* and *sablés* topped with icing sugar and home-made apricot jam – are brought out to accompany the fruit.

Oncle Pierre stands up suddenly and authoritatively jangles a fistful of keys. 'Right, I'm off.' He looks at his watch. 'How are you going to the beach?'

'By bus,' my mother replies.

Pierre makes the click of the tongue that, in Turkey, means no. 'The *müdür* will drive you, or give you his car,' he decrees.

The *müdür* is the manager of the hotel. Although a helpful man, he is a former colonel in the Turkish army and is not, by training or inclination, a chauffeur. 'Pierre, there really is no need,' my mother protests. 'Besides, the children like going by bus.'

This is not true. We much prefer travelling by car – preferably Pierre's car, an air-conditioned, petrol-guzzling Chevrolet with an aquamarine front bench seat and a dark blue sunband at the top of the windscreen.

'Never!' my grandmother exclaims. 'Take the *müdür*'s car!'

Dursun, the cook, comes in with cups of Turkish coffee. (Her name means 'Stop', her parents having had their fill of children when she was born. Trained by my grandmother, she is a well-paid and highly sought-after freelancer.) Meanwhile, my mother and Amy help Fatma, the housemaid, to remove the dishes. In spite of years of mopping the eternal floors of the hotel by hand, Fatma is strong, wiry and flexible. She is probably in her fifties. Her eyebrows are thick and united, and her hair, beginning to grey, is always bunched out of sight inside a headscarf; my mother says that Fatma has never cut it and that it falls to her waist. Fatma's recent promotion to the key position of housemaid has been a success, although my grandmother says that *la Présente* (as Fatma is called when she is within earshot) depresses her with relentless tales of woe. Fatma, who is a Kurdish Turk, comes from a village in the east and still suffers from homesickness. At the age of thirteen, she married a fellow twenty years older than her. He died before any children were born. Fatma remarried another old-timer, a man (as she never ceases to repeat) older than her own mother. They have had six children. One daughter committed suicide; one son is

mentally disabled; another son, in his late teens, is a source of constant anxiety and trouble (gambling or drug troubles, Fatma
reckons) which, it is hoped, military service will iron out. Fatma's
husband refuses to work. Thankfully, she has a son who works hard
as a mechanic and who has bought her a washing machine, although
Fatma worries that the one day the good son will snap and kill the
bad son. Fatma worries a lot. She has never really got over the death
of a little granddaughter who ran in front of a car.

I don't learn any of this until years later. All I know for now is
that if Fatma wishes to make a phone call she asks me to dial the
number since, like Dursun, she has never learned to recognize
numerals or letters.

Auntie Olga, meanwhile, has brought out a fan decorated with
peacocks. Her makeup, which climaxes in a fiery streak of lipstick,
is under threat from the high temperature. 'What heat, what heat,'
she says. 'Darling,' she says to Ann, 'pour me a glass of water.'

Oncle Pierre, who has lit up a king-size American cigarette,
frowns and looks at his watch again. 'That's it, I'm off. I'll see you
all this evening.' He strides away rapidly, to the bank he is building.

Moments later, footsteps from the hallway announce somebody's
arrival: it is the *müdür*, a sheen of sweat on his brow and a smile on
his face, graciously insisting that we take his car.

'That's settled, then,' Mamie Dakad says. While we get ready for
the beach, she and Isabelle and Olga drink more Turkish coffee and
respectively smoke Pall Mall, Kent and Dunhill imported cigarettes
while Fatma polishes the cutlery and the plaques awarded by the
municipality to Georgette Dakad for being the proprietor of the
hotel in Mersin to pay the most corporation tax in a given fiscal year.

I remembered these scenes on a morning in August 1995. I was
alone in my late grandmother's apartment on the top floor of the
hotel, breakfasting on white cheese, olives, bread, and a glass of
milkless Black Sea tea. My solitude was heightened by the shutting
off of the top floor to paying guests. The decision was Mehmet
Ali's, who for two or three years had been running the hotel for his
own profit. Oncle Pierre, who was spending most of his time in
Paris, had lost interest in the business and, in a not entirely selfless

move, he let the hotel to Mehmet Ali at a near-nominal rent. Mehmet Ali, it was felt, had earned his break: not only was he efficient, trustworthy and enthusiastic but, most importantly, he had looked after my elderly grandmother in her last years with unflagging kindness – running errands, ensuring she took her medicines, assisting her with her domestic arrangements.

I got up from the breakfast table and went out to the balcony. The view of the sea was obstructed by the Panorama Apartments, eight storeys of luxury accommodation that rose from the middle of the hotel's terrace. The White Sea (as Turks call the Mediterranean) used to run up to a strand at the base of the hotel, where banana trees grew, but in about 1960 a tract of a land was reclaimed from the sea by Dutch engineers and transformed into a park. A crab-infested ridge of rocks served as a shoreline, and, quite far out at sea, large breakwaters created a haven. Over to the left were the docks and piers. They were dominated by a huge grain elevator that, with its classical white columns and majestic proportions, had always struck me as beautiful as any building in the city.

The Panorama Apartments stood on the site of the hotel's old swimming pool. When Oncle Pierre built the pool – a deep, cobalt box with an adjacent kidney-shaped paddling pool – it was the first swimming pool in central Mersin, and for the few years of the pool's existence, in the late 'sixties and early 'seventies, the modern Toros Hotel saw its heyday. But Oncle Pierre noticed that the businessmen who used the hotel rarely went for a dip and figured that there might be more profitable uses for the land taken up by the pool. And so there emerged the small skyscraper that changed the skyline of Mersin to such effect that postcards depicting it were run off by the city's tourist board, and beneath the apartment block there materialized the first upmarket shopping mall in Mersin. The ancestral land was still being put to profitable use.

I retreated from the balcony, which was suddenly too hot, into my grandmother's apartment, which was suddenly too sultry. Over the years, everything had been tried to cool down that hellish space. Air-conditioning, electric fans, a dogsbody with a water-hose spraying the roof – nothing had worked. Nor was the stuffiness helped by the wintry *fin de siècle* furniture (specially made in Istanbul) that my grandparents had favoured since the 'fifties: heavy armchairs and sofas, and heavy wooden sideboards with a matching dining-table and chairs.

'But isn't it very hot?' The waiter, Huseyin, arrived to collect the breakfast remains. I signalled my agreement with the pained wrinkling of the brow and the twisting of the hand that means, 'How long must we put up with this torment?'

Huseyin had been working at the hotel for over fifteen years and had escaped the round of redundancies introduced by Mehmet Ali when he took over the hotel. During Oncle Pierre and Mamie Dakad's time in charge, firings were very rare and the bulk of the staff would stay on for decades. Few quit. Employment at the hotel, which was fully unionized, was well paid and well insured, and the pension arrangements were hard to beat. Now, however, the future of the hotel was very much in doubt. Business was nothing like it used to be. New, competitive air-conditioned hotels had sprung up around the city and the Toros Hotel, although clean and well-situated, had become old-fashioned and uncomfortable.

I left my grandmother's apartment and went down to the hotel saloon, on the first floor. The saloon had remained practically unchanged in the quarter century I'd known it. The bar still featured revolving stools bolted to the ground, a display of ageing bottles of liquor, an icebox packed with bottles of cherry juice, apricot juice, beer, and Pepsi. The massive gilt mirror hung, as ever, by the entrance; next to it was the flaking, gilt-framed eighteenth century painting of camels arriving at a waterfront; over there were the rugs scattered on the cool floor, and there the pile of antique cushions and armchairs. The 'sixties breakfast tables were present and correct, and the defunct fan hung from the ceiling of the television alcove, where lonely businessmen still killed off evenings in dense clouds of cigarette smoke.

I had an appointment later that morning with a man called Salvator Avigdor, who had worked at the Toros Hotel during the Second World War, and with some time to spare before my meeting, I drank a small glass of tea and looked at my notes. I had, by this time, spoken to a number of Mersin old-timers who had known my grandfather, and gathered together photographs and a very few written documents I'd found in a large manila envelope in my grandmother's sideboard. I had not yet dug out the manuscript that, years previously, Phaedon and I encountered in the depot. The keys to the depot were missing and my mother was looking for them.

What I knew so far was that Joseph Dakak was born on Christmas day, 1899 – 'In Capricorn,' Amy said, 'the business sign.' His mother was Caro Raad. The Raads were an old family from the Syrian *grande bourgeoisie*, but the early death of Caro's parents left her and her sisters *désargentées*, and consequently the Raad girls married men who were considerably older than them. Eugénie Raad married into the Kandelaft family, who belonged to the *soyeux*, silken, class of Lyon and lived in a huge medieval chateau. Caro made a humbler match with Basile Dakak. Basile worked as a *transiteur des douanes* – a customs agent of some kind – in Iskenderun, a port to the south-east of Mersin; but not much else was known about him or the Dakak family, who were Greek Catholics from Aleppo or, possibly, Damascus.

Basile and Caro initially lived in Iskenderun, where three children were born: a daughter, Radié, who was five years older than Joseph, who himself was five years older than Georges. In about 1910, shortly after the family had moved to Mersin, Basile Dakak died from tetanus contracted by opening a rusty-topped bottle of *gazeuse*; he was perhaps fifty years old. The family was plunged into a financial crisis. Radié was taken by her mother to Istanbul to seek a favour from a cousin who was one of the Sultan's ministers; they stayed at the Pera Palace, the luxurious hotel built to accommodate European train travellers, and were grandly received. More mundanely, Caro rented out rooms to *des gens biens*. Her house, a handsome two-storey limestone building, was not in Mersin's upscale Greek quarter but in the Maronite quarter, not far from the Catholic church. The rental income only went so far, and Caro sold her jewels in order to pay for Joseph's fees at boarding school in Aleppo. Papa loved her specially as a consequence, my mother said.

But the money from the sale of the jewels also ran out, and

Joseph was forced to leave school at sixteen. It was the Great War, and my grandfather found work as a bookkeeper in Belemedik, a spot in the Taurus Mountains where Ottomans and Germans were building railroad tunnels. After Belemedik, where he picked up German, Joseph worked for a while as an interpreter for the Red Cross; it was unclear for how long and unclear, generally, what he'd done during perhaps the most mysterious time in Mersin's history, the French occupation from late 1918 to January 1922, a time which I knew nothing about other than that it saw Radié and Georges' departure from Mersin to France, and Caro's death, in early 1921, of a brain haemorrhage suffered in a cinema. She was forty-two years old. By 1923, grandfather was left in Mersin without a family.

Joseph's sense of abandonment was perhaps reflected in a document, dated 23 March 1923, that I'd found in my grandmother's apartment. It was a manuscript transcription by Joseph of a poem by a French poet – Jacques [illegible] – called *Renoncement*, in which the speaker bade an emotional, self-pitying farewell to his departing lover. The poem was of doubtful literary merit and was on the face of it unlikely to have been inspired by Georgette Nader, who was only fourteen in 1923 and who, in her unbudging devotion to Joseph, was the opposite of the poem's inaccessible, fleeting love object. And yet the fact remained that my grandmother had preserved the poem; and it was in the 'twenties, when she was still a teenager, that she began to carry a torch for Joseph Dakak. She loved his style and his authority, and he was drawn to this attractive and spirited young woman (ten years his junior) who had excelled at school. '*J'étais sérieuse, pas flirteuse,*' my grandmother had once told me. '*Je n'étais pas tralala.*' Exactly how Joseph earned his living at this time was not certain – his children could only assume that he was engaged in commerce of some kind – but at any rate, he got by. He was a *débrouillard*, his niece Ginette had told me, a man who could make do and make things happen. A seemingly eternal romantic involvement began between Georgette and Joseph. It grew to be the talking point of Mersin, since Dakak refused to commit himself to marriage, even when he was well into his thirties and financially secure. He had two main sources of income. The first was the hotel, which he founded in 1933 (in the old Nader property, which he rented) and initially called the Bellevue Hotel. The clientele consisted mainly of Turkish businessmen: in the two decades before the Second World War, the movement of foreigners into and around the Turkish Republic was strictly controlled. The second source of Joseph's wealth was income derived from acting for a German company, or companies, building sewer systems in and around Mersin and other Turkish towns. It was this line of work, Oncle Pierre believed, that led Joseph Dakak to go on a business trip to Berlin in around 1934 – a trip about which the only thing known by the family was that it took place.

Meanwhile, the 'thirties passed and Joseph still clung to his bachelordom. He played the field, rode his horse, and enjoyed his freedom – none of which prevented him from exercising dominion over Georgette. He made her quit her job helping out in a shop, and when she played cards he would appear at the door and simply say

My grandmother in her twenties

(in Arabic), 'I have come.' Unless she was losing heavily and needed to play on, she would gather up her chips and leave. Then, in 1939, when he was thirty-nine and she thirty, they married. *'Enfin! Enfin! Enfin!'* my grandmother's friend Lolo Naccache exclaimed when she me told the story. 'Seventeen years he kept her waiting – seventeen years!'

Soon after the marriage came the Second World War; and in 1942, Joseph's mysterious incarceration.

In 1945, he returned to Mersin from Palestine by train. My mother, five years old, accompanied her mother to the railway station to meet her father. He alighted from the train and walked along the platform towards them weeping.

Afterwards, Joseph could not do very much. He opened an import–export office, but the enterprise failed. He was distressed and gloomy. For a year or so he compulsively stalked backwards and forwards for a distance of around twelve feet, staring at the ground as he strode and swivelled, his hands behind his back, his face bunched into that dark, forbidding expression. He began to receive treatment for heart problems.

The one document surviving from this time was his recipe for marmalade to be made from six bitter oranges (*turunç*), three sweet oranges, and one lemon.

In 1947, Joseph accompanied Lina to Lyon, where she was due to start at a new school. They rowed out to the ship in a lighter loaded with trunks and cases filled with food for the French relations, who were subject to rationing. It was a therapeutic voyage for my grandfather. He went to Paris, and he visited his brother and sister in Lyon, from where he wrote a letter home in October. The first part of the letter was a rushed, somewhat curt response to three letters he had received from Georgette – 'I did not write a long letter from Paris as I had hoped, so don't expect one.' He explained that his return would be delayed by a week due to a cholera outbreak in Alexandria, and confirmed that he would still be arriving in Mersin via Beirut. He assured his wife that Lina was very happy and that she needn't worry about the little girl. Then the letter changed tack and concerned itself with a problem at the hotel that the Vali, Tewfik Sirri Gür, had brought to Joseph's attention, namely that complaints had been received about hotel guests going to the hotel's communal toilet wearing their pyjamas.

The old Toros Hotel, *circa* 1950

Returning to Mersin with Tarzan the Great Dane, Joseph concentrated on the business of the hotel. Life, as they say, returned to normal. Joseph opened a patisserie at the hotel, complete with a Greek chef, but it didn't work out. 'He was ahead of his time,' my mother said. Mersin changed only very slowly, and in letters written at the Toros Hotel in 1954, Freya Stark described the town as 'just two streets, one tidy and one dingy, and merchants' houses in gardens beyond. . . . It must be like the age-old life of little ports here . . . [I]n another year or so the big roads will be made and even more changes. I am only just in time.'

The final document I had found in my grandmother's apartment was dated 1 November 1959 and written in French. It was from a Walther Ülrich in Weissenfels (a mining town near Leipzig, in East Germany), with whom Joseph had not been in touch for 'at least ten years'. Neither I nor anyone else had heard of Walther Ülrich, and all I could deduce from the letter was that he'd visited Mersin in the past and that Joseph had in turn visited Herr Ülrich at his home in Saxony – presumably in 1934, the year of my grandfather's trip to Germany. Walther Ülrich informed Joseph that he and his wife had become old (seventy-five and sixty-five respectively) but were still healthy. 'You know that I lost my boys and all my fortune in this terrible war,' he wrote. 'I am thus forced to work right to the end, and count myself lucky to still have my position at the office. . . . And you, my friend, how are you and your family? How is business and who is still alive of those good people whom we count as our mutual friends, the Brazzafolis, Gioskun, etc. etc.? Much has changed in the world since we had the pleasure of your visit. . . .'

Indeed, by 1960, Mersin had finally started to change, and at the forefront of the developments was the new hotel, which was being built with a low-interest government loan procured thanks to the intervention of my grandfather's good friend, Mr Okyayüz, the Vali. That year also saw the dramatic death of Tarzan. The dog was dying of cancer and it was decided to put him down in the mountains near Gözne, where he had been happiest. Joseph, distraught and tearful, did not have the heart to shoot the animal himself and instructed two locals to perform the task. They took Tarzan to a neighbouring valley and shot him there. Unfortunately, they botched the job. Tarzan survived and, bleeding from the gunshot wound, somehow managed to walk the three kilometres back to his master's summer house, where he lay on the steps and died.

My grandfather never spoke about the war. Once, when a friend broached the subject, it brought tears to his eyes. 'Leave this old story alone,' he said. '*Laisse tranquille cette vieille histoire.*'

I closed my notebook and got to my feet. It was nearly midday. The time had come to see Salvator Avigdor. I walked down past the reception and headed out into the heat.

A visitor to Monsieur Salvator, who lives with his wife in an apartment not a pistachio shell's throw from the Greek Orthodox Church, will quickly learn that he is a survivor of a multiple bypass operation (four veins removed from his leg and transplanted into his heart) and brain surgery (a tumour 'the size of an orange' excised). Monsieur Salvator, pale and contented and bald as a melon, will tell you that his family comes from Adrianople (Edirne), in European Turkey; that his uncle was a tailor to Sultan Abdul Hamid II and was awarded a gold medal (which Monsieur Salvator can show you if you so wish) for services rendered; that his father was a watch-maker with a sideline in revolvers; that his son went to Harvard and now runs a huge garment business in the United States; that another uncle worked the boat from Marseille to the United States and spoke twenty-four languages. Sipping a *limonata* and mopping his brow – a surgical scar runs across his cranium like a bicycle track – Monsieur Salvator will tell you these things and indeed many other things that may come to his mind: his loquaciousness, he explained to me, was a side-effect of the heart surgery.

Monsieur Salvator said that he and his wife were the last two Jews left in Mersin. The synagogue had disappeared, as had the seventy Jewish families who lived in the town when Salvator joined the Toros Hotel as an eighteen-year-old on 9 September 1935 – a time when Mersin was a marvel, Monsieur Salvator said, a cosmopolis where you'd hear three words of French, four words of Turkish and three words of Arabic, and when Joseph Dakak, a punctilious but fair boss, caroused until three or four in the morning and didn't emerge from his rooms in the hotel loft until noon. There was a staff of five: a Christian, a Muslim woman, a Kurd, and two Jews. Monsieur Salvator, the bookkeeper, found the ethnically diverse atmosphere uncongenial.

In 1940, Monsieur Salvator recalled with a sigh, the Toros Hotel was the place to be. It had twenty rooms and a first-class restaurant with a chef who had cooked for Mustafa Kemal. On Sunday nights there was dancing to tunes played by musicians from Stamboul on the terrace overlooking the sea. The hotel buzzed with Mersin soci-ety, travellers and foreign so-called businessmen. Leaning forward with not a little excitement in his voice, Monsieur Salvator revealed that the Turkish authorities forced Monsieur Dakak to engage a man – Moharem, he was called – who was an agent of the Turkish secret police and whose job it was to spy on the goings-on at the hotel; that an Austrian resident of Mersin called Gioskun Parker, mentioned in Herr Ülrich's letter as a friend of Joseph, was an agent of the Germans and quite possibly a double agent of the Turks; that in 1940, Monsieur Salvator quit his job because the secret police wanted him to intercept letters and inform on the guests staying at the hotel. The most eminent of these guests was the German ambassador, Franz von Papen. He, Salvator Avigdor, a Jew, had personally accompanied His Excellency and Frau von Papen on a motoring trip down the coast in the direction of Silifke, stopping at the spectacular caverns known as Heaven and Hell.

I asked Salvator whether my grandfather ever expressed opinions about the war.

'Never. It was out of the question. At the hotel, there would be a German here, an Englishman there, and an Italian in between. You couldn't open your mouth. You never knew who was working for who.'

I said, 'What about my grandfather? Do you think he worked for anyone?'

Monsieur Salvator said, 'Well, he was Germanophile, that's for sure. His German was fluent, and he'd speak to the German visitors at the hotel.' He continued pleasantly, 'I personally think that he probably did work for the Germans. You see, once you've given a little information, that's it, you've crossed the line.'

Monsieur Salvator didn't elaborate on his speculation. Instead he stood up and made an aerobatic motion with his hand. 'Every day an Italian plane flew over the port, counting the ships. You must understand, Mersin was an important place. It was full of intrigue, like Lisbon. Mersin,' Mr Salvator said, pointing upwards, 'was like Casablanca.'

Walking back to the hotel from Monsieur Salvator's, I reflected that pretty much everything I had heard about Joseph suggested that he saw himself as a man apart, and indeed that *seeing himself* must have been an essential procedure of his psyche. It wasn't that, Narcissus-like, he fell in love with his own reflection; it was rather that, in order to generate and project an image for which there was no local model, he would have needed to dream up an imagined version of himself by which he might gauge his style and conduct. To judge from his reputation as a self-cultivator, this relationship with his imaginary double must have been a powerful one; perhaps as powerful and enduring as any he knew. The question was: what was the character of this modular other? Who was he?

The notion of my grandfather as a fantasist made me think of certain other fantasists I encounter in my working life – the kind who wind up on the wrong end of allegations of fraud. What often marks the downfall of these men – almost invariably they are men – is not a cold ambition to enrich themselves at the expense of others but a fatal susceptibility to their own deceptions: a crazy, romantic belief that their get-rich-quick schemes, however flawed and tricky, will result in champagne for all. Could the same thing have happened to Joseph? Could some dreamlander's misapprehension have led him astray – into espionage and subsequent imprisonment? I thought about what Monsieur Salvator had said about Casablanca. I was, of course, thinking about the movie, about a well-dressed man in a white tuxedo who tries to steer a neutral and profitable course through a sea of vultures, gamblers, desperadoes, lovers, black marketeers, drinkers, secret agents, beauties, idealists, rumour-mongers. Humphrey Bogart, as Rick, the owner of Rick's Café Américain, had been almost exactly my grandfather's age; and Casablanca was set in December 1941, precisely when my grandfather was running the Toros Hotel and, unless I was mistaken, only months before he was arrested.

I ran into my mother at the Toros Hotel reception. 'Did you find the key to the depot?' I asked. My mother reached into her hip pocket. 'I have it here,' she said.

With the key in my hand I ran up the hotel's handsome granite stairs just as, twenty-one years before, I ran up the stairs clutching a telegram from Ireland that a waiter had handed me. I was in tears as I sprinted up to my grandmother's apartment that day, because the telegram from my uncle said, 'DAD DIED YESTERDAY STOP FUNERAL ON SATURDAY STOP BRENDAN'.

2

Now never marry a soldier,
a sailor or a marine,
But keep your eye on the Sinn Féin boy
with his yellow, white and green.

— Anonymous, 'Salonika'

In summer, around Inishannon, the Bandon could be a jungle river. Rank, swollen trees – beech, oak, willow, ash, sycamore, horse chestnut, various evergreens – gather heavily over the banks, the trunks enveloped by vines and dangling plants, the forked branches supporting huge thunderheads of foliage. Everything is overgrown: river boulders and sandbars sprout bushes and weeds, the water surface is clogged with pale yellow blooms, and elongated strands of green vegetation run underwater. Further west and upriver, the Bandon slips along through meadows and copses and is only patchily visible from the main road. At Bandon, the old British garrison town of which it used to be said that even its pigs were Protestant, the river passes under Bandon Bridge. It is still remembered that in 1641 English troops tied 88 Irishmen of the town back to back and threw them off the bridge into the water, where all were drowned. Upstream beyond Bandon town, the river meanders by such townlands as Coolfadda, Shinagh and Laragh on its northerly bank and Castlebernard and Killountain on its southerly. It is briefly reunited with the highway, at Baxter's Bridge, before twisting off again on a path of its own. The road, meanwhile, has started to resemble the secretive river it shadows – narrow, sinuous, and hemmed in by thickets and dense, overarching trees that barely admit daylight. Black-feathered birds drift like ashes out of the way of cars. The surrounding hills are obscured and the highway is reduced to a succession of blind turns. It's enough to lead you, kept in this leafy dark, to imagine a conspiracy to conceal the world through which you travel – West Cork.

Finally, a valley opens up ahead. A ruined mill appears on the right. You are coming to the village of Enniskean. If you take a left, towards the gentle uplands there, and follow certain hedged-in lanes, you will arrive upon the townland of Ardkitt, where my grandfather Jim O'Neill was born and the O'Neill farm, now occupied by my second cousin Pat O'Neill, may still be found. If you drive straight on, through Enniskean and the even smaller village of Ballineen, you will come to places where my grandfather, long after he had left the country to live in Cork city, returned on nights when neither the moon nor the floods were up, to steal salmon on the Bandon river.

Jim usually took with him a son or two; often, too, his regular poaching sidekick, Dan Cashman, whose ready compliance with my grandfather's commands outweighed the fact that he could neither swim, nor drive, nor see beyond the palm of his hand. The fishing party pulled up in the twilight at Manch, where the Bandon twists close to the road and where the fishing rights and riparian lands were the property of the Conners of Manch House. (Manch was also where Tom Barry's Flying Column, having marched in rain through Shanacashel, Coolnagow and Balteenbrack, crossed the river after the Kilmichael ambush.) Arrival at dusk, when a car with no lights shining would not attract attention, was vital; the car's electrics were doctored so that the brake lights could be turned on and off by a special switch under the dashboard.

My grandfather, Dan Cashman and my uncle Brendan quickly

jumped out. They took two nets – darkened with a product actually called Nigger-Brown Dye – from the boot and skipped over the stile. They passed through the hedge and crossed the single track of the Cork, Bandon & South Coast Railway. There was the water, only a few dozen paces away through furze and long grass. Meanwhile another uncle of mine, Jim Junior, drove on and parked the car in a spot he hoped was both innocuous and discreet. Only fourteen, he would wait there anxiously until the others returned later that night.

Night fell. Nevertheless, it was possible to see clearly, since a night sky is navy, never black, and eyes grow quickly accustomed to the dark. Rain fell intermittently, which was good. The last thing the poachers wanted was the moon hanging there like a button on a blazer and lighting up the river.

My grandfather pegged one end of a net into the ground. Then he took the net's weighted line and threw it over the water on to the opposite bank, which was thirty or so feet away; he did the same with the jackline of the other (unpegged) net. He and Brendan forded the river by stepping on a gravel isle and wading knee-deep across the remaining stretch. Once they'd crossed, Brendan unspooled and worked the first net so that it stretched across the water like a submerged tennis net. (The net could drop ten to eleven feet underwater in meshes of seven and a quarter inches.) Meanwhile my grandfather picked up the second, unpegged, net and signalled to Dan Cashman to do the same on his side of the water. Then Dan Cashman and my grandfather dragged that net through the water towards the tennis net.

Ever since the time he was carried away by the current, Dan Cashman would only enter the water in an emergency. Dan was lucky, that time, to wash up on a fluvial island. My grandfather had to wade into the freezing water and swim over to him. He tied a rope around Dan's waist, swam back to the bank, and hauled Dan through the water like a calf.

In between the two nets was the Key Hole. If the salmon were anywhere, they would be there, slowly twisting where the river was ten to twelve feet deep. These were the trade secrets that my grandfather knew from his childhood: the location of the pools where the salmon congregated – the Key Hole, the Forge Hole, the Rock Pool, the Flat of Kilcascan – and the fords and the dangerous currents. He learned from his father, who acquired the knowledge and the poaching knowhow from his own father.

The three poachers stealthily went about their work. The river was unquiet, haunted by sounds and movements that made everybody jumpy. The wind stirred a roar in the riverbank trees, somewhere waterhens chirped, downriver a startled heron flapped up; and, of course, the water itself, dark and restless shapes of trees reflected monstrously in its sheen, was always rustling. Rain snapped in the trees.

My grandfather was not out on the river at midnight, chilled and soaked and running the risk of catastrophe, for the fun of it. He was there because Jim and Brendan had their confirmations coming up and another son, Padraig, his communion, and the boys hadn't a stitch to wear.

As the nets came together, salmon could be felt tugging in the meshes. Eventually the nets were dragged out. 'Jesus, they're heavy,' my grandfather said. And they were, because they were crammed. A rogue shaft of moonlight shone on the netted fish. 'Look at that,' my grandfather said, 'a rosary.'

On they went, to another pool further down the river, and then another. Each time the fishing was good. By the time the catch was totally landed, thirty-three salmon were tallied. It was a record-breaking haul.

My grandfather made a sack from his herringbone overcoat and filled it with fish. Afterwards, their smell would not leave his jacket. My grandmother would say that the cats of Cork followed him around for a month.

'What happens if the bailiffs come?' Brendan asked his father.

My grandfather pulled out a revolver. ''Twould be a poor night for any bailiff that walks here tonight.'

Although on this occasion two nets were being used, usually just the one sufficed: the poachers would suspend the net in the middle of the pool for about half an hour, waiting for the salmon to entangle themselves on the principle that salmon are never still. (It was not unknown for a dog to be thrown into the river to frighten the fish towards the net.) Sometimes a guest poacher would accompany the O'Neills and the outing would take on a social dimension. Tomás MacCurtain Junior, the IRA man and son of the Lord Mayor of Cork shot dead by the British, went poaching with my grandfather, as did Brendan's brother-in-law, Seán O'Callaghan, after his release from seven years' imprisonment.

Poaching was not restricted to the Bandon. In August and September my grandfather fished for blackberries, as the late season fish were called, at Skibbereen. There, the river Ilen is tidal and the channel forty-five yards across, and two nets had to be tied end to end to cover it. The channel could not be forded: my grandfather had to swim naked with the jackline in his hand. Still naked, he would pull the nets over with the jackline and remain on the far bank for half an hour of fishing; then he'd swim back.

The thirty-three salmon were taken to the fishmongers, who would pay anything from £2 to £5 for each fish. That was a lot of money.

A fishmonger once tried to cross Jim O'Neill. Jim sent Brendan to Mortell's ('If It Swims, We Have It') with three salmon. Mortell only paid for two, asserting that the third was a slat – a dud fish. My grandfather took issue with this and returned to Mortell's on two or three occasions, claiming payment or the return of the salmon. 'It'll cost you a lot more than one salmon,' he finally warned Mortell. Mortell shrugged and continued serving his customers. After all, what remedy did Jim, as a thief of the fish, have? But Mortell miscalculated. There and then, in a full shop, my grandfather toppled a skyscraper of egg-crates and the shop was flooded in a lake of yolk. 'Now,' my grandfather said, 'you can keep your salmon.'

But there was no problem selling the thirty-three salmon. The O'Neill boys made their sacraments dressed to kill.

Poaching was not always this lucrative or easy. The danger and awful thrill of it lay in the ongoing battle of wits with the fishing bailiffs who patrolled the river at night. To my uncles Jim and Brendan, these nocturnal escapades from the middle of the last century are as vivid as ever, and they are still able to give detailed and amazed accounts of their close shaves and run-ins with the forces of law and order, stories of flashlights and car-chases and gunshots fired in the air – stories that nearly always end with the bailiffs foiled and flat on their faces like cartoon goons.

Even the time uncle Jim was caught is retold as a triumph of sorts. One night in 1957, they were netting the river just west of Bandon, near the Welcome Inn – my grandfather and his sons Jim and Brendan, twenty and nineteen years old respectively. The river at that place turns like a horseshoe, with a gravel strand on the inward bank of the turn. Engines and other hitches had been thrown on to the bed of the pool to stop poaching, but my grandfather knew exactly how far down the hole the net could be dropped without snagging. Two fish were twitching on the gravel when suddenly the bailiffs' torches were bearing down on them. Brendan, who was on the far bank, immediately bagged the fish and pulled the net out of the river. 'Lie down or I'll fire,' he shouted, bluffing, and the two approaching bailiffs dived for cover.

My grandfather ran upriver and uncle Jim went downriver, splitting the patrol. When uncle Jim got some distance away, he turned round and shouted obscenities to attract attention to himself and give the others a chance of getting away. Sure enough, the bailiffs both turned on him and, joined by a third bailiff, soon had Jim cornered in a field. When asked who he was, Jim asked them who were they to ask. 'We're water keepers,' they said. 'Well, so am I,' said Jim. They grabbed him by the scruff of the neck and marched him away. Jim stumbled and fell. 'I can't see a thing,' he complained, 'could you shine a light?' The bailiffs complied, and the flashlights alerted Brendan and my grandfather to their pursuers' whereabouts.

Uncle Jim was led past the hidden getaway car to the Welcome Inn. Phone-calls were made, and just as the bailiffs were about to take Jim back to the river for further questioning, four uniformed guards appeared. They asked Jim who he'd been poaching with. 'Well,' Jim (a teetotaller) said, 'I was in the pub, addled – I was after drinking a few pints – and a fellow I knew to see asked me whether I wanted to make a few shillings. Jesus, I wouldn't know his name at all. The third fellow,' Jim informed the guards, 'was a fellow we picked up in Bandon. John was his name, I believe.'

Two of the guards rolled up their sleeves. 'Right, you're going to tell us what happened.'

'Lads, take it away,' an older officer said, 'he's only a young fellow.' He took Jim aside. 'Listen, son, the judge will go easy on you if you help us out. You're only carrying the can for the two others.' But Jim stuck to his story, and after the interrogation ended, he asked whether there was any chance of a lift to Bandon. 'Ah, sure why not,' the guards said.

Once in Bandon, my uncle starting walking. Even though his feet were killing him – he wore oversized Wellingtons – he took an indirect route home, via Toureen, in case he was followed. (On the morning of 22 October 1920, five British soldiers were shot dead in Toureen.) It wasn't until he'd tramped the eight miles to Toureen in the darkness that a car finally drove by. He stuck out a thumb and the car came to a halt. Who should be in it but the chief fisheries inspector and his assistant – Scanlon and Buckley. Even though they knew young Jim had been out poaching, they drove him into Cork and dropped him at the door of the house. If Jim was expecting a warm and relieved welcome when he got home, he was disappointed. His father and brother were in bed, fast asleep.

The next day, water bailiffs found the nets Brendan had stowed in a ditch two fields south of the river. Salmon scales in the net were sent for analysis to Dublin, where they were identified by Dr Wendt as the scales of two salmon. Uncle Jim was summoned to court and charged. He didn't comply with the summons and on the day of the hearing was in West Cork, looking for guns for the IRA campaign in the North. He learned about his convictions on four charges – poaching, possessing a net, and possessing parts of two salmon – and his fine (£21 10s. 10d.) from a headline in the *Evening Echo*.

Uncle Jim, on his wages of £7 a week, was unable to pay the fine. He wrote to the Minister of Justice, explaining that he was the eldest of ten children and his earnings weren't his to keep. The Minister replied that the best he could do was grant Jim an extra three months in which to pay the fine.

Three months was all Jim needed. Three months took him into the next fishing season. On the first night of the new season, they caught enough salmon to pay the fine and plenty more.

My uncle Jim's decision to draw the bailiffs to himself was not a spontaneous self-sacrifice but the implementation of a plan that, whatever else happened, my grandfather was not to be caught: two years before, Jim O'Neill Senior had picked up a conviction and a large fine for poaching, and a second offence would have had very serious consequences. The irony was that his conviction arose from an entirely innocent visit to the river. My grandfather, at that time, was working at the ESB marina power station, where he befriended a man from Donegal, Jimmy McCloughlin. Jimmy was set on buying a car, even though he couldn't drive. My grandfather said to him, 'I know where there's a nice little car for you; and I'll teach you to drive.' So Jimmy bought a 1946 Hillman Minx for £40 and my grandfather obtained full use of the vehicle for the duration of the driving lessons. In the course of one such lesson, they decided to go for a spin in West Cork. It was a beautiful summer's evening, and the two men were accompanied by their wives. The lure of the river was always with my grandfather and as usual he couldn't resist casting an eye over it. The day-trippers were sitting on a bank of the Bandon, admiring the scenery, when bailiffs appeared and asked what they were doing. 'I'm out showing these Donegal people West Cork,' my grandfather truthfully answered. Nevertheless, the next day there was a raid on the O'Neill house. By chance they uncovered two coal bags with scales of two salmon in them. Jim O'Neill was convicted and fined £48. It was a massive penalty, but it was the first and last time they ever caught him.

The time my grandfather was arrested was the only time his son Kevin, my father, saw him drunk. My father (the third oldest son, after Jim and Brendan) said that he was occasionally taken poaching. 'I hated it,' he said. 'It scared the hell out of me. For me, West Cork was about ambushes and murders and the Black and Tans. It was a bloodstained, haunted kind of place – spooky. The roads and fields were dark and isolated. Men were shot and buried there. I wasn't like Brendan,' my father said. 'Brendan was fearless, as crazy as my dad.'

Jim O'Neill wasn't frightened in West Cork. He was at home there day or night: at home in townlands around Enniskean like Curraghcrowley, Desertserges and Farranasheshery, and at home, too, in further-flung Clonakilty, Kilbrittain, Drimoleague, Skibbereen.

To my ears, these place-names continue to have the lyricism of the unfamiliar, even though I've now been to the villages and small towns they identify; and although I've seen the bunting that over-hangs their streets and seen their houses sunlit in fresh coats of coral and mustard and avocado, and noted, furthermore, the signboards that designate them as Heritage Towns, Development Zones or West Cork Trail attractions, I continue to think of them, and places like them, as grey-brown, inward-looking, and vulnerable to flooding by a past that, like the local water-table, lies just beneath the surface.

It might be said that the persistence of these notions, and their romanticism, show me up for what I am: an outsider. I'm not sure about that. If mythic West Cork abides anywhere, it is in its own people, who, it can sometimes seem, are apt to ascribe some history to its every rut, puddle and tree. Some spots give voice to the past by their names, like the inlet in the Bandon known as the Punchbowl because centuries ago wines and spirits were poured into it by banqueters at Togher Castle and for two days after the locals drank freely while they swam; but most places are dumb. The uninformed visitor cannot know that Meehan was thrown from his horse at that gate and died, that the derelict cottage by the road is what splits the O'Herlihy family. Nor can the visitor guess that the petrol-station stands where there was once a British barracks; that twelve Thompson guns with rounds of ammunition were dumped for years beneath those rhododendron bushes; that the farmhouse in that copse was a training headquarters for the IRA; that a Big House stood among those diseased elms until it was burned to the ground; that in the square were deposited the three McCarthy girls, tarred and feathered for dancing with the enemy; that the stony furlongs of that mountainside were tramped by Tom Barry's Flying Column; that in that bog were placed the bodies of three men executed as informers.

In some locales history is visible. For example, there is a little valley known as Beal na mBlath (the Mouth of Flowers), which you reach by driving along a deserted country road north of Dunmanway, turning right at a crossroads marked by an inn, and stopping a further hundred yards or so along the road. There is a grassy bank on one side of the road and a wooded bank on the other, and, as happens on so many West Cork lanes, there is the sound of a brook shivering in a thicket somewhere. It was here, a memorial stone reminds us, that, on 22 August 1922, Michael Collins met his death. A few miles north-west of Beal na mBlath is the road from Dunmanway to Macroom. At a remote point in the road, not far from a crossroads, you'll see a monument shaped like an enormous tombstone. This commemorates the Kilmichael ambush: in November 1920, Tom Barry's IRA Cork No. 3 Brigade, for the loss of three men, surprised and killed eighteen British Auxiliaries, burned two armoured lorries, and seized arms and ammunition. The whole fray can be re-imagined by reference to a relief model of the terrain that's been placed on site, complete with electric lights of varying colours to illuminate the positions of the two lorries, the IRA command post, and the three points on the roadside rocks from which the IRA men fired; it is apparent, if you walk down the exposed road in question, just how well chosen was the ambush site and how little hope the Auxiliaries had of escape. The monument to the boys of Kilmichael was unveiled in around 1970. To mark the occasion, several hundred marchers paraded in a military formation. At the front walked Tom Barry and Jim O'Neill and, attached to his hand, Jim's oldest grandson. At a certain point I broke free of my grandfather's grip and ran on ahead, leading the column on my own; turning around, I saw the marchers salute as they passed the monument and so I saluted, too.

I have no memory of my grandfather at all, and the Kilmichael incident is known to me only through the chuckling recollection of my grandmother. She related the story as we stood together at the monument on a chilly, drizzling November day. As my sturdy, beloved grandmother described my younger self marching on this road, I was surprised by a surge of gratification which, had I not uneasily suppressed it, would have come close to euphoria. In however tiny a respect, my trajectory had intersected this rough land and its people, who had granted me uncomplicated admission into their ranks; and, for whatever reason, I was suddenly engulfed by a feeling of kindredness and racination that was unaccustomed and thrilling. This was something other than a simple wave of pleasure set off by an encounter with one's cultural origins; it was, rather, an intense recognition – or what *felt* like recognition – of a primitive affiliation to a political and historical community, an affiliation so pure and overwhelming that for an instant it felt as though I had stumbled upon a solution to a riddle.

Then again, I'm open as anyone to the spells places can cast. When, in March 1995, I flew into Cork city for the first time in years and looked out of the aeroplane window to see the two channels of the river Lee dazzling among my birthplace's low hills and the sun shining on one half of the city and the rain falling on the other, I was bewitched. My entrancement continued in the taxi from the airport, for as we descended into Cork a rainbow, the biggest and most fiercely striped I'd ever seen, made a miraculous half-circle from the valley down below to the highland on my right. I could not help associating this iridescent loop of vapour with the optimistic political atmosphere in the country. The ceasefire declared by the IRA and its paramilitary loyalist counterparts was over six months old. Daytime patrols by the British army in the North were waning, troop numbers were falling, and the talk was of exploratory talks between the British government and Sinn Féin. True, some issues looked troublesome, in particular the insistence by London and unionists that paramilitary organizations had to disarm prior to their participation in all-party talks; but the general view was that the benefits of peace had proved so substantial that, however tough and protracted the road ahead might be, a return to violence was out of the question. Things were looking up.

The taxi drove me to my grandmother's house in Ballinlough, a district of Douglas in south Cork dominated by a large estate of tidy, pebble-dashed houses built forty or so years ago. I arrived to find a Sunday evening family gathering in full swing. Crowded into the living room were three uncles, Jim, Terry and Padraig, and their wives, Kitty, Mary and Joan; my aunt Angela, down from Dublin for the weekend; my aunt Marian and her husband Don; and, of course, my grandmother, who gripped my face as I stepped over threshold and gave me two fervent kisses. I was happy to say little as the family talked amongst itself. The chatter – incessant, cheerful, uncontentious – ranged from the terrible weather (for two golfless years it hadn't stopped raining) to local politics to the question of whose looks were inherited from whom. As I observed the goodwill and talk flowing around the room, I wondered how my warm and open family could ever keep things from each other – things that might amount to secrets. As I found out, they did; and it was as though, by some trick of chiaroscuro, the very brightness of such talk served to plunge unspoken matters all the further into obscurity.

Sometimes it appears that political convictions may be genetically transmitted characteristics, like a certain crookedness of the nose or the ability to swing a stick at a ball. My grandfather, great-grandfather and great-great-grandfather, the story went, was each imprisoned in the cause of Irish freedom. There was a nuance: although his father Peter was a rebel, Jim O'Neill's republicanism mainly descended from the family of his mother, Annie O'Driscoll. Her father, William O'Driscoll, was a famous Land Leaguer, and on his release from Cork Gaol a crowd carried him shoulder-high into Kilbrittain and named him William the Conqueror.

I discovered that stories circulated plentifully among the O'Neills. My grandmother was their collector and teller-in-chief. It was she who told them earliest and shaped them longest, and she who was invested with the authority of having been there. Born on 19 May 1912, she was, in a manner of speaking, there in 1916 for the Easter Rising; there when the Irish Republican Army came into being, there during the Anglo-Irish War – in which Tomás MacCurtain Senior was shot dead in front of his family, and Terence MacSwiney, MacCurtain's successor as Lord Mayor of Cork, died on hunger-strike – and during the Civil War. My grandmother was party to these mythic episodes and they were part of her. She said – and she wasn't joking – that her terror of thunderstorms and loud noises in the night stemmed from the times when she cowered indoors while the British forces ran wild in the deserted streets of Dunmanway, hammering down doors and drunkenly shooting and murdering and causing mayhem.

Grandmother's view of the world was profoundly political, if not downright Manichaean. Everywhere she saw the forces of justice and good locked into an unending, many-faceted conflict with the forces of injustice and evil. Approaching her ninetieth birthday, she continued to follow current affairs, taking sides on a wide range of issues: Balkan warfare, Central American flood relief, local industrial disputes, the persecution of gay broadcasters, the treatment of Rumanian immigrants. She made a point of buying *The Big Issue*, the magazine for the homeless, and knew all about the life of her regular vendor, Christy. When she visited me in London at the age of eighty-three, she instinctively befriended the two tramps – immense, bearded, raucous drunks – who slept at the corner of the street I lived in, and for years asked how 'those two lads' were getting on. Her consumption patterns were shaped by a variety of boycotts (against governments and corporations) and sympathies (for Irish-made products), and the time I flew over to Cork on RyanAir she did not hesitate to criticize me for using an airline that was bad to its workers. The war between right and wrong was without limitation, and whenever I visited my grandmother I was treated to up-to-the-minute despatches from the front. Very often the bulletin concerned some showdown, skirmish or exchange of words in which Grandma had been personally involved: an encounter with Conor Cruise O'Brien, the Catholic arch-unionist ideologue who denounces Irish nationalism as 'Catholic imperialism', whom she once upbraided in the streets of Dublin; or some occurrence whose very banality revealed the boundlessness of her ethical concerns. For example: in 1996, when she was eighty-four, my grandmother went to the Aran Islands on her annual jaunt with 'the girls' (her sisters Nance and Enda). Whereas some might return from the Aran Islands with stories of their haunting beauty, what Grandma spoke of was, first, the rejection of a ham sandwich at the hotel ('*Ham?* Ham my eye, it was all gristle') and a further rejection of what purported to be a 'salad' sandwich; and, second, of some argy-bargy that took place on the ferry to the mainland. The boat was crowded and Grandma approached a German couple who were occupying a three-person seat for themselves. '"Excuse me," says I, "could you and your wife move along so that I can sit down too?" "No," the man said. I laughed, because I thought he was joking. Then I realized he wasn't. "How *dare* you," says I. "You're on an Irish boat, sailing on Irish waters, and you're on holiday – yet you won't make room for me?" "No," the man said, "you will not sit there." "You are an arrogant German bastard. As long as you're alive Hitler isn't dead." That did it. They moved along then.'

My grandmother also talked about the deep past. She told a story that, like a horror movie, started with a prelapsarian scene of innocence and domestic tranquillity: her father reading to her in bed at the family home in Dunmanway, West Cork. This was a rare treat. Although Timothy Lynch, a quiet man, doted on his children, he worked a six-day week as a foreman for a bread company in Bandon, coming home at around five on a Saturday and going out again Sunday evening. Every weekend he had to cycle twenty-one miles each way, rain or shine. (He was something of an athlete: he played on the Cork football team in 1911. My grandmother played camogie, the women's version of hurling, with less success: a goalie, she once conceded fourteen goals to Macroom.)

As Timothy was reading his children a bed-time story, there was a hammering at the door. It was them – the Black and Tans. They were dragooning men to fill in the craters in the road. Timothy was pulled away and herded with others in the main square of the town. It was like Hitler, my grandmother said, all the able-bodied men were rounded up and forced to work for days at a time, and their terrified families might have no idea of their fate or whereabouts. As Timothy was led away, some of the children – there were eleven of them, seven girls and four boys – began to cry. This infuriated one of the Tans. 'Shut up!' he shouted. But the crying continued. The Tan became enraged. He drew out his pistol and shot the cat in the head.

My grandmother had another childhood recollection of the Black and Tans. One freezing December day, a local Catholic cleric, Canon Magner, took his dog out for its daily stroll. Some time later, the dog returned home without its master, whining and whining. The housekeeper sensed something was wrong and a search party went out. They found blood on the road. Then they found the canon's body in a ditch; he had ice on his face. He'd been stopped on the road by an open lorry of British soldiers, questioned, and shot. A lad called Tadhg Crowley was also at the scene. The search party found his body, too.

'That was my political education,' my grandmother said. 'My family and the Black and Tans.'

It wasn't difficult to guess what education my grandmother received from her family. Her uncles Dan and Bob Lynch were interned in the North in 1921 during the Anglo-Irish War, and three of her brothers, Jack, Tadhg and Paddy, came to be interned during the Second World War. The only non-republican Lynch was Ellen Lynch, my great-grandmother. She was born a Kingston and there was Protestant blood in her; but even she had Fenian cousins, the two Quill brothers, who abandoned their nail factory in Dunmanway and disappeared – to America, in the family's best guess.

More than one of my grandmother's children observed that she rarely spoke about her husband, Jim O'Neill. For example, Grandma had no ready tale about her courting days with Jim, which is perhaps why, when I broached the subject, she spontaneously said, 'What did I know about him? I knew that he was beautiful.'

She must have known that he was a republican, too, because she'd see him at the Gaelic League Hall, where you spoke Irish and danced Irish dances, and at Tomás Ashe Hall, the republican club in Father Matthew Quay, named after the Easter Rising veteran who died from forcible feeding during a hunger strike.

Eileen Lynch was eighteen when she met Jim O'Neill. She had

just moved with her family from Dunmanway to Cork city, where she worked in a shop. She wasn't entirely without metropolitan sophistication: Grandma said that the Black and Tans' womenfolk had introduced West Cork to rouge, powder, lipstick and bobbed hair. ('Don't go looking like a Black and Tan's wife!' the nuns would say to schoolgirls who wore make-up.) But Eileen and Jim didn't go with each other immediately; there were other liaisons first. It wasn't until she was twenty-one and he twenty-three that romance, as they say, blossomed. On 8 July 1934, at the Church of the Immaculate Conception in the Lough, Eileen Lynch married her beautiful republican.

My grandmother quickly took to her parents-in-laws, Peter and Annie O'Neill, who lived up at Ardkitt. 'Annie was a very kind woman who would bake cakes for the tinkers and happily put them up in the hay-shed,' Grandma said. ('In those days,' she said, 'itinerants were not like they are today: they'd come and be friendly with you and mend your pots and pans; tell you your fortune if they were women.') But Grandma's real admiration was reserved for Peter O'Neill. 'What a man he was. What a man. He was a rebel; a lovely rebel. And he had the brains of – how many? – five professors.' This was the Peter O'Neill story: that, in essence, my great grandfather was a scientist rather than a farmer. It had even filtered through to me growing up in The Hague: how he harnessed the stream that ran through Ardkitt and generated hydroelectricity for the farm; how he grew tobacco – tobacco, in West Cork! – and turned an enormous £300 profit for his first crop; how he cultivated tomatoes and mushrooms and kept honey-bees; how he was the only farmer for miles around who didn't have a bush in the gap; and, most famously, how he invented and crafted a mahogany-framed egg incubator that hatched a hundred chicks and won first prize at the 1932 Cork science fair but, unhappily, could not be patented for want of money. 'He was altogether unlucky with money,' Grandma said.

But then I heard from my uncles that Peter O'Neill was an alcoholic who drank every penny he made. Every first Thursday of the month was creamery day and Peter would go off early in the morning to collect his money. The next time he'd be seen was in the evening, asleep between the milk churns as the unpiloted pony pulled the cart home.

My grandmother kept a framed photograph of Peter and Annie O'Neill and some of their ten children. Peter O'Neill, a ringer for my father, sits with patriarchal pride at the centre of a cluster of youngsters (Peig, Kitty, Nora, Paddy, Peter) and other relations. In the background, the ivy-clad frontage of Ardkitt farmhouse looms like an old college wall. There is no sign of young Jim, my grandfather, or his sister Mollie. By the time the photograph was taken, these two were living in Kilbrittain with their uncle and aunt, William and Mary-Ann O'Driscoll. My grandfather was farmed out when he was seven. Grandma explained, 'There was such a lot of children at Ardkitt and his uncle in Kilbrittain had no children. So he was adopted – well, not adopted exactly, but he went to live at the Kilbrittain farm.'

A little surprisingly, nobody suggested to me that Jim's early separation from his parents adversely affected him. The redistribution of offspring from overpopulated to underpopulated homes was not an unusual occurrence in the country in those days and it made economic sense for young Jim to be reared by his uncle and aunt, who were short of manpower and had nurturing energies to spare. Also, the arrangement gave young Jim the chance to acquire an interest in the Kilbrittain farm, eighty odd acres of dairy land known as Graunriagh: the O'Driscolls were childless and in need of an heir.

But Jim never did inherit Graunriagh. When he was twelve, his uncle William O'Driscoll died from peritonitis: it was the time of the Tan War, and the cratered state of the roads meant that William could not be transported to the hospital in Cork on time. The farm had to be sold. Mary-Ann O'Driscoll did not neglect her youngsters: provision was generously made that Mollie and Jim would each receive £500 at the age of twenty-one. The children never benefited from their inheritances. Mollie died, aged nineteen, of tuberculosis; and though Jim collected his bequest in Skibbereen, he immediately went to the office of a solicitor called Neville, in

Cork, and transmitted the entire sum to his father, Peter, who needed to pay off farming debts and to stock Ardkitt with seven calves. The payment to Peter was made not as a gift but as a loan, and a promissory note in favour of Jim was executed by Paddy O'Neill, Jim's eldest brother and, as the heir to Ardkitt, the ultimate beneficiary of the loan. The promissory note was entrusted to the custody of Neville. It was agreed that repayment would fall due when Paddy got married and came into a dowry. (In those days, many marriages amongst the farming class – which saw itself as a class apart – were fixed up by matchmakers, with the size of the dowry depending on the size of the bridegroom's farm.)

However – there's always a *however* in these stories – triple adversity struck. In October 1944, Peter O'Neill died intestate, with no provision made in respect of his debt to Jim. Second, in the late 'forties Paddy married Ellen Hennigan, universally known as Baybelle. Baybelle started trouble in the home from day one, according to Grandma, and Paddy, who had hitherto been a wonderfully friendly uncle to Jim and Eileen's children and had invited them round to Ardkitt every summer, refused to pay back the loan, even though Baybelle's dowry was £500, exactly the amount required. Third, Paddy was able to get away with non-payment because the office of Neville, the solicitor, had burned to the ground together with all documents stored there; and Neville himself was in a mental hospital and couldn't remember a thing about any promissory note. The dispute came before the High Court in about 1949, but my grandfather's claim was dismissed.

There was a further dispute with Paddy over property. Another uncle, Jim O'Driscoll, left my grandfather the deeds to a house in Bandon. However, the keys to the property were held by none other than the bugbear, Paddy. Even though he had neither the deeds nor good title, Paddy sold the house and pocketed the proceeds.

But it didn't end there. The most bitter feud of all arose from Paddy's treatment of his and Jim's mother, Annie (who, incidentally, had brought a £500 dowry to *her* marriage with Peter O'Neill and was grandly wed by fifteen priests). The root of the problem lay in the ill-feeling between the mother-in-law and the new bride. Annie found a bottle of hair-dye under the staircase and immediately she guessed that Baybelle was not as young as she claimed to be: a serious matter in West Cork, where in the view of some it was a mortal sin for a wife to be older than her husband. Bad blood was also caused by Annie's intrusions into the housekeeping. When Annie commented to Baybelle that she shouldn't put red clothes into the pot with white ones, Baybelle told Annie to mind her own business.

It was around this time, my grandmother said, that 'Baybelle hunted the itinerants from Ardkitt. The woman itinerant said, "All right so, we won't come back – but there'll be grass growing at your door and nobody'll enter it." And that came about.'

Then, in the 'fifties, came the egg money dispute. When Peter O'Neill, died, it was understood by all that his widow Annie was to remain at Ardkitt and, in accordance with another country tradition, that the egg money was hers to keep; that is, the small proceeds derived from the farm's sprinkling of chickens and turkeys. But Paddy (Grandma: 'a skinny, nondescript person, God rest his soul, I couldn't describe him') demanded the egg money for himself. Annie tried furtively selling eggs on her own account, but when she returned from the market and lied about how many she'd sold, Paddy (who had counted the eggs) hit her.

Eventually, Annie fell ill. My grandfather cycled out to Ardkitt to see his mother, whom he loved dearly and would often bring a small bottle of whiskey as a gift. He stayed the night. In the morning he went out to the yard to chuck his shaving water; turning back, he found that the only door into the house had been locked by Baybelle. So he smashed the door down. Three days later, he received a letter from Bandon solicitors threatening him with an injunction if he set foot in Ardkitt again. Then, after a couple of months had passed, my grandparents received a telegram from Jim's sister Peig, who lived near Ardkitt: Annie was very ill and my grandparents should travel out immediately. So the following morning they took the train on the West Cork railway to Desertserges Station. Peig told Jim that she was horrified by what she'd seen at Ardkitt: their sick mother locked away in her room like a prisoner and neglected by all except Paddy's kids.

Ardkitt, when my grandparents arrived, was empty except for Annie in her bed, Baybelle having fled to a nearby cottage when she saw her in-laws approaching. 'I decided to make a cup of tea,' Grandma recounted. 'As I waited for the kettle to boil, Paddy came in. "Who gave you the authority to make a cup of tea?" says he. "I'm making it for your mother," says I. "You're making it for that old bitch upstairs?" "Sit down, Paddy," I said, "and we'll have a chat. Your mother idolizes you." But Paddy ranted and raved, roaring and screeching that she was an interfering old bitch who should be long dead. Jim came down the stairs and heard him. Paddy ran off, but Jim ran around the table and caught him, and gave him a few wallops. "Don't, Jimmy, don't, don't," Paddy whined. I shouted, "Kill him, Jim, he doesn't deserve to live!"' My grandmother laughed at herself.

A short while afterwards, Jim received a summons to appear in court on a charge of assault. After hearing the evidence, said Grandma, District Justice Crotty put his spectacles on his nose and turned to Paddy. 'Do you mean to tell me that you came here and stood in that witness-box and all the while your mother suffered? How dare you come here. You should hang your head in shame. You must treat your mother in a humane way, and let her son visit her. A son has that right. But you're not to assault your brother,' he said, turning to Jim. 'There's no justification for that.' Jim was acquitted, Grandma said, and it was Paddy, the complainant, who was bound over to hold the peace.

Uncle Brendan gave a slightly different version. 'Of course he wasn't acquitted,' he said. 'How could he have been, when he beat his brother unconscious? He would have received a suspended prison sentence.' Brendan – a socialist with, I guessed, a political antipathy for the rural fetish of private property – also took a hard-nosed view of Ardkitt. In his view, there was a suspicion of grabbing about the way the O'Neills acquired an interest in Ardkitt in the first place. The original tenants of the farm, the Slyne family, were facing eviction, and Peter O'Neill's father, seeing an opportunity, married the widow Slyne and moved in. In later years she, the widow Slyne, lived with a great-aunt of Brendan's and was kept well away from the family.

Years after the Ardkitt incident, when he was dying, Jim O'Neill asked his son Terry if he could do him a favour. 'Of course,' Terry said. 'Make sure,' my grandfather said, 'that Paddy is barred from my funeral. Will you promise me that?' Terry was a little taken aback by the request – and surprised that he, and not Brendan, had been entrusted with the responsibility – but he resolved to carry out his father's wishes.

Jim O'Neill's children believed that he took an inestimably heavy blow when Graunriagh slipped away from him, a hurt aggravated by the loss of his O'Driscoll inheritance to Paddy. Decades later, he would drive past houses in Catwell, a district in South Cork, and say, 'Now one of them should be mine; they were going for £300 in the 'thirties.' Displaced to the city, my grandfather was left with an inextinguishable yearning for West Cork and a haunting sense that he had been unfairly thwarted in his vocation to farm his own land. He never really reconciled himself to the diminished horizons that the city held out for him as an unskilled labourer, educated to primary level, working in the three bleakest economic decades of the century.

Nevertheless, prior to his internment my grandfather was in

My grandfather (right), walking with a brother and nephew,
in the late 'forties

amenable employment. He drove a lorry for the Roads Department of the Cork Corporation, transporting men and materials from place to place. Although not a patch on farming, it was a satisfactory job. He was popular with the men, the hours (eight to six, five and a half days a week) were tolerable and the pay was sound. He comfortably provided for his wife and his first three sons. In 1936, when young Jim was born, my grandparents moved from a flat in the Old Blackrock Road to Wellington Road, St Luke's. Their next move was to a flat at Wesley Terrace, next door to the IKA man, Tomás MacCurtain Junior, and finally, in 1939, to Friars Road, Turner's Cross. But on my grandfather's return to Cork in November 1944, after nearly five years as a prisoner, things were very different. The Cork Corporation refused to give him his job back, and it took him six months to find work as a casual labourer in Distillery Field, in Cork – a fairly heroic feat, given his post-imprisonment depression and the widespread reluctance of employers to hire known political trouble-makers. (Phone calls would be placed by Special Branch officers to warn prospective employers against republican job applicants.) My grandfather mostly worked as a self-employed builder's labourer, going from job to job with his spade and bicycle, desperately trying to minimize idle periods in between. Precisely whom he worked for, and when, was in retrospect unclear; it was thought that at one point he worked for Lingwood, a builder and decorator of shops, doing refurbishment work. About three years after his release, my grandfather was re-engaged by the Corporation as a driver of garbage trucks, works lorries and other vehicles. Jim became active in (possibly even the leader of) the Cork Corporation branch of the Irish Transport and General Workers Union, and it may be that this fuelled the hostility of Philip Monaghan, the city manager. For whatever reason, Monaghan apparently had it in for my grandfather and fired him in about 1950 for accepting a bag of potatoes from a market gardener to whom Jim had delivered some goods as a favour. The hard times returned and Jim, by now in his forties, was forced back to intermittent labouring work. But during the course of the 'fifties, his technical flair, which ranged from knowing how to wire a house to understanding the workings of the combustion engine inside out, finally began to pay off. He worked for the South of Ireland Asphalt Company, maintaining plant and machinery on jobs that took him all over the country. He worked for McInerney's, a company from Clare, and, doing a mechanical fitter's job, in Foynes, Co. Limerick, for John Browne Engineering – the British company for whom, thirty years later, my father would work as the project manager of pharmaceutical construction projects worth hundreds of millions of dollars. In around 1958, he worked at Whitegate in East Cork, where a refinery had been built. It was around then that Jim, in his late forties, was paid to undergo a one-year apprenticeship as a pipefitter. A Dutch company, Verolme, was building ships at Rushbrook, near Cobh, and there was such a shortage of skilled labour that the government and the company invested in extensive training of the workforce. Not long afterwards came trade union recognition of single-year apprenticeships and my grandfather at last became an officially recognized skilled worker. From then on he easily found employment as a pipefitter on construction sites, and by the end of his working life, in the early seventies, his technical adeptness had led to work on weighbridge installation and calibration. In around 1968, Jim's work took him abroad for the only time in his life. He went to Holland for Foster Wheeler – the company that had given my mother her first job in Mersin – and spent a few months in Rozenburg, near Rotterdam. In the only letter he ever sent to my father, my grandfather complained of the monotony of the experience, which was only broken, he wrote, when my grandmother visited him for a week.

Jim was born on 16 October 1909, 'in Libra, the sign of balance,' my aunt Ann said with a little laugh, because in fact her father was an agitated, moody man prone to explosions of temper. He was rarely at ease. Sitting about, relaxing, was out of the question: there was always a chore to finish, always something to be done. Punctual, he was intolerant of tardiness in others: if you were late for an appointment, he wouldn't wait for you. He followed a strict morning routine: get up, turn the potatoes, eat breakfast, get to work early. When he returned home in the evening he went straight to the

bathroom, washed, changed, and then came down for his dinner. He
never ate in his work clothes and on Sundays he wore a three-piece
suit and a hat. He sometimes smoked a pipe. He took great care of
his appearance: he was a very handsome man with a fine physique –
slim hips, broad shoulders – and not without vanity. He liked his
children to look the part, too, insisting that they were always dressed
well: he would tell Grandma (who made pretty skirts that the girls
loved to wear) that they couldn't afford to buy cheap clothes. He
changed the soles of the children's shoes himself: he'd buy the
leather from O'Callaghan's, cut it rough, let it soak overnight, and
stitch it on the next day surrounded by the aromas of hemp and
wax. Strips of bicycle tyres would be glued on to the soles for extra
protection. Jim could fix just about anything, and his skills
extended to woodwork and making furniture: my grandmother's
oak and glass china cabinet, still in use, was his handiwork. He was
a disciplinarian, stern and domineering with his family, which (in
Jim Junior's phrase) he ran like an army. He was very authoritarian:
his children said that fumes would come out of his ears if you tried
to discuss something with him. 'Don't answer back!' he'd snap,
even though they might not be contradicting him. His daughters,
growing up as teenagers in the 'sixties, sometimes felt he was anti-
everything unless it was Irish. He'd yell if he caught them listening
to Radio Luxembourg. If he heard a band playing *It's a Long Way
to Tipperary* he'd aggressively go up and tell it to stop, intentionally
causing a rumpus. He was a hard case.

That was the word that everybody used in connection with Jim
O'Neill: *hard*. It applied to practically everything about him: his
work, his times, his life, his luck.

My elder sister Ann remembered a soft moment: when her
grandfather devoted an entire Christmas day to teaching her how
to ride a bicycle; and my younger brother David remembered that
he made him a catapult. 'Those things would make sense to him,'
my father said. He was physical man. He believed in physical
things.

He believed, for example, in using physical force on his sons. If,
driving his car, you braked going into a curve, he'd whack your ear

from the passenger seat. 'Whack you? He'd *murder* you,' was my uncle Terry's laughing refinement. Terry recalled an occasion when my father was behind the wheel and exclaimed, 'Look at the meadows!' My grandfather swung and connected with the back of his hand. 'Keep your eyes on the road,' he barked. Kevin did not get on with his father. Terry told me with a smile, 'Your dad was kind of lackadaisical. We all seemed to have specific jobs, specific roles – I'd be in charge of this, Jim might be in charge of the other – but I don't remember how Kevin fitted into that scheme.' Kevin wouldn't kow-tow to his father (an aunt said) and this independence of spirit was regarded as an infuriating form of insubordination: Jim, with his limited education, was not one to view argument as a vehicle of enlightenment. Even allowing for this, my father still couldn't exactly fathom what my grandfather's problem was. 'Joe, he was so irrational; I couldn't rationalize the violence at all.' My father told me this one morning in 1996. We were driving to Oxford, where later that day the university would confer a degree on my younger sister, Elizabeth. He spoke in a straightforward, open way, even though what he was saying was difficult and cathartic. 'I used to dread him coming home at night. I was petrified he'd find some reason to punch or kick me. Your mother said to me, Maybe you had misconceptions. Well, those right hooks and left crochets were not misconceptions.' It was raining, and my father, a tassel of thick silver hair falling over his brow, leaned forward to wipe mist off the windscreen to help my driving vision. He sat back in his seat and added, 'We didn't really see eye to eye on many things. Take the poaching. It makes a great story now – how we went "mushroom picking" along the river when the net was to be collected, how, with the Hillman stinking of fish, my father gave a lift to Inishannon to a guard who said he going to raise the alarm about poachers – but I saw no justification for it. I thought it was wrong. When the bailiffs and the police came to the house that time they found the scales in the net – and by the way, I was blamed for that, I got a real walloping – I should have slammed the door in their faces; but I didn't. I had this sense of respect for authority, a sensitivity about wrongdoing. That was the thing about my dad,' my father said. 'I felt he was always trying to get me to do things I thought were *wrong*.'

Driving, I said nothing. 'As I started to succeed at hurling, things improved,' my father continued. 'When I reached around seventeen or eighteen years of age, his invincibility crumbled. I lost my fear of him. Years later, I came back to Ireland as a married man and I took him out for a drink. "There are some things I'd like to clear up," I said, and I asked him why he'd behaved in the way he had. He said things like, "You've got to be cruel to be kind." I said to him, "Everything you did in your life, I swear I'll do the opposite." And that's how it has turned out. His intolerance, his failure to explain anything – they've acted as spurs for me.' We sat for a little while in silence, travelling in rain. Then my father said – and here his ambivalence about Jim, whose name he gave to my younger brother, surfaced – 'You know, having said all that, if he walked through the door today I'd be very comfortable with him. I'd have no problem having a beer and a chat. And if he hadn't been my father, I'm sure I'd have liked and respected him as a friend. There was a lot about him that was admirable.' My father examined his hands. 'There came a point when I started going back to him; when I realized that he needed my help. Keep in mind that opportunities were very limited, Joe. Ireland in those days was a different world, you wouldn't believe how narrow and bleak things were. Yet, in spite of it all, he managed to bring up a family of ten kids. It wasn't perfect – we'd have to borrow schoolbooks and look over classmates' shoulders – but the way he provided for us was a great achievement. He was a relentless worker,' my father said. 'He worked for us night and day.'

Jim O'Neill's children were unanimous about this: their father was an unstinting provider. 'He didn't deny us one brown ha'penny,' Jim Junior said. But the responsibility of doing well by his family – the responsibility, as uncle Jim put it, of having to go to every extreme to earn a shilling – incarcerated my grandfather: he never really felt free to rest. Aunt Marian said, 'He looked on life as a chore; I don't know if he ever really enjoyed himself.' Even whist drives had to be taken very seriously as earning opportunities. A good player, Jim would often win a Christmas turkey and sometimes pick up as much as £10. But more subtly dispiriting than his economic entrapment was the question of his social status. It gnawed at Jim O'Neill that he did not own his home – he, a farmer's son. He felt, in his heart, that it was beneath him to live in a corporation house, amongst people who lived in corporation housing. He was a territorial man. Tradesmen – the breadman, the milkman – would not be allowed past the threshold: 'these people's place is at the door,' he would say. When a neighbour, Mrs O'Sullivan, put up clothes to dry on the rail of the fence that divided her front garden from that of the O'Neills, my grandfather stormed over, knocked at her door and said in his abrupt way, 'Mrs O'Sullivan, I want you to remove those clothes off the railing.' 'Why?' 'They're unsightly.' 'The railing is as much mine as it is yours,' Mrs O'Sullivan pointed out. 'Well,' my grandfather said, flushing, 'would you please hang your clothes on your side of the railing, then.'

The O'Neills – which is to say, Grandma and four boys – only moved into corporation housing because with Jim interned they couldn't afford the rent at 39 Friars Road, Turner's Cross. Their first corporation house was at Mount Nebo Avenue, in north Cork.

North Cork, the old, tilting half of the city built on the elevations north of the Lee, reveals itself in sudden, often deceptive vistas: banked cottages appear airborne, a colourful row of parked cars rears up a hillside like a Ferris wheel, and, looking down treeless Mount Nebo Avenue, a distant rural landscape looms mirage-like at the bottom of the road. Mount Nebo Avenue forms part of a large housing estate built in Gurranabrahan in the 'twenties and 'thirties. Gurranabrahan (the Brothers' Walk) is sometimes called the Red City after the red sprawl made by its tiled roofs when viewed from a distance; but red is not the dominant colour once you're inside Gurranabrahan – grey is. The houses are grey, as are the pavements, the roads, the lamp-posts and the walls. Even other colours (brown, cream, umber) are grey versions of themselves. Still, the seventy-year-old neighbourhood – encapsulated for me in the spectacle of dishevelled, rained-on schoolboys trudging uphill beneath cables drooping from telegraph poles – has an old-fashioned communal appeal. The streets are kept clean and the houses, their front gardens featuring stout palm trees, topiarized hedges and well-tended shrubs, are shipshape. The former O'Neill residence at Mount Nebo is not atypical. Part of a terrace of houses, the front door is reached by walking up some cement steps and then a few feet of pathway. A low hedge grows tidily around the garden's perimeter railings. There are two storeys and three bedrooms. The frontage is covered in that familiar, rough, grey-brown pebbledash. Window and door trims are painted white. Patterned net curtains hang in the windows. All in all, the building looks well.

At Mount Nebo, the children went to primary school in Strawberry Hill and Sunday's Well, and to secondary school at North Monastery. They played Gaelic games at St Vincent's GAA Club and worshipped with their parents at St Vincent's Church. My grandfather had a nearby plot of corporation land, on which he grew vegetables. In 1953, the family left Gurranabrahan and moved into 22 Churchfield Terrace East, a three-bedroomed corporation house in a newer estate in nearby Churchfield. The Churchfield house had a parking-space for one car and a passage leading directly from the front to the back garden, where there was a shed. There was a downstairs bedroom (for the parents), a living room at the back, and two bedrooms upstairs. The five eldest boys shared two double beds, with the youngest of them, Terry, squeezed contentedly between two of his brothers. The young girls (Ann and Angela) shared the other bedroom with little Declan; and in due course baby Marian joined them. In the loft, accessible through a ceiling hatch, my grandfather removed bricks in the party wall so as to create an emergency getaway tunnel into the Twomeys' house, where a further breach in the brickwork created a further secret exit to the Sutton place. The escape route was never used.

These days, the O'Neill house is occupied by Mary O'Sullivan. Now in her late fifties, she grew up next door with her nine siblings (and, she told me angrily when I called on her, her mother had five miscarriages). 'The O'Neills were a fabulous crowd,' she said. 'If we didn't have butter, the O'Neills had it; if there was no milk, the O'Neills had it. At night we'd hear the door closing and my mother

The escape hatch at Churchfield Terrace

would say, "There he goes, we'll have a few bob tomorrow."' Mary's words for Jim were 'hard-working, good-looking, hunky, and cranky.' 'He was short with you, kind of dominating,' she said. 'If he was home before Mrs O'Neill, he'd come round and snap, "Where are the children?" "Mr O'Neill, they've had their bread and butter," my mother would say. He'd say, "That's not enough."' Another neighbour, Rita Twomey – like Mary, still in Churchfield Terrace after forty years – chipped in and said that Mr O'Neill was very strict: 'You'd have to duck.' 'Mrs O'Neill was marvellous,' Rita said. 'She never missed a day of washing the floor of the hall and kitchen.' Rita and Mary said that Mrs O'Neill had her own mind but she did everything that Mr O'Neill said. 'Things like that were different in those days.' Mary O'Sullivan said, 'He wasn't one to do any painting or washing. He might do the gardening.'

Gardening, in this context, meant the cultivation of vegetables. Jim grew potatoes, onions, lettuce, rhubarb, beetroot and cabbage, and enjoyed it. Another pleasure was his greyhound, Cora, who occupied a luxurious kennel equipped with a raised, straw-covered timber bed, and who was treated (uncle Terry said) like a princess.

He tried to breed pups from Cora, but they died of distemper. On Sundays, Cora would be taken harecoursing, and my grandfather, surrounded by the ranges of West Cork, would be happy. He also became very involved with St Vincent's Gaelic games club and was on a steering committee for fund-raising. My grandfather took great pleasure in watching his boys play. He would run along the touch-line urgently declaring, 'That's my son! That's my son!'

The children's memories of their North Cork days were of pleasant, impecunious, rough and tumble times: of riding and falling off a box-cart shooting down the hill at Mount Nebo; of getting it in the neck for tearing holes in precious jackets and taking heels off shoes; of horses straying into gardens; of neighbours treating other people's children as a social resource, pressing them into errands (shopping, minding prams, looking after youngsters) and even, if necessary, clipping them across the ear; of near-misses with eviction (one time my grandmother's brother Tadhg cleared the rent arrears just as the furniture was being put out into Mount Nebo Avenue); of Terry getting into a fight with Jackie Buckley, and Mrs Buckley grabbing her son by the collar, saying, 'Come in, there's an army of them.'

22 Churchfield Terrace East

In Churchfield, as in Mount Nebo, everybody knew everybody, and my uncle Terry could still name the people who lived on the street – the Wisemans, Coghlans, McCarthys, Dennehys, Mrs Conch, the O'Learys, McGraths, O'Connells, O'Donovans, Linehans, Drummonds, Nations. The O'Neills nearly always had a car, starting with a second-hand Hillman 1946. The cars were mostly Hillmans because Jim Junior got a job as a Hillman agent and would see a bargain coming in. My grandfather had a functional, unsentimental approach to any vehicle he owned. He would taxi men to work for a fee, transport salmon, and use the car as an ambulance or hearse for neighbours. Except for the Sweeneys, the O'Neills were the only car-owners in the neighbourhood. The family stood out in another respect: at Easter, theirs was the only house in Churchfield with a tricolour flying out of the window. On Easter Sunday all O'Neills wore an Easter lily ('Whether we liked it or not,' said my aunt Ann) and marched from the Grand Parade to the republican plot in St Fintan's cemetery. At the cemetery a volley of shots would be fired by men wearing green fatigues, Sam Browne belts, and hats with one side of the brim fastened up.

'Republican politics was the boys' domain,' Ann and Marian remembered. 'Dad never really engaged in any proper discussion with Mum about politics. They were in it together, and that was that. If he hadn't been so headstrong he would have appreciated how supportive she was of him. Mum should have been a politician. She was the most fantastic housekeeper, mother, cook, all-round manager, and diplomat. She'd be the calming force, and he the one to blow up over things.'

Sometimes explosions were caused by my grandfather's jealousy. One day he stopped the car to talk to Jimmy MacDonagh. Jimmy MacDonagh had a soft voice and, leaning into the car, he said to my grandmother, who was all made up, 'Eileen, you're blooming.' Jim drove away in a rage and there was a flaming row. And if Grandma went into town she'd be cross-examined: 'Where did you go? Who did you meet?'

In truth, my grandfather never had a jot of a cause to be jealous; and neither, for that matter, had my grandmother, although I'd heard her gently teased about Pat Buckley, the landlady of Jim's favourite bar in Shandon. When I mentioned Jim O'Neill to Pat Buckley – a lively, attractive woman in her sixties – she had trouble placing the name, but once she'd called him to mind she remembered my grandfather clearly. 'He was a lovely man to speak to,' Pat Buckley said, pouring me a complimentary pint of my grandfather's drink, which she remembered was Guinness. 'He was very sincere. He was a hard worker, supposed to be fantastic at his job. The first time he was ever here was with Dinny Kelleher, who came with him here many times. Jim O'Neill asked for two pints and put his hand in his pocket. "I have no money," says he. "Don't worry," says I, and gave him a fiver. He had an honest face, and I knew he was genuine by his eyes. He had beautiful eyebrows, like you do. From that day on he always came here. He normally wouldn't drink during the week – he didn't drink much, he couldn't afford to. He was an interesting man and would speak about current affairs; he'd have opinions on things. He never mentioned his own political activities. Often he'd meet his brother-in-law Jack Lynch,' Pat Buckley said, 'and I heard his wife was lovely. I met her two years ago, at a funeral. He always drank here,' Pat Buckley said, patting the bar where I stood. 'He was not a lounge person. They weren't lounge people,' she said.

After my grandfather moved south of the river, to Douglas, in 1962, he also drank regularly at the Orchard Bar, on the Ballinlough Road. I went there with Terry, who remembered the times his mother waited in the car with clambering and brawling kids while his father drank a couple of pints. According to John Barrett, proprietor of the Orchard Bar since its establishment in 1961, Jim was quiet about his politics and certainly not a pub republican (a mouthy, ineffectual type). Jim would take collections for the Prisoners Dependents' Fund in bars, not hopefully jingling the cup but charting a silent, effective course through the drinkers. 'They'd shell out for Jim,' John Barrett said, 'because they knew he'd suffered.' Terry said, 'He'd do the same at work, to the dismay of his colleagues. His commitment to the movement was relentless,' Terry said, 'he wasn't a fair-weather friend.' When Jim had a cold, John

Barrett recalled, he'd drink four hot toddies (whiskey, cloves, lemon, hot water) and the cold would clear up in a couple of days. 'His drink of choice was Guinness,' John Barrett said, 'often with a shot of Paddy whiskey. Rough, but they were rough men.'

Jim O'Neill's new home in South Cork was a detached three-bedroomed house in a new estate of privately owned houses. It had a garage, a front garden and a large back garden that gave onto a playing field. He could afford to buy it because he was in regular work and because his older sons were now working and able to contribute to the family finances. My grandfather was very proud finally to be a man of property; it made him feel independent, free. Grandma and he called the house Dún-Ard in reflection of their respective origins in Dunmanway and Ardkitt. Jim strained the soil in the front and back garden and grew vegetables. His relations with my father became more benign. Returning to Cork in his mid-twenties, my father would say, 'I've been around the world but I still can't get a proper haircut,' and Jim would put a towel around his neck, bring out the scissors, and, putting to use a skill developed during his internment days, cut my father's hair. As money ceased to be a real problem, my grandfather gave up poaching and drove out with his family to West Cork for blameless outings and picnics. They went out there every weekend they could. In the mid-'sixties, Jim even tried to buy a property in Ross Carbery to build a summer home but, jinxed again in the matter of land, was beaten to it by a German. He bitterly predicted that the country would be bought up by foreigners. My grandparents started to take short holidays together and to relate in an easier way. Sometimes my grandfather sang,

> I'm a rambler
> And a gambler
> And a long way from home
> And if you don't like me just leave me alone
> I'll eat when I'm hungry
> And drink when I'm dry
> And if Mountjoy don't kill me
> I'll live till I die.

Just as he was approaching retirement and just as, in aunt Marian's words, he was realizing there is life, my grandfather became ill, and died.

In November 1995, I went on two trips in West Cork. The first, accompanied by my grandmother, was to Kilbrittain. It was a softly overcast Sunday morning, with the sun reduced to a pool of ivory in the clouds. We took a roundabout route, via Halfway and Kinsale. I'd heard it joked that it was after the defeat of Hugh O'Neill, the Earl of Tyrone, at the Battle of Kinsale (1601) that our family scattered in Cork.

In Kinsale, we stopped for Mass. It was a novena Mass and the priest urged the congregation to pray for the souls of those in purgatory who had not yet received their just reward. We, the living faithful, could assist these souls: papal indulgences could be earned by praying for the departed at certain cemeteries, and acts of mortification and intercession would also promote the transit of souls. My grandmother said prayers on her knees, her thick bottom lip wavering as she whispered with closed eyes, and of course I wondered if she was praying for the soul of my grandfather.

After Mass we drove across the immense waterway that the Bandon river forms as it flows into the ocean. We passed Our Lady's Shrine at Ballinspittle, where a six-foot-high statue of the Virgin Mary, located in a grotto above the road, was said to move miraculously. On we drove, past sugar-beet fields and banks brimming with rusting ferns, to Kilbrittain. Kilbrittain is a small village of a strongly rural character, its buildings huddled inconsequentially on the exposed slopes of a bare valley. I followed my grandmother's directions and soon we came to Graunriagh House, where my grandfather had been raised, a pretty, solid, two-storey farmhouse with seashells and shards of glass embedded in the dashed walls for decoration. We drove slowly into the yard behind the house. Dogs ran up barking. A man with frizzy, greying hair came out, his windreddened face peering at us in bafflement until he recognized Grandma. That was Dan-Joe Holland, who owned and worked the farm – eighty acres of grazing – with his wife Joan. Over tea, Joan and Dan-Joe talked to Grandma about the changing times – the lack of interest of their six children (four in London, two in Ireland) in taking on the farm, the exorbitant price of All-Ireland tickets, the decline of football and hurling in Cork, the rabble that are priests these days (a view my grandmother did not go along with) and the shower of rogues that are politicians. The house, which Dan-Joe guessed was around two hundred years old, was solidly built, with even its internal walls two feet thick. It was decorated in a typical country way: the floors were covered with bright, densely floral carpets, and the walls with patterned wallpaper that was also pasted on the top of the kitchen refrigerator. The two front rooms were packed with armchairs, and on the table of the living room I noticed an opened book about the shooting of Michael Collins.

After a while, we all strolled out to the front yard. 'When Jim O'Neill used to visit the farm,' Dan-Joe said, 'he would walk straight past the house, go through the gate at the back and immediately walk the land.' Dan-Joe gestured in the direction of a bare, muddy hill loomed over by a grey sky. Grandma pointed in the opposite direction, to the front garden. 'That was where the orchard was. Jim always used to say to me that even when the Black and Tans were in Kilbrittain they'd hang a tricolour in the trees. In those days they'd burn down your house for that. But Kilbrittain was a hotbed and they never could stop people holding meetings here.' Beyond the front garden, clearly visible a few miles below, was the green and rumpled ocean. The island known as Heart's Rock was pointed out to me. 'It was not far from there,' Grandma said, 'that the *Lusitania* sank.'

We said goodbye to the Hollands and drove away through the village. On our left we saw Kilbrittain National School, the tiny, two-roomed cottage, still in use, that was my grandfather's sole alma mater. The schoolhouse enjoyed a clear view of the valley: a small river, some pastures flecked with sheep and crows. We headed out on the narrow road along which, seventy years before, my grandfather drove cattle to the Bandon mart, a tricky job since the cows would be through any gap in a shot.

Grandma at Kilbrittain National School

A few days later, I drove through Bandon again, this time with uncle Brendan. We were going to Ardkitt. As a boy, Brendan travelled there on the railway. Sometimes the train back to Cork was used to transport salmon. The O'Neill brothers carried the fish in suitcases and would switch carriages during the journey to avoid detection.

Ardkitt (from the Irish, Kit's Height, Kit – or *Ceit* – being a champion of ancient times) is the name of the hill over which the farm of the same name spreads itself in a series of fields bordered by hedgerows. With a maximum area of 55 acres, Ardkitt is, by the standards of the Bandon valley, by no means a large farm. To reach it, you turn from a small lane on to a still smaller lane which climbs the hill. On your left, as you gently ascend, a stream runs largely unseen down to a spot where steam engines formerly used to draw water. Two fields on that side of the road belong to the O'Neills. On the right side of the road is the farmhouse's tree-lined front yard, which encloses a hedged, tree-filled garden; a stone pigpen (now in ruins); an old, stone cattleshed, where bulls used to be kept and cows milked; and the Victorian farmhouse itself, a pretty, whitewashed, two-storeyed stone building with a slate roof and yellow-painted trims to the windows and chimney-top and front door. Behind the house, a touch downhill, is the orchard of apple trees. Close by, accessible by a separate entrance, is a cottage that until recently was owned by the Lordans, our cousins. As with Graunriagh, the pastures of Ardkitt are only visible once you have tramped up to the crest of the land rising gently at the rear of the farmhouse.

Driving into the yard, we were greeted by the two friendly, barking dogs whose presence seems compulsory in country houses in West Cork. Pat O'Neill, son of the demonized Paddy and Brendan's first cousin, welcomed us in and gave us tea and bread and jam. Pat was living on his own and his bowling trophies provided the principal decorative touch in the living room. This was not bowling of the lawn or ten-pin variety but road bowling, a traditional West Cork game of which the object is to propel, with a windmilling underarm action, a 28-ounce cast-iron ball along a given stretch of country lane in as few throws as possible. The sport requires a particular skill and strength, and Pat – long, low-slung arms, broad shoulders and enormous hands – had the right physique for it. When Pat stood with his fists pressed into his jeans pockets and his level shoulders in a hunch, Brendan whispered to me, 'Look at him, that's your grandfather there. That's him now, that's him exactly.'

I took a walk in drizzle beyond the house, up towards the fields. A large corrugated iron shed loomed on my left – the barn? – together with low outbuildings. Mud caked and sucked at my rubber boots. Just walking on this ground was a slog. Hundreds of small puddles pocked the mud. I made out the tracks of tractor wheels and cattle. There was no sign of cattle in the flesh. I came to the fields. They ran aslant the hill and were bounded by hedgerows that limited the distance you could see across Ardkitt. Still no cows. The rain started falling more heavily. I felt dull. Farming phrases I'd heard uttered by my father and his brothers in connection with childhood summers spent here before the feud with Paddy – threshing, mowing the fields, growing wheat and barley and oats, milking the cows, feeding the cows, pulling the flax (yes, in West Cork: local cultivation of flax was promoted during the Great Famine as a means of providing employment for the starving locals), picking mushrooms, making hay – failed to make sense of these wet, empty fields. And yet this was the site of golden memories for my father. He and the older O'Neill boys, who were no more than about ten years of age, took working holidays on the farm, and loved it from the moment they awoke in the Lordan cottage to the moment, at the end of the day, they washed their feet in the cold water of the well, which was in the Well Field across the lane from the farmhouse. A special treat for the boys was driving the donkey and cart down to the scutching mill in Enniskean, and of course the threshing day was a great day. The crop would be brought to the haggart – the yard by the cow-shed – and threshed in a steam-powered threshing machine equipped with a huge flywheel and spectacular driving belts. Wood from ash trees fuelled the steam engine, and my grandfather would carve hurleys for his sons from spare pieces of ash. The neighbours would help out, and so would children from Enniskean, mere blow-ins whom the O'Neill brothers, led by Brendan, would beat up. In the evening there would be a big dinner (turkey, goose, ham from the Ardkitt ham room, masses of potatoes), porter, and dancing to tunes made with an accordion and a fiddle. In the days immediately fol-lowing the threshing day, Jim and his boys would go to the neighbouring farms and help out there. 'It was idyllic,' my father said. But all I sensed, standing on the brow of the hill in the rain, was that this was a place that exacted hard physical effort. I began to feel cold. I turned back through the muck to the house.

A short while afterwards, I got into the car to leave. Brendan was still talking to Pat by the front door of the farmhouse. Then Pat went into the house while Brendan stamped his feet at the thresh-old. A few moments later, Pat returned with a white towel in his hands. He handed the towel to Brendan. They laughed, and then Brendan came over to the car. Brendan got into his seat and slammed shut the driver's door. He dropped the towel on my lap. I felt a weight amongst the folds. I unfolded the towel. A rusted revolver sat between my knees. I looked at my uncle. 'Colt .45,' he said, starting the engine. 'That's the gun that shot Admiral Somerville.'

3

. . . exaggerated suspicions are paranoic or true to reality, a faint private
echo of the turmoil of history . . .

Theodor Adorno, *Minima Moralia*

In early January 1942, a freeze of a ferocity not seen for twenty
years destroyed the citrus fruit crop of the Çukurova region. By
February, only a few rotting specimens dangled in the gardens that
surrounded Mersin.

One effect of this calamity was a dramatic rise in the price of
citrus fruit; another was a small killing for Joseph Dakak. Just
before the frost set in, he and Halil Eser, a business associate,
had bet against mild weather and bought six hundred cases of
lemons.

Inspired by this success, Joseph Dakak noted that the war and
consequent collapse of the European export market had caused a
crash in the price of Palestine lemons. Whereas one lemon sold in
Mersin for 25 kurus (a kurus being one hundredth of a Turkish
lira), its Palestinian counterpart could be bought for only one kurus.
Joseph Dakak understood what this meant: that anyone who succeeded in importing the fruit from Palestine was looking at an

extraordinary return on his outlay. He decided to go to Jerusalem and buy two hundred tonnes of lemons for resale in Turkey.

However, there was an obstacle. Travel through Syria (i.e., Greater Syria, a territory covering modern-day Syria and Lebanon) and Palestine, was under British control, and in order to get to Jerusalem my grandfather required visas from the British Consulate in Mersin. It was far from sure that these would be granted. As recently as the autumn of 1941, Joseph Dakak, who had recently opened an import–export office, had unsuccessfully applied to Desmond Doran, the British passport officer in Mersin, for transit visas for a business trip to Egypt. No reason was given for the refusal.

Not long after this rebuff, Joseph Dakak found himself at the office of Hilmi Bey, the chief of the political section of the Mersin police, on a routine matter. On Hilmi's desk was a photograph of Doran and a shooting licence; Dakak joked that Doran shouldn't get the shooting licence until he granted Dakak the visas to Palestine. Hilmi Bey smiled and said nothing.

A little while later, Dakak bumped into Olga Caton at the Toros Hotel restaurant; she was dining with a friend, Togo Makzoumé. Seeing my grandfather, she snatched her British passport from her bag and taunted him with it: 'You can't get a visa, but I can – and a diplomatic one, at that.'

The next time Dakak visited Hilmi Bey – on another routine matter – the police chief asked why it was that Madame Olga had been able to obtain a visa for Egypt while Dakak had not. Dakak replied that he'd heard that she was off to Egypt on an important mission; and because Olga herself had freely gossiped about her activities, Dakak felt able to ask Hilmi whether it was true that her mission was on behalf of British intelligence. Hilmi Bey simply smiled. Dakak asked a second question: was Togo Makzoumé, who'd lately been Olga's constant companion at the Toros Hotel, also working for the British? Again, Hilmi Bey gave a knowing smile and said nothing.

After the war, my grandfather learned that Olga Caton's job in Egypt was running a women's internment camp, a post she owed to her lover – the British passport officer, Desmond Doran.

In any event, in February 1942, my grandfather applied to the British Consulate for visas for Palestine. One morning in early March, he ran into Arthur Maltass, a consular officer, in the market. 'Mr Doran has gone to Beirut,' Maltass said. 'He has asked me to tell you that he's doing his best to procure your visas.' A few days later Doran returned from Beirut with visas for Joseph Dakak.

On the afternoon the visas came through, Joseph Dakak was again approached in the market – this time by a Turk, Osman Emre Bey. 'So,' Osman Emre Bey said, 'you've got what you wanted, you're off to Palestine to make a fortune.' Dakak made a non-committal gesture. Osman squeezed his arm. 'It's thanks to the good word I put in for you with Doran that he was persuaded to grant your visas.' Osman continued to press against Dakak. 'As you know,' he said, 'I've got a lawsuit coming up from trial, and I need to pay the lawyers. Give me money, Dakak. If you don't, my sister will lose her orchards. You owe it to me.' Dakak frowned and moved away. 'I'll think about it,' he said. In fact he was reflecting that, far from being indebted to Osman, he was in credit to the tune of one hundred liras: Osman had yet to repay a loan fully documented by a receipt kept in Dakak's office. But Osman wasn't going to be fobbed off. The next day, and the day after that, he came to the hotel and repeated his demands for money. Finally, to be shot of the man, Dakak said, 'Look, I don't have the money at the moment. I'll think about it when I get back from Palestine.' Agitated, Osman said, 'But that's no good to me, my trial won't wait, I need the money now.' 'I told you, I don't have it,' Dakak said brusquely. At that, Osman Emre Bey turned around and left in a fury.

On 24 March 1942, Joseph Dakak departed for Palestine. To cover his expenses he carried £150 obtained from the Ministry of Finance. He travelled, first class, on the Taurus Express.

A couple of things need to be made clear. First: the incidents described above come straight out of Part I of Joseph Dakak's written account of his arrest and imprisonment, which he entitled *The Departure*. Second: although I'd rediscovered and photocopied the entire testimony in the summer of 1995, it was not until January 1996 that I began to have access to its contents, and then only in instalments. From time to time I received in the post a chunk of text translated from Turkish into French by my aunt Amy – who, like her brother and sister, had never read the papers before. 'It's going slowly,' Tante Amy said when she called me from her home in Geneva. 'It isn't easy work, you know.' She made a throaty noise, and I realized that she was struggling with tears. 'Anyway, you've got everything I've done so far. I'll send the rest to you as soon as I can.'

A photograph stapled to a train pass dated 7 March 1941 (issued in the name of Joseph Dakak, and not his new name, Dakad) helped me to guess at the image my grandfather projected as he took his seat on the Taurus Express. The photograph showed a man wearing a double-breasted, chalk-striped grey suit, a white handkerchief in his breast pocket, a white shirt with a buttoned-down collar, and a tie with diagonal stripes. His hair, still not grey, was brushed immaculately back and his moustache was trim. His fellow passengers would have received the impression of a gentleman travelling on business had it not, perhaps, been for this feature: dark circular sunglasses that covered his eyes and gave him a cool, somewhat sinister look; to those of a dramatic cast of mind, the look of a spy.

This was not as fanciful as one might think. In 1942, mystique and the promise of adventure were attached to train journeys. Illicit romantic encounters, skulduggery in the dining-car, identical suitcases exchanged on steaming platforms, cat-and-mouse in the corridors of trembling wagons: how many old movies and books contained such tropes? In 1949, for example, a British soldier called Richard Pearse published an idiosyncratic memoir of his wartime experiences entitled *Three Years in the Levant*, and it was clear that he, at least, saw spies everywhere. A member of the Field Security Service of the Intelligence Corps, he served for a time as a security controller on board the Taurus Express. It was a crucial railway connection. Excluding the Far East, there were four frontiers between Allied-held territory and neutral states: the border in Ireland; the Russian–Turkish frontier; the Iraqi–Turkish frontier; and, last and most important by far, the Syrian–Turkish frontier. Twice a week, this line was crossed by a train from Istanbul to Baghdad via Aleppo, where another train could be caught to Tripoli, Beirut and Jerusalem. In the absence of shipping traffic, the railway served as the funnel for travel from the Far East to the West and from the Northern Mediterranean to the Gulf. As a consequence, the luxury end of the train was occupied, Pearse reported, by 'Prime Ministers, diplomats, engineers, Arab princes, Turkish princesses, Egyptian professors, mystery men and beautiful blondes (some of the spy fiction type)'. Eastbound travellers came from Germany, Sweden, France and Holland with the latest news from Europe; westbound travellers came from China, Afghanistan, India and Iran. During its transit through northern Syria, the train was sealed and an armed British sentry stood at every door. 'It was well known,'

Pearse explained, 'that the Taurus Express had already carried in its luxury sleeping- and restaurant-cars more international agents and spies than any other train in the world.'

As the train slowly made its way south-east, my grandfather no doubt thought about Georgette, who was eight months pregnant, and the very real chance that he would come home to a second child; about the arrangements made for the care of the hotel and the racehorse in his absence; about the windfall that, all being well, he stood to make from the lemon deal, a capitalistic enrichment of a kind that running a hotel could never produce; and, of course, about the state of the war. My grandfather would have been aware that, in the words of the British Consul in Mersin, Norman Mayers (writing home on 29 March 1942), 'The rumours are going around of a possible invasion by the Germans of Turkey, or Syria, or what not'. He would have known that the German invasion in the Soviet Union had been checked by the Red Army's counter-offensives but that there remained a very real risk of a German advance to the oil-rich Caucasus and, from there, to Turkey and the Middle East. He would have known that Rommel had taken Benghazi in January 1942 and that a German drive across North Africa, to the Suez Canal and the Holy Land, was apparently imminent.

Nevertheless, my grandfather went ahead with his venture. When he married, Georgette had made him promise to give up taking business risks – Georgette, the gambler *par excellence*! – but what possible downside was there to this once-in-a-lifetime opportunity? (Joseph had not, incidentally, kept his promise to his wife: unbeknownst to her, he'd dabbled in the tin market and furtively stored away a substantial quantity of the metal.) Moreover, it was exciting to travel to Jerusalem, a city he'd never visited, on the Taurus Express, a train that offered the vivid contrast of wild and beautiful country on the outside and, indoors, polished wood, crisp white sheets, good food and (in these interesting times) stimulating and exotic company. For Joseph Dakak, a man not fully tested by Mersin's provincial demands, such a trip, in such a milicu, was more than a commercial outing: it represented a fulfilment of his cultural potential. Was he not, after all, a man of the world?

Joseph Dakak arrived in Beirut at 5 p.m. on 26 March 1942. He deposited his luggage at a hotel and paid a visit to a cousin, Alida Hannah. Alida immediately insisted that Joseph check out of his hotel and stay the night with her and her son, Rico.

There then occurred the first of a series of encounters between Joseph Dakak and oddly animated, oddly politicized strangers. After dinner, Alida's neighbour, a Dr Saliba, dropped by for the evening. Dr Saliba, who worked at the American University of Beirut, made it clear in conversation that he was anti-English and pro-German. My grandfather wrote: 'Since I didn't care for this subject, I didn't give Saliba's utterances much thought; but on

reflection, his insistence on manifesting his Germanophilia did
seem a little strange.'

Early the next morning, Dakak travelled in a horse-drawn carriage to the train station. Rico Hannah helped him with his luggage.
He advised my grandfather that the place to stay in Jerusalem was
the Modern Hotel.

On train between Haifa and Jerusalem, a stranger engaged Dakak
in conversation. Soon Dakak found himself being interrogated in
detail about the political situation in Turkey – in such detail, in fact,
that he finally promised the stranger that as soon as he returned to
Turkey he would be sure to make special inquiries at the Turkish
Ministry of Foreign Affairs. It dawned on the stranger that Dakak
was being sarcastic, and he fell silent.

On 27 March 1942, Dakak arrived in Jerusalem. Perhaps drawn
by its name, he went directly to the place recommended to him by
Rico – the Modern Hotel. It was there, in the lobby, when he was
checking in, that a voice loudly proclaimed, 'Why, if it isn't Joseph
Dakak! How are you, my dear?'

Dakak turned to see a woman approaching him. 'You don't recognize me?' she cried. 'It's me, Olga, the sister of Nicole Panayoti
of Antakya!'

Dakak knew a Panayoti who ran the Tripoli branch of Catoni,
the old Iskenderun shipping agency; but this woman? Then it came
back to him: he had met her once in Mersin, a long time ago. She
was Olga Husseini, 'a notorious adventuress' active in the Arab
nationalist movement. Her husband, Mustapha Husseini, was a
nephew of Haj Amin el-Husseini, the Mufti of Jerusalem. Dakak
had heard somewhere that Olga had accompanied her husband to
Iraq and even India to whip up support for the Palestinian cause.

Olga continued to behave like a long-lost friend. She organized a
session of *concain* in Dakak's honour ('Maybe,' my grandfather
speculated, 'she knew that I often played this card-game in Mersin').
The game was spoiled, my grandfather recorded, by Olga and
Mustapha's incessant talk of politics – tirades against the English,
advocacy of the Arab movement, praise of the Germans. Turkey,
they pronounced, had done well not to declare war on Germany and

not to allow itself to become the pawn of the English. It would be better still, they said, if the Turks opened the way for the Germans to come down through Turkey and Syria to the aid of the Palestinians.

Every time Joseph Dakak tried to change the subject, Olga and her husband returned to it. This state of affairs continued for the remainder of Dakak's stay at the Modern Hotel. For twenty days, Arab nationalists – all friends of Olga, all pro-German – gathered in the evening and spoke against the English and in favour of the Mufti, who at that time was in Germany.

In his account, my grandfather did not spell out but certainly knew the essential facts of the Mufti's situation. Amin el-Husseini received the life appointment of Mufti of Jerusalem in 1921 from Ronald Storrs, the Governor of Jerusalem. If Storrs believed that the responsibilities of office would moderate el-Husseini's political stance, he was wrong. The Mufti became the leading figure in the Palestinian anti-Zionist movement and was instrumental in the Arab rebellion of 1936. In 1937, facing arrest and imprisonment, he escaped to Beirut, where he continued his political activities. In 1939, he relocated to Iraq and set up a shadow Palestinian government in Baghdad. Then, in May 1941, after participating in the failed uprising against the British in Iraq, the Mufti was forced to go on the run to Teheran. In September 1941, after British and Soviet troops entered Iran and installed Mohammed Reza as Shah, the Mufti disappeared yet again, by now with a bounty of £25,000 on his head. Refused entry into Turkey, he somehow resurfaced in Italy in October 1941. The following month he was in Berlin, where he quickly assumed responsibility for notoriously virulent propaganda broadcasts to the Middle East.

At a certain point in his testimony, my grandfather suddenly veered to the subject of oranges: it was his habit, he said, always to keep a bowl of these by his bedside at the Modern Hotel. One night, he discarded an orange that had a strange and unpleasant taste. He tried a second orange but it, too, was inedible. Three more oranges were sampled and they all had the same foul taste. That night, Dakak fell violently ill. Suffering from severe stomach pain, diarrhoea and wind, his heart kicking in his chest, he vomited all night. By morning he was exhausted, and he spent the whole day in bed. The following day his stomach ache persisted and he asked Mustapha Husseini to take him to a doctor. Husseini took him to a Dr Dajani, whose surgery was only a hundred metres away. 'Dr Dajani speaks German very well,' Husseini said as he escorted my grandfather to the doctor. 'He studied in Germany.' It was Dr Dajani's opinion that Dakak had caught a cold and he prescribed pills for stomach ache. 'Unfortunately,' my grandfather wrote, 'not yet understanding the cause of my problems, I didn't mention the oranges to the doctor. And yet it certainly was my first poisoning.'

My grandfather explained this dramatic statement by relating the following incident. One evening, Olga was playing cards with some Greek soldiers who had checked into the Modern Hotel. She called Dakak over to her table. 'Have you heard the latest?' she said. 'Turkey has entered the war.' 'I hope that isn't true,' a Greek colonel said anxiously. 'It'll mean an end to the food parcels I send from Istanbul to my parents in Greece. They'll starve to death.' Dakak didn't get excited. 'Let's wait for the official news tomorrow,' he said; and sure enough, the next day saw no report of any Turkish declaration of war. The whole episode, my grandfather asserted, had been Olga's attempt to trick him into revealing (by his reaction to the bogus news) whether Turkey would enter the war – and, if so, on whose side.

It was here that my aunt Amy's first chunk of translation came to an end, and here, too, that I realized that I was lost – lost in the intricate, cryptic place into which the testimony had dropped me, a zone in which Arab conspirators, Greek soldiers, Turkish secret policemen, Levantine businessmen, British consular officials and German sympathizers loomed and drifted. What was the connection between the events in Mersin (dealings with the British consulate; conversations with the chief of the secret police; an attempted extortion) and Jerusalem (poisonous oranges; Palestinian intrigues)? What linked Olga Caton at the Toros Hotel to Olga Husseini at the Modern Hotel? And what was the significance of the peripheral figures – pro-German Dr Saliba, the inquisitive stranger on the Jerusalem train, German-speaking Dr Dajani, cousin Alida? Were we to understand that Alida's son Rico – who had, after all, advised my grandfather to stay at the Modern Hotel – was somehow in collusion with Olga Husseini's crowd? And with whom was that crowd in cahoots? I assumed that, as I continued to read the testimony, express answers to these questions would be forthcoming. But they weren't. It was as if my grandfather never succeeded in gaining a clear perspective on the blurred circumstances leading up to his imprisonment, and that, like a moth that has flown into treacle, he remained forever stuck in the opaque, viscous events he described. Certainly, he never satisfactorily answered the unspoken, anguished questions his story raised: What was behind my downfall? What did I do to deserve this?

It was my mother who brought up the name Wright. Mr Wright, she said, had been the British consul in Mersin during the war, and occasionally Mamie Dakad had fondly mentioned that this monsieur had assisted her in the matter of her interned husband. 'Mr Wright was a young man at the time,' my mother said. 'You never know, he might still be alive.'

So in February 1996 – only a few days, incidentally, after a massive explosion in the London Docklands had brought the seventeen-month-old IRA ceasefire to an abrupt and fatal end – I consulted the *Diplomatic and Consular Year Book* of 1943. I saw that D.A.H. Wright, Vice-Consul in Trebizond, assumed duty as Vice-Consul at Mersin on 5 May 1943, in succession to Norman Mayers.

I took a look at the post-war Foreign Office Lists. Wright served as acting consul in Mersin from 1943 to 1945 and afterwards went on to a distinguished diplomatic career, serving as ambassador in Addis Ababa and Tehran. Could it be that he was still alive? I turned to *Who's Who 1996*. There he was: Sir Denis Arthur Hepworth Wright (born 1911), an Honorary Fellow of St Antony's College, Oxford, and the author of two books on Anglo-Persian relations. I immediately wrote to him. Three days later, a reply arrived inviting me to visit him; and the following weekend, on 17 February 1996, I drove up to Haddenham, Buckinghamshire.

Haddenham, I discovered, was a large village swollen by modern estates, but its old centre was an extraordinarily idyllic spot where a church with a tower overlooked a pond inhabited by white ducks and a pair of swans. A narrow lane led down from the pond to the ancient low-lying house where Denis Wright lived with his wife, Iona. I was met by a straightforward, initially gruff man – 'What are you writing, exactly? A novel, or a proper book?' – who, even in his mid-eighties, was tall and athletic. Wright still wrote and regularly travelled abroad with Iona to places like Russia and Greece. He straightaway led me upstairs to his study and asked me how I had got hold of his name. I recounted what my grandmother had said about the assistance he had given her. 'I remember your grandmother very well,' Wright said, much to my surprise. He turned towards his desk and pointed at some volumes. 'This is what I've got.' There were carefully bound typescripts of his letters home from Mersin; a typed and bound and footnoted autobiography; essays on the politics of wartime Turkey; and albums of carefully annotated photographs and cuttings. As a personal documentary record of wartime Mersin, these papers almost certainly had no equal.

Mersin's significance in the Second World War, Sir Denis told me, arose out of the wider political situation in Turkey. By a series of non-aggression and friendship treaties, mutual assistance pacts, trade agreements and non-committal manoeuvres, the Turkish Republic, led by President Ismet Inönü, adroitly managed to maintain its neutrality. It wasn't an easy thing to pull off. Churchill, in particular, had a 'bee in his bonnet' about securing Turkish participation in the war – in Wright's view, this would have been a generally counterproductive development that would have achieved nothing for Turkey other than the destruction of its major cities. Turkey's diplomatic skill was such that it not only resisted the strong pressure exerted by the Axis and the Allies but also managed to take the benefit of Allied offers to strengthen its military infrastructure – offers to build roads and airfields, and to supply aircraft, tanks, armoured cars, AA guns and training teams. These projects gave rise to a problem: how to ship the necessary materials into the country? With the Italians in Rhodes and the Dodecanese and the

Germans in control of Bulgaria and mainland Greece, Turkey's main ports, Istanbul and Izmir, were within range of Axis aircraft. And so two points of entry into Turkey were identified as safe from the threat of air attacks: the sister ports of Iskenderun and Mersin. It didn't matter that Mersin did not have a proper harbour and that vessels had to anchor half a mile or so offshore and discharge their cargo into lighters; large quantities of military and other essential equipment were nevertheless shipped in, usually from Alexandria, usually in Greek ships, and usually in secret.

It is a little-known fact, Wright said, that one of the undercover infrastructural projects was based near Mersin. As Axis forces advanced in south-east Europe, the danger arose that they might invade Turkey on their way through to Syria and the oilfields of the Middle East. In response to this threat, the Allies drew up contingency plans with Turkey whereby the line would be held in the Taurus Mountains and reinforcements from Syria and Egypt would be quickly sent up by rail and road. Thus, in July 1941, a party of around forty men of the British Royal Engineers set up camp just outside Mersin with the task of blasting a tank-friendly road through the Taurus Mountains and improving the roads and bridges that connected Mersin, Tarsus and Iskenderun. To keep the operations in ostensible accordance with the neutral status of the host country, the construction party wore civilian clothing and held itself out as Messrs. Braithwaite & Co., Civil Engineers and Contractors of London. There were other sensitive Allied operations in Mersin. These included the exportation, mainly to the United States, of Turkish chrome – vital for manufacturing armaments – and the shipment of timber and railway sleepers from the Findikpinar forest in the Taurus Mountains to the British in the Middle East. Such mercantile activities were overseen by the United Kingdom Commercial Corporation (UKCC), a wartime corporate vehicle for the United Kingdom. The UKCC, Wright said, was represented in the consular staff in Mersin, as were a number of key Whitehall ministries – the Admiralty, the War Office, the Ministry of War Transport, the Ministry of Economic Warfare. The consulate also housed agents of SIME (Security

Intelligence Middle East) and MI6. These agents, and indeed practically all British military personnel working in Turkey, entered the
country from Syria, on the Taurus Express.

This last fact was confirmed to me by an old friend of Denis
Wright named Bill Henderson. In 1941, Henderson, an architect in
the Royal Engineers, was posted as a junior staff officer to Ankara,
where his duties included meeting soldiers (dressed as civilians)
disembarking from the Taurus Express at six in the morning. In
1942, when Henderson was transferred to Cilicia to work on the
Taurus road, he discovered that the British had German counterparts in the vicinity, who were undertaking huge water supply and
irrigation schemes around Mersin under pre-war contracts. On one
occasion, Henderson recalled, his Turkish foreman got hold of
surveying equipment from helpful Germans. 'All that cloak-and-
dagger stuff and all those false identities were something of a
charade,' Henderson said. 'Everybody knew what was going on.'

Everybody, in this context, meant the German diplomatic and
intelligence corps, which was headed by the Reich's ambassador,
Franz von Papen – the Chancellor of Germany for a brief time in
1932 and then Vice-Chancellor in Hitler's first government from
January 1933 to the summer of 1934. The principle objectives of
the Germans were, first, to ensure that Turkey did not join the
Allies, and, second, to monitor and if possible influence the military
situation in the Middle East. Paul Leverkuehn, the Chief of the
Istanbul Station of the Abwehr from July 1941–44, considered that
his most important task was to guard against the risk of Turkish
entry into the war on the Allied side. The strength and distribution
of the British and Free French forces in Syria and Iraq was, accordingly, of vital interest to German intelligence. Arab observers along
the frontiers with Turkey carried out reconnaissance, and travellers
to and from Egypt, which continued to trade with Turkey, were also
a rich source of information. Agents of intelligence organizations –
Abwehr, Sicherheitsdienst and Auslandsorganization – operated
from German consulates. There was no German consulate in
Mersin, where the Axis powers were represented by an Italian consulate headed by an aristocrat named Aloisi. The Italians, Wright

said, engaged a man to swim out and attach limpet mines to the hulls of Allied merchantmen moored in the waters off Mersin. In the event, they only damaged one ship.

British counter-espionage was largely in the hands of SIME agents. One of these was C.T.C. Taylor, SIME's man in Adana. Taylor wrote in his unpublished autobiography:

> The enemy had a considerable number of sympathizers among the Arabs, many of whom remained faithful to the Grand Mufti of Jerusalem, who had fled to, and was operating from, Germany, and Italian Levantine families with members on either side of the [Turkish-Syrian] frontier. My organization's job was to spot enemy agents, or their various forms of communication and propaganda, and prevent them from penetrating far into territory held by us . . .
>
> [The frontier with Syria] was the chief route for agents and propaganda amongst the Arabs and Egyptians. In Adana the leading German agent was Paula Koch, who had been matron of the hospital in Aleppo before the war and who became most annoyed, I learned, when I christened her the Mata Hari of World War II. She had a milk-brother and informer, Joseph Ayvazian, who owned a hotel and restaurant up in the hills above Iskenderun at Soğuk Oluk.

Taylor arrived in Turkey in January 1942. On the Taurus Express to Istanbul, he bumped into another SIME agent, an Irish aristocrat from West Cork, Lieutenant-Colonel Sir Patrick Coghill, Bt. Coghill had arrived in Turkey on a control espionage job for Colonel R.J. Maunsell, the head of SIME, who was based in Cairo. In Istanbul, Coghill reported to Lieutenant-Colonel Guy Thomson ('a disappointed, venomous man' Coghill thought), who gave him the job of vice-consul at the British consulate at Adana. Coghill's mission was to find out how the enemy got its people across the Turkish border into Syria, and to tip off the British forces in Syria as to where and when enemy agents might be picked up. He was

greatly assisted by the Turkish authorities, whom he found much
more inclined towards the Allies than the Axis, specifically, Coghill
enjoyed privileged contacts with the Turkish secret police. The
secret police – under the direct and personal control of the prime
minister, not the cabinet – supplied the Allies with information
they could not obtain for themselves, such as complete lists of passengers leaving the country by rail or by air. In a stab at maintaining
neutrality, information was also passed on by the Turks to the Axis
powers, but this intelligence was not, both Coghill and Taylor
thought, of the same quality as that supplied to the Allies.

Sir Patrick Coghill's short spell in Adana led him to conclude
that there were two classes of spies travelling to and from Syria: a
riff-raff of smugglers, whose stories were unreliable; and high-up
agents who, like Joseph Dakak, travelled with neutral passports on
the Taurus Express.

After three weeks in Jerusalem, Joseph Dakak obtained an
export licence from the authorities in Palestine and concluded
a contract with a local merchant for the supply to Mersin of two
hundred tonnes of lemons. With his return visas in his pocket, he
set off on the train home, to Turkey.

He was arrested at Rasnakura, on the Palestine–Syria border.

That same night he was taken to Haifa, and the next day, back to
Jerusalem, where he was registered by the Palestine CID (Criminal
Investigation Department). The commander of the detention
centre was an English sergeant-major. He took Dakak's wedding
ring and another ring, saying that these would be returned later;
they never were.

My grandfather was held in Jerusalem for seventeen days. The
food was terrible – 'not fit,' he complained in his testimony, 'for even
the worst of murderers.' There was nowhere to sit or sleep: the choice
was between standing and lying down on bare cement. He repeatedly
asked to see the Turkish consul and was repeatedly told that he could
do so tomorrow. He was shown a warrant signed by the police chief of
Jerusalem, Arthur Giles, which stated that he was held in custody 'on
suspicion' pursuant to section 17(a) of some Act.

There were eight other detainees in this prison, most of whom were Jews. Only later, my grandfather wrote, did he realize that they were all spies and that their primary concern was to find out whether he, Dakak, was connected to Jewish anarchists.

I was startled to read this. What possible reason could there be to suspect Joseph Dakak, a Turk of Arab origins, of supporting the Zionist underground in Palestine? The allegation went unexplained, because here Part I of the testimony came to an end and Part II, called *In Beirut*, began.

On the seventeenth day of his detention in Jerusalem, Dakak was told that he was being taken to the Turkish border. But the following day, 8 May 1942, he was driven instead to the military prison of the Free French in Beirut. Technically, he remained in British custody.

Dakak was taken to a cell occupied by eight others. Among them he recognized a Mersin millionaire called Nazim Gandour. Gandour – a Muslim of Lebanese, not Turkish, nationality – hadn't shaved in four days. He had been arrested at the Syrian border by Desmond Doran, the British passport officer, who had travelled on the train with him. Gandour said that his visa had been inscribed with unusual numerals to alert the Syrian authorities that he should be arrested. 'You see?' Gandour said to Dakak, 'your passport has the same stamp.' Gandour said that Doran was an evil man who had corrupted quite a few people in Mersin, including certain Turkish police officers. 'Doran's the one behind all this,' he said.

The food at the Beirut prison was dreadful. One day Gandour – who enjoyed the unique privilege of a mattress and pillow apparently provided by his family – returned from a meeting with the prison governors and said to Dakak, 'Don't worry. From now on, I'll be receiving food prepared by my family, and I'll give you some.' And after that day three kinds of mezes (appetizers) and abundant quantities of fruit and baklava arrived at the prison. My grandfather wrote: 'It was well known in Mersin that I very often ate baklava; and in this way Gandour tried to gain my confidence.'

Because he suffered from stomach disorders, Dakak asked Gandour whether he might be able to get hold of some plain boiled potatoes. Gandour was able to oblige. One day, however, the potatoes tasted a little strange, and soon Dakak was seized by intense stomach pain, vomiting and diarrhoea; his heart started beating rapidly and he broke out into a drenching sweat. My grandfather's agony continued for three days. A doctor from Aleppo who was locked up with him took his pulse and diagnosed an upset stomach; but as he lay ill, Dakak remembered the incident with the oranges in Jerusalem and everything became clear to him: he had been poisoned, and all his fellow inmates, who had not eaten the potatoes but nevertheless had pretended to vomit, were in the pay of the English.

I didn't know what to make of this. Was it possible that *all* of my grandfather's cell-mates were informers?

The leader of this ring of stooges, my grandfather asserted, was Nazim Gandour. Every Saturday morning, when the prisoners were let out to air their blankets, Gandour's parents would be present a little distance away, play-acting: the mother carried a handkerchief and constantly wiped away tears. Gandour, meanwhile, questioned Dakak about the prominent people of Mersin and about the likelihood of the Germans invading Syria via Rhodes and Cyprus. 'Not having powers of divination,' my grandfather noted, 'there was no way I could possibly answer him.'

'This charade lasted for a month and a half,' my grandfather wrote.

All the while, the prisoners circulated terrifying stories about the English: how suspects were made to disappear, how their bodies were hacked up and dumped in the sea. There wasn't a machination, my grandfather wrote, that wasn't used to terrorize him and impress on him that he, too, could meet with this fate. On one occasion he overheard an Armenian sergeant in the neighbouring cell loudly declaring that he had worked as a butcher in Adana during the French occupation.

A few days after the poisoning incident, my grandfather continued, a pretext was used to transfer him to a cell in a building used for criminals convicted of serious crimes. Wary of the food, Dakak did not eat anything. He did, however, accept a glass of water that an Armenian orderly had filled up. After taking a mouthful, Dakak registered a strange sensation. His lips and his tongue began to swell and burn, and his breath began to rasp in his chest. He poured away the remaining water.

An hour or so later, my grandfather heard a conversation in the adjoining cell. Two men were giving instructions to the guard. 'At four in the morning, a car will come. That's when his time will be up. You'll put him into a sack and load him into the car. Once on the road, you'll shoot him twice in the head and finish off the job the poison started. Make sure you run the engine to muffle the sound of gunfire. Once you've chopped him up, throw the pieces into the sea off a cliff between Beirut and Tripoli.' The guard sobbed loudly and cried out, 'How can you ask me to do such a thing?'

My grandfather snapped. In his pocket was a small metal blade he kept for cleaning his nails. He cut himself with the blade, slashing his skin in twenty-five places. The blade was blunt and he used his teeth to tear his veins further open. With his blood, he smeared on the wall, *I AM INNOCENT.*

At five in the morning, a passing soldier noticed the blood and the semi-conscious prisoner. Soon more soldiers arrived and carried my grandfather to a room where his wounds were roughly bandaged. Instead of taking him to a hospital, they returned him to his old cell with Nazim Gandour and his cronies and laid him down on the bare ground with just two blankets.

Dakak was very weak. The spies in the cell tried to take advantage of his condition by gathering around him and asking questions about photographs they thrust before his face. Unable to take it any more, Dakak eventually cried out, 'I know who you are! I know that you're all working for the Intelligence Service!' At that, they stopped their interrogation.

But that same night Dakak awoke to find Gandour and two others looming nearby; and one hurriedly pocketed a gadget the size of a magnifying glass. 'As you'd been sleeping for so long,' Gandour bluffed, 'we thought we'd wake you up.' 'I later realized,' my grandfather wrote, 'that they'd drugged me in order to extract revelations from me. It wasn't the first or the last time,' my grandfather asserted, 'that this tactic was used on me.'

Three days after Joseph Dakak cut open his veins, he was forcibly removed from his cell and driven to a place called the Prison of the Sands (*Prison des Sables*). Two guards accompanied him. One said, 'The day after tomorrow, we're taking you out to sea and we're not going to waste more than two bullets on you.'

Upon arrival at the Prison of the Sands, Dakak spent half an hour in the infirmary. In spite of his injuries and loss of blood, he was placed alone in a cell equipped only with a pillow and two blankets. Once more, he had no choice but to sleep on the ground.

He was watched day and night. Anybody approaching the cell would be told to move on. From time to time the guard would look through the peephole and whisper, 'There's no escape'. After three days, my grandfather – confused, broken in spirit and not really conscious of his actions, he wrote – tried to hang himself from the door using a pyjama belt. The guard quickly realized what was happening and entered the cell to put a stop to it. The next morning, Dakak mutilated himself again, reopening his wounds with a rusty piece of metal ripped from the bottom of the door. On seeing the blood, the guard removed Dakak from the cell. The prisoner's wounds were bandaged and he was taken to a cell in another building.

The new cell was painted completely black. A large crucifix hung on one wall and at the centre of the crucifix was written, in Turkish, '*Tonight*'. That night a guard opened the peephole and said, 'You see that bearded face on the wall? An Armenian murderer scratched that picture with his nails on the night before his execution. At four in the morning, he was taken away and hanged.'

Dakak, worn out by lack of sleep and malnourishment, spent that night and the days and nights that followed in terror of execution. He also suffered from dehydration: it was August, the black cell was a furnace, and he was given nothing to drink from six in the evening to six in the morning; only in response to his cries would a mouthful of water sometimes be poured through the hole in his door.

He went on hunger strike and shouted for his consul. After ten days of fasting and protest, he was informed that his consul was coming. He stopped his hunger strike. However, when the visitor arrived three days later, Dakak became afraid and did not believe that he was the consul. 'As a consequence,' my grandfather wrote, 'I did not speak freely to the gentleman or voice complaints about how I was being tortured.'

After three months in the Prison of the Sands, Joseph Dakak was returned to the French prison in Beirut and placed in a cell with four other so-called detainees. Although his mental well-being had improved after the consul's visit, returning to this environment sent Dakak rapidly into reverse. As ever, he had to listen to his cell-mates' horror stories, and on the second day one of them (who claimed to be from Adana) said to the guards in a stage whisper clearly audible to Dakak, 'Tell the commander that enough is enough, it's time to finish with this man; hanging, shooting, it doesn't matter, just so long as it's done.' The guard returned a little while later and said, 'Everything's arranged. It's all been set up for four o'clock tomorrow morning.'

Shocked, Dakak ran to the balcony and threw himself down into the prison's interior courtyard. My grandfather wrote: 'I preferred to kill myself than face the rope or the bullet. It wasn't until later that it dawned on me that everything they did was part of a strategy of psychological torture.'

In its hallucinatory, ghastly, and temporally fluid progression, the testimony uncannily corresponded to a nightmare; and reading it, I was by now fighting for my breath. The suicide attempts, the mental torture, the self-mutilations, the cell transfers, the food poisonings, the suspicions, the unceasing distress at the centre of it all: repetitive and demanding and interminable and horrifying, my grandfather's grievances filled the pages like fumes. A part of me was irritated by the author of this airless, woebegone account, which made an incoherent and overly direct claim on my pity and too readily assumed assent to its tormented speculations – and, of course, a part of me consequently felt guilty: for I recognized in myself the strange mercilessness of the disobliged reader. However, I wasn't an ordinary reader. I was the writer's grandson. I couldn't flee the scene. I had to persevere and attempt to understand

something about Joseph's ordeals, which he had taken such trouble
to record.

My grandfather could not remember exactly how he threw himself over the balcony in the French Military Prison. When he came
to, after four hours of unconsciousness, he was back at the infirmary
at the Prison of Sands. His right leg was broken and he had a cut by
his right eyebrow. The next day he was transferred to the government hospital in Beirut, where his leg was put in plaster.

Joseph Dakak stayed at the hospital for seven months (which
suggested injuries more serious than a simple broken leg). He was
nursed by a Spanish nun called Sister Inias. She visited him every
night for two hours of prayers and conversation. The talk covered
a variety of subjects and ranged from religion to politics to the stories in the Beirut newspapers which the nun smuggled in every day.
Sister Inias would ask Dakak his opinion of current events – in
particular, how he expected Turkey to act. Other times, she would
tell him stories of how the Turks had slaughtered hundreds of
thousands of Armenians. She told him that the Turks did not like
Christians and that as a Christian he should not expect anything
from his consulate.

My grandfather concluded that Sister Inias was a spy, and that
she was saying these things about Turkey in order to demoralize
him and tempt him into a betrayal of his own country.

During the last weeks of his stay at the hospital (in March and
April 1943), a patient called Aram Hachadourian was put in the bed
next to my grandfather. Hachadourian had hardly lain his head on
his pillow before he'd revealed that, although a native of Gaziantep,
he had lived in Iskenderun for the last forty years and was the uncle
of the wife of Joseph Ayvazian, the proprietor of a hotel at Soguk
Oluk in the Amanus mountains. Hachadourian said that Ayvazian
had been mistreated by the Turks, who wouldn't permit anyone
stay at his hotel because of remarks he'd allegedly made in favour of
the Germans.

I was startled to read this: Ayvazian was the man identified by
C.T.C. Taylor, the SIME agent, as a German spy.

Hachadourian quizzed Dakak about the well-known people of

Iskenderun and about Turkish Armenians photographed in a magazine published in 1937 or 1938 called *Armanian*. Dakak didn't recognize any of them. Aram Hachadourian complained to my grandfather that in 1939 the Turks had forced him to leave Iskenderun and had frozen the bank account credited with the proceeds of the sale of his house, money which there was now not the slightest hope of recovering. 'Aram Hachadourian,' my grandfather wrote, 'came up with any old anti-Turkish rubbish because he, too, was a spy.'

At around this time, Sister Inias arranged a visit by Joseph Dakak's Beirut cousin, Alida Hannah. The nun told Alida, 'Don't be too long, I'll take care of the guard next door'; and to Dakak's astonishment the guard, who had never before left his post, disappeared. Joseph and Alida spoke for ten minutes. She assured him that Nazim Gandour and his brother Fazil were being tortured and were in a pitiful state. Nazim, Dakak retorted, was nothing other than an English spy.

Hachadourian, in the bed right next to Dakak's, listened to every word. My grandfather subsequently came to the sad realization that his cousin and Hachadourian were working together and that everything she'd said had been for the Armenian's benefit. 'There is no doubt at all that this was the arrangement,' my grandfather wrote in his testimony.

Two weeks later, Joseph Dakak was removed from the hospital and transferred to Palestine. On 5 May 1943, they brought him to a monastery situated between Jerusalem and Ramle, in a village called Emuas.

The monastery was surrounded by barbed wire and held thirty-three men, including Greeks, Germans, Albanians, Arabs, Serbians, Poles and Italians. By this time, my grandfather stated, he had come to understand the devious ways of the English and the subterfuges they used to extract information from him. It did not take him more than a day, therefore, to realize that the thirty-three men were all spies for the English and that at their head was none other than Nazim Gandour. As soon as a newcomer arrived a the camp, he would ostensibly be mobbed for news. The conversation would then be manipulated in such a way that the new arrival ended up by questioning Dakak. In this way, over the course of one and a half years, the number of inmates rose from thirty-three to eighty-eight. At the rate of about two a fortnight, fresh agents were sent to the monastery to do their work.

A familiar feeling of dismay overcame me – the feeling lawyers get when their witness comes out with a statement that abruptly deflates the balloon of credibility he has laboriously puffed up. It was simply impossible that an entire internment camp might be devoted to extracting information (information about *what*, incidentally?) from one prisoner. My grandfather was clearly a writer in the grip of paranoia.

I felt a strong pang of pity. That Joseph – an authoritative, punctilious man who (in Amy's words) never exaggerated and never said that he had eaten three figs if he'd only eaten two – had been reduced to this state of miscomprehension was a measure of the depth of his fall.

But this development did not lead me to distrust the whole of his testimony. A witness may be reliable in certain respects and unreliable in others. My grandfather was not *lying* about the role of his fellow prisoners; he was simply deluded about it. His paranoia therefore did not make me especially sceptical of his version of physically observable events (*especially*, because I was always conscious that the testimony was, as lawyers say, a self-serving statement), but of course it made his interpretation of them doubtful – doubtful, but not necessarily wrong. The fact that a man is paranoiac does not mean that he is immune to conspiracies to harm him.

My grandfather continued his story of his persecution in saddening detail. They used a variety of ruses to question him, he stated. One bizarre trick was to give the prisoners names that were exactly, or almost exactly, the same as the names of the political leaders of their country in the hope that this would subconsciously induce Dakak to volunteer information about the men in question. They had another strange ploy: they would bring in so-called prisoners who bore a striking resemblance to persons about whom they sought information. For example, long ago there had been in Mersin an Italian consul called Moki, and so there materialized an

Italian prisoner who looked exactly like Moki and who began to speak to Dakak in Italian. And another Italian 'prisoner' strongly resembled the Italian consul who succeeded Moki in Mersin. Joseph Dakak wrote:

> During the two and a half years that I spent in the monastery, they used these and any other ruse you could think of in order to extract from me the slightest piece of information about events that were taking place in every corner of the world and about the people involved in such events. As time went by, I understood better and better what was going on, namely that the English would go to any length to uncover anyone who might have some connection to the Nazis or who might be Anglophobic. Names would be suggested to me in conversations or in the newspapers and magazines that were brought to me, and my reaction would be noted. The spies surrounded me incessantly, and chief among them was, of course, Nazim Gandour. This is how the days passed.

He continued:

> Because of the pressure, intimidation, psychological torture and poisonings that I endured, my heart weakened and I contracted the condition which I suffer from to this day. Instead of providing me with medical care, they did everything to wear me out and aggravate my cardiac condition. Every time they found reason for dissatisfaction, they stepped up the torture: they put a spade in my hands and despite my poorly condition made me dig in the field next to the monastery, carry rocks, and unload wood from lorries. To ensure the destruction of my physical and mental health, they made me suffer every torture imaginable, the spies taking it in turn to seize on to the most trivial matter to vex me and pick an argument. This programme was carried out so systematically and relentlessly that it would have been

the easiest thing in the world to surrender one's sanity. They
lodged me on the second floor of the building in order to
force me to climb up and down the stairs if I wanted to do
the slightest thing. When the doctor finally examined me, I
was told that there was nothing wrong with me, that it was
all in my mind. They did not grant me the privileges that the
other spying inmates enjoyed and constantly assigned me the
hardest work, inventing pointless and demanding tasks for
this purpose.

Joseph Dakak was alone in the basement when a guard told him
that the war was over. Three days later, they once again moved him
to the upstairs floor, and it was there that he read in the newspapers
that the legislation authorizing internment without trial had been
repealed and that internees had been freed. However, a month
passed and still Dakak was not released. He wrote a letter to the
Turkish consul and, when this went unanswered, a second letter.
Finally, four months after the end of the European war, he wrote to
a letter of protest to Major Prendergast at the Defence Security
Office in Jerusalem.

Two nights later, the prison commander, Captain Sylvester, said
to him, 'Get ready, you're off tomorrow.' Dakak replied, 'Could
you please inform the head of your office in Jerusalem that I wish
to see him.' 'I see. Might I ask why?' 'For three and a half years,
you have kept me imprisoned,' Dakak said, 'even though I am
innocent. You have caused me great psychological and financial
damage, and on top of all this, you've made me suffer from this
malady of the heart. I wish to claim damages and interest in
respect of these losses.' The Englishman smiled unpleasantly and
said, 'I'm going to give you some advice. Ask your Turkish
government for compensation.'

The next morning, Dakak was called into Captain Sylvester's
office and presented with a typed letter to sign. By this point, his
belongings were in the waiting lorry outside and they were shouting
at him to get a move on. Even so, he cast an eye over the paper and
saw that it asserted that he had been well looked after during his

detention and that his property had been restored to him in full. My grandfather said, 'No, I won't sign that. I cannot betray my conscience. If it was simply concerned with money, I would sign without hesitation. But this letter does not tell the truth about how I have been treated and I will not sign it.' At this, another document was quickly typed in triplicate. Dakak read it and, seeing that it mentioned money and nothing more, put his name to it. He dashed to the waiting lorry and climbed quickly aboard. It was only after he'd set off that it occurred to him that there were blank spaces on the page he'd signed where the English could insert anything they wished. But it was too late now to do anything about it.

Travelling with my grandfather were Nazim Gandour, a Hungarian Jew, and an Arab. At the Miye Miye camp in Saïda, my grandfather and the Hungarian got off and Nazim Gandour and the Arab were driven on to Beirut. After four days at Miye Miye, Dakak and the Hungarian were driven to Beirut, where they caught a train to Aleppo. There, the two prisoners were placed on board the Taurus Express and accompanied by a soldier and an English sergeant to the border town of Meydan Ekbez. The sergeant observed to Dakak that Turkey had tough laws and pitiless justice. Dakak replied: 'I am prepared to appear not only before Turkish justice but before any court of justice.' It was the last trick the English had up their sleeve, my grandfather wrote; had I shown the smallest sign of fear about returning to Turkey, the sergeant would have been convinced of my guilt and would have returned me to the British. This was, after all, his assigned role; and the Hungarian Jew played his part very well, too.

My grandfather's testimony ended as follows:

I was a prisoner for exactly three and a half years. During my detention not a single cigarette, a single handkerchief or a single piastre were granted me. I was forced to buy everything with my own money, and other valuable possessions were taken from me and stolen. An innocent man, I was unjustly imprisoned. By systematic and unceasing torture, by repeated poisonings in small doses and by the failure to treat to my heart condition, I suffered physical and psychological injury. I was made to suffer by means that contravene the laws of humanity, by methods incompatible with the dignity of mankind. It is worth pointing out that during my entire period of detention only twice did an English commanding officer meet me and only once a French commander, and then but briefly. What most enraged me were the insinuations directed at making me believe that my own government had delivered me to the English. They also wanted me to believe that the reach of the Intelligence Service knew no bounds, and that even in Turkey I was within its grasp.

As a Turkish citizen, it is my duty to inform you of the foregoing.

Accurate or not, the testimony finished on a note of relative coherence and sang-froid, and even the somewhat absurd complaint about the handkerchieflessness of his captivity sounded like a beginning of a return to fastidious form. Most importantly, my grandfather's grievances came to a point, albeit an unusual one. The testimony was not, as I'd initially suspected, a statement of a claim for compensation. It was simply a *notice,* addressed to the Turkish authorities, of grievous wrongs committed on a Turkish citizen by 'the English' and of loss and injury suffered thereby.

But what was the Turkish government supposed to do about this? Take up the matter with the British on a diplomatic level? Pay compensation for torts it did not commit? Either course seemed very improbable. The more I thought about it, the more puzzled I became by the function of this document and the precise nature of my grandfather's relations with the Turkish state, to whom the testimony was presumably addressed. As I re-read the final paragraph, one sentence stood out: '*What most enraged me were the insinuations directed at making me believe that my own government had delivered me to the English.*' I did not understand the relevance of this strange remark, or why my grandfather had chosen to end his testimony with it.

On 3 February 1942, around the time my grandfather was making his fateful visa application to the British consulate in Mersin, Sir Patrick Coghill, the SIME agent based in Adana, visited Beirut. The baronet learned, to his 'stupefaction and horror,' that he had been appointed head of the British Security Mission in Syria. The BSM had been founded by Arthur Giles, the head of CID Palestine Police, and had accompanied the invasion force into Vichy-controlled Syria in the summer of 1941 with a view to assuming the counter-espionage activities of the Vichy Sûreté. In the event, the Sûreté records were destroyed before the British could get their hands on them. Coghill noted that, at the time, the loss of the records 'was a bitter disappointment – but looking back I wonder whether we were not better off without them. As practically all the French agents and informers were Lebanese Christians, all their reports were hopelessly biased and distorted – yet if we had taken them over we would certainly have believed them and relied on them.' At any rate, it soon became apparent that the Axis had no significant espionage capability in Beirut or elsewhere in the region. Little trouble was experienced from its agents, which, Coghill speculated, was perhaps due to the large number of 'suspects and known pro-Axis sympathizers' held in 'internment camps for Enemy Aliens and Agents and Suspects'.

The administration of the camps – indeed, practically all internal administrative power in Syria – was in Free French hands. Nonetheless, when Sir Patrick Coghill assumed command of the British Security Mission in the summer of 1942, he was from that time on responsible for the continued detention of Joseph Dakak. Not surprisingly, there was no mention of my grandfather in Coghill's autobiographical papers, which I read in an Oxford library. There was, however, another omission which did strike me as a little curious. Although he referred frequently to his life and home in Castletownshend, West Cork, and to his family, Sir Patrick Coghill made no reference to his uncle, who also lived in the village of Castletownshend, Admiral Somerville.

4

There are crimes of passion and crimes of logic.
                                                    – Albert Camus, *The Rebel*

Shortly after nine o'clock on the evening of Tuesday 24 March
1936, the occupants of The Point, Castletownshend, County
Cork – Vice-Admiral Henry Boyle Townshend Somerville and his
wife – heard footsteps on the gravel path outside their dining room
window. Mrs Somerville said to her husband, 'Perhaps that's one of
the boys coming to see you' – the boys, in this case, being the young
men of the locality who dropped by to ask the Admiral's help in
joining the British navy. 'I'll go and see,' the Admiral said. He rose
to his feet to receive the visitors personally: the cook and the housemaid were out for the evening at a play presented in the village by a
travelling company. There was a knocking at the door. Admiral
Somerville picked up an oil lamp, crossed the hall, and stepped into
the porch at the entrance to the house. Mrs Somerville, who
remained in the dining room, heard an indistinct voice outside the
glass-panelled front door: 'Are you Mr Somerville?' 'I am Admiral
Somerville,' Somerville replied correctly. Mrs Somerville heard
gunshots and the sound of glass shattering. She grabbed a lamp

and rushed into the hall. As she entered, a strong gust of wind blew in through the open door of the porch, extinguishing the flame she carried. Mrs Somerville found herself in complete darkness. She called her husband's name – 'Boyle! Boyle!' – but received no response. All that was audible was the sound of footsteps – the steps of two persons, was her impression – retreating down the gravel avenue towards the gate of the house. Mrs Somerville advanced in the darkness towards the porch. She saw her husband lying motionless by the doorway among the broken remains of his lamp.

Alongside the body was a piece of cardboard on which letters cut from newspapers had been glued. The message read, 'This British agent has sent 52 boys to the British Army in the last few months.'

By order of Chief Superintendent McCarthy, the Corkman initially in charge of the investigation, the body was left untouched until the arrival from Dublin, on Thursday, of Chief Superintendent Woods of the Special Crimes Department, and Chief Superintendent Sheridan, Head of the Technical Bureau of the Civic Guards. Friday saw the arrival of Commandant Stapleton, the Free State army's ballistics expert, and Dr John McGrath, the State Pathologist, who carried out a post-mortem examination.

At the inquest held later that day in the Somerville home, Dr McGrath gave evidence that the body was that of an elderly man, 5 feet 11 inches in height, dressed in a dinner suit and a bloodstained white dress shirt. On examination, the pathologist found six wounds. The first was a bullet wound in the left groin at the level of the pubis. The direction of the wound was from the left of the deceased towards the right, and downwards. The bullet was extracted from muscles in the right thigh, having travelled through the belly cavity, puncturing the intestine twice, and through the pubic bone. The second wound was situated at the crest of the ilium on the left side. This wound also tracked in a downwards direction. Dr McGrath found the bullet in the muscles on the right side of the small of the back. Wound number three was in the chest, situated 1½ inches to the left of the midline and 2¾ inches above the nipple line. This wound went partly through the breastbone, then through the membranes that covered the heart, then it punctured the left artery of the heart at a point above the heart. Then the track went under the lining and through the back of the chest wall between the third and fourth ribs; it continued through the muscles of the back and the shoulder-blade bone, and terminated in the muscles at the back of the shoulder-blade, where a bullet was lodged. The fourth and fifth wounds (an entrance wound and an exit wound on the left upper arm caused by a bullet passing through and breaking the bone) were the only horizontal wounds. The sixth wound was at the angle of the lower jaw, an inch in front and below the left earlobe. The track of this wound was through the jawbone, which was broken, then downwards and rightwards and through the front of the spine, and through the tissues of the neck and the right shoulder blade, and finally into the muscles on the right side of the spine. Here another bullet was found. In total, at least five shots were fired.

The State Solicitor, a Mr T. Healy, addressed the inquest jury at length. He described Admiral Somerville as 'the descendant of a proud family, the descendant of people who won distinction at home and abroad, the descendant of one of our incorruptible band who had fought to keep in this country a Parliament which had legislated for the entire country, the descendant of one who had disdained rank and wealth in order to fight for that Parliament which legislated for 32 counties and not for a dismembered and partitioned country.' This was a reference to a great-grandfather of the deceased, Charles Kendal Bushe (1767–1843), the Lord Chief Justice of Ireland from 1822 to 1842, who in January 1800 spoke in the Dublin parliament against its forthcoming union with the English parliament. People also noted that the Admiral's father, Tom Somerville, had been a friend of a local republican hero, Jeremiah O'Donovan Rossa (1831–1915). O'Donovan Rossa died in New York, and it was on the occasion of the repatriation of his remains, at Glasnevin Cemetery, that the republican Patrick Pearse famously proclaimed, 'Life springs from death; and from the graves of patriot men and women spring living nations . . . [T]he fools, the fools, the fools! They have left us our Fenian dead, and while Ireland holds these graves, Ireland unfree shall never be at peace.'

The deceased, Mr Healy continued, was a man who 'had acted as a kindly gentleman to all, and everybody who came to him for help and aid was assisted by him'. The suggestion that he was a recruiting agent for the British armed forces was, Healy stated, false. 'Admiral Somerville never asked, sought or induced any person to join that army or navy, but when people came to him and asked him for a recommendation he gave it freely in so far as it lay in his power where he knew people, and when he did not know them he told them the procedure to be adopted. But he used no influence to get any man or boy into the English navy. Now, if every person who had signed a recommendation for boys to join the English navy is to be shot, I am afraid there will be a great number of people in this country who will be shot, because men in all stages and positions, clergy, have signed such recommendations. Surely, the least that might have been given to the deceased was a warning that his action was distasteful, and was regarded as unworthy of the conduct of Irishmen. No notice or warning was given to the deceased, but instead he was hurled to his death. No stain will lie on the memory of the deceased where he was known, and throughout the country the action which has taken place is abhorrent, and I again repeat that every effort will be made to trace the authors of it, though goodness knows, with modern means of communication, the assassin has the advantage on his side.'

The State Solicitor's gloomy remark was directed at the fact that the killers had fled in a car that two schoolgirls had seen driving away from the house at great speed. It was not until the following day that guards arrived. A minute investigation began. Castings were taken of the tyre-marks left by the car, photographs and measurements were taken of the scene, fingerprints and footprints were thoroughly examined. A week after the homicide, forensic searches were still being carried out at Point House.

While the detectives went about their work, more details began to emerge in the press about the late Admiral. He was born in Castletownshend in 1863, the son of Lieutenant-Colonel Thomas Henry Somerville (who served as High Sheriff of Cork in 1888) and Adelaide, daughter of Admiral Sir Josiah Coghill, Bt. Ships on which the Admiral served included the HMS *Shandon*, the

Agincourt, the *Audacious*, the *Heroine*, the *Sphinx* and the HMS *Sealark*. He had seen active service in the Chilean–Peruvian war and the first Egyptian war, and as a hydrographic surveyor had sailed in waters by China and Ceylon and in the western and eastern Pacific Ocean. During the Great War he had commanded the *Victorian*, *Argonaut*, *Amphitrite* and *King Alfred*. He was awarded the CMG and made an officer of the *Légion d'Honneur*. After his retirement from the navy in 1919, the Admiral was employed by the Hydrographic Department at the British Admiralty. He wrote several books, including dictionaries of languages spoken in New Hebrides and New Georgia, Solomon Islands. Writing ran in the family: Edith Somerville, co-author of the Somerville and Ross books, was his sister. Boyle – the Christian name he went by – Somerville was a Fellow of the Royal Anthropological Society and a Vice-President of the Cork Historical and Archaeological Society. He was a charitable man and frequently contributed to the funds of the Skibbereen Conference of the (Catholic) St Vincent de Paul Society.

And indeed the assassination outraged the Catholic Church. In an address that was read out in every parish in his diocese, the Bishop of Ross stated that in respect of the crime there was 'no single circumstance to palliate guilt in the slightest. It was not the result of sudden and overwhelming passion, an outbreak of uncontrollable excitement, momentarily taking away the full use of reason. No. It was a well-planned, carefully thought out and deliberately organized crime, with every move coolly forecasted and every precaution taken to ensure the subsequent safety of the perpetrator. It bore every mark of the crime of the coward, who will strike only when assured of impunity. . . . It is to be hoped,' the bishop said, 'that this awful crime will be a warning to our young men, who may be tempted to join Secret Societies, so often and deservedly condemned by the Catholic Church.'

Condemnation also came from the political establishment. In the Dáil, a government spokesman sympathized with the relations of the victim of 'this cowardly crime', and Cork County Council also passed a resolution expressing its sympathies. Councillor D. O'Callaghan said that the Admiral, whom he'd known for fifty

THE CORK EXAMINER, THURSDAY, MARCH 26, 1936.

AGED VICE-ADMIRAL SHOT DEAD AT THE DOOR OF HIS HOUSE

KILLED INSTANTLY.

PATHETIC STORY TOLD BY TRAGIC WIDOW.

"A VOICE—THEN SHOTS."

Unknown Assailants Escape In Motor Car.

THE WEST CORK TRAGEDY.

Widespread Investigations By The Civic Guard Authorities.

A tragic story was told yesterday by the widow of Vice-Admiral Henry Boyle Somerville, who was shot dead at the door of his residence on Tuesday night.

At about 9.15 p.m., she said, when she and her husband were seated together in the diningroom. They were the only occupants of the house at the time. She happened to leave the diningroom to go to an ante-chamber, and while there she heard footsteps in the yard at the rear of the premises.

She returned to the diningroom with a small reading-lamp, and while there she again heard the footsteps.

Then there was a knock and her husband went to the door. She overheard a man asking: "Are you Mr. Somerville," and her husband's reply: "I am Admiral Somerville."

"Immediately," said Mrs. Somerville, "there was the sound of the firing of several shots and the accompanying sound of falling glass."

WEST CORK SHOOTING SENSATION.—A close-up view of the entrance porch of the residence at Castletownshend, where Vice-Admiral Somerville was shot dead on Tuesday night. Note the bullet-hole in door panel.
("Examiner" Photo).

years, never did anything in his life that either Catholic or Protestant could be ashamed of. He was an idol of the people. He was not a recruiting agent for the British. Mr O'Callaghan himself had recommended persons to British armed forces for the last twenty to thirty years, poor men who came home with a pension of £300 and £400 to support their families. Senator Fitzgerald, speaking on behalf of Fianna Fáil, stated that even if the Somerville family differed from the rest of the country with respect to the national outlook, there must be room in this country for all shades and classes of opinion. (Hear, hear.) Mr O'Mahony, who wished to be associated with the vote, said that the Somerville family had, in the past, suffered for its convictions as far as Irish nationalism was concerned. Mr O'Mahony did not agree with the Admiral politically, but it was a terrible thing that he had received no warning.

The Admiral's funeral took place on 28 March 1936. The *Cork Examiner* showed a photo of a procession of hundreds following the coffin down the main street. Among the mourners, the newspaper reported, was the nephew of the deceased, Sir Patrick Coghill, who had travelled from Britain for the funeral.

The furore continued in the newspapers, and politicians and priests urged anyone who knew something to come forward. Rumours began to circulate that inquiries had extended into Kerry and that an arrest was imminent. But nobody was ever arrested for the murder of Admiral Somerville.

In time, one important fact entered the public domain: action of some kind against Admiral Somerville was authorized by Tom Barry, then the IRA OC (Officer Commanding) in County Cork. Decades after Somerville's death, Barry went on record that an IRA squad had been instructed to 'get' the Admiral, but that 'the leader of the IRA squad, not the most stable of men, apparently was carried away, and interpreted his orders quite literally, and shot the Admiral dead'.

What most intrigued me about Barry's oddly vague account was its attempt to introduce a morally significant distance between him and the killing. Ordinarily, Barry had no qualms about the republican use of 'physical force'. What was it about this particular incident that led him to disown it?

At the beginning of 1936, the IRA was a diminished and strategically confused organization. Morale had fallen sharply since the early 'thirties, when the IRA regrouped effectively for the first time since the Civil War and, animated by socialist ideas, held rallies and mounted sometimes violent campaigns against prison warders, police officers, the courts, and English imports such as sweets and newspapers. The threat to the institutions of the Free State grew so serious that in late 1931 the Dublin government set up a Military Tribunal to try political cases, since juries were unwilling, out of fear or ideological persuasion, to convict republican defendants. Then, in February 1932, Éamon de Valera's pro-Republican Fianna Fáil came to power and legalized the IRA. Everything changed. There was a boom of recruitment into the IRA, whose activities were limited to resisting the political advance of the Blueshirts, the followers of a pro-Treaty, fascistic organization that called itself, successively, the Army Comrades Association, the National Guard, and the Young Ireland Association. There were riots, bitterly-fought street battles and, very occasionally, fatalities. But by the end of 1934, the

Blueshirt threat had been effectively eliminated, and the IRA (which still asserted a right to bear arms in the face of the continuing British presence in Ireland) began to lose its direction. Drilling and training faltered and membership fell sharply. Some men left for the communist-inclined Republican Congress group, but a greater number drifted to Fianna Fáil. Although Fianna Fáil had not delivered a republic, for many republicans its anti-British measures (most notably, economic sanctions and the abolition of the requirement that members of the Free State parliament swear an oath of allegiance to the British Crown) represented acceptable progress. In 1935, relations between the IRA and the government – by now characterized by uneasy mutual tolerance – worsened. In February, IRA men, acting in support of a group of tenants threatened with eviction, broke into the house of a land agent in Edgeworthstown, Co. Longford, and shot dead his son. Then, in March, came a direct confrontation with the authorities: IRA men, siding with striking bus and tram workers in Dublin, sniped at Free State army lorries in use as public transport, and wounded two police officers on patrol. The government finally acted against its Civil War comrades-in-arms. Throughout 1935, arrests, surveillance and harassment of the IRA – still not an illegal organization – increased; and so, correspondingly, did IRA antagonism towards de Valera and Fianna Fáil, now seen as traitors to republicanism or, at best, its unfit trustees. By early 1936, republican logic dictated that it fell once more to the IRA to advance the cause of an Ireland united and free from British rule.

Here one came to Tom Barry's difficulty: how to leap from this premise to a necessarily remote and terrible spot in the ethical landscape – the shooting of an elderly Irishman in his home. (It is a vital and appealingly pluralistic tenet of republican ideology that Protestants in Ireland like Admiral Somerville, however unionist or 'West British', are as Irish as the next man.) The reason given by Barry for the Somerville killing was that the victim had 'sent' Irish boys to the Royal Navy as an 'agent of the British'. But this did not really make sense. Somerville's sending of Irish boys to the Royal Navy was a mischief that could have been stopped without shooting him dead. The fact that nonetheless the IRA undertook the perilous and dreadful course of homicide suggested that it was not really concerned, in this instance, with stopping recruitment. What if the objective had not been to *stop* Somerville but to *punish* him? Again, this did not stand up to scrutiny. Somerville's actions were, in practical terms, harmless. There had been no systematic IRA engagement with the British since 1921, and the continuing British presence in Ireland was not even slightly dependent on the Royal Navy's enlistment of young men from West Cork or elsewhere in the country. Somerville was, therefore, a purely ideological offender, at most guilty, as the state solicitor put it, of distasteful conduct unworthy of an Irishman. By the ethical and judicial standards operative in non-repressive societies (standards espoused by the IRA), causing ideological offence was not a capital crime; and it followed that any 'execution' of Somerville, particularly in circumstances where he received no warning, would bear no rational relation to the gravity of his offence.

But it seemed unlikely that Tom Barry's embarrassment would have been caused simply by the problem of irrationality. Although preoccupied by his image in history as a disciplined soldier who played by the rules, Barry was also a hardline republican. Hardline republicans are disinclined to throw doubt on their own or their comrades' actions. They are convinced of the justness of their cause and of the good faith in which their fellow volunteers act, and they know that misjudgements, even irrational misjudgements, are a regrettable, unavoidable fact of war, and they do not hold themselves peculiarly responsible for that fact. It seemed, then, that Tom Barry must have been defensive about something other than the (irrational) reasons given for the shooting – which meant that the Admiral must have been shot for some other, unmentioned, reason. But what reason was it?

Although the answer to this question was obvious and terrible, it was not until much later that I was able to see it. What I knew, in the first instance, was that the death of Admiral Somerville had historic consequences: together with the fatal shooting, on 26 April 1936, of a suspected informer, John Egan, in County Waterford, it led to the final collapse of the relations between the IRA and Fianna Fáil. On

18 June 1936, the IRA was declared an unlawful association by the government, and has remained unlawful in Ireland ever since.

Uncle Brendan did not elaborate on his pronouncement that the Colt .45 unearthed at Ardkitt was the weapon used to shoot Admiral Somerville. He said that he was going to do a little bit of research into the matter. I didn't press him. Streams of confidential information run underneath all families, but the very integrity of republican families depends on secrecy. Leaks are avoided by restricting the movement of sensitive information to approved channels and, just as importantly, by the cultivation (conscious or unconscious), by those not in the know, of a measured incuriosity about certain things that others might be up to. This complicity perhaps comes naturally in large, claustrophobic families, where not everybody can or wants to know everybody else's business, and where mutual, unintrusive loyalty is an essential familial glue. 'You've to stick together for better or worse,' my grandfather would say to his sons. The reservoir of O'Neill republican confidences was Brendan. He was the son whom my grandfather trusted, and to whom he vouchsafed knowledge of certain matters so that Brendan might bear witness to them and, it could be inferred, keep them in memory until they might safely emerge at the lit surface of history. But when is this kind of disclosure timely? This was a matter for Brendan's judgement and, in relation to the circumstances surrounding the death of Admiral Somerville, quite a responsibility. Sometimes, I discovered, O'Neill sensitivities are anomalous, so that even though an event might be a matter of public record it remains subject to our internal hush; thus we have secrets that elsewhere have become non-secrets and we treat as out-of-bounds territory trampled by the rest of the world. The discrepancy is understandable: why should the family's boundaries of discretion, staked out in times of extreme jeopardy, follow the shifting contours of a public discourse that embodied the political values which for so long brought us danger and hardship? But in relation to Admiral Somerville, we had not been overtaken by public knowledge. The public had no idea about the Colt .45 or who had pulled its trigger.

When I asked her about it, my grandmother could not to tell me

whether the story about the gun was true or not. 'We were never told anything,' she said. She did, however, remember the 'hulla-baloo' that the Somerville shooting caused; and she also knew – from what source, I didn't know – that the car used by the assassins had been finally abandoned at Rathduff, a small village north of Cork city, close by the house of her father's sister.

Not long after the Ardkitt trip, another thing surfaced. Breaking a silence he'd kept for a quarter of a century, my uncle Billy Pollock said that when he became engaged to my aunt Ann O'Neill a fellow remarked to him, 'Do you know you're marrying the daughter of the man who shot Admiral Somerville?'

My grandfather's childhood was a wartime childhood. From around 1918 until the truce in July 1921, he lived through the Anglo-Irish War and – after nearly a year's imperfect peace – through the Civil War. County Cork, sometimes referred to as the Cork Republic, was a centre of fierce resistance to the Anglo-Irish Treaty of December 1921, which provided for the partition of Ireland into an independent Irish Free State (comprising 26 counties) and a province of the United Kingdom (comprising six Ulster counties) to be called Northern Ireland. But the rebels' resistance did not last long. Free State troops arrived in Cork in August 1922 and, notwithstanding the death of General Michael Collins and instances of extreme violence, took physical control of the county with relative ease. By May 1923, the fighting was as good as over and the great majority of the IRA was in captivity.

During these conflicts, Cork was by far the most violent county in Ireland. From 1917 to 1923, the IRA in Cork killed 195 and seriously wounded 113 people, and blew up 211 bridges and 301 buildings. The British army killed 93 and wounded 155, the Royal Irish Constabulary killed 108 and wounded 145, and the Free State army killed 70 and wounded 175. The combined forces of the Crown destroyed 237 buildings. The total number of serious casualties came to around 1,600, which is to say around one victim per 240 persons – a much higher rate than that suffered in Northern Ireland since the troubles there began in 1969.

The Anglo-Irish War was much bloodier and more terrifying than the Civil War. The IRA's guerrilla campaign was ruthless and unpredictable and calculated to cow not only the Crown forces but also their perceived civilian supporters – most notably, Protestant families, whose Big Houses were burned down in reprisals against British actions. Faced with an effective and intangible enemy, the British imposed martial law and terrorized the local population by official and unofficial reprisals, death squads, and the raiding and destruction of homes. A good part of the centre of Cork city was burned down as a reprisal for the Kilmichael ambush. I learned something of the scope and deadliness of the violence by leafing through the newspapers of the time. On 16 February 1921, for example, the *Cork Examiner* ran the following headlines: CORK TRAIN AMBUSH – SIX PASSENGERS DEAD, TWO ATTACKERS KILLED, MILITARY WOUNDED · MOURNEABBEY CONFLICT – CIVILIANS DEAD AND CAPTURED · SHOT DEAD IN CORK FIELD – ANOTHER LABELLED BODY FOUND · REPORTED SKIRMISH NEAR CORK.

The day before, 15 February 1921, the *Examiner* carried the following story:

> BANDON DOUBLE TRAGEDY – TWO YOUNG MEN
> SHOT DEAD
> Bandon, Monday – Another appalling tragedy is reported
> today from Breaghna, Desertserges, which is in the
> neighbourhood of the place where Thomas Bradfield, of
> Knockacoole House, was found shot about a fortnight ago.
>
> It appears that the two sons, James and Timothy, of a
> highly respectable farmer named James Coffey, were taken
> from their beds about two o'clock this morning by masked
> and armed men and immediately afterwards shots were
> heard, their dead bodies being found subsequently in a
> neighbouring field. They were aged 19 and 22 years, and
> were quiet and inoffensive. Much sympathy is felt for their
> bereaved parents and relatives.

The question of who killed the Coffey brothers (who, it later emerged, were in fact aged 22 and 25) was raised in the House of Commons on 22 February 1921, but the British government had no information then, or at any subsequent time, as to the identity of the killers. The O'Neills simply said it was the Black and Tans. We had a view on the matter because the Coffeys, who lived very close to Ardkitt, were Jim O'Neill's first cousins, and, a fact not mentioned by the newspapers, IRA volunteers. Their deaths, not forgotten, were part of the family's narrative of itself.

My grandfather was eleven years of age and living in Kilbrittain with his O'Driscoll aunt and uncle when his cousins died. It required a conscious effort on my part to think of him at that age, and all that came to my mind was the cinematic image of a boy in shorts tramping alone across a field in Graunriagh. I could not picture his face or guess what his thoughts were. I knew that he was growing up without his mother and father, that two of his cousins had met death in the most nightmarish circumstances, that at night he heard gunfire and roaring British armoured cars and shouting enemy soldiers; that his name, James O'Neill, appeared on the list of occupants tacked to the front door of Graunriagh by order of the British; that the Kilbrittain company of the IRA was one of the most active in the country; that in a year his uncle would die, and that he would leave school at fourteen and be once more uprooted, and that he never knew life to be easy or certain. These frightening, internecine circumstances were utterly removed from my experience of growing up, and I hesitated to draw too many conclusions from them; but I thought they were a clue to why, by the time he was a man, my grandfather had developed a character and outlook calculated, first and foremost, to withstand and reduce the world.

After Graunriagh, Jim went back to Ardkitt. In his late teens, he quit the farm and went to Cork city. At some point between 1930 and 1932, when he was in his early twenties, he joined the IRA. Although at this time many republicans were throwing their weight behind Fianna Fáil (my grandmother recalled her brother Tadhg campaigning in West Cork in the 1932 election), my grandfather never trusted Éamon de Valera. As the 'thirties passed and de Valera did little to progress the unification of Ireland, my grandfather's distrust developed into loathing. 'He hated him; he really, really hated him,' my grandmother said.

Jim O'Neill threw himself into paramilitary life with characteristic determination. With his single-mindedness, physical strength and easy way with machinery, he was a very competent and respected volunteer and known for being a strict disciplinarian. By the mid-'thirties, he was an IRA company OC and TO (training officer). Training took him away for weekends to special camps, and he would often come home from work in the evenings only to set off immediately for a drilling session in West Cork, where his knowledge of the country complemented his expertise with a Lewis machine-gun. When the civil war in Spain started in July 1936, Jim O'Neill toyed with the idea of fighting against the fascists. But the IRA forbade its members from travelling to Spain (a prohibition of limited effect: around 400 Irishmen, mostly ex-IRA, fought in the International Brigades, 42 dying in action), because volunteers were required for active service in Ireland. Only months after the killing of Admiral Somerville, the first anti-British military campaign since 1921 was to be launched.

The first step was to be a raid on Gough Barracks, in County Armagh, by 26 men from the Cork active service unit. Among the select few was Jim O'Neill.

The Corkmen packed their bags and went to confession and bought train tickets for Dundalk. However, when the women's republican group Cumann na mBan – which was not supposed to know anything about the raid – requested to participate in the raid, it became apparent that the attack was an open secret. The Armagh raid was cancelled. My grandfather always regretted this lost opportunity, just as he always regretted not having fought for the Spanish Republic – even though its cause was doomed and nothing he could have done would have affected the outcome of that war.

The Armagh raid was the idea of Tom Barry, the new IRA Chief of Staff. His right-hand man was my great-uncle, Tadhg Lynch, the IRA adjutant-general. I knew from family talk that Tadhg was an IRA man but I only learned what a prominent national figure

he'd been from reading historical literature. I read, for example, that
in May 1937, he marched alongside his friend Frank Ryan, recently
returned from the Spanish Civil War, at the head of the anti-
Coronation march in Dublin. There was a huge brawl with the
police, but the marchers made it to the Smith O'Brien monument in
O'Connell Street, where Tadhg, 'his coat and shirt a mess of blood,
but voice, mind and body vibrant with the passion of a great work
well done' (*An Phoblacht*), chaired the meeting. Fighting broke out
again and Tadhg was knocked out. Waking up next to Tom Barry in
hospital, my great-uncle got out of bed and mobilized the Dublin
unit for another march the next day. A *New York Times* headline
read: 'Dublin Republicans Battle Police in Anti-British Rallies'.
Tadhg no doubt appreciated the effect of such media coverage:
that year he edited a new series of *An Phoblacht*, the newspaper that
still remains an important IRA mouthpiece.

My grandmother said that Tadhg was an analytical man, into
strategy: he wouldn't be a fellow to go out and do the shooting. Her
brother Jack, she implied, was different. Jack was a man of action.

Everybody loved Jack Lynch. They loved his cheerful, straightforward take on the world, they loved his devilment and courage. It
was Jack who was always on the run, always getting into scrapes
and, most of the time, getting out of them – shooting his way out of
a tight spot in Drimoleague from the back of a roaring motorcycle,
clambering on to the roof of MacCurtain Hall in Cork as the
Special Branch poured into the building. It was Jack, abroad in
West Cork, who one night was warned by a ghost not to go to a
place surrounded by waiting security forces. It was Jack who holed
up in a dugout at Ardkitt and took breakfasts from his great
admirer, Peter O'Neill, Jack who was happy-go-lucky. When,
during active service in England, his false identity became known to
the doctor who removed his appendix, the doctor, a man called
Keyes, turned out to be a Dunmanway Protestant and for some
reason gave him the wink. Jack was across in England for two or
three years, Grandma said, working undercover as a navvy. In 1940,
when the police tried to arrest Jack and his friend Denis Griffin in
Dunmanway at the rear of O'Driscoll's pub, Denis Griffin was

caught, losing a finger to a bullet; but Jack escaped. 'Jack was quick,' Grandma said.

These colourful anecdotes did not reveal the wider significance of great-uncle Jack and, in particular, his activities in England. Jack Lynch was appointed the IRA's commanding officer for Great Britain in 1937. He was based mainly in Liverpool and Manchester and Birmingham, and his pseudonym was Buckley. On 12 January 1939, the IRA formally served Lord Halifax with a demand for the British military evacuation of Ireland within four days. The demand was not met, and on 16 January 1939 the IRA responded by blowing up electrical lines and power stations. In February, time-bombs were set off at Tottenham Court Road and Leicester Square underground stations, seriously injuring two people; at the end of March, two major explosions struck Hammersmith Bridge, bombs blew up in Birmingham, Liverpool and Coventry, and seven further explosions hit London. In May, fifteen people were treated as a consequence of tear-gas attacks in Liverpool, four explosions shook Coventry, four magnesium bombs were set off in a Birmingham cinema, and London cinemas were damaged. In June, the postal system was attacked: letter bombs were posted, and twenty pillar boxes, a mail van in Birmingham and a sorting office in London were blown up; three banks in central London were smashed by huge explosions, and Madame Tussaud's was damaged by a balloon bomb. By 24 July 1939, there had been 127 incidents, one fatality, and serious injuries to 55 people. Two days later, bombs went off at Victoria Station and King's Cross Station, where a man was killed. A day after that, in Liverpool, a bridge was blown up and a post office reduced to rubble. Then, on 25 August 1939, a bomb intended for the destruction of a power station detonated in the middle of a busy Coventry street. Five people were killed. Two members of the Coventry unit of the IRA, Peter Barnes and James McCormack, were arrested and hanged.

On 2 September 1939, the day after the German invasion of Poland, a state of emergency was declared in Éire (as the Free State was now called). Worried that the IRA's activities compromised the neutrality of the State, de Valera acted decisively against militant republicans. IRA men were selectively arrested in the autumn of 1939 and the winter of 1940. In a countrywide haul in June 1940 and in continuing arrests thereafter, practically all known republicans were locked up.

Jack Lynch, who returned to Ireland in 1939 to take command of the Cork IRA, managed to avoid capture until 1942. Jim O'Neill was not so lucky. On 2 January 1940, six months before the general round-up, a Special Branch detective arresting Tomás MacCurtain Junior was mortally injured, and in retaliation Cork's senior IRA men were immediately seized. At three or four in the morning, armed detectives knocked on the door at Friars Road. Jim O'Neill, who had played snooker earlier that night at the fire brigade, was in his bed and in a state of undress. As he fumbled to put on his new Christmas shirt, one of the detectives told him to hurry up. 'You'll wait as long as it takes,' my grandmother snapped. 'We didn't send for ye.'

James O'Neill, who refused to recognize the jurisdiction of the court, was found guilty of membership of an unlawful association and was sentenced to three months' imprisonment. He was taken to Mountjoy Prison in Dublin. During his spell there the Supreme Court declared that the Emergency Powers (Amendment) Bill, which empowered the state to intern Irish citizens without trial, did not contravene the Constitution. The Bill was duly signed by President Douglas Hyde. My grandfather was re-arrested on his release from Mountjoy and taken to the internment camp at the Curragh, in County Kildare. My grandmother was notified by telegram that her husband would remain interned until further notice.

Nine months later, in December 1940, Jim O'Neill was released on parole for a few weeks to receive dental treatment. He was delighted to be home. His teeth were fixed, he visited old friends, and he took his three young sons on outings to West Cork. A fourth son, Padraig, was conceived.

My uncle Jim recalled this interlude with peculiar vividness. He was playing on the street with his kid brother, Brendan, when a black car came down Friars Road. Jim had only ever seen cars stop on the street when a family took delivery of a baby from the hospital, so when the black car halted outside the O'Neill house, he pointed and said to Brendan, 'Look, we're getting the baby.'

It was the Special Branch, in a Black Maria. In an instant, armed soldiers were running through the garden and taking positions on rooftops. A jeep screeched to a stop and more soldiers sprang out, holding rifles. The house was surrounded and then occupied. The soldiers waited. My grandfather, returning from an errand to buy cigarettes and records for his fellow internees, was seized before he could set his foot through the door.

A search of the premises was carried out. Under the saddle of a doorway, they found a dismantled machine-gun and rounds of ammunition that (without my grandparents' knowledge) had been secreted there by Jack Lynch and an IRA carpenter.

The following day, my grandmother went with her three children to see Jim at the Bridewell in Cornmarket Street. They were told that dinner was being served to the prisoners and that they should return in an hour. The young family went outside to wait. Cornmarket Street is adjacent to the North Channel of the river Lee. Young Jim noticed that there was a lot of activity in the Channel, with boats in the water and a crowd gathered round. For some reason a man was in the river, repeatedly diving and resurfacing in the pea-coloured water. A little while later, the O'Neills returned to the Bridewell. As they sat in the waiting-room, the body of a drowned boy was brought in, wrapped in a blanket. My grandmother put her hands over her sons' eyes.

When my grandfather came into the visiting-room, flea-bites covered his face, his hands, his throat, his ears.

He was transferred to Collins Barracks. My grandmother made him an apple pie and went to visit him with the three boys. No visiting on a Sunday, she was told. The pie, a suspicious object, was not passed on to her husband. The boys ate it.

That night, at three in the morning, there was a hammering at the door. It was Jim Moore, the Special Branch detective notorious for his vindictiveness and lechery. My grandmother refused to let him in. Jim Moore shouted, 'We're moving James to the Curragh.'

It was four years before James and Eileen saw each other again.

When they looked back on the perplexing circumstances in which the machine-gun had been discovered at Friars Road, they came to the conclusion that a person must have informed on them. They also began to wonder whether Jim's release had not been a trap and whether he had not all along been a dupe of the Special Branch. Jim had always been a careful man, slow to take people into his confidence, but after his internment this caution turned to suspiciousness. Years without privacy, without respite from the anxiety of being spied on by so-called comrades ('Your best friend could betray you,' Grandma said), years of being subjected to false and vicious rumours concerning his wife, and of seeing the worst side of his fellow internees, left him disillusioned and untrusting. 'He came out very, very bitter,' Grandma said. 'He was very bitter about what one Irishman would do to another.' This fear – of betrayal, of being tricked – stayed with my grandfather. In the late 'forties, money was so unaccountably tight that he concluded that Grandma was being blackmailed – whereas in fact she simply did not have the heart to tell her husband that, even though he was working so hard, there was just not enough to make ends meet. Even in the 'sixties, when he moved into his own house in Douglas, my grandfather's paranoia continued. The back garden of the new house abutted the garden of Mr Sparrow, the policeman, and this worried him: 'Draw the curtain,' he would direct, 'he might be looking down at us.' After the Curragh my grandfather was plagued by suspicions – suspicion of his loving wife, suspicion of his neighbours, suspicion of the authorities – and was never entirely free of an inkling that a deception was being played on him and that things were not what they seemed.

In March 1995, I got in touch with my great-uncle Paddy Lynch. Paddy was my grandmother's younger brother and I knew that he'd been interned at the Curragh with his brothers, Jack and Tadhg, and my grandfather. I had never met Paddy but was told he was a terrific fellow who loved a yarn. He lived in Maynooth, Co. Kildare, with his wife Peig (herself described by my grandmother as 'a staunch one'), and I wrote to him asking if we might meet.

After I'd received no reply, I gave him a call. I wasn't expecting an especially warm response – I was, after all, a virtual stranger with an English accent – but, even so, the depth of his feeling took me by surprise. Right from the off, he was agitated and antagonized. 'Haven't you received my letter?' he asked. I had not, I told him. 'Well, I've no intention of discussing the camp in any shape or form, or having any dialogue about it whatsoever.' Before I could think of anything to say, Paddy quickly added, 'When I left the camp, it was dead and buried and never going to be resurrected. It's fifty years since I left and you won't get me to mention one iota about it. I've been pestered down the years by fourteen or fifteen people, by people well up in the writing business, offering me a lot of money. I won't do it. I could do with the money, but I couldn't take one cent. It would be blood money. If you want to talk about Gaelic games or horseracing, my pet subjects, we could spend three to four days talking about them. But that's all. You're perfectly welcome to come round, I wouldn't want to put you off. But we'd have nothing to talk about except the weather.'

A few days later, Paddy's letter – which had been held up in a mail strike – arrived.

Dear Joseph,
I was released from the Camp fifty years ago come 3rd of next May. As I was walking across the plains of Kildare, I stopped for a moment, looked back, and said 'Paddy, everything in there is dead and buried for ever.' I have no intention to resurrect even one word to anybody.
If you have visions of dialogue between us, hoping to prise me open, it's not on. End of story.

Some months later, in September 1995, I travelled from Cork to County Kildare. I drove in a bewildering alternation of hard rain and extraordinarily pure sunlight that suddenly turned the plain at Cashel bright as Africa. I passed through grey, half-pretty towns – Fermoy, Urlingford, Durrow – and, taking a detour from the main road, through villages that had not sloughed off the old colonial topography: the long, high wall that runs by the road as you enter the village, with tall woodland behind the wall; the continuation of the wall for an unseemly distance; a gate in the wall with a lodge and a lane leading to a Big House obscured by trees; the resumption of the wall and treetops; then the grey, treeless village: a petrol station, bungalows, and old cottages with pebbledashed walls made of a hotchpotch of brick and mortar and stone.

County Kildare gave the appearance of being devoted entirely to horses and their riding, breeding and training. Signboards advertised pony shows and gymkhanas and race meetings and stud farms, and in places the white railings of gallops ran alongside the road before nimbly curving away into intensely lush grassland. I passed through Kildare town, and not long after I saw a sign giving the direction of the Curragh Camp – still in use, as it had been during the Emergency, as the central military barracks of the army of the Irish State. I had no idea what to expect. I had never been to the Curragh – the plain which gave the Camp its name – and had not yet read anything about the Camp.

I turned down a side-road and moments later was presented with a desolate spectacle. Before me was a broad, featureless belt of heathland traversed by a single empty road. The road led to a distant wood of pine trees. Within the wood and visible above the treetops was the unmistakable silhouette of a military tower. A few sheep stained with turquoise dye grazed on the thin grass of the heath. On the rainy eastern horizon were the Wicklow Mountains, whose charcoal shapes seemed to have smudged the grey sky above them. As I drove slowly across the plain, I began to feel apprehensive. My approach was clearly visible to anyone in the red-brick tower, which looked like the Victorian tower of my Cambridge college, a suicides' favourite that, student rumour had it, was the work of an architect of prisons and lunatic asylums. A sign asserted, *NO PHOTOGRAPHS ON PAIN OF IMPRISONMENT*. I came to the wood. Abandoned concrete huts pocked a hollow to my left. I drove on slowly. I stopped at a cross-roads surrounded by a cluster of buildings that included a post office and a general goods store. Young men in civvies and number one haircuts slouched on concrete steps. Barriers blocked the road to the left and right, which were restricted to *AUTHORIZED VEHICLES ONLY*. I was at the centre of the camp, and I realized what made me so uneasy. It was the proximity of incontestable power.

By leave of the camp commander, I had a meeting arranged with a Corporal Seoirse Devlin at the Curragh Military Museum, which was located in a large, one-roomed brick building. Corporal Devlin was a small, compact, extraordinarily enthusiastic man in his thirties. The Museum, he explained, opened in 1955 after an American millionaire called Chester Beatty donated one of the top eight weapons collections in the world to the Irish nation. Corporal Devlin was the curator of the collection and looked after it practically single-handedly. 'It was worth the trouble,' he said, gesturing eagerly at the exhibits. Housed in glass cases was a startling variety of exotic instruments of destruction: African and Dayak swords, daggers from Caucasia and India, clubs from Polynesia, Japanese muskets (especially fine, these, the corporal said), and a whole arsenal of bejewelled, ancient and otherwise precious spears, knives, cutlasses, pistols, scimitars, battle-axes and bludgeons. In addition to the Beatty exhibits, some of Corporal Devlin's private collection of military memorabilia was on show: handguns, a Lewis machine-gun of the kind Jim O'Neill used to teach his men to assemble and disassemble, military motorbikes, rifles, military uniforms and jackets that included old Irish Volunteer and IRA tunics. It was an extraordinary feat of accumulation, given the limited time and money available to a corporal in the Irish army and the limited interest of his employer in its own cultural history.

I mentioned that there didn't seem to be anything in the Museum about the old internment camp. There was a certain amount of material, the Corporal said, and he showed me a photograph of a group of cheerful young German officers being served tea by a waiter wearing a white jacket and a bow tie. Seeing my astounded expression, Corporal Devlin explained that from the summer of 1940 onwards, about 40 RAF men (who included Poles, Free French and Canadian fliers) and 60 Germans, mainly Luftwaffe men, were interned at the Curragh in accordance with

Ireland's neutrality policy. These fellows – most of whom had crashed in Ireland or its territorial waters – had it pretty good. The Germans received their salaries in sterling, and every RAF man had his own room and received pay of 35 shillings a week. Food, which included roast beef once a week, was never in short supply, and drink could be bought cheaply by the Allies at a bar stocked by the Dublin British Legation. One man even shipped his wife over to Ireland, spending the days with her in Newbridge, which was just a mile or two away, and returning to the camp in the evening in accordance with the terms of his parole, which allowed internees to leave the camp so long as they came back at night. The internees would cycle into neighbouring towns and work on nearby farms. Once a month they were allowed to catch a bus into Dublin. Although there was no fraternization, the two opposing sides (in the only instance in the war of their co-imprisonment) greeted each other amicably. A schoolboy's code of honour governed their relations with their Irish captors. If an escaping prisoner knew he had been spotted, in deference to the guards' lack of ammunition and the obvious pointlessness of any bloodshed, he surrendered on a 'bang-bang, you're dead' principle (an American who bent the parole rules to escape to Belfast was sent back by his superiors). Whereas Allied internees were released in mid-1943, the Germans were held until the end of the war. 'At first,' Corporal Devlin said, 'the Germans plotted and attempted one or two escapes, but soon they settled down. They didn't have such a bad time of it, in the end.' Indeed, only a short while ago a group of former German prisoners had revisited the Curragh to relive the old days. All this was fairly well documented, Corporal Devlin said, and two books had been written about the Allied internees alone.

'What about the war-time Irish internees?' I asked. The corporal touched his round glasses. 'Well, that is still a sensitive subject,' he said. 'It so happens that I've done some digging around, but I haven't come up with anything. A lot of documents have been burned.' 'So there's no record of the IRA internments? Only of the Allied and German?' The corporal nodded. 'And there isn't a monument or anything of that kind? Some acknowledgement?' Devlin touched his glasses again. 'It isn't talked about,' he said. 'It's a non-subject.' I asked whether there was any chance that I could see the site of the old republican internment camp. 'I'm afraid not,' he said apologetically. 'It's in a security area and you'd need authorization to go there. You're not missing much,' Corporal Devlin said. 'There aren't any huts left.' Then he retrieved a book and showed me a sketch plan which showed the lay-out of the camps..

I left Corporal Devlin in his museum and walked back to my car, which was parked by the crossroads at the centre of the camp. I decided to try my luck. I went to reception office and asked for permission to see the old German internment camp. A couple of phone-calls later, I was being driven to the south part of the Curragh Camp by a soldier who'd been detailed to give me five minutes of his time. He led me into a field bespattered with sheepshit. 'Here we are,' he said. 'Here's the old German camp.'

We were at the perimeter of the camp. To the south was half a mile of open plain where sheep grazed and a horsewoman cantered; tall trees and a village, Brownstown, marked the limit of the plain. To the east were the Wicklow Mountains; to the north, the body of the military camp, with its redbrick buildings; to the west, a misty plain.

I entered the field and walked around for a few minutes. The foundations of the camp buildings, concrete ridges that protruded from the grass, were still visible; the wooden superstructures of the huts had all disappeared. Slabs of concrete marked the locations of the stoves around which the internees had huddled. Nettles, thistles and weeds grew everywhere. The only structure of any size left standing was the red-brick chimney the Germans built for the cook-house. Then I walked towards the neighbouring field, which was the location of the old republican camp. The two camps were separated by a deep trench that still contained ancient curls of barbed wire. I walked to the edge of the trench and gazed out at the site of my grandfather's five-year captivity; for unspecified security reasons, I was allowed no closer. I could make out the foundations of the huts in the grass and, in a slight dale at the edge of the campsite, the old playing field.

I turned back and returned to my car with a feeling of relief. The whole of Curragh Camp, not just the old internment grounds, had a charmless, depressingly defective air, and I could understand why the troops nowadays preferred to commute into work from the surrounding towns. Even if they'd wanted to live here, much of the picturesque red-brick Victorian terraced housing designated for their accommodation was no longer fit for human habitation. The camp had been built by the British in 1855, and it seemed to me that the place was still clouded by its years of service as the principal barracks of the foreign power and the headquarters of the Black and Tans.

As if to confirm this thought, the sun emerged from a blue gash of sky as I drove out of the camp. The day was suddenly a glorious one and the clouds white as cricketers. I noticed the grandstand of the Curragh racetrack a mile or two away and the pale H's of rugby posts rising here and there on the heath.

I drove on to Dublin. I entered the city centre and then, crossing to the Liffey's northern bank, drove to Arbour Hill, which rose just north of the river and whose atmospheric old working-class housing was becoming fashionable. I paid a visit to Arbour Hill Prison cemetery. It was a peaceful, tree-lined place. There was a carefully tended lawn and a memorial wall inscribed with the Proclamation of the Provisional Government of the Republic of Ireland read out in public by Patrick Pearse to launch the Easter Rising:

Irishmen and Irishwomen, in the name of God and of the dead generations from which she receives her old tradition of nationhood, Ireland, through us, calls her children to her flag and strikes for her freedom.

Having organised and trained her manhood through her secret revolutionary organisation, the Irish Republican Brotherhood, and through her open military organisations, the Irish Volunteers and the Irish Citizen Army, having patiently perfected her discipline, having resolutely waited for the right moment to reveal itself, she now seizes that moment, and, supported by her exiled children in America and by gallant allies in Europe, but relying in the first on her own strength, she strikes in full confidence of victory.

We declare the right of the people of Ireland to the ownership of Ireland, and to the unfettered control of Irish destinies, to be sovereign and indefeasible. The long usurpation of that right by a foreign people and government has not extinguished the right, nor can it ever be extinguished except by the destruction of the Irish people. In every generation the Irish people have asserted their right to national freedom and sovereignty; six times during the past three hundred years they have asserted it in arms. Standing on that fundamental right and again asserting it in arms in the face of the world, we hereby proclaim the Irish Republic as a Sovereign Independent State, and we pledge our lives and the lives of our comrades-in-arms to the cause of its freedom, of its welfare, and of its exaltation among the nations.

The Irish Republic is entitled to, and hereby claims, the allegiance of every Irishman and Irishwoman. The Republic guarantees religious and civil liberty, equal rights and the equal opportunities to all its citizens, and declares its resolve to pursue the happiness and prosperity of the whole nation and all of its parts, cherishing all the children of the nation equally, and oblivious of the differences carefully fostered by an alien government, which have divided a minority from the majority in the past.

Until our arms have brought the opportune moment for the establishment of a permanent National Government, representative of the whole of the people of Ireland and elected by the suffrages of all her men and women, the Provisional Government, hereby constituted, will administer the civil and military affairs of the Republic in trust for the people.

We place the cause of the Irish Republic under the protection of the Most High God, Whose blessing we invoke

upon our arms, and we pray that no one who serves that
cause will dishonour it by cowardice, inhumanity or rapine.
In this supreme hour the Irish nation must, by its valour and
discipline and by the readiness of its children to sacrifice
themselves for the common good, prove itself worthy of the
august destiny to which it is called.

The signatories of the Proclamation – Thomas J. Clarke, Sean
MacDiarmada, Patrick Pearse, James Connolly, Thomas
MacDonagh, Eamonn Ceannt, Joseph Plunkett – were executed by
firing squad and their remains, treated with quicklime, were buried
here, at Arbour Hill Prison, where a memorial stone with inscriptions in Irish and English recalled them. When I first came across
the text of the Proclamation, as a twenty-one year-old student in a
Cambridge University library, the surge of emotion I felt was so
strong that my scalp and cheeks and ears prickled, and it's even possible that my eyes clouded over. I cannot fully account for these
intense sensations of patriotic exhilaration, but I know that it's only
once you are buoyantly swept away in their simplifying current that
you realize quite what a burden it is to wade through that other,
finicky, obstructive, futile, morally muddy world, and what an
absolute relief it is to be quickly towed by certainty and feel
significant. No matter how familiar I grow with it, I am always
moved by the Proclamation of Independence and grateful for it.
    It so happened that a film touching on the Easter Rising, *Michael
Collins*, directed by Neil Jordan, was being made in and around
Dublin at that time – September 1995. The film was causing great
excitement, and not simply because of the presence in Ireland of its
stars, Liam Neeson and Julia Roberts. The eponymous hero himself
had captured the imagination of the public. Newspaper stories,
magazine features and TV programmes about Collins and his times
were hungrily absorbed, and the media somewhat bizarrely
reported the substance of the movie's eighty-year-old plot as if it
were breaking news. The nation was developing a new appetite for
its history. The paramilitary cease-fires of August and September
1994 had just passed their first anniversaries, and it seemed that the

events of the Anglo-Irish War and even the Civil War could at last be consumed without distress. When the call went out for unpaid extras to appear in crowd scenes in *Michael Collins* – notably for the Bloody Sunday scene in which British troops fired into the crowd at a Croke Park football match, killing twelve – large numbers of people from all over the country presented themselves in suitably old-fashioned attire, eager to take part and take fresh narrative possession of the national past. This light-hearted new enthusiasm for history had another consequence: it facilitated the appearance, in 1997, of *The IRA in the Twilight Years, 1923–1948*, a book that decisively disturbed the long stillness surrounding the Curragh internments. Published by a former Curragh internee named Uinseann MacEoin, the book contained the reminiscences of more than thirty men about their internment days, and, taken together with information I gathered from Curragh veterans I met in Cork and Dublin, enabled me to piece together something of my grandfather's experiences in Tintown, as the internment camp was called by the internees.

I walked from the cemetery at Arbour Hill to a decrepit hospital in north Dublin. In the wasteland behind this ruin had been built the most spectacular set for *Michael Collins*, a simulacrum of the O'Connell Street area as it appeared shortly after Easter Sunday, 1916. The set was open to the public, and I joined the sightseers strolling in the dusk on pseudo-cobblestoned streets that were sprinkled with sawdust. We looked at tramlines, a shop selling boaters, a hotel with a hammam, and, of course, a burned-out General Post Office. It was an agreeable way to spend a quarter of an hour. On my way out, a speaker crackled into life and began to broadcast a speech spoken by Liam Neeson in a West Cork accent. It was Michael Collins addressing a street-crowd, but the sounds of his passionate words travelled indistinctly in the unseasonally warm breeze and very few of the people leaving the cardboard Dublin of old paused to listen to what was being said.

Jim O'Neill, who arrived at the Curragh from Mountjoy Prison in March 1940, was among the very first prisoners to be taken to

Tintown. He was initially detained in the Glasshouse, a purpose-built cell-block that held fifty-two men and was later used as a punishment centre. In around April, Jim was moved to a settlement of seven wooden huts. He lodged there while a much larger encampment of twenty-four timber huts was completed. In August 1940, when 171 new internees arrived from Cork Gaol, the new camp came into operation. Each hut was divided into two sections that separately contained thirty prisoners, one bucket latrine and a pot-bellied stove. The men slept on beds constructed from the trestles, boards and mattress with which they were issued on arrival. Not all of the huts were residential. Two were cookhouses and others were in use as an infirmary, a chapel, a laundry, and a library, where stool-pigeons would pass on information. Smaller huts served as wash-houses and latrines. Just south of the huts were playing fields with goal-posts for hurling and Gaelic football. The perimeter of the camp was lit up at night and guarded by strips of barbed wire and a wide deep trench. Observation posts looked down on the camp, and prison guards could be heard calling all through the night: 'Number 1 reporting, all is well.' 'Number 2 reporting, all is well.' The camp held a shifting population of anywhere between 300 to 500 republican prisoners at any one time. In the five years that the internment camp operated, not one managed to escape. An internee was, however, free to leave if he 'signed out' – i.e., undertook to desist from republican activism. Jim O'Neill never signed out. He stuck it out until about November 1944, when, following his father's death the month before, he was granted parole. Most internees were offered and accepted extended parole at around this time. A hardcore of about seventy men, who were regarded as a continuing military threat, remained in Kildare until mid-1945.

Like everybody else, Jim passed his internment in a buttonless Free State army shirt, string-laced boots that forced their wearers to shuffle, and a grey, misshapen Martin Henry suit that was inadequate in the winter and uncomfortable in the summer heat. Not that overheating was a common occurrence. The encampment was situated on a bare, wind-blown, exposed place that always felt chilly, even in summer. The cold may have contributed to the constant hunger from which the prisoners suffered, even though they received the same rations as their guards: a quarter loaf with a lump of butter and an egg for breakfast; for lunch, stew; for dinner, a quarter loaf with a lump of cheese. Food was served in the cook-house, and since all men had to be inside their huts during hours of darkness, in winter the meals were consumed between 9 a.m. and 4.30 p.m., leaving the men unfed for interminable nights. They went to great lengths to get extra food, plucking wild sorrel from under the barbed wire fence and, in the case of one man, trapping a bird and eating it stuffed and roasted. Once a week the prisoners took a much-needed lukewarm shower. In the smoky, reeking, unsanitary huts, lice was endemic and illnesses, unpleasant rashes and infections were easily communicated. Medical attention was patchy, and the camp doctor was called Dr Doolittle. The shithouse was called Gerry Boland's, after the Minister of Justice. It was daily hardship rather than mistreatment that was the most trying – although misbehaviour would result in a spell in the Glasshouse, where the prisoner was kept in solitary confinement and fed bread and water. Jim O'Neill and his friend John Varian spent time in the Glasshouse for reasons that were no longer clear.

The prisoners – who had no radio – had a variety of contacts with the outside world. Each hut received one newspaper. Priests came in for Mass on Sundays and confessions on Saturdays. Attendance at Mass was very high, partly because anyone who stayed behind in a hut might be suspected of being an informer. According to my grandmother, the Quaker Society was very good to the men, and brought them gramophone records and other useful items. (If ever Grandma were to change religion, she said, she'd become a Quaker.) Only closed visits were permitted – i.e., visits during which the parties were separated by a wire mesh and not allowed to touch – and the majority of the men refused these. When open visits were finally introduced in around July 1943, Grandma was not able to see her husband. It was a long way to the Curragh, and what with the children, no bus service and money very tight, the journey was simply impracticable. Instead she wrote to Jim every day, posting her letters once a week. Internees were allowed to send one letter a week. Jim wrote to Eileen one week and to his mother the next. The letters Eileen received were censored, and whole sentences would be crossed out.

My grandmother's situation in Cork was very difficult. She had the boys (four boys with Padraig's birth in August 1941) to look after, rent to pay and, aside from welfare payments of a few pounds a week, no regular income. For the first six months, Jim's work colleagues at the Cork Corporation took a collection for her, and a little money came in from the Republican Prisoners' Dependants Fund. Grandma struggled along with the help of the family. Sometimes she received money (and a bottle of cod liver oil) from Tadhg after his early release from the Curragh and cash-in-hand from Jack (when he was still on the run). Eileen's parents and her sister Kay Coletta helped out with groceries, and Jim's parents sent potatoes and parcels of eggs from Ardkitt. Her sister Mae, in Dublin, and her aunt and uncle in Dunmanway, the Kingstons, were also very good to her: they took in young Jim after he had broken his leg and looked after him until her husband's return from the Curragh. Although Eileen earned extra money by knitting, hunger was not always avoidable; my uncle Brendan remembered a time when the family had five Oxo cubes for three days.

The demands of poverty did not deter Eileen O'Neill from political activity, and Friars Road was used as a safe house for Jack Lynch and others. They would stop for a day or two at a time, staying indoors and sleeping on the ground floor for easy access to the sash windows that gave on to the garden. Grandma also kept a printing press and copies of the republican *War News*, which carried details of arrests, internments and other matters of interest to republicans that received no coverage in the heavily censored official press. On one occasion Grandma's place was surrounded by Free State soldiers and she threw the press and the pamphlets over the hedge to her neighbour (the horrified and distinctly non-republican but nevertheless co-operative), Mrs Neenan. The soldiers charged in and trampled over the clothes hanging on the line but found nothing. 'At Turner's Cross we were raided morning, noon, and night,' Grandma said. 'I should have charged for all the entertainment I gave them!'

Even after Grandma left Friars Road, Turner's Cross (rent 12s. 6d.) for the corporation house at Mount Nebo Avenue (rent 3s. 6d.), money was still hard to come by. Republican bazaars would raise money by selling brooches and rings and handbags made by Curragh internees. Rings (often Claddagh rings and snake rings) would be shaped out of spoon heads or coins, which in those days contained a significant element of silver: small rings were made from one-shilling pieces and larger ones from two-shilling pieces. 'Jim made a lovely wedding ring for an American girl, Eileen O'Reilly,' Grandma said, 'and engraved her name on it. They gave Jim old-fashioned clippers,' Grandma said, 'and he made a box for them and acted as the camp barber.'

In addition to passing the time with crafts activities, internees had the opportunity to study sociology, economics, history, German and Irish (notable Gaelic scholars were interned at the Curragh). My grandfather did not appear to have taken classes or to have gone down other roads that promised a broadening of intellectual horizons. He did not, for example, join one of the numerous Irish-speaking huts, where any utterance of English was strictly forbidden. He joined a Cork hut, Hut C1, commanded by his brother-in-law Tadhg Lynch. It was a fateful decision, because Tadhg, and Hut C1, came to be at the centre of the most bitter division of the camp.

In early December 1940, a handful of senior IRA officers, including Larry Grogan and Peader O'Flaherty, arrived at the Curragh and took over the camp leadership. Not long afterwards, the internees' butter ration was cut from one half ounce to one quarter ounce a day. Even though the ration of the camp guards had been reduced by the same quantity, it was decided to stage a protest by burning down huts. Jim O'Neill and Tadhg Lynch suggested to O'Flaherty (who urged the arson with the cry, 'We'll show them are we men or are we mice!') that only huts that were unoccupied and had no escape tunnels beneath them be burned; but in the event, on 14 December 1940, seven huts, some occupied and containing the belongings of the men, were burned to the ground, and an extensive network of tunnels was exposed. The camp authorities responded with predictable aggression. They herded the men into the remaining huts – including a concrete-floored hut known as the Icebox – and locked them in, with no beds or extra clothes or fuel for stoves, for two freezing days and nights. The older men, in particular, found the ordeal very hard. On Monday 16 December 1940, the men were finally allowed out. As they were queuing for a meal at the cook-house, the guards for some reason shot dead an internee, Barney Casey, as he stood in line. When the internees returned to their huts, the guards continued to their offensive, striking the men, shouting, rattling batons and leaving lights on throughout the night; this prac-tice continued indefinitely, as did the evening roll-call of prisoners in their huts, when even a slight movement of the head led to trouble. Henceforth the internees slept on their palliasses on the floor, since their burnt bedboards were not replaced for two years. Grogan and fifty-one other ringleaders of the fire were taken to the Glasshouse and kept in solitary confinement for ten weeks as they awaited trial for arson. In Grogan's absence, a man called Liam Leddy was made camp leader.

A great change came over the camp after the fire. Morale wors-ened and discipline broke down: marching to the cookhouse in military fashion came to an end, as did the closing of ranks around men who signed out. Most significantly, a split appeared between Hut C1 and the new camp leadership. In January 1941, Liam Leddy issued the order that huts should refuse the reduced ration of turf (peat) for their potbellied stoves. Tadhg Lynch, who failed to see the point of such a protest in freezing weather, disobeyed the instruction. As a consequence, Leddy ordered that Tadhg be ostra-cized for 'co-operating with the State'; but the rest of Tadhg's hut, around twenty men (including Jim O'Neill and Paddy Lynch), stood by their OC and disobeyed Leddy's instruction to leave the hut. They, in turn, were ostracized; which is to say, nobody spoke to them, played Gaelic games with them, responded to their overtures or otherwise acknowledged their presence.

Hut C1 never got out of Coventry. However, others soon fell out with Leddy's group, and new men arriving at the Curragh often preferred the less rigid, more diverse regime that operated on the dissident side. Some of these were communists, others were men, often regional commanders from the North, who were used to doing things their way and did not relish the idea of surrendering their power or rank (the camp rule was that all men fell back to being ordinary volunteers). In time, the unofficial faction came to outnumber the orthodox group. Tadhg Lynch, meanwhile, was able to avoid much of this unpleasantness. He applied for and obtained extended parole within weeks of the turf incident and was never re-interned. I never understood how or why my great-uncle was able to get out in this way; but it seemed that his release may have been sanctioned by the IRA command, because in 1941 Tadhg and his brother Jack apparently participated in the court-martial proceedings against Stephen Hayes, the IRA Chief of Staff suspected of treason.

Some observers felt that the split between Lynch and Leddy reflected their respective loyalties to Tom Barry and Seán Russell. Seán Russell had been elected leader of the IRA in April 1938. Barry strongly opposed Russell's election and (on the grounds that there were plenty of targets in British-occupied Ireland) Russell's plan for the bombing campaign in England. Less clear is what stance, if any, Barry took in relation to Russell's dealings with Nazi Germany. These began in October 1936, when, during a visit to the United States as the IRA Quartermaster-General, Russell wrote to the German ambassador in Washington regretting the refusal by the 'puppet Irish Free State government' of landing rights to German aeroplanes, 'a right apparently conceded without question to England, the traditional enemy of the Irish race'. This diplomatic overture was followed up in February 1939 when Russell, now IRA Chief of Staff, sent an agent to Berlin to receive instruction in the procurement of small arms and hand grenades and to try to secure the provision of German military supplies. When the Second World War broke out, Seán Russell was on the run from the authorities in the United States, who had served him with a deportation order. He finally escaped that country by accepting a German invitation to travel via Genoa to Berlin, where he arrived in May 1940.

Russell took bomb-making classes with the Abwehr and sought out German assistance for the IRA. In August 1940, he set off to Ireland by U-boat. He never made it. On 14 August 1940, the leader of the IRA died from perforated ulcers and was buried at sea wrapped in the flag of the Third Reich.

On board the submarine with Russell when he died was Tadhg Lynch's old comrade from the 1937 anti-Coronation march, Frank Ryan. Ryan had had an extraordinary few years. In the late summer of 1938, he was captured by fascist forces in Spain. For nine unimaginable months he was one of a group of eighteen prisoners of whom nine were shot dead each morning and replaced by nine others. In July 1940, after representations from the Irish and German governments, the frail and deafened anti-fascist was released to Nazis and driven to Berlin, where he joyfully met up with Russell and accompanied him on the fateful U-boat journey to Ireland. After Russell's death, Frank Ryan returned to Germany, where he died in a sanatorium in 1944 and was buried in a grave bearing his German cover-name, Francis Richards.

The circumstances of Ryan and Russell's deaths had, of course, a symbolic resonance. They stood for the ease with which political extremists can lose their way and, in the case of Seán Russell, the fallibility of the tenets of Irish republicanism as a general guide to political conduct. Directed by the imperative of breaking the connection with England, it didn't occur to Seán Russell – a devout man with no personal vices – that England's misfortune, in the context of war with Nazi Germany, might have a significance other than Ireland's opportunity. Once removed from the backwaters of Ireland and Irish America, Russell and the organization he led were in every sense out of their depth.

It so happened that there was, in the dissident faction at the Curragh, a group of internees who took a wider view of international affairs. The Connolly group was led by Neil Gould, a communist who had lived in the Soviet Union, and its members absorbed and discussed left-wing literature and closely followed developments on the Eastern Front. Following their ideas through to their logical conclusion, some even argued that the right course of

action would be to help the Soviets to defeat the Nazis by signing out
and joining the British army. Even for the relatively flexible IRA
camp leadership on the dissident side, this went too far. Gould was
refused permission to teach Russian and, eventually, removed from
the Curragh. The Connolly group had a strong Cork element, and
Hut C1 was pro-Soviet, and Jim O'Neill was a socialist; nonetheless,
it was doubtful that my grandfather came significantly under Gould's
influence. Described by one veteran as a man with a strict sense of
discipline and little interest in political development, Jim would most
probably have approved of the decision to remove Gould and quash
any talk of IRA men joining the British army. Certainly, he never discussed Neil Gould with his wife or even his son Brendan.

Nor did he discuss the Germans, whose presence at the Curragh
was barely recorded in the reminiscences of Irish internees. To a
degree, this was an understandable hiatus – after all, the men had
plenty to say, and plenty that needed to be said, about their own
day-to-day experiences, and it might have been that they were
simply according themselves a natural historical priority. Even so,
given the proximity at the Curragh of the two national groups –
separated only by a trench, they were within shouting distance of
each other – and the extraordinary dimensions of the world war, it
seemed wrong-headed to relate the story of the internment without
meaningful reference to the events occurring beyond the Irish
encampment's barbed wire: the very events, in fact, that were the
cause of the men's internment. It was remarkable how republican
discourse, although influenced by the transnational principles of
socialism and Roman Catholicism, was impermeable to ulterior
narratives. Of course, there was an obvious reason for the non-
appearance of the German internees or, for that matter, the Second
World War, in the movement's self-history: these subjects raised the
issue of the IRA's complicity with Nazi Germany.

I had no reliable idea of where Jim O'Neill stood on the IRA
dealings with Nazi Germany, which very few, if any, Cork volunteers knew much about. But in the course of a conversation about
Ardkitt in the old days, Grandma said to me, unprompted, 'During
the Second World War, we didn't know how bad the Germans were;

Jim O' Neill

we saw it only after, on the screens, and heard it on the radio. What Hitler did . . . Oh, my God, what he did.' Grandma was sitting in the front room with clasped hands, next to the photograph of her husband aged around fifty: with his smiling, chiselled face, and his white shirt, dark tie, cardigan, and checked tweed jacket, my grand-father was the very image of the hard, handsome IRA man. 'At the time,' Grandma said, 'anyone that was beating the English, we were for them. We thought that way. But how wrong we were. How wrong we were.'

5

Something very wrong must have happened to make my life take so false and unnatural a turn.

Thomas Mann, Letter to the Dean of the Philosophical
Faculty of the University of Bonn, 1937

One evening in 1939 before the outbreak of the war, the Hittitologist John Garstang and his wife were having dinner at the Ankara Palace Hotel, in Ankara, when Franz von Papen, the recently appointed ambassador of the Third Reich to Turkey, walked into the restaurant surrounded by animated and fawning officials. The group sat at a table in full view of the Garstangs. Mrs Garstang, an excitable, disapproving Frenchwoman from Carcassonne, looked on with increasing fury as Papen was toasted and congratulated by his fellow diners. Eventually unable to restrain herself any longer, she strode across to Papen's table and, wagging a finger at his face, berated him and the regime he represented. The famously suave Papen took the reproof with a smile. He had been in, and extracted himself from, far stickier situations before.

John Garstang, a small, elderly, burly man with a full beard, did not pay much attention to the German diplomat. Garstang took no

real interest in politics. He was absorbed, to the exclusion of almost
everything else, by the Hittites. He didn't care for card-games or tea
parties, and his preferred conversation – over breakfast, lunch and
dinner – was archaeology. His principal diversion was methodically
to practise his golf swing with the iron he always brought on his
digs. Occasionally, however, the extra-Hittite world had to be reckoned with. In 1907, the year he travelled on horseback through
north-east Turkey in search of Hittite monuments, Garstang's
application for a dig was frustrated by the Kaiser, who personally
procured the relevant permits from the Sultan for the German ori-
entalist Hugo Winckler. Another setback for the Englishman
occurred in 1936, when the Arab Revolt obliged him and his young
nephew, O.R. Gurney, to flee their dig at Jericho and escape, via
Syria, to Turkey. Forced to look for something new to do, John
Garstang arrived in Mersin in December 1936 to prospect for sites.
He stayed at the Toros Hotel and befriended its owner, a refined
and helpful man with an enthusiasm for antique civilizations. In the
winter seasons of 1937–9, Garstang dug in Mersin at the ancient
mound of earth called Yümüktepe, which was situated alongside the
Soğuk Su (Cold Water) river that trickles through Mersin; then the
world war intruded and he was forced to drop the expedition until
1946. That year, Garstang met O.R. Gurney off the boat in Bootle,
Liverpool; when the two met (Professor Gurney told me with a
mild smile when I saw him at his Oxford home) *without pause*
Garstang began to talk about his latest research in Hittite geography,
not once inquiring where his nephew had been for seven years.

And yet, for all of his preoccupation with work, John Garstang
was distressed and embarrassed when he learned, on his return to
Mersin in 1946, of Joseph Dakak's experiences at the hands of the
British; and he urged his Turkish friend to seek redress. On 9 April
1947, Garstang wrote to my grandfather from Ankara, stating that,
as promised, he had spoken to the British embassy and had been
heard out with some sympathy. The upshot was that Monsieur
Dakak was invited to write to the Head of Chancery at the embassy.
'Be brief, polite and direct,' Garstang advised, 'and don't discuss
the matter with anyone.'

As a consequence, my grandfather wrote the following letter (in English), dated 15 April 1947:

Sir

1.   I left Mersin on the 24th March 1942 with a Turkish passport and British visa for Palestine in order to buy lemons.

2.   After spending three weeks in Palestine and having arranged my business, I was arrested on my exit in Nakura and brought back to Jerusalem where I was detained as a suspect.

3.   After spending various periods in several prisons in Palestine and Beirut I was returned in April 1943 to a special detention camp in the monastery of Emwas (between Ramleh and Jerusalem) where I remained until the middle of September 1945, 4½ months after the official declaration of the end of war in Europe and the Middle East.

4.   Each time I was interrogated I requested that I should be returned to Turkey or given a trial in order that I could prove my innocence, but the answer received on each occasion was that the investigations had not finished.

5.   My sympathies are and always have been for the Allies and if I had been pro Axis it is quite certain I would not have applied for a visa for Palestine.

6.   All the investigations made against me during the 3½ years of my detention proved nothing. With the result I was returned to Turkey which proves my innocence.

7.   Previous to my leaving Turkey and being detained I was the owner of an Export and Import office, part owner of Günes and Korum Cinemas, owner of Toros Hotel and Restaurant; but as a consequence of my detention and having no one to look after my various business undertakings, my wife had to 1. Liquidate my Export and Import Office. 2. Close the restaurant at the Toros Hotel. 3. Cancel my partnership in the working of the Günes and Korum Cinemas. Only the Toros Hotel was left to my wife to run

and as the income from this was not sufficient to support my
wife and three children also to have money sent to me in
detention through the British Consulate in Mersin, my
savings had to be used.

8.   As a consequence of my detention, and my emotions as
an innocent man, has left me nervous and also with a weak
heart which has disabled me for the rest of my life and which
makes it necessary for me to see specialists in Istanbul from
time to time.

9.   Although my losses are much larger and such questions
as mental suffering, loss of health could not be compensated
by any amount, I estimate the very lowest and reasonable
amount for the losses described in paragraph 7 at £5,000, but
I leave it to your judgement and consideration to assess an
amount which you may consider has been actually lost owing
to my wrongful detention and I am sure you will deal with
this on traditional British lines and see that I am justly
compensated for the losses I have had.

I am Sir,

Yours obedient servant.

This letter, together with Garstang's letter and a very few other
papers, turned up in my grandfather's old safe in the Toros Hotel in
the spring of 1996. I was impressed by the clarity and conciseness of
my grandfather's letter to the British embassy and, one or two shaky
moments aside, by his grasp of English, which extended to a feel for
legal phraseology and tone; and I caught a glimpse not only of the
appealingly adaptable intelligence for which he was remembered but
also of a less commemorated streak of courage. By an act of will, the
spooked narrator of the testimony had been discarded and replaced
by a self-possessed, measured complainant who made the best of a
not very strong case: because, for all of the claim's careful assertiveness, its central proposition – that the claimant's innocence was
demonstrable from his repatriation – was, of course, flawed.

   I called up Amy and asked if she knew anything about this
letter. Amy told me what she had learned from Pierre: that,

contrary to Garstang's advice, her father decided to notify the Turkish authorities of his proposed request for compensation because he simply didn't dare proceed without their assent. When the authorities advised him to drop the matter, Joseph complied, and the letter of claim to the British embassy was never posted. 'What about the testimony?' I asked. 'Was that ever mailed to the powers that be?' Amy didn't know, and neither did anyone else. Joseph, it was said, was very cautious with officialdom. When Ginette Salendre (the daughter of his sister, Radié) visited Mersin shortly after the war and became friendly with a woman archaeologist who was *mal vue* on account of her subversively liberal views, Joseph was anxious and disapproving. 'Be careful,' he said to Ginette, 'they could make trouble for me.' He took pains to stay on the good side of the mayors and governors and steered clear of non-conformist types. According to my family, Joseph, for all his commercial boldness and authoritarianism and social gravitas, had a timorous nature. He went around in fear of illness, of contamination of his food, of the authorities, of things turning out badly. He was a *froussard*, in the word used fondly, and with noticeable unanimity, by Ginette, Amy and Pierre to describe him – and to explain why, in their view, he could never have been involved in espionage, an offence that was, after all, punishable in Turkey by death. My grandmother had once said the same thing to my mother: she was convinced of her husband's innocence because he simply would have been too frightened to become involved in anything.

This assessment of my grandfather was unverifiable and, of course, potentially wishful. Nevertheless, Joseph Dakak's temperamental frailty was perfectly evident from his testimony; and it seemed pretty unlikely that he would have been able to tolerate the stresses of double-dealing. But not all spies were thieves of top secret information acting under extreme pressure. Take, for example, a man with the job of keeping an eye on the number and kind of vessels anchoring in the roads of Mersin; such an agent would be dealing in sensitive but non-secret information available to anyone with a view of the nautical horizon – the kind of view, it so

happened, that could be enjoyed from a south-facing window of the
Toros Hotel.

It became clear to me that Joseph Dakak was amazingly well-
placed and well-qualified to act as a German spy. First, like Joseph
Ayvazian, the German agent in Iskenderun, he was a hotelier and
restaurateur, which gave him excellent access to the people and
news that passed through the town. Second, from the autumn of
1941 he operated an import–export business – Nazim Gandour's
line of work – an enterprise capable of lending a sheen of commercial legitimacy to inquiries concerning the movement of goods
and people in and out of the country. Third, he spoke German,
was fond of Germans (and German-speakers: Walther Ülrich's
letter from Weissenfels established that my grandfather was
friends with Gioskun Parker, the Austrian rumoured to be a
German agent in Mersin) and had a long history of working with
Germans. Relevant, here, were two further documents from my
grandfather's safe. The first, in the stationery of the *Gesellschaft
für den Bau von Eisenbahnen in der Türkei*, was in French, and
provided detail about a well-known but sketchy episode in my
grandfather's life:

Belemedik, 15 February 1919
We certify that Mr Joseph Dakak has worked as a bookkeeper for Office of the Central Magazine of the 1st
Division for the Construction of the Baghdad Railway from
5 September 1916 to 15 February 1919.

During his time with us, Mr Dakak has always been equal
to his responsibilities and we can only commend his zeal and
application to his work.

Mr Dakak leaves us of his own accord, free of all
obligations, by reason of which we present him with this
certificate.
Signed: the Chief Magaziner and the Chief Engineer of the
1st Division

Belemedik, I knew, was high up in the Taurus Mountains and

was the site of a grave of 43 German and Austrian soldiers, a nurse, and an English corporal who had all died between 1914 and 1918. Two and a half hazardous years in the wilderness, alongside hundreds of men and camels and mules labouring in snow and heat to blast rocks and shift rubble and lay sleepers, had been Joseph's first real experience of work and the adult world. It would inevitably have been an unforgettable and formative time and, judging from the reference he received, was one in which the teenager struck up a good relationship with his German bosses. My grandfather's sense of solidarity with and admiration for Germans – his Germanophilia, some said – later stood him in good stead professionally. Also preserved in the safe was a letter written in German on the notepaper of Lenz & Co., a construction company with offices in Kurfürstenstrasse, Berlin, and Istanbul. The letter, dated 10 March 1930, was addressed to Herr Josef Dakak, Mersina:

We hereby confirm that, with effect from 7 March 1930, you shall be retained by ourselves for the monthly fee of 150 Turkish liras. As soon as your travel papers are in order, you shall travel from Mersina to Malatya, where you shall report to our construction manager, Herr Dipl. Ing. Lender. Your retainer shall take effect as soon as you receive instructions from him. Your appointment shall be terminable without notice.

Expenses incurred in travelling to and from Malatya-Mersina shall be reimbursed by ourselves.

Here was confirmation that Joseph had acted as a German agent – for commercial purposes, at any rate. There was nothing odd about this, particularly as, in the run-up to the Second World War, Germany was by far Turkey's greatest trading partner. But long-standing German construction works around Mersin continued during the war and, just as Braithwaite & Co. had been used by the British as a cover, German corporations must have served the Reich, which gave rise to the possibility that the nature of Joseph Dakak's assistance to these corporations might also have shifted.

This was, after all, a man who retained an affection for German culture after having travelled to Germany in 1934, when an intense and ritualized romantic nationalism flooded the country and when, in August, a plebiscite upon the death of President Paul von Hindenburg resulted in 38 million Germans voting for, and only four and a half million voting against, the consolidation of the offices of president, chancellor and commander-in-chief of the armed forces in the fulminating, maniacally anti-Semitic person of Adolf Hitler. Who was to say that my grandfather had not been swept along, or at least doused, by this historic surge?

The summer of that year – 1934 – saw another, less dramatic change in the political landscape which Joseph Dakak probably registered: the resignation by Franz von Papen of the office of Vice-Chancellor of the Reich. An arch-conservative Westphalian aristocrat, Papen had served without particular distinction in the Prussian Landtag for eleven years and, according to the French ambassador in Berlin, 'enjoyed the peculiarity of being taken seriously by neither his friends nor his enemies'; but in June 1932, in the aftermath of the resignation of Heinrich Brüning, he suddenly found himself, at Hindenburg's invitation, Chancellor of Germany. Papen lasted until December 1932, when he was succeeded by General Kurt von Schleicher. Then, on 30 January 1933, Hindenburg withdrew his support from Schleicher and authorized the appointment of Adolf Hitler as Chancellor of the Reich and Franz von Papen (who was not a member of the Nazi party) as Vice-Chancellor. Papen remained in office until July 1934, when he accepted a job as a special envoy to Austria, where his brief was to manage and exploit the flux created by the recent assassination of the Austrian Chancellor by Austrian Nazis. Papen remained Hitler's man in Vienna until March 1938, the month of the *Anschluss*. In April 1939, he began his stint as the Reich's ambassador to Turkey. His arrival would certainly have been noted by Joseph Dakak; and my grandfather would have been very excited to learn – at some time in 1939 or 1940, going by Salvator Avigdor's recollection – of the former Chancellor's decision to pay a visit to Mersin and to stay, in the company of his wife, at the Toros Hotel.

The distinguished visitors would have received a warm and appropriate welcome. My grandfather would have gone to great pains to ensure that all was to the satisfaction of Herr and Frau von Papen, and no doubt he put himself personally at their service. It would not, I guessed, have taken Papen very long to ascertain that Monsieur Dakak was remarkably capable and well-informed and well-situated, and that an attempt ought in due course to be made to secure his discreet co-operation on a range of matters. Espionage, it so happened, was something of a Papen speciality. In the Great War, as Germany's military attaché in Mexico and then the United States, he set up a comprehensive network of North American agents to inform him of shipping schedules and cargoes leaving the United States. He forged passports and, to prevent the Allies from receiving American armaments, he incorporated a company to buy up all the hydraulic presses on the market. He authorized acts of sabotage that included attempts to blow up the locks of the Welland Canal in Canada to delay the arrival of Canadian troops in France and to destroy Vanceboro Bridge, which ran between the United States and Canada. So disruptive were Papen's activities that eventually, in December 1915, he was expelled from the United States. Thirty years later, Papen oversaw the activities of Cicero, the Albanian valet to the British ambassador Sir Hughe Knatchbull-Hugessen and perhaps the most spectacularly successful spy of the Second World War: from October 1943 to March 1944, Cicero supplied the Germans – at a price of up to £15,000 per film of 36 negatives – with photographs of his master's Secret and Top Secret papers, which included minutes of the Teheran Conference held in November 1943 by Churchill, Stalin and Roosevelt.

Of course, my grandfather was not to know any of this as he sat on the terrace of the Toros Hotel with the Papens, making small talk about archaeology, perhaps, or the Great War, in which the two gentlemen had served alongside the Ottoman forces, or about Germany or Berlin. Even if Joseph had always sympathized with the Allies (as he claimed in his letter to the British embassy), there was no sign that he was equipped, as Mrs Garstang was, with the kind of ideological aversion to Nazi Germany that was probably required to keep in perspective Papen's enormously flattering attentions. Papen was not only invested with the charisma of a man touched by history and fame, he was also quick-witted and personable and winning – sufficiently winning, in fact, to have persuaded both Hitler and a very doubtful President Hindenburg of the merits of installing a Hitler–Papen government.

To cap it all, the ambassador was a first-class horseman – good enough to have had excelled in the steeplechase as a youthful *Herrenreiter*. His best-known photographic portrait showed him with his horse in the Zoological Gardens, Berlin. A tall, slender man with a greying moustache and eyes set close to a long, upturned nose, he stood with one hand rubbing the animal's head and the other clutching a crop. He wore a cap, a bow-tie, a jacket with matching breeches, shining knee-length leather boots, white gloves, and a handkerchief in his breast pocket. In this get-up he bore an odd resemblance to another immaculate, gloved, whip-carrying horseman I had seen: Joseph Dakak. Was this him? Was Franz von Papen, with his private charm and public accomplishment, Joseph's idealized self made flesh? It was, at any rate, easy to imagine a polite exchange, in German or French, in which the hotelier humbly put his filly at the disposal of the chivalrous German – just as he put his young bookkeeper, Salvator Avigdor, at the Papens' disposal to act as a guide on their jaunt west of Mersin. I wondered if it had occurred to Joseph how this act of hospitality might look to others. True, a drive to the ancient, tiny port of Silifke, the site of a notable Byzantine castle, would traverse an archaeological and sightseeing paradise; but – assuming Papen's visit occurred in wartime, which was not certain: it could well have taken place in the summer of 1939 – the route was also of strategic interest. The state of the road, the accessibility of the shoreline to shipping and landing crafts, the presence or absence of any construction workers or troops, the general lay of the land, these were all useful things to know. My grandfather might have openly assisted Papen in a valuable reconnaissance exercise.

Was this simple guilelessness or something more sinister? The question also arose in relation to the occasion, in late 1941, when

Joseph Dakak, with Tayara

Joseph light-heartedly asked Hilmi Bey, the chief of the political police in Mersin, if Olga Caton and her friend Togo Makzoumé were working for British intelligence. What possible business was this of Joseph Dakak? Was my grandfather being idly inquisitive, or was he pressing the police chief out of a real need for the information? Either way, he was acting with a recklessness that was completely inconsistent with the prudence that had been generally attributed to him. Joseph Dakak's three-week-long fraternization with the Arab nationalists at the Modern Hotel was also strikingly suspect – on a par, in terms of giving an impression of his political sympathies, with travelling to Cork and hanging out night after night with the Lynches and O'Neills at Tomás Ashe Hall. There was something else. On 21 June 1940, the Mufti, Haj Amin el-Husseini, wrote to Franz von Papen from Baghdad seeking to establish friendly relations. The contact proved fruitful, and very soon after he arrived in Berlin in November 1941, the Mufti established an espionage and sabotage network that covered Turkey and Palestine. His agents worked in close contact with German intelligence, operating in Iskenderun, Antakya, Adana, Diyarbekir – and Mersin. In Istanbul, meanwhile, Paul Leverkuehn, the Abwehr chief, established contact in Istanbul with Musa Husseini, the Mufti's nephew and heir-presumptive (and not to be confused with the nephew whom Joseph Dakak met, Mustapha Husseini), with a view to obtaining intelligence about troop movements in Syria and Mesopotamia. What more likely German–Arab conduit of information could there have been than a Syrian with strong German connections and an inability to mind his own business travelling on the Taurus Express from Turkey to Palestine?

In his testimony, Joseph gave a very specific – and, I thought, entirely credible – account of his reasons for going to Jerusalem. But he was at a loss to explain his dealings with Hilmi Bey and the Husseini family, portraying himself – a worldly, well-informed and socially adept man – as a maladroit innocent who had feebly been sucked into political conversations he didn't want to have, louche company he didn't want to keep and, ultimately, the meshes of a vast, mysterious net of injustice he was powerless to escape. It was true that the testimony had been written when Joseph was in a profoundly confused and desperate state, and true, also, that it remained unclear what acts of espionage, specifically, he was supposed to have committed. Nonetheless, it did not *look good* for my grandfather; and it was obvious why British intelligence might have formed suspicions about him. Which brought me to a question I hoped Sir Denis Wright might be able to answer: who were the people in British intelligence in Mersin in 1942?

Wright proved to be amazingly helpful. 'There was a whole mob of curious characters at the consulate,' he said. 'The Consular Shipping Adviser, a secretive fellow called Piggott, was the Admiralty's man, responsible for naval intelligence; Geoffrey Maltass was the Ministry of War Transport's man; Arthur Maltass, Geoffrey's cousin, acted for the Ministry of Economic Warfare; Captain Gerald Calvert, whose family owned an estate in Troy, was the War Office's Movement Control Officer; there was a SIME agent called Geoffrey Williams; and there was Desmond Doran, the Passport Control Officer and MI6 agent.' Williams and Doran sent their Secret reports back to their respective bosses in Istanbul – Lieutenant-Colonel Guy Thomson and Colonel Harold Gibson. 'Doran had left for Egypt by the time I came on the scene,' Wright said. 'I knew him slightly from Rumania, where he was posted before Mersin. He was blown up by the Stern Gang in the end,' Wright added with no visible sadness, 'in Palestine.' Wright didn't know Olga Caton or the secret policemen Hilmi Bey or Osman Emre Bey (the man who had pestered my grandfather for money to fund his lawsuit). Arthur Maltass, on the other hand, he knew well. 'When I came to Mersin, Maltass had taken over the MI6 function from Doran, who was his friend. Maltass was a slippery, effeminate sort of fellow, charming in his own way, I suppose; a homosexual. Before the war he ran a boarding house in London. He was posted to Mersin because it was believed that he spoke Turkish, which he

Denis Wright (centre, standing) surrounded by his consulate staff in Mersin. Arthur Maltass (wearing a tie) stands next to him.

didn't.' Wright added, 'He was an Anglo-Greek from Izmir – a Levantine, not pukka British. The Turks contemptuously referred to him as *tatli su Ingiliz* – literally, sweet-water Englishman. His English had an unmistakable accent.'

As a Foreign Office man, the consul was not responsible for overseeing the intelligence agents. However, although Wright was 'not a clandestine chap at all', his work in Trabzon had put him in good standing with the intelligence chiefs in Istanbul, and they let their men in Mersin know that they could count on Wright's cooperation. As a result, the agents showed Denis Wright the Secret and Confidential reports which went to Istanbul each week. Wright wasn't impressed. The reports struck him as superficial, gossipy and very much alike. 'It soon became clear to me' Wright said, 'that the separate reports sent by Maltass, Williams (the SIME man) and Piggott (naval intelligence), which appeared to be mutually corroborative, in fact nearly all flowed from a common source: William Rickards, the Lloyd's agent in Mersin, and his cousin.'

I knew of William Rickards. He was Olga Caton's brother and a well-known member of my family's Mersin circle.

Wright continued, 'Rickards was about fifty years old, I would say, and lived with his widowed mother and sister, Dosia Grigsby. The Rickards family was the only British family native to Mersin,' Wright said. 'I remember they owned a valuable collection of the works of Richard Burton. William Rickards was a slippery piece of work at the best of times – a homosexual, it was said, but I wouldn't know about that. He was greatly disliked by the Syrian fraternity, and a great gossip. His reports were full of stuff about who was sleeping with whom, but nothing of substance.'

Denis Wright acted quickly. In a Secret and Personal letter dated 29 June 1943, he wrote to Maltass' MI6 boss, Harold Gibson, 'Mersin is, as you probably know, a hotbed of malicious gossip and I have been very much disturbed to find how much of this gossip is passed on as reliable information.' In order to 'sift fact from fiction', Wright requested and was granted authority to vet Maltass' reports before they were sent to Istanbul for redistribution; and the transmission of unreliable information out of Mersin was immediately reduced. Which brought me to a question I had never directly posed before.

'What about Joseph Dakad? Are you aware of any evidence that he was a spy?'

'I have no proof about Dakad,' Wright said. 'He got put in the bag before I got there, and I never got involved. There were, I remember, very strong feelings.' He paused, thinking back to half a century before. 'Dakad may easily have been the victim of Byzantine goings on. Maltass may have been a nigger in the wood-pile,' Wright said unselfconsciously, 'and I'm sure that Rickards was gunning for his enemies and feeding Doran with information which Doran took at face value. And it *may* be that Rickards, who kept in with the Turks, had information planted on him by Turkish authorities, who had no use for the Syrians and were quite capable of planting material about people they didn't like. I sensed this straight away; one has certain antennae.'

Unsure what Wright meant exactly, I did not immediately follow up on this last observation about Turkish antipathy for 'Syrians', his persistent, and unsettling, term for the Mersin Christians. Instead, I rang my mother in The Hague and spoke to her about William Rickards. My mother – who came to know Rickards when he was 60 – remembered him as a very English man who spoke French and Turkish with an English accent. She was genuinely taken aback at the notion that he was unpopular. 'I never heard my father say anything bad about him,' she said, 'and in fact he and my mother were great friends with William's youngest sister, Rosie, and her husband, Riri Levante.'

At my mother's suggestion, I paid a visit to William Rickards' nephew, Patrick Grigsby. Patrick was Dosia Rickards' son and had spent his earliest years with his widowed mother in his uncle's house in Mersin. Nowadays he lived with his wife Beryl in a large redbrick Victorian house in Sutton Coldfield, a town near Birmingham. He had extraordinarily bushy grey eyebrows, a broad flat nose, and, even though he'd left Mersin at the age of 14 for school in Istanbul and afterwards made his life in England, retained that distinctively rich Levantine accent. He had recently sold up his small business of importing and distributing mechanical parts and was now semi-retired. We shared a strangely similar Irish–Turkish ancestry: his mother, Theodosia Rickards, was from Mersin and his father, a master mariner named Henry Grigsby, was from Cork. (Patrick, born in December 1931, had no memory of Henry, who drowned at sea off Haifa in 1933.) Like all of his generation, he remembered Mersin of the 'thirties and 'forties as a leisurely, intimate 'paradise' of orange groves and beaches and gardens where he played with Fonda Tahintzi and Roger Vadim, the future filmmaker, who was the son of the French consul, Plemianikov. As a young child, Patrick said, he and his mother were invited by Joseph Dakak to the curtain-raiser at the Günes Cinema, Walt Disney's cartoon *Who Killed Cock Robin?* This struck me as uncanny: there was a famous scene in *Sabotage*, Hitchcock's 1936 adaptation of Conrad's *The Secret Agent*, in which the secret agent Verloc, a cinema proprietor, screened exactly the same film.

Patrick told me that his grandfather Henry Rickards, a general's son, arrived in Mersin in the 1880s and invested his gold in the Mersin–Adana railway. Henry married Maryam, a sixteen-year-old Syrian from a humble family of builders who was girlish enough to attend school on the morning of her wedding. Horrified by a union that was inappropriate in every respect, the Rickards family cut off Henry. Even so, he managed to live comfortably on the income from his investments and to educate his four children in France and England. Henry Rickards died from pneumonia in 1939. 'He wasn't the sort of person I would like,' Patrick Grigsby said. 'He was a disciplinarian and a very strong Presbyterian – very English, very much the product of the Empire.'

From what I was told by Patrick Grigsby and others I spoke to, it was clear that, like his father Henry, William Rickards was a difficult, inflexible, eccentric man. Every morning he went for a constitutional walk with a Panama hat on his head and an English newspaper under his arm, striding without acknowledgement past acquaintances he came across. The walk was followed by a cold shower and a fruit juice. Lunch, taken at noon on the dot, was followed by a *sieste*, for which he would don blue pyjamas. Then he would have another cold shower and present himself at the dinner table to be fed by the women of the family. He never did anything for himself; domestic work was for women, whom he regarded as mindless, chattering cretins. At 9 p.m. – no later – he would go to bed. He adhered strictly to this routine. Like his father Henry, William disliked work and lived off the proceeds of family properties. He was an intensely self-absorbed man who embraced with great seriousness a succession of belief systems: he joined the Fabian Society and the Freemason Brotherhood (he was the grand master of the Nicosia Lodge), and finally he was drawn to the mystical and contemplative practices of Mevlana, with their emphasis on tolerance, simplicity, love and charity. Perhaps this accounted for William's frugality – when he died, his worldly possessions amounted to a chamber-pot, a safe with some money, a cupboard, and a bed – and for his philanthropy: he paid for the education of various of his sisters' children. Otherwise, he had difficulty in translating his spiritual principles into action. William Rickards' unfeeling and anguished disposition was perhaps rooted in his experiences of the Great War. He served as a volunteer at Ypres and Passchendaele, in Belgium, from 1914 to 1918. 'It must have affected him all his life,' Patrick Grigsby said.

Patrick did not know that his uncle had been a British informer during the Second World War or, for that matter, that he'd held the Lloyd's agency in Mersin. He knew of Arthur Maltass, though, and remembered him clearly. 'Maltass was a likeable individual. He dressed immaculately, like the actor Edward Everett Horton, who played diplomats and butlers. His dinner table, I remember, would be laid with flowers. He was fantastical about his background and went to great lengths to impress. He would say that his parents were titled and living in England with servants and stately homes. I remember he told a story about his father asking the butler about the absence of cruet at the table. "Can you see anything missing, Roberts?" "No, sir," Roberts said. "Well, get a ladder." Roberts got a ladder. "Now, climb the ladder and have another look".'

Patrick remembered Desmond Doran, too, as a tall, sandy-haired, handsome man. It was news to Patrick that his aunt Olga

Caton had been Doran's lover, but he wasn't surprised, because
Olga loved the company of men and had led a notoriously tangled
amorous career. Wherever she went, it seemed, she got into a passionate, ill-starred romance. After nursing college in Whitechapel,
London, she was employed in 1933 as a nurse-companion to a girl
who'd been paralysed in a riding accident. The girl's family were
landed gentry and Olga, by her own account, mixed in grand circles,
received a proposal from the Duke of Bedford, and fell in love with
the son of the house, who later died in the North African desert. It
was during this time in England that Olga looked into her origins
and learned that the Rickards family had a coat of arms – a tower
with, appropriately enough, a Saracen's head – and was based in
Norfolk; but when she arrived at the family seat in Norfolk ('a
grand pile,' Olga reported), her aunts would not see the woman
with a strange accent, and Olga was turned away at the door.

By the time she returned to Turkey in 1939, Olga Rickards had
acquired a taste for the grand life and a streak of snobbery and
racism that led her to look down on Turks and Jews ('I *hate* Jews,'
she'd hiss) and Arabs, her mother's people. She had a disastrously
short-lived marriage with John Caton, Britain's Honorary Consul
in Mersin, bore a daughter, and had her affair with Doran. After her
wartime service commanding a women's internment camp, Olga
took a job as the matron of an English boarding school for girls –
Tolmers, near St Albans – so that her daughter might be educated
there. In 1958, Olga arranged for my mother, who was then
eighteen, to spend some months at Tolmers. 'I taught French conversation and took A-level courses in English and History,' my
mother said. 'I used to watch TV with Olga in the evenings. She
was always nice to me.' My mother added, 'She was a single mother.
She always had to fend for herself and daughter.'

My mother did not mention that Olga was a terrible gambler
and – Patrick's phrase – 'an exceedingly lavish person'. In the 'sixties, when she returned to Mersin, Olga would take a carriage to the
Club every evening, not leaving until three in the morning. She
lived with a maid in a modest apartment and kept a photograph of
the Queen of England on her sideboard. Olga retired to England in

the early 'eighties and moved into a residence for the elderly in Bedford: she didn't want to die in a Muslim country, she said. At the time, I was a student in Cambridge, which is not far from Bedford, and my mother urged me to visit Olga: 'It would give her such pleasure, Joseph, you must go.' But I never got round to it, even though the journey would have been easily made and Olga, trapped in her unapproachable homeland, would have been thrilled to see me. She surfaced a final time before she died: my parents and I were in the car in The Hague one Sunday morning when the BBC World Service played a request by Olga Caton for *O Silver Moon*. Aunt Olga died not long afterwards. Her last wish was for her ashes to be returned to Mersin.

Olga's passing represented another unravelling of the Levant, a realm, as was implied by its very name – from the French for the rising sun – that was a creature of the occidental mind. In its narrowest sense, the Levant designated the eastern littoral of the Mediterranean; but the term was also applied to places (typically, ports and trading centres) that, although remote from the littoral, shared its distinctive ethnic, religious and linguistic diversity and flavour. Cities like Salonika and Alexandria and Adrianople could be considered to be in the Levant, as could Istanbul. The British diplomat Sir Charles Eliot wrote of the Ottoman capital in 1907:

Nothing, perhaps, gives one a better idea of its inhabitants than what is styled an *Almanach à l'usage du Levant*. Every leaf which is daily torn off [. . .] bears inscriptions in six languages: Turkish, French, Bulgarian, Greek, Armenian, and Spanish in Hebrew letters. It records the flight of time according to five systems [. . .]. Nay more, the *Almanach* extends the same large impartiality to all religions. It registers the disagreeable ends of Greek, Bulgarian, and Armenian martyrs, and bids the believer rejoice, according to his particular convictions, over the Immaculate Conception of the Blessed Virgin, the Prophet's journey to heaven on a winged steed, and the dedication of the Temple of Jerusalem – all these exhilarating events being commemorated on the same date. Besides this, it informs us that the day in question is the thirtieth after Kassim, that twelve o'clock Turkish, or sunset is at 4.30 à la franca, and that midday is 7.23 Turkish [. . .]. The little Levant almanack does, it is true, give a certain pre-eminence to Mohammed and his celestial tour; he sprawls over the middle in triumphant Arabic flourishes, crowding the Bulgarian and Armenian martyrs into corners, and casting vowel points and spots parlously near the Immaculate Conception. But though recognizing the predominance of Islam, it addresses a public which has no one language, religion or code of institutions.

Looking back from the vantage-point of a Turkey that was at least 99 per cent Muslim, the world evoked by Eliot seemed scarcely credible. But the official Ottoman data bore it out. In 1886, for example, Istanbul's Muslim population (itself by no means exclusively Turkish) stood at 385,000, whereas the combined population of Greeks (153,000), Armenians (150,000), 'foreigners' (129,000), Jews (22,000) and miscellaneous Christians and Bulgars exceeded 460,000.

Eliot's cheerful celebration of this ethnic and religious plurality was exceptional. Until the mid-nineteenth century, a Levantine meant a European national resident in the Levant: Arthur Maltass and William Rickards fell into this category. The term then acquired a broader and pejorative sense, connoting a person – usually a Greek, but he might equally be an Armenian or an Eastern Christian or any half- or pseudo-European generally – who formed part of the transnational commercial scum that floated on the clear seas of pure Turks and Arabs. The Levantine was typically an unwholesome, repellent type – Joe Cairo in *The Maltese Falcon*, Mr Eugenides in 'The Waste Land' – with a malign, tapeworm-like effect on his host society. Sir Mark Sykes (of the Sykes–Picot agreement 1916, by which France and Britain settled on the post-war carve-up of Syria, Lebanon, Iraq and Palestine) described him as 'this mule-brained jackanapes who is destined to influence and corrupt every attempt that may be made towards raising the fallen people of Asiatic Turkey', and in January 1920, the magazine *Near East* pronounced:

> The failure of Turkey is the failure of Rome. Rome fell
> because there remained no Romans, Turkey fell because in
> Constantinople there remain no Turks. They have become
> 'Levantine-y'. A Turk will trace in his family, perhaps, a
> Circassian mother, an Egyptian grandfather, here a rich Greek,
> always an Albanian or a Jew. He differs only in this respect,
> that he forms the aristocracy of 'Levantinia'. Throughout the
> centuries many people have come to the city, the city of the
> Great Whore has sucked most of them in and spat them out
> Levantines – a people without honour, talking myriad tongues
> in jargon, the sole people of the world without one virtue.

Joseph Dakak, born in the quintessential Levant port of Iskenderun, undoubtedly qualified as a Levantine in the pejorative sense. He spoke numerous languages, cut a suave figure, ran a hotel, did a bit of opportunistic import–export business, and generally made a living at the intersection of east and west. As a metropolitan, uprooted Syrian he did not count as a proper Arab, who was to be found in the warlike, desert-loving tribes further south. Indeed, 'The main characteristics of a Syrian,' a 1902 travel handbook asserted, 'are ease and courtesy, lightheartedness, hospitality, childishness, indolence and deceit. Under the exterior air of politeness and candour, there lurks in every Syrian an ingrained spirit of deceit. There is a common saying in the East that a Greek will get the better of 10 ordinary Europeans; a Jew will beat 10 Greeks; an Armenian will get over 10 Jews; but that a Greek, a Jew and an Armenian together are no match for a Syrian.'

In their propensity for intrigue and deception, half-Syrian Olga and William Rickards were stereotypically Levantine – and, so far as Joseph Dakak was concerned, destructively so. But, driving back down to London from Patrick Grigsby's house, I felt no hostility towards these lost, disconnected siblings.

In the middle of December 1941, after John Caton had enlisted with the British army and left his wife Olga to her own devices in Mersin, his successor as consul in Mersin, Norman Mayers, alighted from the Taurus Express at Yenice, a railway junction between Tarsus and Adana at which, a little over a year later, Winston Churchill would meet President Ismet Inönü and vainly urge him to commit the Turkish Republic to the Allied cause. It was six in the morning and raining heavily; blind to the future historic significance of his location, His Majesty's newly appointed consul felt like a man abandoned at a country junction in Ireland. When Mayers finally reached Mersin on the local train, he was dismayed to discover that the conveyance awaiting him was a dilapidated carriage drawn by two horses. His dejection worsened when he arrived at the consulate – a cold, dark, dank building in the interior of the town that overlooked a small cobbled square in which caravans of camels, led by a braying donkey, would discharge their loads in the morning rain. He decided that the house, which consisted of an office on the ground floor and living quarters above, was the worst thing he'd seen since his posting as a new vice-consul in Beirut.

By the following Sunday, Mayers was feeling a little less sorry for himself. A local British resident, William Rickards, had invited him to a picnic in the orange gardens of a Turkish friend, and on Sunday the three men sat in a wooden kiosk high above the treetops, drinking beer and munching on bread and cheese and tinned fish. They enjoyed the views: the sea to the south, the snow-tipped mountains to the north. The pleasantness of the occasion was made complete when, shortly after Mayers returned home, a basket of lemons and oranges was delivered to the consulate by his Turkish host. The consul turned some of the fruit into candied peel for Christmas pudding and further busied himself making plum-puddings and mincemeat for the consulate Christmas party. Three small turkeys were delivered and kind locals supplied him with fruit salad and Russian salad. Norman Mayers began to dislike Mersin a little less.

On Christmas Eve, the consul went to a party given by William Rickards' sister, Olga Caton (who was 'more Syrian than English but very Britannic for all that, [and] who is supposed to have done more damage than ten in Mersin with her tongue, which has a great appetite for scandal'). There was a Christmas tree, good food, good cheer, lots to drink, and some bridge. Then, on Christmas Day, it was Mayers' turn to entertain. A buffet of turkey, chicken, plum-pudding, cold mince pies, salads, cheese, sweets, various cakes, cold tongue was set out and talc was sprinkled on the tiled floors to encourage dancing. The party, attended by the British flock, went well, thanks in part to the enlivening presence of a few 'kittenish Syrian-Mersin-Turkish *jeune filles*'. On New Year's Eve, Mayers ran into these girls again at a party given at a 'Syrian' house. He was pleased to note that black tie and evening frocks were worn and astonished when, at midnight, the lights were dimmed and the foreigners sang Auld Lang Syne. Everyone then stumbled off to the Club, where the cream of Mersin society was present. At three in the morning, a carriage took the consul home through heavy rain. He later heard that at five in the morning a great *bagarre* had broken out at the baccarat table which was eventually quelled by the Chief of Police himself.

From the very first day of the new year, Mayers noted, the weather turned extremely cold; and by the twelfth day of 1942, the frost had destroyed the orange crop. Luckily for the consul, he'd already made a large quantity of 'MMMM' – Mayers' Medicinal Mersin Marmalade.

I found Norman Mayers' letters home at the Middle East Centre of St Antony's College, Oxford (where the papers of Sir Patrick Coghill and C.T.C. Taylor were also kept). They were filled with vivid, somewhat fiddling accounts of food, furnishings, parties, the weather and the inadvertently hilarious activities of Mersin's 'O so provincial' 'Syrians'. (There was that unsettling term again.) Christmas festivities notwithstanding, Norman Mayers despaired at the uneventful and inconsequential character of the place to which he had been posted. He devised the humorous theory that Mersin, as a glance at an atlas would confirm, was the motionless hub around which the world at war revolved.

It seemed that the consul, as he boiled greengages into jam, organized soirées and battled with quartermasterly zeal for mince pies and Cypriot brandy, fell victim to a kind of diplomatic somnambulism; or, at any rate, was slow to wake up to the shadowy activities taking place before his eyes at the consulate. It was not long before he realized that Mersin was not as dead as it looked; and by August 1942 he was writing home, 'It is really amazing how in my time at Mersin this place has changed from a complete backwater to – still a small place, but one busy with work, intrigue, visitors and all sorts of opposing forces.' At the forefront of Norman Mayers' mind, when he wrote these words, was the controversial detention by the British of a certain Mersin businessman, Nazim Gandour.

I discovered that the details of the Gandour affair were preserved in one of the small number of embassy and consular files concerned with wartime Turkey kept in the Public Records Office at Kew, in south-west London. The contents of the file – memoranda, letters, notations on minute sheets – provided a remarkable insight into the workings of the organization responsible for the arrest of Joseph Dakak.

The story began on 23 May 1942, when Norman Mayers wrote to the British embassy declaring himself to be 'exceedingly troubled about the news that Gandour was arrested when he crossed the [Syrian] frontier with our visa over a fortnight ago':

> The indefiniteness of the whole matter, and the consciousness that Nazim Gandour has been the object of suspicion all that time that I have been in Mersin, without any proof being offered so far as I am concerned, arouses all my apprehension. . . .
>
> Doran says that it is a question of espionage. I am not going to say that Gandour is innocent. I do not know him very well. But I do know that he is an exceedingly clever businessman who is closely connected with the timber and chrome business of the UKCC. His business affairs and his fortune are in our hands, and the majority of his relatives are in Syria and Egypt. If this man has done espionage for the

Italians or Germans, he cannot have done it for pecuniary interest. I do not believe that he would work for our enemies out of political conviction. There remains only the possibility that he has been subjected to pressure by them. In the last connection I would say that Gandour is quick enough to take a lot of catching in that way.

The matter must be brought into the light, and it must be brought into the light quickly. That is the British way of doing things, don't you agree?

Two days later, Mayers wrote again to the embassy:

You may ask what is worrying me so much in the matter. It is the fear that we have got hold of a man who is at least innocent of the serious charge of espionage; and the fear lest this whole inquiry be conducted on arbitrary lines. In the case of Gandour I can get nothing but 'suspicions' out of Doran, and I am beginning to think that there may be against him nothing more than suspicions. . . .

The embassy in Ankara did not share the consul's anxieties. The minister, J.C. Sterndale Bennett, thought that Mayers was 'getting altogether too worked up about this', and the counsellor, A.K. Helm, did not 'think we need be too tender-hearted about these Levantine traders. The profits are no doubt well worth the risk.' Nevertheless, the embassy could not afford to brush off its man in Mersin, and the decision was taken to look into the matter. It was at this point that the trouble, and the dark farce, started – when the diplomats undertook the seemingly straightforward task of fathoming why was Gandour arrested. Wading into an apparently shallow pool of inquiry, they finally emerged soaked, mud-spattered, and spitting weeds.

On 27 May, the military attaché, Major-General Alan C. Arnold, reported the following to Sterndale Bennett:

With reference to the arrest of Nazim Gandour, British

Security in Syria have considerable evidence that Nazim
has been working for a considerable time for the Axis. This
is confirmed by the Turkish Secret Service authorities who
far from being horrified, as Mr Mayers suggests, have
urged us to put an end to his activities. As I have frequently
pointed out to Consuls, proof as known in peace time law
courts can very rarely be produced against enemy agents in
a neutral country. All that you can do is to take the sum
total of evidence available and if it is sufficiently damning
act. It is better that one innocent man in twenty should be
interned rather than the lives of British sailors should be
endangered.

Gandour's particular line of country as far as I can
remember was acting as intermediary between Lebanese,
Syrian, and Palestine caique crews and the Axis agents in
Mersin. . . . I am only passing on to you what I believe to be
the views of Security second-hand and I will ask Lt.-Colonel
Thomson [of SIME] to come and see you personally about it
when he arrives tomorrow.

But Lietenant-Colonel Thomson was not able to help, and
Arnold wrote to SIME in Beirut for further information. In
response, he received a Secret letter dated 30 June 1942 from
Colonel R.J. Maunsell (the head of SIME and the chief spycatcher
in the Middle East) in Cairo. However, Maunsell's letter was unil-
luminating. In the end, Helm could do no better than simply – and
misleadingly – inform Norman Mayers that there existed 'detailed
evidence from the competent authorities regarding the reasons for
the arrest of [Gandour].'

But as soon as Mayers had been swatted away, another problem
presented itself: an Istanbul lawyer engaged by Gandour's family,
Miss Süreyya Agaoglu, travelled to Beirut to see the prisoner. The
lawyer was 'of considerable repute and *persona grata* with Turkey's
leading political figures, including the Prime Minister' and,
although not allowed to communicate with Gandour, was received
with great courtesy in Beirut by Sir Patrick Coghill. Coghill

informed her that Gandour was charged with having (1) sold wood
to the UKCC at exorbitant prices; (2) passed on to the Axis information regarding UKCC transactions; (3) passed on to Axis sources
information regarding British dealings in chrome; (4) sold to the
Axis manufactured goods imported from Egypt. Coghill also suggested that her client's predicament was, at bottom, down to two
people in Mersin: Desmond Doran and Norman Mayers' picnick-
ing friend, William Rickards.

On 7 September 1942, Gandour's lawyer had a lengthy interview
in Ankara with the minister, Sterndale Bennett. She argued that,
since she had received assurances from the Turkish Ministry of
Foreign Affairs that the Turkish authorities had submitted no evidence against Gandour, it was clear that information had been laid
against Gandour by business enemies.

Sterndale Bennett was stumped by the wealth of detail amassed
by the Turkish lawyer and was, he afterwards noted, 'somewhat
handicapped in discussing the case by the fact that it was a matter
dealt with entirely by the military authorities [and by the fact that I
am] not aware of the exact nature of the charges or the evidence'.
The minister – who noted that the 'Turkish authorities will, of
course, never admit that they laid any information against
Gandour' – decided to take the advice of the military attaché,
Arnold, on how best to proceed, although he acknowledged that
'Colonel Maunsell or Sir P. Coghill alone will probably have
detailed knowledge of the case'.

By now, things had descended into absurdity. Norman Mayers, it
had become clear, relied on the diplomats in Ankara for his information; the diplomats (Sterndale Bennett, Helm, etc.) relied on
briefings from their military attaché, Arnold; Arnold depended on
'Security' personages – Thomson and Maunsell – who relied on
Coghill, who in turn relied on Doran, who himself relied on information produced by his local sources – Turkish sources and/or
William Rickards – whose own sources were unknown. What passed
as reliable intelligence was, in fact, an erratic pendulum of hearsay
by which second- and third- and fourth-hand information of
uncertain origin swung from Mersin A (Mayers) to Ankara to

Istanbul to Cairo to Beirut to Mersin B (Doran) and back again to
Mersin A.

It came as no surprise, then, to learn that the military attaché
confessed to Sterndale Bennett that he did not know whether the
charges described by Süreyya were in fact correct. The attaché
robustly suggested that perhaps the solution lay in deporting
Gandour as soon as possible. Helm regretfully responded, 'I should
be afraid that removal to Africa is no longer a cure by itself.' It was
decided, in the end, to 'choke off' Gandour's lawyer. When Süreyya
tried to see the British ambassador on 3 November 1942, she was
informed that His Excellency was very busy; and on 7 November
1942, the first secretary in Ankara, D.L. Busk, wrote to Colonel
Thomson in Istanbul instructing him to 'continue the choking-off
process at every opportunity'.

Meanwhile, the problem of Norman Mayers had returned. The
tenacious consul reiterated his 'conviction' that Gandour was not
guilty of espionage and commented that, although Süreyya blamed
Doran entirely for instigating the case against Gandour,

> she should lay the blame, unless I am very much mistaken,
> on other quarters nearer home. It leaves me with my old
> distaste and sense of shame, for it points to local jealousies
> and suspicions as the source and origin of Gandour's
> troubles.

Quarters nearer home? Jealous locals? Mayers never made
explicit what he was hinting at. Instead he made a practical
proposal: a reconsideration of the evidence by an independent
'British legal personality'.

The counsellor, Helm (who noted that 'Mr Mayers has for years
had a bee in his bonnet over such cases'), replied as follows:

> I can say at once that, in normal times, we should have
> complete sympathy with the case which you put up. These
> times are, however, anything but normal and, whether we
> like it or not, we have to face the fact that principles which

are perfectly good in peace-time have to be scrapped or
weakened under the exigencies of war. This applies
particularly in matters affecting security and I am sure you
will agree that under this head no avoidable risks can or
should be run.

This does not mean that I am making any excuses for the
handling of the Nazim Gandour case. For perfectly good
reasons security is confined to special people and in the case
of Gandour we are completely satisfied that this man is by
no means as innocent as your letter suggests. Moreover, and
also for very good reasons, it is neither practicable nor
desirable in matters of this kind, under war conditions, to
have the whole story brought out.

Against this background I would just like to emphasize
once more that the case against Gandour is *not* based on
information derived solely, or even principally, from
Turkey. . . . If Mlle. Süreyya should return to Mersin and
try to discuss the Gandour case with you, we must ask you to
take the line that, while you can listen to anything she has to
say, you are precluded from discussing it as it is being
handled by other authorities.

There, it seemed, the matter effectively came to end – or, perhaps, not. The Gandour file at the Public Records Office contained
two blank documents consisting of one page and two pages respectively. They were marked 'closed until 2018'.

The Nazim Gandour papers made no mention of Joseph Dakak.
But they clarified that Gandour was (contrary to my grandfather's
fearful belief) an authentic prisoner and not a British stooge, and
also that Gandour had correctly maintained to Joseph that Desmond
Doran was instrumental in their arrest and internment. More generally, the Gandour affair undermined any notion that the fact of
internment was some kind of indication of the existence of *good
grounds* for internment; because the closer one looked into the matter,
the more apparent it became that the smoke surrounding Gandour
was traceable not to inculpatory fire but to the fumes produced by

the wilful confusions of the attachés and the secretaries and the lieutenant-colonels. In the end there was little doubt that the treatment of Nazim Gandour was, applying normal notions of justice, almost comically unfair. He was not charged with, let alone convicted of, any offence. He was denied access to a lawyer. He was detained indefinitely, by security forces accountable to no one, on the grounds of mere suspicion. He was not properly, if at all, informed of that which he was suspected of having done; and – most bizarrely of all – the suspectors themselves were unsure about what specific wrongs they suspected Gandour of: after all the enquiries and memoranda and Secret letters and consultations and relayed messages, not one of these bureaucratic Chinese whisperers was able to grasp or spell out precisely what the case against Nazim Gandour was. Then again, there was never a *case* against Gandour as such. He was not the subject of a juridical process. On the contrary: his fate – from his arrest to his eventual release – was in the hands of persons with no real interest in (as Norman Mayers put it) 'the furtherance of justice'; and Joseph Dakak, it could be assumed, was subject to the same regime.

But there was, it had to be acknowledged, a limit to the criticism that could be levelled against the British authorities. It was true that, once Gandour's situation was brought to their attention, they acted obtusely and without any regard to the well-being of the 'Levantine trader'. Against that, however, they were fighting a war – a just war, it might safely be said – and, as is well known, the efficacy of war depends precisely on the massive and systematic infliction (and endurance) of undeserved personal suffering. In such circumstances, the moral sense may only with difficulty be attuned to the lot of any particular individual, which can seem of minuscule significance – particularly if the lot in question is that of wrongful internment, which is not the worst fate to befall a man in times of war.

But this kind of macro-rationalization was unlikely to help or even occur to the wronged individual. Joseph Dakak, certainly, did not regard his situation with philosophical resignation. He experienced his captivity as an unmitigated physical and mental catastrophe. My grandfather was terrified and angry and bemused and incredulous

and shocked by what was happening to him. He could not relativize
his situation, or go with its flow, or ascribe to it a rational or even, as
appeared from the opening words of his first (and only surviving)
prison letter home, an earthly cause. The letter – which Amy found
and copied to me from Geneva – was written in French and addressed
to *Ma Georgette chérie, mes petits amours*:

> The Lord has wished to submit me to the most terrible
> ordeal to which a human being could be submitted – may
> His will be done.
>
> My dear Georgette, I received your letter of 15th
> September in which you express your fears concerning my
> health. Alas, even the strongest will and the most robust
> constitution would be shaken by the mental and physical
> suffering I have endured these past six months.
>
> To have not done a thing, to have a clear conscience and
> yet to be in the state I am in, that is very hard.
>
> How many times, when I have awakened in the morning,
> have I asked myself in a half-sleep if I was not dreaming, but
> alas, hard reality was not slow in affirming itself.
>
> I have wept so much, thinking of you and of the little
> darlings, that my tears have run dry. Me, to whom their
> cooing and caresses were a whole world.
>
> Our consul-general has brought me the two flannels, your
> letter, money. He came to see me and was very kind to me, I
> did not know how to thank him.
>
> My dear Georgette, don't weep or fret, what will be will
> be. Maybe we shall meet again one day, if God permits and
> adversity is less cruel.
>
> Kiss my little angels and remind Lina not to forget me in
> her bedtime prayers.
>
> Thank you for all that you are doing on my behalf, and
> pray for your Joseph, who loves you all and does nothing but
> think of you, at home in Mersin, day and night.

The letter was dated 8 November 1942. It was written at the

Hôpital du Liban, Beirut, while my grandfather was convalescing after his final attempt at suicide.

It was thanks to the Turkish consul in Beirut that my grandmother received the letter. In September 1942, Georgette Dakad temporarily entrusted the children to her sisters and boarded the Taurus Express in an attempt to see her husband in Lebanon. On the outward journey, she met *un monsieur très raffiné* who, no doubt intrigued by the well-dressed young woman travelling in mysterious solitude, propositioned her. My grandmother rejected the advance; but once the distinguished gentleman became aware of the purpose of her trip, he introduced himself formally as the Turkish consul to Beirut and put himself at her service. The consul, Rifki Bey, was not able to secure for my grandmother access to her husband, but he did pay a personal visit to the prisoner and passed him a letter and various items sent by Mamie Dakad. He also conveyed Joseph's letter to Mamie Dakad. It was the first time she'd heard from him since his arrest more than five months earlier.

My grandmother had been facing an ordeal of her own. Georgette Dakad was a strong woman – as a strong as a man, her friends used to say – but she was devastated by her husband's disappearance; and things got no easier after 28 April 1942, when she gave birth to a third child, Amy. (Whom, in fact, she named Claude. When the little girl finally met her father at three and half years of age, she was renamed after a nurse who had been good to him. 'Your name shall no longer be Claude,' her father informed her. 'You are Amy now.') In their father's absence, the three children grew up surrounded by women. Their grandmother, Teta, lived in the house, and their mother's spinster sisters Isabelle and Alexandra were a constant presence. My mother said that she was a happy young child. When she grew old enough to ask about her father, she was told that Papa was away on a business trip. Then one day a spiteful girl said to her in the course of a kindergarten tiff about hopscotch, 'At least *my* father isn't in jail.'

Prices in Mersin were very high and Georgette was forced to make savings. The racehorse, Tayara, was sold, as was the shop in which the valuable hoard of tin had been secretly deposited by my grandfather; and so (the story went) a fortune was mislaid. Georgette also had to take over the business of the Toros Hotel. This was not without its complications. The British, Mamie Dakad would later tell my mother, posted a spy in the hotel. Masquerading as a customer, he occupied the room near the office and stayed for some time, peeping and prowling around. One day, Georgette entered her office to discover that there had been a break-in. The safe was open, papers were scattered everywhere, but strangely the thousands of lira kept in the safe (a sum large enough to buy a property) were untouched. On another occasion, she was greeted on

Georgette and Joseph, 1940. A family friend holds my infant mother.

the stairs of the hotel by an eminent Axis guest – the German or
Italian ambassador, my mother thought – and she immediately went
to the British consulate to report the encounter before they heard it
from anyone else. Otherwise, Mamie Dakad effectively withdrew
from society. She saw to the hotel in the mornings and stayed at
home in the afternoons, when she would do housework and play
cards with trusted girlfriends like Kiki and Dora and Lolo.
According to Lolo, my grandmother was right to be cautious. The
war split Mersin into factions, and a partisan or ambiguous gesture
or flippant remark could lead to trouble with the Turkish authorities.

In May 1943, the same month that Joseph Dakak was moved
from the military hospital in Beirut to the monastery at Emuas,
Denis Wright took over from Norman Mayers in Mersin. This was
a significant development: according to my grandmother, Monsieur
Wright helped her with sending and receiving letters, and he
advised her not to invest hope and money in trying to secure her
husband's release but, rather, to await the end of the war. 'I don't
remember giving her that advice,' Wright said to me when I raised
the subject, 'but if I had advised her, that is the advice I would have
given.' 'What do you remember?' I asked. 'I recall seeing her from
time to time about her husband,' Wright said. 'I don't recall much
else.' He added with a smile, 'I take it you've read my letter about
that party in Gözne.'

I had read it, in Wright's volume of his letters home from
Mersin. On the first weekend of September 1944, Wright went up
to Gözne for 'an end-of-season party arranged by the Vali but paid
for by the Syrians':

> The Saturday evening dance took place in the garden of the
> coffee house: the Club orchestra was there and the
> refreshments were all prepared by the Syrians who
> complained that the Turkish women had done nothing to
> help with the fête. . . .
>   It was a rollicking party with a full moon shining down on
> us and all Gözne was there. The Syrians were as noisy as ever

but seemed happier and less restrained in their own Gözne. I had a dance with Mme Dakad, the Toros Hotel woman whose husband is in one of our concentration camps in Syria or Palestine: it was the first time she had really amused herself in public since his arrest and the excitement of it all and the odd drinks she had had (and I gave her one which perhaps I shouldn't have done) went to her head. She had a fit of crying and a sort of hysterics (by this time she had been removed from the dance floor to a room in the pub) shouting *'J'ai dansé avec M. Wright! Vive M. Wright! Vive le Consul d'Angleterre!'* and repeating all this until she was forcibly taken home by Mme Carodi. She had recovered yesterday morning when I saw her playing poker – these Gözne Syrians play morning, afternoon and night daily and lose or win anything up to 300 liras a session, probably more. Mme Dakad has won about 3000 liras [about £410, which was more or less Wright's annual salary] in the last few weeks, they say.

Denis Wright's letters of the autumn of 1944 portrayed a more relaxed Mersin. The blackout was lifted, cricket matches were played at the 'Braithwaites' construction camp, and the consul represented Mersin in a tennis match. A jazz band played on the 'millionairish' seafront boulevard that was being built under the direction of the new Vali, Tewfik Gür. Jewish refugees bound for Cyprus passed through Mersin, and another excitement was the defection of an Austrian couple and a German who were working for German intelligence in Turkey – Herr and Frau von Kleckowski and Wilhelm Hamburgher. (The Americans had asked the British to smuggle them out of the country, and the trio stayed at the consulate before heading off to Syria on the Taurus Express.) Otherwise, life at the consulate passed quietly. On 11 November 1944, Mr Busk at the Ankara embassy noted, 'The importance of Mersin has in the past lain in the fact that it was one of two accessible ports. We may hope that the Aegean will be shortly opened up and when this happens the importance of Mersin will sink to almost nothing.'

The old seafront at Mersin

And so, in January 1945, Denis Wright left Mersin for London. Before he left, he received a letter from my grandmother dated 9 January 1945 which he kept and later pasted in his album of memoirs. Mamie Dakad wrote (in French):

> Mr Wright,
>   I have just learned of your departure and unfortunately there is not enough time to see you and thank you for all that you have been good enough to do for me. I hope that you will not forget me in Syria, because I must receive news from my husband.
>   Bon voyage and good luck.
> Best wishes
> G. Dakak

In May 1945, the European war ended. Still Georgette waited for her husband. Four months later, she was in the mountains, in Gözne, when she received a letter informing her of Joseph's release. She was so absorbed by the letter that she didn't notice a creature slithering in the vine overhead, and didn't even flinch when the serpent suddenly fell and landed at her feet. My grandmother enjoyed telling her daughters this story, with its connotation of Eden regained.

The northern extremities of the Red Sea consist of two fingers of water that point, respectively, at the Mediterranean Sea and the Israel–Jordan border; and wedged between them is the triangle of the Sinai desert. The easternmost finger is the Gulf of Aqaba and at its very tip is the Israeli holiday destination of Eilat, a conglomeration of hotels, purpose-built lagoons and concrete apartment blocks generated by the proximity of coral reefs and submarine wildlife. I flew there from London on 7 April 1996, Easter Sunday. The British capital was passing through a tense, unpleasant phase, and I was glad to be leaving. A few days before, special stop and search laws, rushed through parliament that same week, had come into force: it was the eightieth anniversary of the Easter Rising, and intelligence reports suggested that the IRA planned to mark the occasion with violence. Londoners feared the worst. The IRA ceasefire had ended on 10 February with an explosion at South Quay, in the Docklands, in which hundreds had been injured and two killed. The city was subjected to further disruption and violence. Walking home one evening, I found that Soho was blocked off to traffic and that an 'explosive device' was being defused in a telephone booth I passed every morning on my way into work. Then, on Sunday 18 February, the 171 bus (which I used to take daily when I lived in south London) blew up at the Aldwych near Bush House, again at a place I walked by most working days. The explosion injured six and killed the carrier of the bomb, Eddie O'Brien, a twenty-one-year-old from Gorey, Co. Wexford. For a few days after, the spectacular carcass of the bus remained on the road, a fantastically mangled mass of strawberry metal coated with flakes of fine snow.

But the place I was flying into was far more dangerous than the one I was leaving. In nine days in February and March, Hamas suicide bombers had killed sixty-one people in Jerusalem and Tel Aviv. These events triggered – as they were probably designed to – measures from the Israeli government that were as retaliatory as they were defensive, most notably the imposition of very strict restrictions on the movement of Arabs out of the West Bank and Gaza. With many thousands separated from their families and jobs, the military and political crisis grew ever more bitter, and it seemed that further bomb attacks were imminent.

But there was no sign of trouble as I drove out of Eilat and across the stony heights and crumbling sandy hills of the Negev desert – only of ostriches, donkeys, camels and hovering hawks. I drove through Sodom and then, passing Masada, along the western shore of the Salt Sea into Judea. When the Salt Sea came to an end I turned westward; for some distance now (my map told me) I had been travelling in the Autonomous Territories. The desert was now freckled with bushes. Grazing lambs and nomad encampments appeared on the hills, and the roadside bloomed with poppies and shrubs with mustard- and lavender-coloured flowers. I passed through a couple of Israeli army checkpoints, and then, abruptly, I was in Jerusalem.

Jerusalem was more beautiful than I had ever imagined: a place of elevations and drops and, at its centre, where the walled Old City rose out of the green, bucolic depths of sheep-strewn valleys, extraordinary juxtapositions of pastoral and urban scenes. There was something else that I hadn't anticipated. Because of planning regulations introduced by the British and evidently still in force seventy-five years later, buildings in the central districts of the city were constructed, or at least clad, in limestone, and as a consequence Jerusalem still presented to the world the pale stone exterior that used until a few decades ago to be so typical of the cities of the Levant. Ambling in tranquil, sunlit nineteenth-century districts in the New and Old Cities, I was overcome by visual and atmospheric echoes of old Mersin. It felt faintly absurd to apprehend the city in such humble terms, but as I walked amongst the dramatic throngs in the Old City – outlandishly outfitted monks and clerics, minuscule and bonneted old Greek women dressed entirely in black, East African pilgrims in long robes and turbans – and noted with amazement that the Arab, Christian, Jewish and Armenian quarters actually contained ancient populations of Arabs, Christians, Jews and Armenians (each attired in distinctive robes and hats and shawls), it occurred to me that this was precisely the vivid commingling of races and nationalities and religions and languages that had so powerfully struck travellers to nineteenth-century Mersin. The link between this city and the little Turkish port of my child-hood became clear: they were both profoundly Ottoman places. The gulf between modern, uniform Turkey and the culturally var-iegated Levant in which my grandfather grew up revealed itself. To trace his fate, I was beginning to realize, I needed to look deeper into that Ottoman world – in which, after all, Joseph Dakak had passed the first third of his life.

I stayed in the New Imperial Hotel, an attractive edifice in the Parisian style situated just by Jaffa Gate, in the Christian quarter of the Old City. Built in 1889 for Greek Orthodox pilgrims, the hotel was still the base for flocks of Greek women arriving for the Greek Orthodox Easter, who every morning and evening cawed and rus-tled in the hotel's cavernous salon. There were remnants of the 'Deli' that used to operate here, and a sign persisted in proclaiming the availability of non-existent BEVERAGES! and SHAKES and DELI-SANDWICHES. On the balcony, lantern spheres adver-tised the croissants, brioches, cakes and ice-creams of yesteryear. The hotel motto – in English, like the other old signs – was painted on the wall of the ground floor entranceway: *Yesterday is already a dream and tomorrow is only a vision, but today well lived, makes every yesterday a dream of happiness and every tomorrow a vision of hope.*

My main objective in coming to Israel was to track down, first, the Modern Hotel in Jerusalem, and second, the monastery at 'Emuas' where my grandfather had been locked up for the best part of three years. With respect to the former, I held out little hope: investigations I'd made from England had made it pretty clear that the Modern Hotel was no longer in business and had, as far as one could tell, entirely disappeared. The owner of the New Imperial Hotel, a courteous man in his fifties named Mr Dajani, had no knowledge of the Modern Hotel, and neither had the people I spoke to at the Ron Hotel or the Golden Jerusalem Hotel or the Kaplan Hotel or the American Colony Hotel or the King David Hotel.

Meanwhile, I ran into an unexpected difficulty regarding the monastery: there was no sign, on the detailed maps I consulted, of

a village called Emuas or Emwas on the road between Jerusalem and
Ramle, and all that the young Jewish woman I spoke to at the
Tourist Information Office could suggest was that I go to
Damascus Gate. 'Ask the Arabs there,' she said; 'they may be able
to help you.' Although puzzled about why she would think that
random Arabs might know more than a tourist information expert,
I went to Damascus Gate, a crowded, rowdy place where minibuses
to Ramallah and other Palestinian destinations gathered. Fairly
soon, a scrum of experts had gathered around my road map; but
none could point to the place called Emuas. 'Go here,' one man
said; 'go there,' another said, indicating different points in the map.
Confused, I thanked my would-be helpers and returned to my car
to mull over the conflicting advice I'd received. Just as I was opening the door of the car, a man who had not previously spoken
urgently approached me and said with conviction, 'Go to Latrun;
Emuas [he pronounced it Amwas] is there'; and having no better
lead, I followed his advice.

It was a faultless, warm day. The drive to Latrun was on the Tel
Aviv highway, a poppy-lined road that ran through a series of
gulches and ravines, their sun-bleached rockfaces decked out with
cypress groves, clusters of pines, and acacia bushes with flowers the
colour of New York taxis. Eventually this rocky landscape suddenly gave way to a vast plain of chequered farmland. LATRUN, a
signboard announced. I swung off the highway. Before me, on a
raised plateau, stood an unpleasant block-like building with two
watchtowers and fortified perimeters. I decided to drive over.

I stopped in the car-park of the military base. There were many
Jewish families around, unpacking picnics and trooping through
an entrance in the fifteen-foot-high stone wall that surrounded the
base; above the wall, a row of tanks loomed and flags of Israel hung
from thirty flagpoles. 'Is there a place here called Emuas?' I asked
an official-looking middle-aged woman standing at the entrance
with a walkie-talkie. The woman shook her head. 'There is somewhere called *Emmaus*, I think, over there, maybe' – she pointed
back across the highway – 'but not *Emuas*. Emuas I don't know
about. This place, Latrun,' she said, 'was the fort and detention

centre of the British in the Mandate days. Prisoners of war –
Germans, Italians – and Zionist guerillas were held captive here
during the Second World War. Nowadays, it is a tank museum and
memorial to the valour of the Armoured Corps Division of the
Israeli Defence Forces. Desperate and repeated efforts were made to
capture Latrun from the Arabs in 1948,' my guide said, 'but these
failed, and many men lost their lives. Over there' (the woman gave
an indication with her head) 'is a wall where you will see the names
of those who died. In the museum is a computer where family and
friends have typed in their memories of the dead soldiers. Not all of
the dead have been remembered,' the woman said, adjusting her
glasses. 'Many of the forces that attacked Latrun were fresh from
Europe and had not even been officially registered anywhere before
they came here and were killed.' The woman's speech was blunt and
grooved, and she had plainly made this talk before. 'It was not until
the Six Day War in 1967,' she said, 'that Latrun, and the Latrun
corridor to Jerusalem, fell to Jewish troops. Latrun was a strategically crucial spot, since it controlled the main supply route into
West Jerusalem.' She pointed back at the highway I had driven
down, where the road entered a narrow pass between two wooded
hills. Then I noticed on the southern hill, gleaming amongst trees,
a spectacular brick building with over forty west-facing windows, a
red roof, and a towering chapel: a monastery, surely.

I thanked the woman for her help and went quickly back to my
car. In a state of some excitement, I drove into the monastery's
grounds and went slowly uphill through beautifully tended gardens dense with trees and vivid flowers. Then shadowy cloisters
and huge columns appeared; this was a grand, almost palatial place.
In the reception area, I found a young man, a French speaker, selling wine and honey produced by the Trappist monks who, he told
me, had inhabited the monastery since its foundation in the 1890s.
He flatly denied that the place had been a British camp during the
war. 'Never. Impossible.' I was baffled. So where was the village of
Emuas, then? 'On the other side of the highway,' he said, confirm-
ing what the woman at Fort Latrun had said. He gave me a careful
look. 'To be accurate, it's not a village any more. It is a park. I think

that the Israelis destroyed the village in 1967.' 'Is there nothing left, nothing at all?' 'There's an ancient basilica there,' the young man told me, 'and, I think, a house.'

I got back into the car and, a couple of minutes later, crossed the highway. After coming to the park mentioned by the receptionist at Latrun Monastery – Canada Park, built and planted thanks to the donations of Canadian Jews – I doubled back on myself. Not far from the highway, I noticed for the first time a gateway to a property. There was a sign – *La Communité des Béatétudes, Emmaus Nicopolis* – and, beyond an open gate, an ancient ruin of some sort, in which a priest and a group of tourists bowed their heads in prayer. That ruin was, presumably, the basilica that the man at the Trappist monastery had mentioned. Then, as I got out of the car, I caught a glimpse of something further up on the hill: an elegant building of white stone, surrounded by cypress trees. I walked past the tourists up the steep and curved gravel path that led to the yard at the front of the building, a two-storey block flanked by two protruding towers. On the ground floor were eight arched and barred windows and a huge front door. On the first floor, a handsome terrace, fronted by a series of columns and arches, was recessed into the building; circular, porthole-like windows gave on to the terrace from the central block. Crenellations ran along the top of the frontage, giving the house – which was in immaculate condition – an austere, embattled look that spoke of Crusades and infidels. I noticed that the stones surrounding the well in the front yard were arranged into the shape of a cross.

I climbed the steps to the front door, a grand affair with enormous silver hinges. I rang the bell hanging by the door. A man in his forties – he introduced himself as Yves-Marie Villedieu – appeared, and I briefly explained the purpose of my visit. Monsieur Villedieu said that the building might indeed have been used by the British during the war but that he himself knew little of its history. In that regard, I ought to speak to Monsieur Florent Arnaud, he said, scribbling a Jerusalem address on a piece of paper. Nowadays, he explained, the building housed a religious community consisting of two French families (whose children attended the French school in Jerusalem), some monks and some nuns. 'Here, let me show you,' he said, and he led me to a modern chapel that was incorporated into the west wing of the house, a simple, elegant space with new stained-glass windows. Then I followed Monsieur Villedieu out of the chapel and into the cool of the house's spacious entrance hall. Monsieur Villedieu said that I could not see the private areas of the building but was welcome to go up to the terrace. We went up the stone staircase to the first floor. Overhead, light flooded through the high porthole windows; underfoot, black and white tiles gleamed. I could have been in a clinic. I came to the terrace, maybe eighty feet lengthways and ten feet deep, and rested my hands against the thick ledge. Below was the gravel yard where I had stood minutes before, and, in the distance, clearly visible between the tops of palm trees, cypresses and fruit trees that grew about the house, Fort Latrun, its shrunken tanks squatting like cockroaches. The Fort was just like its counterpart at the Curragh: the same strategic location and coldly functional set-up, the same phantasmal presence of the British and their internment camps.

The grounds beyond the immediate vicinity of the house consisted of a few acres of thickly overgrown meadowland that ran downhill to a boundary of stone walls. If there had been a prison here during the war, all of this vegetation would have been cut down, which meant that the Latrun detention camps, with their floodlights, barbed wire and trudging columns of prisoners, would have been a constant and oppressive spectacle. I tried to blot out the birdsong, the smell of wildflowers, the all-enfolding serenity. I tried to imagine another scene: the bewildered figure of my grandfather, unaccustomed to manual labour, toiling away on the hillside in the heat, in the rain. I tried to imagine him, with his troublesome heart, struggling up and down the stairs I had just climbed. It was not easy. The flowering greenery, the odours and sounds of nature, the cool, all had a tranquillizing effect; and, of course, I wasn't even sure that my grandfather had been here at all.

I left the house and drove around Canada Park, looking for a sign of vanished Emuas. Following a trail inside the park, I travelled through an almost dreamlike setting of limestone escarpments,

cultivated terraced hillsides, copses, and wild meadows where storks
paused in the grass and cows and sheep grazed. During twenty
minutes of driving through a landscape apparently untouched since
biblical times, no human being appeared other than soldiers of the
Israeli army packed into a patrol jeep.

Back in the clamour of Jerusalem the following day, I paid a visit
to Haidar Husseini, who, I'd been told, was a member of the
famous family of the old Mufti, Haj Amin el-Husseini. I found
Mr Husseini in his office at the Lawrence Travel Agency, which
was situated on the ground floor of the Lawrence Hotel, on Salah-
a-Din Street in East Jerusalem. A distinguished-looking man in
his sixties wearing a blazer, a grey-checked cardigan and a purple
tie, he was not familiar with the names of Mustapha and Olga
Husseini. However, when I mentioned that Mustapha and Olga
liked to meet with Arab nationalists at the Modern Hotel, he interrupted me and said, 'The Modern Hotel? I remember it well. It was
on Mamilla Street, and if I remember rightly it was the property of
the Islamic waqf; the lease was in the name of Hassan Ahweida.
Mamilla in those days was the centre of Arab Jerusalem, a very
busy place,' Mr Husseini said. 'Near the hotel there used to be a
patisserie and a coffee house, and every day there was a card-game
next door, at the house of Zeronian, whose children, Jerry and
Diana, I knew well. They fled after the occupation in 1948. We all
left the area at that time, of course. I was young, fourteen or fifteen
years old; my father had been a judge in the High Court of Justice
under the British Mandate.' Haidar Husseini picked up a pen and
paper. Prominently displayed behind his chair, I noticed, was a
photograph of the travel agent shaking hands with Yasser Arafat.
'The Modern Hotel would have ceased to operate in 1948, I
believe,' Mr Husseini continued. 'It was a three-star hotel, in
today's terms. You'll see it if you go to Mamilla street; it is still
standing, but it is old and empty. I think the Israelis intend to knock
it down.' Mr Husseini drew me a map. 'This is Mamilla, here,' he
said, sketching. 'And here' – he made an X – 'is the building you are
looking for.'

I walked back to the New Imperial Hotel and, sitting in its

gloomy, chair-infested old saloon, I reread my grandfather's testimony for any mention of Mamilla Street. There was no such reference, but something else did catch my attention. When my grandfather had been 'poisoned' by the oranges he'd eaten, he was taken to see a Dr Dajani, whose surgery was about 100 metres from the Modern Hotel. Dajani: wasn't that the name of the proprietor of the very hotel I was sitting in? It was a long shot, but I went to see him in his office and asked him if, by chance, he could throw light on the matter. He said unhesitatingly, 'that doctor would be my uncle, Dr Mahmoud Dajani.' 'Did he speak German, or did he study in Germany?' I asked, remembering my grandfather's assertions to this effect. 'He spoke a little German, perhaps,' Mr Dajani said doubtfully, 'but he was not educated in Germany. But I am sure my uncle would be your doctor,' Mr Dajani said conclusively. 'There would be no other Dr Dajani. He had a large house, now knocked down. He ran a clinic from there. It was down below, on Mamilla Street.'

Mamilla Street was a five-minute walk west and downhill from the New Imperial. It ran east from the junction of King David and Agron streets to Jaffa Road. Completely blocked off from pedestrians and road traffic by metal barricades, Mamilla was a street of ruins. Its western side had been completely razed, leaving nothing but mounds of weedy earth, and only a handful of buildings on its eastern side were standing: crumbling arcades, commercial premises and houses that dated back, I guessed, to the last decades of the Ottoman empire. The Modern Hotel was an elegant stone wreck. Shuttered-up old shops took up the ground floor, and the hotel, running to a width of seven shops, occupied the two storeys above. Immediately behind it was a wasteland, and next door was a fine, square, gutted house – the Zeronian place that Mr Husseini had mentioned? – with tired red tiles still adhering to its rooftop. All that remained of the Modern Hotel's roof was a disintegrating lattice of timber beams. The arching windows of the hotel were tall and windowless and dark, and empty doorways opened onto the vestiges of balconies. The occupants of the west-facing rooms had no doubt sat on those balconies looking down on the crowded road and

pavements below, a spectacle of urban vitality that, peering on tip-
toes over the barricade from the street below fifty years after the
event, was hard to envisage. My difficulty was more than topographical. Mamilla Street not only fizzled out into a cul-de-sac of
barriers and earthworks but also, it seemed, into a historical dead-
end. For nearly fifty years, the ghostly thoroughfare had borne
witness to the territorial and moral convulsions of 1948, when
Mamilla, the venue of anti-Jewish riots, became a dangerous no-
man's-land occupied by squatters and overshadowed by Jordanian
guns; and 1967, when Jerusalem was 'reunified' by Israeli forces
and the Mamilla squatters were controversially and forcibly
removed to high-rise buildings on the edge of the city. But now a
decisive rescripting seemed afoot. I could see that a road-building
operation was underway at the bottom of Mamilla Street, and the
long, spindly arm of a red crane hovered in the sky, a wire line
dropping from its tip like a line of ink from a nib in flow. The line
reached down into a body of pale concrete rising just below
Mamilla Street, where signs in Hebrew and English announced the
construction of a new, truly modern hotel. The plan, I discovered
from the *Jerusalem Post*, was that within two years the Mamilla
neighbourhood – a century ago 'the beating social and commercial
heart of Jerusalem' where 'Jews and Arabs once cohabited as merchants, shopkeepers and customers' – would 'once again brim with
stores, hotels, entertainments and sidewalk cafés'. Supermarkets, a
park, hotels, underground car-parks and luxury apartments with
German kitchens would be built on the sites of old Israeli and
Jordanian sniper outposts. It remained to be seen, the *Post* reported,
to what extent the development would, as was hoped, form a bridge
between the Arab and Jewish communities. There was no mention
of the fate of the building of the Modern Hotel.

On the morning of 12 April 1996, I met Florent Arnaud, whom
Yves-Marie Villedieu had advised me to speak to about the home at
Emmaus. Monsieur Arnaud worked at the offices of the Pilgrims'
Commission in a building across the road from the New Gate, next
to the church of Notre Dame de France. He was a man in his fifties,
and in his *fonctionnaire*'s blazer and tie and goldrimmed glasses he

displayed a Gallic neatness that set him apart from the sartorial jamboree taking place in the street outside. For eighteen years, he explained, he had been the secretary of the commission that had established relations between Israel and the Vatican. 'Dakak,' he said, as he began to flick through the pages of the testimony, 'is a commonplace name – *un nom banal*. There are plenty of Dakaks in Bethlehem, Muslims, I believe, who mainly work in tourism and often marry foreigners; and are there not Christian Dakaks in Aleppo?' He read on for a little while, sometimes skipping pages and at other times lingering on paragraphs with eyebrows at a critical arch. I suddenly felt embarrassed for my exposed grandfather. 'There are certain things about this document that immediately strike me as bizarre,' Monsieur Arnaud said decisively. 'Opening an import–export office in late 1941? Applying for a visa to go to Egypt? You'll excuse me, but that seems to me a little. . . .' He pointed a whirling index finger at his temple. Then Arnaud retrieved some typed notes of his own from his desk and, consulting these, began to speak in the manner of somebody giving a lecture. 'The story of the property of Emmaus-Latrun really begins in the nineteenth century,' Monsieur Arnaud said. 'The Crimean War (1856) and the construction of the Suez Canal (1860) led to a great influx of westerners to this area. Among these was the Princesse La Tour d'Auvergne, who lies buried in the Mount of Olives. She summoned a French architect, Bernard Guillemot, from France. It was Guillemot who, in 1885, carried out the dig which resulted in the discovery of the ruins of the Old Church which you now see at the entrance to the property. At that time, the land, owned by the Carmelites of Bethlehem, was marshy and, aside from a small building occupied by a hermit, deserted.' Monsieur Arnaud cleared his throat. 'The Pères de Betharran –' Monsieur Arnaud said, 'Betharran being near Lourdes – established themselves in Bethlehem as a consequence of the separation of church and state in France. In 1932 or 1933, they built the house at Emmaus as a holiday retreat. Perhaps it is not quite accurate, therefore, to speak of it as a monastery. At the back of the mind of those building the house was the thought that a carmel might also be built in the grounds; but nothing came of that, apart from a door and archway which you will find in the perimeter walls. I have done a little research of my own,' Monsieur Arnaud said, 'into the somewhat neglected architects of the church buildings in the Holy Land. The house at Emmaus was designed by a very fine architect, Favier, whose other buildings include the French consulate in Jerusalem and the carmel of Haifa. The house at Emmaus has several notable features – including, as you will have seen, the magnificent silverwork on the door, made possible by a gift from the Belgian court. Unfortunately, the building is poorly constructed. The land there is at a sharp incline and the earth is unstable and slippery. As a consequence, the house is a *danseuse*. The cellars are now dangerous and have had to be closed, and all of the dividing walls are cracked or broken. Indeed, it is perhaps not an exaggeration to say that the building is in danger of falling down. In 1940,' Arnaud said, 'the Pères de Betharran were deported to France or to Italy and the English requisitioned the building. They used it not as a prison camp but, to be exact, as a concentration camp; and it must have been the place where your grandfather was held. After the war ended,' Monsieur Arnaud said, 'the Pères did not return. So you see, the drama of the house at Emmaus is perhaps this: that it has never fulfilled its vocation.'

The next day, I drove out to Latrun for a second time. It was another warm and sunny day and the traffic flowed quickly. There was no indication anywhere that, three days before, on 10 April,

Israel had suddenly launched Operation Grapes of Wrath, a ferocious aerial and artillery attack directed at Hezbollah guerrillas in
south Lebanon which, by 15 April, would result in the deaths of at
least twenty-two people and the displacement of around 400,000. I
had personally felt a gust of the political violence stirring in the air.
The previous day, 12 April, which was the day after my meeting
with Haider Husseini, a bomb exploded directly above the
Lawrence Travel Agency in room 27 of the Lawrence Hotel. The
explosion shattered every window on the second floor of the hotel,
spewing glass on to Salah-a-Din Street, and the doors of all ten
rooms on the second floor were ripped from their hinges and scattered. It was first thought that the occupant of room 27, who
crawled out of the room covered in blood, was a British citizen
called Newman; but investigations would subsequently reveal that
the man – who lost his legs, an arm, and the use of his eyes – was a
Lebanese Shiite called Hussein Mohammed Hussein Mikdad, and
a Hezbollah operative.

I arrived at the junction of Latrun and turned off in the direction
of the Trappist monastery. Following a suggestion made by
Monsieur Arnaud, I asked the receptionist at the monastery if I
might see Brother Guy. 'The old monk is a simpleton,' Arnaud had
said, 'but he's lived in Latrun all his life and might be able to tell
you something of interest.'

I had always associated Trappist monks with silence, but Brother
Guy – a small, cheerful, bald, physically robust man wearing brown
sandals, a stone-coloured ankle-length habit, a black scapula with a
hood, and wide brown cincture that tied at the hip – was loquacious
and excitable. 'I saw it all!' he would exclaim from time to time. '*J'ai
tout vu!* I'm seventy-one, I've been here since I was ten, I tell you
I saw it all with my own eyes!'

Brother Guy walked me up towards the top of the hill on which
the Trappist monastery was built. He was born in Tripoli, in
Lebanon, he told me, and had been brought by his cousin to the
monastery as a *juvéniste*. He had only twice left the monastery: to
study in Jerusalem, in 1942, and to have a brain operation in
France. When a huge bandy-legged lizard scuttled across our path,

Brother Guy noticed my interest and asked in astonishment, 'You don't have lizards in London?'

After a few minutes Brother Guy stopped and pointed back to the plain of Ayalon, where Fort Latrun had come into view. 'I saw them locked up there,' he exclaimed, waving his arms in excitement. 'Four thousand Italians, one hundred Germans, one hundred Pétainistes – I saw them for myself. There were executions – an Englishman was executed, a German, an Arab, a Druse, and one other. There was barbed wire everywhere, and Poles guarded the prisoners. There were seven thousand Poles here!'

Presently, the remains of a castle appeared on the other side of a chasm formed by old Ottoman barracks. 'This is a Crusader castle,' the monk said. 'Richard Coeur de Lion played checkers with Saladin right here. The castle was built by Flemish knights in the twelfth century, to guard the road from Jaffa to Jerusalem. That's where the name *Latrun* comes from, from the name of the castle, *La Tour des Chevaliers*.'

We walked on and reached the very top of the hill. 'The moment the British left in 1947,' Brother Guy said, 'the Arabs built fortifications around this castle. From here the Jordanian artillery, under the command of a German officer, bombarded the Jewish convoys to Jerusalem. The Jews counter-attacked, but it was a disaster. Six hundred Jewish soldiers died on this hill in three hours, as you can see from this commemorative monument.' Brother Guy gestured at a menhir-like boulder held aloft by two metal prongs.

'What about the house over there?' I asked, pointing to the hill of Emmaus. 'Do you remember anything about that place during the war?' 'Well,' Brother Guy answered, 'there used to be barbed wire around that house, too. I'm not really sure who was imprisoned in there – top officers, was the rumour. It was a mysterious place. I never went there. It was at Emmaus,' the monk said, 'that Jesus manifested Himself to the two disciples and took supper with them. There used to be an Arab village there,' he added. 'They were good people, the people of Amwas. Some of them worked at the monastery. In three days, using nine bulldozers, the village was wiped off the face of the earth. The gardens, the olive trees, the apricot trees, all were churned up and destroyed. The chickens and vegetable plots were buried in rubble. I saw it happen,' the monk said. 'I saw it all.'

Brother Guy agreed to accompany me to the house at Emmaus. He turned out to be a knowledgeable guide. As we stood by the ruined basilica just inside the gate of the house, he explained that this was a Byzantine construction from the fifth century, which had been covered seven hundred years later by a Crusader church. 'Emmaus,' Guy said, 'first came to historical prominence in around 165 BC, when Judas Machabeus defeated the Syrians in the famous victory that gave rise to the Jewish feast of Hanukkah. The city was destroyed by Varus, in AD 4, but rose again. The Roman Fifth Legion camped here for two years before attacking Jerusalem in AD 70, and by 223 the Romans had renamed the place Nicopolis. Arab armies established a large military base here in the seventh century, then shortly afterwards a plague broke out and the city emptied. Then it was repopulated and it regained its importance. It was the last station of the Crusaders on their way to Jerusalem in June 1099,' Brother Guy said.

Standing in the basilica, I looked up the hill of Emmaus and saw once more the mock-battlements of the house appearing just above the tops of thick green trees. Leaving Brother Guy down at the basilica, I set off on foot up one of the pair of driveways that approached the house in two separate curves, like pincers.

I walked up the hill reflecting that I was the first in my family to have parted the thick folds of familial pain that had covered this place; and when I thought about the tears that would come to Mamie Dakad's eyes at the mere mention of my grandfather's time here, I became light-headed with sadness. I arrived once more at the house. I thought about ringing the bell and having another look around. There seemed little point. I had been inside once already and, if Florent Arnaud was correct, the cellars in which my grandfather had spent the last months of his internment were now hazardous and out of bounds. The house did not look as though it was in danger of falling down. It exuded solidity and beauty and militaristic Christianity, and there was no sign of its past as

(Arnaud's term) a concentration camp. But it was certainly here
that my grandfather had lived for nearly three years. He had slept
and woken in this building, walked these grounds, and surveyed
the valley below and the encampments at Latrun, and hated it
here. The competition to tell the story of this patch of the planet
was intense: the Jews, the Arabs, the British, the Christian
churches, the Romans, the French – all had laid narrative claim to
Emmaus or Amwas or Nicopolis, and alongside their insistent
sagas my grandfather's small story seemed as miserable and efface-
able as graffiti. But I was glad to have made the journey. I felt I was
claiming my grandfather and his pain from this beautiful doomed
house, and by my presence scrawling on its pristine stone, *Joseph
Dakak was here*.

My last appointment in Israel was at Shamelech Boulevard,
Tel Aviv, where the office of Yitzhak Shamir was situated.
Shamir had agreed to see me after I had written to him briefly
explaining my inquiries into my grandfathers and asking whether
he knew anything about Desmond Doran, the British agent killed
by the ultra right-wing guerrilla organization of which he had been
a member, Lehi (also known as the Stern Gang). He faxed me back,
granting my request for an interview. He added:

> A man by the name of Doran was killed in Tel Aviv during
> 1946–47, when a British intelligence building was blown up
> in Tel Aviv, as part of the actions against British offices. He
> worked in this building.

I was already a little surprised at Shamir's readiness to meet me –
'he treats his past like a state secret,' an Israeli historian had
cautioned me – and when I reached his office, on the tenth floor of
a modern office block, it struck me how low-key, and apparently lax,
was the security for a man who presumably knew something about
assassination and blowing up buildings. I was shown directly to his
room, which was sparsely decorated with a bust of John F.
Kennedy, a large flag of Israel that drooped from a pole, and a

shofar in a case. Bright sunlight filtered through the lowered blinds. Shamir, dressed in a grey suit, blue shirt and dark tie, stood up from his chair with a shy hospitable smile, and I immediately saw that this tiny eighty-one-year-old man was in terrific shape – trim, energetic, mobile and, judging by his handshake, strong.

Shamir didn't have much to say about Doran. 'Doran personally didn't interest us,' he said. 'The operation was directed against the British intelligence office. It was nothing personal.' He raised his hands slightly. 'I wasn't involved in the operation,' he said. 'At that time I was already out of the country, in East Africa.' In the summer of 1946, Shamir explained, he was deported to Eritrea. He had already, in 1943, escaped from an internment in Palestine, and in Africa, the British felt, the arch-terrorist would be out of harm's way once and for all. But they were wrong, because Shamir escaped again. Stowed in a compartment in the container of an oil truck, he travelled over a thousand miles across British-controlled Ethiopia to Addis Ababa; and then he traversed another thousand miles to one of the hottest places in the world, the French Overseas Territory of Djibouti. Granted political asylum, he lingered in Djibouti until the French authorities approved his papers and transported him to Toulouse. From Toulouse he went to Paris, and from Paris, via Czechoslovakia, he returned to Palestine.

I was naturally struck, as Shamir told me his story, by the extreme contrast between the prison careers of Yitzhak Shamir and Joseph Dakak – a contrast that corresponded to the extreme differences in their personal qualities and in their relationship to the political world. On the other hand, Yitzhak Shamir did have much in common with another fearless, politically monomaniacal and possibly lethal military internee, Jim O'Neill – a similarity which even extended to membership of guerrilla movements that had friendly dealings with the Nazis.

In its anti-British zeal, Lehi attempted to form an alliance with the Nazis, who were viewed as mere 'persecutors'. Towards the end of 1940, the leader of Lehi, Joseph Stern, sent an agent, Naftali Lubenchik, to Beirut to meet with von Hentig, a German Foreign Office official based in Vichy Syria. The meeting apparently resulted in Stern's agreement to active participation in the war on the German side on the condition that the aspirations of the Israeli freedom movement were recognized. After the Allied invasion of Syria in June 1941, Stern decided on a second mission to the Germans; he had in mind the very possible scenario of the Germans invading Egypt, the Turks surrendering to Hitler, and the British as a consequence being forced to evacuate Palestine. But the mission failed. The Lehi agent despatched to meet the Germans in December 1941 was arrested near Aleppo, and a few days later Joseph Stern was killed. Yitzhak Shamir, meanwhile, had joined the Stern Gang at precisely the time when Stern decided to continue his pro-German orientation.

I put to Shamir a remark attributed to him: *A man who goes forth to take the life of another whom he does not know must believe one thing and one thing only – that by his act he will change the course of history*. Looking straight at me, Shamir said, 'Active people in the underground are convinced it's their duty to fight. It is very dangerous, and when people expose themselves to dangerous missions they have to be doubly convinced they are right.' 'Was every single one of the killings perpetrated by Lehi justified?' 'Without doubt,' he said unhesitatingly. Shamir's eyes were fixed on mine in a steady, practically hypnotic gaze. 'We would not be here without that. We had to *fight* for the recognition by the world of our right to be masters of this country. Nobody was going to *give* us recognition. And we got it. When I came here as a twenty-year-old student in 1935, there were 300,000 Jews here – now there are four million. We have made large progress in spite of the fact that the British army, then an imperialist army, was against us, and all our Arab neighbours attacked us. In spite of this, we won the war. It's a miracle: this is our country!' He gave me a happy smile. 'It is written in the Bible that all would come back, and it became true.'

That was quite an accomplishment he credited himself with, I thought – and a quite stunning act of narrative to place himself, in effect, alongside the legendary protagonists of the Bible. I asked him about the Palestinians. 'There are twenty Arab countries here,' Shamir said calmly. 'They are all full of Arabs. They are all part of the Arab movement. If an Arab wants to live in an Arab independent country, he can go there. Jordan was a part of Palestine and now it is an independent Arab country with a Palestinian majority. There is not, therefore, a Palestinian nation without a state. But if they want to live here,' Shamir said, 'they have to live in a dignified way. We accept autonomy, and we propose self-government in a federal state, not an independent state. The Palestinians can handle their own rules and rights except for two issues: foreign relations and security matters.' He leaned forward and gently battered the table with a closed fist. 'This country belongs to us historically. We have the right to bring in Jewish people.' Shamir leaned back in his chair. 'We had a double aim: the independence and assembly of the Jewish people in this country. This has still not been implemented. We only have a third of the people. We *have* to bring in the other two-thirds' – here he leaned forward and once more began thumping his desk – 'otherwise we will not be able to resist. It is quite a mission, to bring everyone back. I believe in it. I believe we will get it done.'

I sensed what a formidable, single-minded adversary this octogenarian would still be. I was also struck by how seductive he was. I had never spent a morning tête-à-tête with a famous former head of state before, one who listened carefully to what I said and agreeably asked for my opinions from time to time. I didn't feel like mentioning Lehi's involvement with the Nazis, or pressing him about his strange ideas concerning the rights of Palestinians, whom he had once compared to cockroaches. It occurred to me that the last time a member of my family had been exposed to this brand of charisma was when Joseph Dakak had found himself with Franz von Papen.

'Do you know the Irish language?' Shamir asked with a smile. 'It interests me. We had the same phenomenon with Hebrew, and now, as you see, it's alive.' He gave me another cordial smile and asked whether I was myself involved in the Republican movement. I shook my head. 'You know,' Shamir said, 'when you are in the underground, the support of the community is most important.' He gave me a slow twinkling grin, and it seemed for a moment that he was going to wink. 'A lot of the British police in those days were Irishmen – and not all were very devoted to their service.' After a slight pause for effect, he continued: 'We have been very interested by the IRA. When I was in the underground, I read everything I could about the Irish confrontation with Britain, since Britain, at that time, was our common enemy. I read a lot about 1916, I read about de Valera and Collins. My pseudonym in the underground was Michael, you know, after Michael Collins.' Shamir said, 'They fought a long time, without result. All the Irish resistance move-ment was full of tragedies.'

6

Father . . . was a proud man and a high-principled one, though what his principles were based on was more than I ever discovered.

Frank O'Connor, *An Only Child*

Once, while horsing around at home in The Hague, my father grabbed my thirteen-year-old brother by the wrists and held him captive. 'This is an old IRA trick,' my father gloated; 'I've got you now.' My brother responded by simply banging his wrists together and bringing about a stinging collision between my father's hands. My father let go with a painful howl that turned into laughter – at himself, and at his son's devastating subversion of the mythic organization he'd invoked.

For my father to identify himself with the IRA, even jokingly, was unprecedented, and for an instant a connection – faint but nevertheless a little shocking – arose between him and the sinister body of men responsible for the bombings, kidnappings, robberies and killings which Dutch TV and BBC Radio brought to our attention. Aside from some incidents in Germany in 1978, the violence all took place in Ireland and Britain – that is, until 22 March 1979, when the British ambassador to The Netherlands, Sir Richard

Sykes, and his footman were shot dead in front of the ambassador's residence in The Hague. As in the Somerville shooting, two unknown gunmen ran away and were never caught. Even though Sykes was, at the time of his death, the Chairman of the Board of Governors of my school, the British School in The Netherlands – whose assembly hall was named the Sir Richard Sykes Memorial Hall – his killing quickly faded from my thoughts. Certainly, I didn't in any way link my father to that event. I had heard my father once or twice call himself a republican, but he obviously used the term in a loose and private sense, because he certainly didn't support the Provisional IRA or sing rebel songs or make anti-English cracks or go in for emotional recapitulations of Ireland's sad history. He would sometimes heatedly point out the hypocrisy of British pronouncements on Ireland, but there his visible embroilment in Irish nationalism would end. There was nothing radical or revolutionary or unlawful about him. My father was not a rebel.

Then, nearly twenty years after his friendly scuffle with my brother, I learned that my father had, after all, been in the Irish Republican Army.

The revelation came towards the end of that drive we took together from London to Oxford in 1996, a couple of intimate hours during which my father – who was reflective and open about his day-to-day thoughts and feelings, but not a man prone to reminiscing – disclosed more to me about the early formative events of his life than he had in the previous thirty years. The disclosures began after I asked him whether he knew that his uncle Jack Lynch had been in charge of the bombing campaign in England in 1939. 'No, I didn't know,' he answered, unamused. After a pause, he added, 'Did *you* know that I was in the IRA?' A silence fell in the car. We were south-east of Oxford, in a deeply English landscape of orderly fields and low, cultivated hills. The silence continued as I mentally circled the new information like a stroller who has happened on one of those old mines, buried for decades, that English beaches occasionally regurgitate. Then my father said, 'Son, I'd like to talk about how I saw it, about my perspective; I'm afraid you might have a romantic view of the whole business. In reality, it was seedy and mediocre. There was no philosophizing, no discussion, no rational identification of objectives and how to achieve them. Plus, there was incompetence. The officer in charge of one meeting arrived half an hour late – and this was the guy in charge! I said to him, "How are we supposed to accomplish anything if we start half an hour late?" It was a shambles, it was amateurish. After about a month or so, I just stopped going to the meetings.'

I asked my father whether my grandfather had pushed him towards the IRA. He shook his head. 'No. Nobody asked me to join, or even suggested it to me. I joined by myself, when I was seventeen or so.' 'What made you do it?' I asked, looking straight ahead at the traffic. My father hesitated. 'I was curious, I suppose,' he said slowly. 'Everybody else was involved, and I wanted to find out what it was all about. Also, there was a great upswell of support for Sinn Féin at the time, and I was an idealist, a bit of a dreamer.' He added, 'I was never attracted to the violence, though. Maybe I'd seen too much of it growing up.'

We drove on. Not long afterwards, the spires of Oxford appeared in the rainy distance. A few minutes later, we met up with my mother and my sister Elizabeth, and later still we watched my sister receive a postgraduate degree, in law, with others from her college, Somerville.

It was hard to say whether my father's truest act of rebellion lay in joining the IRA or in quitting it. A story my grandmother told illustrated the depth, and longevity, of his exposure to republicanism. Eileen O'Neill gave birth to my father, her third son, in her bedroom on 26 April 1939. Two nights later, Jim took the baby to see the priest in a borrowed IRA brigade car that was entirely covered in mud and slush: my grandfather had been out that evening in West Cork, leading exercises in snow that fell even as blossoms showed on the apple trees. Father Sheehan was not at the church, so Jim went round to his house. 'There's no christening today,' Father Sheehan said; but after Jim flashed him a wad of money, the priest agreed to perform a baptism. My swaddled infant father was taken from the brigade car to the font and quickly assumed into Christendom – but not, it might be said, before he had first been transported by Irish republicanism and set on a track that would lead, years later, to his presence in a car headed for the North, filled with guns and ammunition and men meaning to use them.

My father's growth into political consciousness corresponded to his growing awareness of his father's absence as an IRA internee. After Jim O'Neill returned to Cork in late 1944, when Kevin was five years old, the political clouds thickened still further in the domestic atmosphere – even though Jim, distraught by his experience of ostracism and infighting at the Curragh, did not rejoin the IRA and did not, in the face of his family's financial crisis and the difficulties of returning to civilian life, have the means or will for activism. But my grandfather's essential republicanism remained intact, and a couple of years after his release from the Curragh he began to support a party that promised to square the near-circle formed by his aversions for the institutional IRA, de Valera's government, and British rule in the North. Clann na Poblachta, founded in the summer of 1946, was led by the barrister and IRA veteran (and future Nobel Peace Prize winner) Seán MacBride. Although the Clann recognized the governmental organs of Eire, with the consequence that membership meant expulsion from the IRA, it was dedicated to the unification of Ireland and the downfall of de Valera's government, and for my grandfather this was enough. In 1948, to great general excitement, Clann na Poblachta had ten men elected to the Dáil and, in one of those bizarre hybrids generated by parliamentary pragmatism, formed a coalition government with the Blueshirt party, Fine Gael. In 1949, the Republic of Ireland came into being. The new State's constitution laid claim to the whole of Ireland as the national territory, but in many republican eyes the declaration of statehood poured juridical and symbolic cement on the border with Northern Ireland. Jim was confirmed in his bitter distrust of constitutional politics, and by 1950 or so, the link between the IRA and the O'Neill family began to revive.

The IRA, at this time, was still trying to recover from the destructive effect of the internment years. No military action of consequence had been taken for the best part of a decade and the membership was fragmented and demoralized. There was little for a volunteer to do other than to participate in commemorations, sell raffle tickets and political literature, and attend apparently pointless meetings. Then things slowly began to pick up. With the Dublin leadership exercising strict ideological control – the socialist activism that characterized pre-Emergency republicanism was no longer tolerated – the organization slowly regrouped. In June 1954, after the famous raid on Gough Barracks in Armagh, in which 250 rifles, seven Sten guns, nine Bren guns and forty training rifles were stolen from the enemy, the IRA once more caught the public imagination. In around August 1954, my uncles Jim (eighteen) and Brendan (seventeen) applied to join the IRA; in September 1954, they were duly sworn in. The brothers joined Cork No. 1 Brigade. 'Because of who we were,' Brendan said, 'we had no problem getting in.'

Like my father, Jim and Brendan said they joined the IRA of their own accord, without their father's prompting or knowledge, even. 'But after we joined,' Brendan said, 'Father never discouraged us. He would drive us out to the training camps, where we would have theory and practical classes in warfare: dismantling weapons, bombs, unarmed combat, and so on. The poaching gave us good fieldwork experience. It was a very serious thing to do with your life at that age,' Brendan said. 'You were liable to be sent off at any moment.'

This was true. Moreover, the success of the Armagh raid was exceptional. In 1953, three volunteers received eight-year prison sentences after being caught in possession of a cache of weapons stolen from Felsted School in Essex (where, over three hundred years previously, Oliver Cromwell had been a pupil); and in October 1954, a month or so after Jim and Brendan joined the IRA, a failed raid on a British army barracks in Omagh, Co. Tyrone, resulted in the capture of eight young volunteers. They were sentenced to ten years' imprisonment. Among them was Seán O'Callaghan, whose sister, Rosalie, Brendan would later marry.

The republican cause received a great boost in May 1955, when Sinn Féin, since 1950 effectively the civilian wing of the IRA, polled over 150,000 votes in elections in Northern Ireland and won two seats in the Westminster Parliament. This was followed, in June, by a good showing at local elections in the South. Republican exhilaration spread across Ireland, and Kevin O'Neill briefly joined his two older brothers in the IRA.

As for the boys' father, he was (in Brendan's words) one of the most reliable unofficial men the IRA had in Cork, someone who could be trusted to dump arms, transport people, raise funds, and quietly put his experience and contacts at the disposal of the movement. Brendan said that Tadhg Lynch, who had also denounced the leadership and placed himself at the periphery of the movement, was likewise able to do much valuable unofficial work.

In 1956, the IRA Army Council decided that the IRA was strong enough to embark on its first major military initiative since the 1939 English campaign. It was resolved that flying columns would penetrate the Six Counties and engage in a guerrilla war. The objective was to disrupt the occupying power's centres of administration by cutting all its lines of communication – telephone, rail, road – and thereby force British withdrawal from the border regions of Tyrone, Fermanagh and South Derry. The designated enemy was the British army; the overwhelmingly Protestant Irish members of the Royal Ulster Constabulary and the B-Specials (a civilian militia) were not targets and were only to be shot as a last resort of self-defence.

On Friday 7 December 1956, Jim and his brother Brendan received notification that IRA men were to present themselves immediately at a place in Mayfield, in the north of Cork city, for active service. The call-up came as a surprise, and Brendan had to ask Kevin, who lay sick in bed, to look after a dinner date that weekend. As Brendan and Jim were packing their things, their mother came up the stairs to the bedroom with a tray for Kevin. She said, 'I know you won't be back this time.' Brendan said, 'We will, Mother, we will, we'll be back on Sunday night at the latest.' My grandmother said, 'I don't care if you get ten years or twenty, but don't come back cowards.'

However, Uncle Jim returned from Mayfield within a few hours, in tears: the Army would not allow brothers from the same family, or newly married men, to go up, and five such volunteers were sent home. Brendan, though, was one of around twenty Corkmen to leave on the night of 7 December in a truck filled with straw. They were driven to billets in Co. Meath, where they stayed until Tuesday 11 December. Then they crossed into the Six Counties and met up with columns from Limerick and Dublin. The combined forces numbered fifty or sixty men. They were split up into units of eight or nine under the command of men who'd already been planted in the North a month or two previously. They were to go into action that night.

Back in Cork, Jim and Eileen O'Neill waited for news. My grandfather, who knew nothing about the raid in advance, was very upset that his sons had not confided in him. 'The worst time was the waiting,' Grandma said. 'Oh, that was terrible. Then the news broke on the radio of the first attack, and I felt relieved.'

The news was that, in the early hours of 12 December 1956, IRA units had attacked, with varying degrees of success, targets such as a transmitting station, a radar installation, a courthouse, a Territorial Army building, a B-Specials' hut, a bridge, and an army barracks. The following day, the IRA issued a proclamation announcing that, 'Spearheaded by Ireland's freedom fighters, our people in the Six Counties have carried the fight to the enemy. . . . Out of this national liberation struggle a new Ireland will emerge, upright and free.' The famous Border Campaign of the winter of 1956/57 had begun.

That first night, Brendan's unit was given the job of attacking Lissanelly Barracks, which was to the rear of Omagh army barracks, and stealing arms. Brendan's task was to take the guard room with a man called Bertie Murphy. In order to penetrate the barracks, a breach had to be blown in its wall, and two men drove off to a quarry at Mountfield, seven miles away, to steal gelignite. 'But,' Brendan said, 'the two fellows never returned; and just as we were getting into position to attack, all hell suddenly broke loose: the attacks had started all over the North and the barracks had gone on the alert.' Brendan's unit withdrew into the Sperrin Mountains, near Gortin, Co. Tyrone, and waited for a few days and nights in the trees, frozen cold.

Brendan returned to Cork in February 1957. He and other young veterans of the Border Campaign were sent on an intensive training course and made training officers. They trained two nights a week and every weekend: the campaign in the North was still going on and replacements were needed for the large numbers of volunteers who were being arrested. The Border Campaign had not, as had been hoped, decisively swung public opinion behind the IRA, and the security forces in the Republic were proving to be assiduous in their pursuit of IRA men who came within their jurisdiction. To make matters worse, internment at the Curragh was reintroduced in July 1957 by Éamon de Valera, who'd been voted back into power in the March election. All but one of the IRA leadership was picked up in the sweep – Seán Cronin, the IRA Chief of Staff, avoided capture by holing up at the Dublin house of Tadhg Lynch.

A year after the introduction of internment, the Border Campaign was still dragging on – but not, in the view of uncle Brendan, anywhere near boldly enough. When a plan he'd devised to ambush an enemy patrol at the border near Belleek, Co. Fermanagh was not sanctioned, my uncle's frustration led him to strike out on his own.

And so, in September 1958, three O'Neill brothers – Brendan, Jim (who had resigned from the IRA in sympathy with Brendan) and Kevin – drove up to Dublin with their uncle Jack Lynch and Brendan's friend Jim Lane. The boot of the car was filled with weapons retrieved from dumps in West Cork. The plan was to spend the night in Dublin with Tadhg Lynch and the next day drive on to the Six Counties, where Jim and Brendan O'Neill and Jim Lane were to engage the enemy. Kevin, who according to uncle Jim had been 'roped' into going along, was to drive the car back to Cork, even though he barely knew how to drive.

Tadhg was not home when the five men reached Dublin, so they stopped in O'Connell Street and had a meal at a pub called the Green Rooster. At midnight they got back into the car and headed back towards Tadhg's. Driving through Dublin at that time of night was a hazardous business, since the laws against drinking and driving made an exception in favour of persons deemed to be travellers – i.e., persons returning home from their 'bona fide', a pub five miles or more from their home – and consequently the roads after closing-time were full of cars weaving their way homeward across the city. The O'Neills were driving along the Ballymun Road when a van suddenly cut across them. There was a smash. Jim and Brendan went through the windscreen, breaking their noses and, in Jim's case, losing consciousness. The van driver immediately restarted his engine and drove away from the scene. Then guards appeared, asking questions and nosing around the scene of the accident. The Corkmen had no option but to keep calm and answer the questions asked of them and hope that the boot of the car was not examined. Eventually the guards completed their inquiries and set off after the hit-and-run driver. My father quickly removed the weapons from the boot and stowed them under the hedge of a nearby garden.

The police caught up with the driver of the van, Connolly, and brought charges against him. At the trial, a barman gave evidence that Connolly had been drinking at his establishment for many years and customarily drank a few whiskies and five or six pints in a night; Connolly's counsel accordingly submitted that his client, with such a pedigree and experience as a drinker, could not have been intoxicated on the night in question, during which his consumption of alcohol had not exceeded his regular quota. The submission was accepted by the judge, and the accused was acquitted of driving whilst drunk and convicted of the less serious charge of dangerous driving. My uncles Jim and Brendan, and great-uncle Jack Lynch, who had broken a wrist, received compensation for the injuries they suffered in the crash, though it was not until 1977 that Brendan discovered that in flying head-first through the windscreen he had fractured his neck in four places.

Despite their injuries, Brendan and Jim checked themselves out of hospital on the night of the accident. Jim was too hurt to travel on and spent three days recuperating at Tadhg's place before returning to Cork by train; Kevin also turned back for Cork.

Brendan and Jim Lane, meanwhile, continued north in a hired car. But the car turned out to be defective and would only go in first gear, and the two guerrillas were forced to dump their weapons and return home.

After their exploits became known, the IRA issued a statement disassociating itself from Brendan O'Neill. When my grandfather raised the matter with an IRA man at a republican commemoration, the IRA man, a cigarette dangling from his lip, answered with an insolent air; and the next thing he knew, an open hand had slapped him across the face and knocked his cigarette from his mouth. The hand belonged to my grandmother.

On Christmas Eve of 1958, only three months after the crash in Dublin, Brendan and Jim Lane set off to the North once more, determined to carry out the Belleek ambush the next day. 'But it was a white Christmas,' Brendan said, 'and the action had to be aborted because the snow cracked underfoot like glass and the target would have been alerted to our approach. We walked the seventeen miles back to Kinlough, hoping for another day. That day never came, and we headed back to Cork.'

Brendan and Jim Lane did not give up there, though. They returned to the North the following year, and, with their friend Charlie Ronayne, participated unofficially in the IRA's Border Campaign. All told, Brendan said, he went up three or four times. Aside from a reference to setting fire to a Territorial Army building in Garrison, Brendan was not inclined to detail the actions his unit had taken. A lot of time was spent subsisting, he said, moving from house to house. When the IRA officially abandoned the Border Campaign in January 1962 (the number of fatal casualties of the campaign – eight IRA men; two civilians; two men from the republican splinter group Saor Uladh; six RUC men – said something about its relatively ineffectual nature), Brendan joined another group and continued his underground activities until 1963. He was involved in securing control of arms that others proposed to give away to Welsh nationalists, and, finally, in a fruitless scheme to capture the newly appointed Unionist Prime Minister of Northern Ireland, Captain Terence O'Neill (no relation).

My father's flirtation with the armed struggle against the British ended with the disastrous venture with his brothers, an episode that afterwards took shape in his mind as pure comedy. As for Uncle Jim, although he never re-enlisted after his resignation from the IRA in 1958, he remained a republican, and when the violence in the North began he sympathized with the Provisional IRA. He never became involved with the Provos but supported them in parades, commemorations, and collections for prisoners' dependants. Then something happened that changed his political outlook. Jim – a gentle man who, after retiring from a long career as a quality controller for Ford, drove a van for disabled people – told me his story when I visited him and his wife, my aunt Kitty, at their house in Cork. My uncle, who began by telling me that Kitty's uncle, Billy Horgan, was shot dead by the Black and Tans, spoke softly and fluently, at dictation speed.

'In 1984, when I was hospitalized for three days for a minor matter, Jim said, I learned from Kitty that the wife of a neighbour, John Cochrane, was looking for me. John was forty-five and a father of eight; he belonged, I knew, to some republican organization – either the IRA or the INLA. When I came out of hospital on Thursday, Eileen Cochrane (who neither supported nor objected to John's politics) said John had been missing since Tuesday. She asked whether I could find out if he was away on IRA business. So I tried to help, and was up till 2 a.m. trying to contact people in the movement; but to no avail. The following day, I went to another contact, who put me in touch with another fellow, who put me in touch with the No. 2 of the Cork Brigade. I met the No. 2. I told him we were worried because John Cochrane suffered from epilepsy. He said he'd look into it. "I'll call you when the Angelus bells stop ringing," he said. At six o'clock, the phone rang. The voice said, "There's no match this weekend, and even if there was, the man you're looking for wouldn't even be a sub." I passed this on to Eileen, and then I accompanied her to the Gardai station at Union Quay. We asked whether John Cochrane was being held; they assured me he wasn't. So we went to the *Cork Examiner* offices with a photograph of John and took out a missing person's notice.

The next day, at lunchtime, I heard screaming outside the house. It was Eileen, screaming that they'd found a body on the silage heap at Ballincollig; and straightaway we were fairly sure. By this stage, I'd learned that John had been an IRA information officer for two years but that he'd been relieved of his post because of his epilepsy. On Sunday morning, the guards came round to ask whether I'd identify the body at the morgue. John's father and brother-in-law came with me. They were not allowed into the morgue, where Dr John Horbison, the State pathologist, was still working on the body. I went in alone. There was so much damage to the head that I had to walk out of the mortuary to compose myself. Then I went back in and identified John. He'd been shot through the temple. They had shot him as an informer. I went back to my contacts to throw a few fucks into their faces and tell them what I thought of their organization. They tried to reassure me that they knew what they were doing, but I later found out that it was a fellow called O'Callaghan from the North who was the informant and to cover his tracks he'd fingered John Cochrane. It was a crowd from Belfast that came down to shoot Cochrane. All the while, the OC here continued to insist that Cochrane was the informer.' Jim paused. His arms were crossed and resting on the table. He said, in the same measured tone he used when reminiscing about his childhood, 'I heard that on Tuesday John was seen running through a department store, running through coat-racks. They left him on a pile of dung and tyres. And that's why I think my father's five years at the Curragh were a waste of time.'

I wondered a little about my uncle's disillusionment, because in the context of the war in Ireland the shooting of a man wrongly believed to be an informer was not a novel or especially atrocious occurrence; indeed, since practically no lethal military campaign can limit its fatalities to enemy combatants, the killing of John Cochrane, taken in isolation, could even be said to be of little significance in the cold business of deciding whether or not the war, as a whole, was justified. But for Jim, republicanism was not a cold-hearted, unemotional business. And although he gave up supporting the IRA, he did not give up his dream of a united Ireland –

literally. My uncle said to me, in a tone of slight amazement, 'When I was in my teens, I had a very vivid dream that the Six Counties were united with the Twenty-six, and that we were marching in the North on a dead straight, undulating road, and there were throngs of people lining the road. When I finally went to the North, in 1985, on holiday, I came across a place that was intensely familiar. It came to me: these were the roads I'd dreamt of, and these were the throngs, with bands and banners.'

'Blow him off the road!' Brendan shouted as a dawdling car in front of us failed to make way. 'Go on, overtake him now! Go on, Joe!' But I held back, unsure about the oncoming traffic and all the while anxious to maintain a prudent distance between our car and the one ahead. 'Keep up, keep up!' Brendan cried in disbelief, 'keep up or somebody'll slip in!' He shook his head in despair. 'Ah, Joe, you'll never make a getaway driver.'

We were on a road trip, heading for the north of the island to revisit some of the places where Brendan had been active, as he put it, in the late 'fifties and early 'sixties and finally in 1969. When I finally overtook the car ahead of us, Brendan's arm suddenly shot out and his hand slammed on the steering wheel to produce a terrific blast of the horn. 'You're nothing but a dirty bastard!' he furiously yelled as we passed the car, his head thrusting out of the window. I started laughing. My uncle, I had discovered, was a comically bad car passenger.

That this trait in him came as a revelation showed up the limits of our previous acquaintance. I only knew Brendan, the brother with whom my father had maintained the closest and most enduring fraternal bonds, in an innocent, avuncular context: as a collector and cracker of terrible corny jokes; as an ex-hurler for Cork (a hard player, not beyond skulduggery); as a runner of marathons (including the New York City marathon); and, especially, as a very useful golfer playing off around a four handicap at the age of sixty and still able to drill a 3-iron a couple of hundreds of yards into the wind blowing through the links of Ballybunion Golf Club, where he was a life member. More recently, I had started to catch sharper views of another, more political life. It turned out that Brendan had been a republican activist from the age of eleven or twelve, when he helped his father campaign for Clann na Poblachta by putting up posters and handing out leaflets. At fourteen, he left school: he found a summer job as a time-clerk on a building site, and when the time came to go back to North Monastery he was determined to stay on. My grandparents, very doubtful about the idea, eventually relented. Brendan's life came to be dedicated to trade unionism and political action of one kind or another. He went to jail for principled non-payment of service charges imposed by Cork Corporation, and he spent the night before Nelson Mandela's release from prison stitching a banner of the African National Congress, of which he'd been a member for twenty years. When dawn broke, the banner's fluttering colours trespassed on the flagpole of Cork County Council. Of course, these stories were irresistible to an establishmentarian and politically sedentary – and politically guilt-ridden – person like me. They revealed my uncle as a driven and adventurous radical who, by his actions, constantly evinced his commitment to the value of political resistance and his distance from the bourgeois conception of life as an economic adventure. So I wasn't surprised when Brendan said that the old IRA campaigns, and in particular the internment experiences of his father's generation of IRA men, should be more widely known and written about, or when he suggested that the two of us embark on outing to the North. 'I'll show you round, introduce you to a few people,' he said, 'and you'll make of it what you want.'

Setting up the trip was a tricky affair: when I arrived in Cork, in late May 1997, campaigning in the national elections was in full swing, and Brendan was heavily involved on behalf of Paddy Mulcahy, a teacher contesting the impoverished constituency of North Cork Central as an independent candidate. Mulcahy's platform – 'DON'T BE SOLD OUT AGAIN – ELECT A PROVEN FIGHTER FOR THE RIGHTS OF ORDINARY PEOPLE. . . . If you want to hit back at the corrupt political establishment vote for Paddy Mulcahy, the anti-establishment candidate with the best chance of taking a seat in Cork North Central' – was set out in a leaflet which also contained an endorsement from Brendan O'Neill:

> Having given a lifetime of service to workers whether employed or unemployed, I am now calling on all my friends and colleagues to come out on election day and give your number one to Paddy Mulcahy. Paddy Mulcahy has always been a great ally and comrade of mine. He went to jail rather than surrender. Put Paddy in the Dáil – he will be a forceful ally to the labour movement and will fight conscientiously for social justice and the rights of the people.

Brendan was particularly concerned about the welfare of travellers, who, he said, had long been the object of discrimination and prejudice in Ireland, 'probably one of the most racist countries in the world'. When I met him after he'd paid a canvassing visit to a travellers' site in North Cork, he was fuming. 'It's a disgrace. The conditions they've to put up with are a fucking disgrace. I can't leave it at that. We've got to do something about it: keep pushing for their recognition as an ethnic minority, keep at them to organize into committees to enable them to decide what they want.'

A few days after the election (at which, not unexpectedly, Paddy Mulcahy failed to win a seat), I drove round to Brendan's house in Blackrock, an affluent neighbourhood in south Cork. The tone of the house – an attractive modernist structure of glass and wood that gave on to the large communal lawn – was an appealing mixture of the zoological and the political. Pets (a cat, a dog, a turtle) milled about, their presence largely due to my animal-loving aunt Rosalie; and, as ever, the exposed brick walls were hung with Brendan's photographically accurate black and white portraits of some of his heroes: Che Guevara, Mandela, Lenin, James Connolly. Brendan's attachment to political father-figures extended to Jim O'Neill. 'My father was a socialist,' he said. 'I'm surprised he never joined the Communist Party.' 'I'm not surprised at all,' Rosalie commented sharply. 'It would have meant excommunication from the Church.'

It was early morning. We were heading north that day. The first

question that arose was whose car to use – mine, with English
number-plates, or Brendan's, with Republic of Ireland plates. From
a security viewpoint, driving in English plates – which closely
resembled Northern Ireland plates – was probably safer. A few
weeks before, two Catholics had respectively been shot and beaten
to death, and it was possible that another loyalist campaign of
random sectarian killings had started. On the other hand, in the
year since the Dockland and Aldwych explosions in February 1996,
violence by republican paramilitary groups had increased dramati-
cally. In June 1996, a huge IRA explosion in the centre of
Manchester injured over 200 people; a month later, a bomb blew up
an Enniskillen hotel; in September, raids of London houses (in the
course of which an IRA man was shot dead) uncovered ten tons of
explosives; in October, two large bombs exploded inside the British
army's headquarters in Northern Ireland, injuring thirty-one; in
November 1996, a 600lb bomb was discovered outside the RUC
headquarters in Derry; in the run-up to the British general election
in April 1997, motorway and airport traffic in England was dis-
rupted by bomb warnings; and in May, an RUC officer was shot
dead as he drank in a Belfast bar. The IRA was not responsible for
all of these actions. The Irish National Liberation Army claimed
the killing of the RUC man, and the Enniskillen hotel bombing and
the attempted bombing of the Derry RUC headquarters was the
work of a republican faction – the 'Real IRA', it came to style
itself – which disapproved of Sinn Féin-IRA's continuing attempts
to reach a settlement that fell short of a definitive commitment to a
united Ireland. It was becoming clearer that the Sinn Féin leadership, whose principal figures were the Provisional IRA veterans
Gerry Adams and Martin McGuinness, was located at the flexible
end of the spectrum of militaristic republicanism.

   In the end, it was decided to travel in Brendan's car, not only
because it was more roadworthy than mine but because Brendan –
although he didn't say so in such terms – was uncomfortable with
the connotations of entering the Six Counties in an English vehicle.
His sensitivity to symbolic acts and the narratives they set in motion
was evident as soon as we set off, when he switched on the radio to

a pre-set Irish language station; and later, to pass the time as we drove through the counties of Limerick, Clare, Mayo, and Sligo, we listened to tapes of various artists singing songs in Irish about emigration and drinking and the Great Famine. Brendan was himself full of snatches of lyrics and verse that he uttered from time to time with emotion that contrasted with the dry and precise tone he liked to use in speaking about his unusual life. He was emphatically intellectually independent and unafraid to challenge orthodoxy. The 1957 Border Campaign, for example, he coldly described as 'dumb. The strategy was to create no-go areas, so that the British would sue for peace and settle. We had too much manpower – there must have been a hundred of us up – and we didn't involve local people. And I always had difficulty with the narrowness of the republican outlook. There was a lack of socialist policy, and the movement often gave the impression that it was only interested in getting the Brits out and handing the North to the employing classes.'

During the Border Campaign, Brendan said, it was a very difficult for outsiders not to be conspicuous. The IRA men had to move from safe-house to safe-house, where they might stay for days or even weeks, subsisting and only sporadically carrying out discreet reconnaissance work. One of these safe-houses was a farm near Kinlough, a village in that wild, littoral sliver of Co. Leitrim that insinuates itself between the counties of Sligo and Donegal. That was the first place that Brendan was taking me.

Leitrim is perhaps the poorest county in Ireland, and it is a saying that even the crows in its skies go hungry. Brendan, relying on topographical memories that were decades old, drove the car along a series of long, forgettable lanes flanked by trees and bushes. The soil was more fertile here than near Sligo, where the fields were separated by rocks unearthed from the land, but there was barely a house to be seen, and no traffic. We drove on, the sense of remoteness increasing as the presence of the Dartry Mountains, bleak, flat-topped heights, grew to the south-east. Then we stopped by concrete gate-posts set into a low hedge that served as a boundary of a farm. 'This is it,' Brendan said.

We got out of the car. There was a closed gate; a field of coarse

grass with a black cow and a white cow; a pair of gravel wheel-
tracks that led crookedly into a copse about a hundred and fifty
yards away, where two small stone cottages could be glimpsed; a
looming table-mountain rising behind the farm; and, in the dim far
distance – it was an overcast, colourless afternoon – another flat-
topped mountain, Ben Bulben, on the far side of which was the
grave of W.B. Yeats. There was no sign of anyone at the farm.
Brendan said that the brothers – if they were still alive – might be
out in one of the fields.

We climbed over the gate. Under a knot of trees to the left was
a monument. A succession of cement slabs rose in steps to a
shoulder-high platform where there was an inscribed stone and a
Celtic cross. The inscription, in Irish, was in memory of a grandfather of the Connolly brothers shot dead on 14 September 1920 by
the Black and Tans, and of an uncle shot dead on 20 March 1922 by
Free State soldiers. We walked up to the farmhouse in the copse. It
was a small, untidy, unfeminized place, and the door was unlocked.
Brendan called out into the musty air of the house and then called
out in the yard. There was no response. We turned back.

As we drove north from Kinlough, Brendan reminisced about his
last trip to the North in 1969. It was a time of protests led by the
Northern Ireland Civil Rights Association against systematic anti-
Catholic discrimination in housing and employment and political
representation, demonstrations, civil disobedience, riots, police
crackdowns and sectarian hostilities. Events culminated in the
explosive violence of August 1969, when the Catholics of the
Bogside threw up defensive barricades in the face of attacks from
Protestant mobs. Barricades also went up in Belfast, which by mid-
August was a war-zone with over a hundred gunshot casualties in
hospital. As civil war and the pogrom of Catholics threatened, the
government in the Republic set up army hospitals along the border,
and Jack Lynch, the Taoiseach, said, 'We won't stand idly by.'
'When Lynch said that we felt untouchable,' Brendan recalled. 'In
August, Eddie Williams (then OC in Cork) and Jim Lane showed
up at the back door, ready to go up, but your uncle Declan was getting married, so I said I couldn't go until Wednesday. At that time

Rosalie was about to give birth and Father advised me not to go up; but if I hadn't gone, I might have regretted it all my life. We got Tom Barry to get us submachine guns, known as can-openers, and they were sent north. They came from sympathizers inside the Irish army in Tipperary. It was £75 for an unwrapped Thompson submachine gun and £75 for a thousand rounds. My pseudonym was Jimmy Neilson, and I wore spectacles with plain glass and my hair brushed down.'

Brendan spent three weeks in Derry that summer, organizing: he wasn't involved in the petrol bombs and stone-throwing, which was for the kids. 'It was a carnival atmosphere,' he said. Some of the Corkmen treated the whole thing like an excursion and had to be sent back.

In December 1969, when a measure of civil order had gradually returned, the IRA Convention, acting in response to the developments in the North, voted to end abstentionism, the policy by which seats won by Sinn Féin in Westminster and the two Irish parliaments were not taken up. Not everybody favoured the change, and the dissident faction split from the official IRA – which, in the eyes of many, was already fatally distracted by Marxist-Leninist notions of unifying the island through class struggle – to form the Provisional IRA.

While he was up in the North in 1969, Brendan stayed for a time with a couple who had sheltered him in the late 'fifties, Frank and Mary Morris. They lived in Convoy, a small market town in Donegal which lies in green, undulating land near the border towns of Derry, Letterkenny and Strabane. We drove there from Kinlough.

Frank and Mary Morris owned a shop and warehouse in the centre of Convoy, and a grocers' wholesale business now largely run by their two sons. Frank was seventy-six years old, a slight, trim, gentle man with a faint voice; he devoted a lot of energy to the Local Enterprise Scheme, he said, and in the recent UK elections he had canvassed for Sinn Féin. Mary was younger, large-eyed, and calm-spoken. She said she was a great admirer of John Hume, the future Nobel Laureate and leader of the (non-violent) nationalist party, the SDLP, and of Mrs Hume, a personal friend. The couple – very kindly, very pleased to see Brendan – looked back fondly but unsentimentally on the days when their place was a safe-house and packed like a fish-barrel with Corkmen. 'The Cork boys were the best and the Dubliners the worst,' Mary said.

After dinner with Frank and Mary, we visited Theresa Peoples, who gave Brendan shelter in the late 'fifties and again in 1969. She lived outside Convoy in a handsome farmhouse filled with unusually fine items of furniture and china. We found Theresa, who was in her eighties, devastated by the death of her brother John-Joe seven months previously; she had not left the house in all that time. Theresa was immensely heartened and moved to see Brendan, and asked anxiously after the mother-of-pearl rosary she'd given him forty years ago. She had recently celebrated her golden anniversary as a Pioneer and she showed us the photograph of the bishop congratulating her. 'The present-day IRA are not like the 'fifties crowd at all,' Theresa said.

We spent the night at the Morris house, and the following morning drove towards the border. We were waved through the British army checkpoint, and very shortly afterwards approached – for the first time, in my case – the city of Derry.

The slogans, spray-painted on walls and hoardings in huge, brutal letters, hit us as soon as we entered the city. *INLA. ALL PARTY TALKS NOW. RELEASE ALL P.O.W.S NOW. REPATRIATE NOW*. We were in the Catholic part of Derry. The Protestant district lay on the other side of the Foyle, a beautiful and immense waterway that seemed altogether too magnificent for the small, gloomy city that rose in clusters of spires above the river's foggy banks. Brendan drove carefully; one false turn and we could have been swept away on a current of one-way traffic across the river. We drove up to the Creggan, as the heights of south Derry are known, and then descended the hill to the Bogside, where the gable end of a destroyed terrace of houses was preserved and painted with the famous words, first daubed during the disturbances in the late 'sixties, You Are Now Entering Free Derry.

Brendan, who has his mother's extraordinary memory for detail, was temporarily disoriented when we came to the Bogside. Changes had taken place since 1969 – blocks of flats had disappeared, new roads had been built – and it took him a few moments to reconcile the quiet new landscape with the urban battleground he had known. But we were in the right place, there was no doubt about that. Bunting strung out from garden rails to rooftops fluttered in celebration of St Columba, a 1400-year-old saint; kerbs and lamp-posts were painted green, white and gold; Irish tricolours fluttered from flagpoles; and huge, impressively detailed murals protested against the Orange parades through Catholic areas and exhorted remembrance of Bloody Sunday, 30 January 1972, when thirteen civilians were shot dead in the Bogside by British paratroopers.

We dropped in on the Bogside Sinn Féin Advice Centre. It occupied a small terraced house and was staffed by four striking dark-haired young women. Brendan chatted to the woman in charge, explaining that this was his first visit to Derry since 1969 and that I was writing a book about the internment days. The young woman smiled and said a few words of welcome, and then mentioned an old-timer, Barney McFadden, who had been in the movement for over sixty years. Barney (born 1921) arrived a few minutes later, and we sat down to talk in the privacy of a back room of the Sinn Féin office. Barney and Brendan found common ground almost immediately, and for an hour or so the two exchanged information and names of old volunteers, almost all deceased. Barney spoke about the historical project that now occupied his time, which was to produce a list of all those volunteers in 1910–30 period – who included a Protestant, he was especially proud to say – who'd never been properly acknowledged by the republican movement.

When we left, Brendan was thrilled. 'It feels great,' he said, as we walked back to the car, 'it's like a warm hug you're getting from the community.' He looked at me with a grin. 'It's a real buzz, isn't it? Don't you feel at home here, really at home?'

I smiled at Brendan. It was intoxicating to have been taken into the very core of the republican struggle and to feel solidarity with my oppressed kinfolk, but of course I did not feel at home on the Bogside. How could I, when simply to open my English mouth exposed me to prejudice and mistrust? When my experiences and my outlook, informed by a middle-class European upbringing, were so different from those of the people here? The Sinn Féin woman at the Advice Centre had remarked to me, 'We're not sectarian here; Derry's not like Belfast,' and I couldn't help marvelling, as we drove anxiously through suburbs daubed in red, white and blue, at the difference between her perspective and mine. As I saw it, a city divided into Catholic and Protestant halves was sectarian in character, and horribly so; and the assertion to the contrary, founded on a comparison with Belfast, was stunning. Was this woman unaware of the norms prevalent in the world outside the North of Ireland?

Brendan drove through Strabane and took a detour to Clady, Co. Tyrone, a small, untidy village that sits right on the border with the Republic. Near Clady, the river Finn is scruffy with weedy isles and broad enough to be spanned by a handsome stone bridge with seven arches. The quirk of the bridge is that its waist-high stone walls are serpentine; they wriggle along the flanks of the road in a series of bulges and nooks into which two or three men might crouch

without being visible from a distance. In January 1957, Brendan's
IRA unit passed the night in these recesses, vainly waiting for
British forces to respond to an explosion the unit had detonated.
'We blew a crater around here,' Brendan said, pointing to a spot on
the bridge. 'The object was to lure the enemy into an ambush. We
waited all night in the cold but British troops never came. In the
end, we narrowly avoided capture ourselves by the Free State
Army.'

   It was another foggy day, and the views up and down the river
were of blurred green farmland. On one bank, just by the bridge,
cows and horses grazed on thick scrub grass. I took a photograph of
my uncle beside a plaque attached to the bridge commemorating an
IRA man called Jim McGinn, 'who was killed on active service' on
15 December 1973. Brendan stood with his hands in the pockets of
his khaki trousers. He was wearing a navy-blue V-necked golfing
sweater and a button-down shirt with fine blue checks. His hair – a
full head, grey and cut short and spiky – was like my father's, and
his eyebrows, silver and thick like my grandfather's, lent further
solemnity to the dour and heavy-hearted expression with which he
gazed into the distance. It was an old-fashioned pose for the camera
that spoke of the gravity of the republican enterprise and of the

respect in which those who have given their lives for it are held, irrespective of how long ago they died; it also spoke of the extraordinary lengths to which the republican movement went to ensure that a volunteer's sacrifices were the tinder of his tragic remembrance. This exclusive emphasis on suffering and self-denial was, of course, a little deceptive, because political activists, even those who may be secretive extremists, generally derive sustenance and gratification from their activities, which are, after all, voluntary, and which inevitably attract a certain kudos. To outsiders, IRA men personified menace; but to those inside the movement, they were good-hearted and lovable figures invested with a certain high-minded nobility – cavaliers, even.

We left Clady and headed south-east, via Omagh, through Tyrone, which genealogical tradition holds to be the ancestral territory of the O'Neill family. Tyrone is a fluvial county, and we crossed or drove by the Mourne, Derg, Strule, Fairy Water and Owenreagh rivers. As we approached the Blackwater river, whose course marks the border for a few miles, I asked Brendan what he thought ought to be the objective of settlement negotiations by Sinn Féin in the apparently imminent event of the IRA announcing a second ceasefire. Brendan said carefully, 'There should be a declaration of British withdrawal from Ireland in twenty-five years' time. Such a declaration, coupled with a ceasefire, would perhaps be a way forward. It would give unionists time to adjust to the reality of it,' Brendan said.

At that moment we arrived at the border village of Aughnacloy, where two armed and camouflaged British soldiers were stopping cars going south. We wound down our windows. 'What is the purpose of your trip?' asked one young soldier, inspecting the driver's licence that Brendan had handed up at his request. 'We're going to Dublin,' Brendan said. 'We've come from Derry.' 'Brilliant, thank you,' the soldier said as he handed back the licence. 'Thank you,' Brendan said politely, taking his time to replace the document in the proper compartment in his wallet. It was, in its way, a small gesture of political resistance: he was not going to be rushed in his own country by any British soldier.

We resumed our conversation. Brendan, elaborating on his earlier statement, said that in twenty-five years' time the likes of Ian Paisley would be dead and a whole new generation would have grown up in the knowledge that the change would take place.

This proposition – that objections to a united Ireland would dissolve in the face of sufficient notice of unification – was obviously problematic, but I didn't argue. Instead, I asked Brendan: 'In what way does the use of violence promote the objective of British withdrawal?'

He began by saying that if it wasn't for the civil rights movement in 1969, nothing would have been achieved.

'No,' I interrupted, 'I don't mean street violence – I mean the taking of life.' I was referring to the three thousand and more people who had been killed by the various armed groups, republican and loyalist and British, since 1969.

'Well,' Brendan said, 'there hasn't in fact been much physical force of that kind used, apart from on the soldiers and RUC men.'

Too surprised to say much else, I said, 'What has the killing achieved, though?'

'Well,' Brendan said, 'it got rid of Stormont, for one thing; and it put Northern Ireland on the map.'

I sensed we were heading for a historical debate, so I said, 'What I can't see is how *renewing* the campaign of violence, after we've had the ceasefire, promotes the objective of British withdrawal.'

Brendan, who was driving, did not respond. A few moments later, seething slightly, he said, 'Do you know, I know it's hatred, but I'd probably want to shoot those two soldiers anyway, even if there was a settlement. I'd just want to do it.'

The atmosphere in the car had suddenly chilled. I decided to press on anyway. It was uncivil of me, but as Brendan well knew, anyone who – rightly or wrongly – expects thousands of others to submit to the experience of death and ruinous injury ought to be prepared to submit to the experience of argument. Besides, Brendan was an unorthodox, independent thinker whom I admired. I wanted to tap into his insights. 'I'm just uncertain,' I said, upping the stakes, 'that the violence has achieved any more than thirty years of civil disobedience would have achieved. That's why I can't say that the killing has been necessary.'

Brendan drove on along the bending, tree-darkened road that took us through the Monaghan countryside. After a long silence, he said slowly, 'Joseph, did you have to do military service in the English army?'

'How do you mean?' I said.

'Oh, that's right,' Brendan said, still looking ahead, dawning comprehension in his tone, 'you wouldn't.'

Another silence descended. Now I was fuming, too, furious at the questioning of my patriotism – of my Irish nationality, even – and of my right to speak on the national question. Wasn't my opinion as valid as anybody's? Wasn't it my country, too?

Then, looking at it from Brendan's point of view, I could see why he might have reacted in the way he had. There are few things more provocative to Irish ears – even ears attached to a person of very mild views – than the sound of a voice in an English accent pronouncing on Ireland, a voice that packs into its drawling vowels centuries of racial condescension and seemingly ineradicable and wilful misconceptions about the rights and aspirations of the Irish people. For an Irishman, it can sometimes seem that there is no arguing with a voice of that kind, because it is precisely the voice of prejudice against arguments made by an Irishman. Did it lie in my English-sounding mouth to question Brendan? Why should he be confident that I was capable of understanding his viewpoint, that I was not regarding him through the eyes of a blinkered, indoctrinated member of the English establishment?

The fact was, I had spent no more that a year of my adult life in Ireland. As soon after my birth as they were able to, my parents removed me from Cork and set off on a global journey that took the family to Africa and Asia and finally, when I was six years old, continental Europe. When my father's project in Rotterdam came to an end in 1975, the family stayed put while he worked in the fjords of Norway, the Borneo jungles and the Arabian deserts, flying back as often as he was able. Aside from a couple of years at the French Lycée in The Hague, I was educated at the British School in The

Netherlands, an expensive yet unpretentious day school, where uniforms were worn and the English educational curriculum was followed. The students were mainly the children of diplomats and of scientists and technocrats working for large enterprises like the European Space and Technology Centre, Shell Oil, and Unilever. It was a multinational set-up: I had British, Italian, Gambian, Australian, Portuguese friends. We were all in the same boat, pleasantly adrift from our native land. Necessarily, our relationship with that place was, to a greater or lesser degree, fantastical. For the non-British, the matter was doubly complicated, since in addition to cultivating an expatriate conception of our place of origin we had to construct a relationship with England, whose culture and educational qualifications we were acquiring at school and whose universities and jobs beckoned. For those of us from two different non-British countries, things were triply unstraightforward; quadruply so if, like me and my siblings, you spoke Dutch and hung out for many years with Dutch friends; and, finally, quintuply tricky if, on top of the aforementioned complexities, you spoke French at home.

But it never occurred to me, faced with Turkish, English, Dutch and French possibilities, to relinquish or even question my identity as an Irishman – not even when, walking as a teenager in The Hague, a couple of Dutch girls I'd never seen in my life shouted '*Vuile Turk!*' (Filthy Turk!) at me. I stoutly refused, as a cub scout of 1st The Hague, to utter the pack's ritual oath of loyalty to the Queen of England. I supported Irish national sports teams, fantasized about an all-Ireland soccer team – imagine McIlroy, McGrath, Whiteside and Brady in the same XI – listened to the Irish records I found at home and, of course, pored over books by Irish writers. Then, in 1980, my father's work took him to Aughinish Island, Co. Limerick, as project manager in the construction of a huge alumina processing plant. In January 1982, he got me a job there, too, as an unskilled 'general operative'. It was a political education of a kind. On my first morning at work I joined the Irish Transport and General Workers' Union, and on my first afternoon I went on strike: some welders had been dismissed by my father for refusing to work in the cold, bright weather, and the shop stewards had called on the men to 'hit the gate' in sympathy. So we did. When I got home that evening, I asked my father what I should do. 'You'll stay on strike until further notice,' he said. 'I'll not have any scabs in this house. One more thing,' he said, opening his newspaper as he sat down on the sofa. 'You're fired.' A day or two later, everybody was reinstated and went back to work.

My Ireland was six months spent in Limerick, a sidekick to Mick O'Sullivan, a mechanic, and Eugene Meaney, an electrician, kind and able men who tolerated the boss' clueless son and patiently milked him at lunch-time poker. By day I lugged toolboxes up tanks, changed the tyres of cranes, and wandered around dazed by tanks, pipes, cables and the innards of malfunctioning machinery. By night, having travelled home in a pick-up truck full of muddied men who made the sign of the cross each time a church or graveyard was passed, I holed up with my father in the Old Rectory of a village called Askeaton. It was a beautiful Georgian house with stables, a faded grass tennis court in the garden, ancient meat-hooks hanging in the cellars, high walls, and a few acres of tall woods where dark birds roosted. My father rented it from the Church of Ireland. It was one of the imposing Anglo-Irish houses whose occupants had for so long thrown a fine net over all Ireland. It was as far away as you could get in Ireland from the Bogside, and I felt at home there.

After Limerick, I went to Cambridge University (in narrow preference to Trinity College, Dublin, which my brother and sister later attended) to study law. Even though I had spent barely a month of my life in England, it was a natural move. My far-off affiliation to Ireland continued as before, and when John Hume came to Cambridge to talk about the need to create an inclusive Ireland (an Ireland that could accommodate a mongrel like me), I was there, cheering him on; and when the time came, in the spring of 1985, my final year, to write a dissertation on ethics and the criminal law, I solemnly set myself the task of answering the question, 'Is the IRA justified in killing people?' – thereby becoming the latest in the generations of O'Neills and Lynches to ponder the means and ends of Irish freedom.

As is so often the case with political ideas formed early in one's life, the conclusions I reached had a lasting influence on me. I concluded, first, that although nationalists in the North might be obliged to obey the laws of Northern Ireland, under no prominent and well-recognized liberal theory of political obligation – theories of social contract and consent (Hobbes, Locke, Rousseau, etc.), or rights theories, or justice and equality theories (Rawls, Dworkin, etc.), or theories of utility – were they *obligated* to. Second, that Northern Ireland was accordingly a morally wrong political entity. Third, that it followed the unionist devotion to the preservation of the status quo was, prima facie, morally wrong and nationalists had good cause to seek to change the status quo. Fourth (on the footing that nationalists were not racists and affirmed the *equal* right to autonomy of national groups, any change that failed to take account of unionist autonomy – e.g., a Dublin-governed united Ireland brought about by force, without unionist consent – would substitute the oppression of one national group for another. Fifth, violence directed at bringing about the unification of Ireland by force rather than by consensus was accordingly morally wrong. Sixth, violence directed merely at disturbing the status quo so as to provoke change short of unification (i.e., change that would reduce the inequality in the autonomy of the two national groups in Northern Ireland) was also wrong, since it could not be demonstrated that non-homicidal methods would be inadequately provocative. This was the point I'd try to make to Brendan; but as things turned out, I was later to have very real doubts it.

Of course, my analysis diverged from orthodox republican doctrine. Most importantly, it was a tenet not just of republicanism but of nationalism – the non-violent mainstream doctrine that a united Ireland is desirable and natural end – that the Protestant population did not really form a separate national group; and that, although they *perceived* themselves to be different from the nationalist Catholic majority (when I wrote my dissertation, only 8 per cent of Protestants identified themselves as 'Irish') and strongly asserted the same – on classic grounds: religion, ethnicity (Anglo-Scottish), political history (loyalty to the Crown), language (their national tongue was not Irish) – their self-perception was at bottom the product of false consciousness 'carefully fostered', in the words of the 1916 Proclamation of Independence, 'by an alien government'. This notion might have had some credence in 1916, but in modern times it was so obviously fantastical that, it seemed to me, no rational person could in all honesty subscribe to it – or inhabit the ideological construct it underpinned.

For a long time I believed that the strength of my analysis was that it was rational, deductive, and non-protagonistic. It didn't well up from inherited feelings of loss and outrage about the division of Ireland or from a received sense that the armed struggle for freedom was prima facie virtuous or evil. Nor did it bother me that I'd never been to the North, because the convictions of many, if not most, Irish people on the subject of the North crystallized before they had set foot there (Jim O'Neill was a case in point). But in the course of my visits to Ireland, I began to have second thoughts. First of all, I realized that the views I'd fastidiously held for a dozen years were inductive and proceeded, in reality, from a gut feeling that the violence I'd observed was for the worst – a gut feeling that could easily have resulted from my participation in British culture; and second, I wondered if I had taken sufficient account of the fact that the virtues of long-term political violence are rarely immediately apparent. What if I had overlooked something – missed, in my narrow rationalism, some wider truth? After all, why should my gut feelings be any more reliable than those of the republicans I'd met? It was not simply that these republicans were obviously kind and good people: it was, as I saw it, that they were undoubtedly *superior to me as moral agents*. They were conscientious and possessed of a sense of societal duty that was much stronger than mine. My grandmother and my uncle Brendan, for example, had spoken up and acted in relation to apartheid and to the rights of workers and ethnic minorities. I, meanwhile, had followed the self-serving, morally unvigorous paths of the business lawyer and novelist; I had enacted no change, done no good, made no effort on behalf of others. What it came down to was this: if their ethical intuitions were so accurate in civilian life, who was to say they had not got it right in relation to question of political violence in Ireland?

Sitting in the car with Brendan, stewing on our disagreeable exchange, I gradually calmed down. It didn't require much of an imaginative leap on my part to see that there *was* something fundamentally enraging about having foreign soldiers in your country, pointing guns at you and interrogating you and making you account for your movements; and, anxious to mend fences with my uncle – and sensing that it was somehow my place to give ground – I said as much to him.

We drove on towards Dublin and checked into a hotel in Rathmines. We ate dinner together, drank a bottle of wine, and played a couple of games of snooker. Towards the end of the evening, Brendan said, 'Joseph, I didn't answer your question today. The truth is, I don't want the unionists to suffer like nationalists have done; I don't want to force them. What I meant to say was that there is a foreign army in my country, and I think I have the right to take on that army and to seek to repel it. I claim a right to do that. It's that basic.' His eyes were wet. 'When my father was dying, he told me he'd like to be propped up on a car seat with a machine gun in his hands and to charge that way into British soldiers. He wanted to die like that, usefully, killing as many as he could.'

'I blame the Camp for his sickness,' Grandma said to me when I got back to Cork.

The trouble started two years before my grandfather's death. At first, he thought it was an ordinary stomach ailment and he went to see Dr O'Connor, who was retired. He examined Jim, put him on tablets, and told him to see Dr Barker, my grandmother's physician. Dr Barker referred Jim to the hospital, and there his true condition was diagnosed.

Jim continued to go to work through his illness, even though the doctors had ordered him to rest. In February 1973, while in lodgings in Tarbert, Co. Limerick he was too unwell to eat the pig's head and onions served by his landlady. My uncle Terry, who had work to do in Limerick, caught a lift up from Cork and met his father for a drink. Terry took care to prolong his drink with his father until the last bus and train for Cork had gone. 'How are you getting home?' Jim asked his son. 'You'll have to drive me down,' Terry said. Then he came out with it: 'I came to bring you back, Dad. I'll tell them tomorrow that you can't work.' 'OK, then,' my grandfather said quietly; which wasn't like him.

It wasn't long before Jim was being treated in hospital for days at a time. My father offered to fly him to a hospital in Switzerland, but Jim stayed on at the South Infirmary, in Cork. He spent the last five weeks of his life there, for a while sharing his private room with his youngest child, Fergus, who also needed medical attention. He fought against his illness to the last. On the morning of the day he died, my father proudly told me, my grandfather summoned the will to shave. He also received a visit from, of all people, a former guard at the Curragh Camp named Dan Daly.

My grandfather died on a Wednesday. He had never once uttered the name of his illness – cancer of the pancreas – and neither, out of solidarity with her husband, had my grandmother. On Friday, his body was removed from the hospital mortuary, where the family accepted sympathies. The funeral was on the Saturday. After Mass was said at Our Lady of Lourdes, Ballinlough, he was taken in a hearse to St Michael's Cemetery, Blackrock. His sons shouldered him through green fields that are now lost under a housing estate. My father was not there, though. Coming from Abu Dhabi, where he'd driven a jeep across the desert to catch the first flight back, he was greatly upset to miss the funeral by hours.

My grandfather's coffin was swathed in the customary pall of the patriot, the green, white and gold flag of Ireland. It was a sunny day, and people threw crisp shadows. An IRA guard of honour marched in step alongside the coffin; they wore berets, tricolour armbands, jackets and ties. Behind them walked my grandmother in a blue dress and a hat. She led a procession of many hundreds of people. There was a great turn-out for the funeral of James O'Neill.

Among the mourners was Dr Barker, who was attending a patient's funeral for the first time. 'I was very disappointed,' she said afterwards to my grandmother, 'to see that nice man was implicated in the IRA.' The security services, by contrast, knew all about Jim O'Neill's republican connections. Expecting IRA men to make an appearance, they were present in offensive numbers, taking photographs and hanging from the trees bordering the cemetery. Somebody made a joke about the Special Branch in the branches.

My grandfather was buried in a plot he had acquired – a double plot. From the grave, the view is of the sky, the water of the estuary of the Lee, and green Cork hills. The headstone carries the statement, IN PROUD AND LOVING MEMORY OF JAMES O'NEILL, DUN ARD . . . . 1ST BATTALION, 1ST CORK BRIGADE. IRISH REPUBLICAN ARMY D. SEPT 1973 AGED 63.

An obituary of my grandfather appeared in a republican publication:

> In the month of September another Veteran Soldier of
> Oglaigh na-Eireann passed to his Eternal Reward without
> seeing freedom coming to Ireland for whom he sacrificed so
> much. He was Jim O'Neill of Briogaid A h-Aoin Corcaigh.
> To his Wife and Family Cumann Briann O'Diolluin

tender their Deepest Sympathy in this their Hour of Sorrow. Their loss is Ireland's loss also because few of her sons have served her better than Jim O'Neill.

I first met Jim O as he was known to us, in the early Nineteen Thirties when I was a young lad in Fianna Eireann. He was even then a Veteran in Ireland's Fight for Freedom. When I joined Oglaigh na h-Eireann in 1937 I served with him in No 3 Company Briogaid A h-Aoin Corcaigh. I served in this Company until I left the Cork area, but I was to meet him again in the Hell Hole of Tintown in 1940. Who can ever really understand what he and his Wife and young Family suffered during those years or the years following his Release while he fought to Re-Build their lives.

In the years that followed he was ever willing to play his part in Re-Building the Republican Movement. When Ireland called her sons to Arms for the present and final fight for Freedom Jim O was one of the first to answer her call. Although now in Failing Health no task was too great for him. He was to the fore in organizing Collections for Northern Aid and An Cumann Cabrac. His car was available at any time it was required. One of his last acts before entering Hospital for the last time was to help Cumann na mBann in Cork to Organize and Run a Bazaar.

His one regret in his final years was that Age and Ill-Health did not allow him to join in a more active way with the young fighting Volunteers in Occupied Ireland, it was with them that his Heart always lay.

Unfortunately the time has not yet come when the full story of the part he played in Ireland's Fight can be written, but please God the day is not far off when it can.

Go ndeanfaid Dia Trocaire ar Do Ainnaim A Seamus.

I was moved by this obituary and by the esteem in which my grandfather was held by his comrades, and saddened for him that even they regarded his life as essentially tragic. But I soon realized that the obituary did not really operate as a sorrowful assessment of Jim O'Neill's life: by casting him in a tragedy, a dramatic mode in which the individual's catastrophic fate is typically the work of an irresistible and often divine force, my grandfather was being granted a form of absolution. His tragic fate was, moreover, provisional, because his full story could only be told once we, the living, had completed his life's unfinished business: and I was reminded of Robert Emmet's patriotic cry from the dock, in 1803, that his epitaph should only be written when Ireland took her place among the nations. Thus suspended in a narrative limbo, my grandfather became a soul whose redemption lay in our hands, a ghost.

But did the full story of Jim O'Neill involve the killing of Admiral Somerville? I had a clue to go on. In the course of our trip together, Brendan had told me that I should speak to Peig Lynch, the widow of my grandmother's brother Jack Lynch.

7

It is quite natural that we should adopt a defensive and negative attitude towards every new opinion concerning something on which we have already an opinion of our own. For it forces its way as an enemy into the previously closed system of our own convictions, shatters the calm of mind we have attained through this system, demands renewed efforts of us and declares our former efforts to have been in vain.

– Arthur Schopenhauer, *Essays and Aphorisms*

A few months after my return to London from Israel, I fixed another appointment with Sir Denis Wright to discuss the Gandour file. Wright had no opinion on Gandour, whom he hadn't known, but he was able to speak about Norman Mayers, his predecessor as consul in Mersin. 'Mayers was a good chap,' Wright said, 'and I admire his guts in the Gandour business. But he was an isolated fellow – a bachelor in his forties, somewhat wet and fussy in his habits – and it may be that loneliness led to his over-friendliness with the Syrians, who were always throwing lavish parties. The Turks became very unhappy about it and in the end Mayers had to be pulled out. I was a vice-consul in Trebizond at the time, and my assignment was to take over from Mayers and clean up the mess.'

When Wright arrived at his new post, he saw immediately that he had to be extremely careful. 'Mersin was a nest of intrigue and gossip. All sorts of strings were being pulled – by the Turks, by our people, by the Syrians, by others – and one was in the middle of it all, which was somewhat exhausting. I decided from the beginning to keep the Syrians at arm's length,' Wright said. 'I created quite a stir by not turning up at a garden party held by one of them on Empire Day, and as a result my stock with the Turks rose sharply. It helped a lot, I think, that Iona and I spoke some Turkish.' He glanced out at his large and beautiful and sunlit garden, where his wife was working on the vegetable patch in which she and her husband grew rhubarb, parsley, potatoes, lettuce, beans and gooseberries. 'Iona,' he added, 'couldn't really bear it in Mersin. She didn't make any chums, and after a few months she returned to Britain. I think she got fed up with the endless tea parties and bridge parties and the silly chatter of the Syrian women.'

So the Turks didn't like the Syrians? I said. I could not get used to this tag.

'They greatly disliked them,' Wright said. 'The feeling was probably mutual, particularly after the *Varlik Vergisi*.' Seeing that I needed further explanation, Wright continued: 'The *Varlik Vergisi* was a wealth tax which came into force in late 1942 or early 1943, and, quite frankly, was used to destroy the minorities. The Turkish authorities assessed the wealth of Jews and Christians in sums that were often many times greater than their actual wealth; and if they reckoned you were dodging payment, you were liable to be sent to break rocks on roads in eastern Turkey. It was a disgraceful episode.' Wright reached over and pulled out some papers from the pile of documentation that he'd prepared for my visit. 'Here, I think you'd better have a look at this.'

It was a report he'd written in January 1944 on the minorities in İçel, the province in which Mersin and Tarsus are situated. Sir Denis Wright stood up energetically ('Right-ho, I'll leave you to it') and wandered out into the garden in his slippers, corduroys, and checked cotton shirt with cuff-links. He exchanged a few words with Iona – the niece of the first Prime Minister of Northern

Ireland, the ultra-unionist Lord Craigavon – then headed off to the hut in a distant corner of the garden where he liked to retreat on a summer's afternoon to rest and work.

Wright's report identified three categories of minorities: Muslim, Other Non-Christian, and Christian. The Muslims consisted of a large Arabic-speaking population of around 25,000 Syrian or Arab Alaouites who lived in their own quarter in Mersin; about 400 families of Sunnite Syrians, including the Gandour family; and an assortment of Greek-speaking Cretan Turks, Kurds and Circassians, each of whose numbers were limited to no more than a few hundred. The Other Non-Christians were Jews (sixty-four families in Mersin, of which thirty-seven spoke Ladino and twenty-seven Arabic) and Gypsies. The Christians consisted mainly of Greeks, Armenians and Syrians, nearly all of whom spoke Arabic and French and Turkish. The Syrians, Wright wrote,

> are disliked, mistrusted and envied by the Turks because of their origin, their religion and their wealth. With a shiny veneer of European manners, if not culture, acquired in Beirut, their way of life is more European than Turkish, they have no feelings of loyalty to Turkey and do little to conceal their contempt for the Turk. The flashiness of their behaviour in public and their group instinct (no doubt the result of persecution in the past) irritate the Turks, with whom they make no attempt to mix or, it seems to the outsider, to understand. They generally send their children to school at Beirut or to Robert College, Istanbul.
>
> They are very conscious of the precariousness of their position here, and, given the chance, most of them would choose to return to Syria. Their present-day claim to be pro-Allied, if anti-French, is probably not very deep, and their gushing friendliness for the British in Mersin is primarily because they see in the British Consulate their only protection and hope against their Turkish 'oppressors', though it is true that they do genuinely find the British more sympathetic than the Turks.

Allegations that many of these people were pro-Axis in the early days of the war should not be taken too seriously, and it should be borne in mind that any reports about their activities emanating from Turkish sources are likely to be coloured. They are not interested in politics, though some of them shewed a passing interest in the recent Lebanon crisis, and their only political concern at the moment is that Turkey shall remain out of the war. Self-interest and financial profit are their only gods. The Turks refer to them as 'Hristian' or 'Arap' with a contemptuous ring in their voices.

My first reaction on reading this was dismay at its portrayal of the 'Syrian' community – to which, after all, my family belonged. Had we really been (and might we still be) such a dreadful, flashy, self-involved crowd? I thought guiltily that in all the summers I'd spent in Turkey I'd only stepped into a Muslim house on maybe three or four occasions, and then only fleetingly; I thought about my grandmother shouting at the servants, about the motorboats and the private beaches and our tiny social circle. No, I could not deny our clannishness or snobbery, or that in the old days my grandparents' few good Muslim friends were drawn mainly from the families of mayors, state governors, university chancellors and landowners (that said, *employés* of any religion were beyond the pale). I did not doubt that, as a group, we could be gratingly materialistic and lacking in the sophistication to which we pretended; but if the Syrians' position was as precarious and marginal as Wright described, then surely for them the financial was political, and making money and spending it with a certain degree of ostentation was a vital form of cultural assertion? Besides, I had no problem with business culture; I knew something from my work as a lawyer about the dreams and exertions that may attach to bills of lading and letters of credit and exportation permits and finance facilities, about the necessity to deal and exploit and broke, to extract, by hook or by crook, a return from the rough world. The so-called Syrians, my mother's people, worked in a very rough world indeed; a terrible climate, lethal diseases, an undeveloped economy, an alien host society: all had to be overcome. Everything was difficult, and everything – the houses they lived in, the port they operated, the churches they attended, Mersin itself – had to be wrought from nothing. Perhaps Freya Stark had sensed this when she wrote from the Toros Hotel, in April 1954, 'There is something very touching in these little hotels, trying to be modern with such difficulties. The traveller is apt to feel cross and tired and wants things different, but when one thinks what a huge effort it is to get as far as they do, one feels very gentle towards them.' Then again, even Stark was sufficiently anti-Levantine to eventually describe Mersin as a 'squalidly rich little town'.

A political curiosity of the report – which, knowing Wright as I did, I took to be fundamentally reliable – was that I had never myself heard the Christians in Mersin talk of themselves or, for that matter, of the Kurds, as an oppressed minority. The Kurdish situation very rarely came up in discussion, even though the war in south-east Turkey had caused around 30,000 deaths since 1984; certainly, there was little sign of sympathy for the insurgent Kurds or for the cause of an autonomous Kurdistan. The fact was that, aside from the odd reference by those in my grandmother's generation to *les Turques*, I had barely heard any talk of the ethnic majority as a group distinct from ourselves; and indeed my cousins, the first generation to have been educated at Turkish schools and to speak Turkish as a first language, would have found bizarre and hurtful the notion that they were not Turkish. What else could they be? No native Mersiner, as far as I was aware, thought of himself as Syrian or Lebanese; Aleppo and Beirut and Tripoli and Damascus simply did not figure as homelands in our communal imagination. Go back to Syria and Lebanon? And do what?

Wright's report continued with an analysis of the 'Turkish Attitude towards the Minorities':

The Turk has an instinctive dislike and distrust of all
minorities. If, unlike nearby Adana, Mersin has never been
the scene of wholesale massacres, the reason is partly that

Armenians, the chief victims of the various Adana massacres, have never been found in large numbers in Mersin, and partly that Mersin has never been a predominantly Turkish town. Syrian influence and sea traffic have played an important part in making Mersin a far more European town than, for instance, Adana.

The largest minority, the Alaouites, being poor and inconspicuous, are, though apt to be bullied, left pretty much alone by the Turkish authorities. The same applies to the Jews, Armenians and Greeks, though they are never allowed to forget that they are minorities.

The Syrians, both Moslem and Christian, but principally the latter, are the real focus of minority feeling in this district. They themselves, by their gregariousness and ostentatious behaviour, encourage rather than allay this animosity, and it is for their benefit that notices are permanently displayed in the Mersin Club insisting that 'Those who know Turkish must speak it.'

The Syrians are, whether they like it or not, the mainstay of all charitable appeals and are expected to pay without demur whatever sum is demanded of them. It is their 'voluntary contributions' which will form the bulk of the fund being raised by the Vali for his Five Year Building Plan. They thus buy for themselves an 'insecure security', and so balance themselves on the edge of a volcano which they feel may erupt at any moment.

Bewildered by this portrait of a Mersin I didn't recognize, I rang up my mother and asked her whether she knew of any law compelling the use of the Turkish language. She didn't recall anything herself, she said, but there was a story about my grandmother's friend Madame Dora, who was sent to prison for a month for snapping in Turkish at a barking dog, '*Türk konus!*' (Speak Turkish!) 'What about the *Varlik Vergisi*?' I asked. 'Oh yes,' my mother said, 'that was a big thing.' It happened at the worst time, she said, when her father was away in Palestine. Mamie Dakad was saved by her

Muslim friends, whose intervention ensured that the sum demanded, although still grossly excessive, was reduced.

I began to see my grandmother's taxpaying trophies in a different light. 'What about Armenian massacres in Adana?' I asked. Denis Wright's reference to these had prompted a tiny recollection of something my great-aunt Isabelle had once said to me, many years ago – something about the river in Adana running red with the blood of Armenians. My mother seemed unsure. 'Well, there were incidents in Adana, a long time ago,' she said vaguely. My mother hesitated. 'I remember Mlle Victorine, a friend of the family who was maybe ten years older than my father, speaking about cries and shouts in the street outside her house. She lived in Adana. And I remember Madame Madeleine once saying that the Tahintzi family had a factory in Tarsus where Armenians hid. Nothing happened in Mersin, I don't think. There weren't many Armenians living there.' She added, 'There were quite a few Armenian girls at my school in Aleppo, including, now that I think of it, the nieces of the man you say was a German agent, Joseph Ayvazian. The Armenian girls spoke Turkish as a first language,' my mother said.

I didn't dwell on the subject of the Armenians; didn't ask myself, for example, what had happened to the now non-existent Armenian settlement in Adana. What I thought about was contrast between the general *unpleasantness* of the Mersin that Wright described and the stories the Mersin people told of the golden, paradisal old days. Something didn't add up.

I didn't know it, but enlightenment was at hand. In the autumn, I caught a train to Paris to meet my second cousin, Olivier Dacade. Olivier, who works as a valuer of antiques and has a strong curatorial streak, had put into order the papers of his grandfather, Joseph Dakak's brother Georges Dacade, and for some time I had been meaning to visit him. I had once or twice met the famously kind Oncle Georges, who died in 1991, but had not got to know him. I was aware that he'd left Mersin for France as a young man and eventually, in partnership with his brother-in-law René Salendre, built up a successful business as a wholesaler and retailer of cloth, garments and haberdashery. The most I was hoping for were some family photographs or letters.

So I was astonished, when I visited Olivier at his apartment near the Bastille, to find a photo of the Mersin waterfront in 1915 (how narrow and deserted and scruffy the main street looked!) and, more striking still, photographs of a hulking German warship anchored off the shore of the town, and of a row of cheerful German pilots looking handsome and glamorous in their flying jackets. There was a picture of a column of Sikh troops marching along a jetty, and another of British officers saluting the arrival of French soldiers. It dawned on me that my grandfather had grown into adulthood in a Mersin fundamentally different to any place I had known or drowsily imagined, a port teeming with German and French and British military and administrative personnel. Evidently, some of these foreigners rented rooms in the house of Caro Dakak: Olivier showed me pictures of my great-grandmother, a sturdily-built woman with dark eyebrows, happily posing for the camera with lodgers wearing French uniforms.

Perhaps the most intriguing document that Olivier possessed was the manuscript text of a speech delivered by his grandfather on 11 December 1919. Oncle Georges, a fifteen-year-old student at the Collège St Antoine, a humble school for boys in Mersin run by the Capuchin friars, had the honour of addressing the following words of welcome to General Gouraud, the commander-in-chief of France's Levant Army:

My General,
   The year was 1521. The Imperial forces had crossed the Ardennes and now threatened Mézières. Their bravery notwithstanding, the troops of François I were on the retreat, and the king's advisers had decided to abandon the town, which seemed too weak to withstand a siege. It was then that Bayard exclaimed with heroic ardour, 'There are no weak places where there are men with heart to defend them!'
   My General, you speak with the same voice! You have

uttered magnificent words in the course of this horrible war, and you have heroically made them good.

You set foot on our Cilician shore aureoled with glory won in so many battles. In you, we salute a *chevalier sans peur et sans reproche* [a fearless, faultness knight]; a hero who more than once, when disaster beckoned, led his armies with victorious deeds to the most brilliant success.

My General, all our admiration translates to a sole cry, a cry that travels beyond your glorious person to that distant land you have just left, to that nation that you have defended, which we, too, love with all our hearts:

Vive la France!

Allow us, finally, to express our confidence in you and, if it is not too bold for a mere schoolboy to tamper with historic words, we say to you, as Bayard did, 'There are no weak places, no desolate regions, where there are brave people to defend and protect them.'

France, Joseph de Maistre said, is the land of astonishing resurrections. Once again, my General, you shall prove that saying true.

Thank you, and *vive la France*.

I was enough of a Turk for my first reaction to Oncle Georges' speech to be one of shock. It was astounding that my great-uncle had cheered on the forces of occupation in this way and, indeed, that the schoolmasters who must have penned his words should have exposed a teenager to the possible consequences of siding with Turkey's enemy in such a public and extreme way: because the comparison of General Gouraud to Chevalier Bayard amounted to an assertion that Mersin was no more Turkish than Mézières, a town in north-eastern France. The notion was so extravagantly colonialist as to be comical; but any wry amusement on my part disappeared after I'd looked into the circumstances in which my great-uncle's speech was made, and the historical spaces opened by his evocation of a battle four centuries past. Then I was simply appalled.

French interest in Cilicia dated back to the Crusaders, who

enjoyed friendly relations with the local Armenian kingdom, an offshoot of Greater Armenia that finally collapsed in 1375. The French-Cilician connection was restored in 1536, when François I – and here one returned to Oncle Georges' speech – acquired extra-territorial privileges, known as capitulations, in Ottoman lands which, since its conquest from the Egyptians in 1515, included Cilicia. French subjects enjoyed liberty of residence and move-ment, freedom of religion, substantial immunity from Ottoman jurisdiction in civil and criminal matters and, most importantly, freedom of commerce. Even though the rival powers enjoyed capit-ulations of their own, France became the dominant trading partner of the Ottoman Empire and French its language of business, com-munications and education: in 1907, my grandfather, a seven-year-old primary school student in Iskenderun, was one of around 70,000 Syrian children attending a French religious school.

By this time, France had long assumed the role of chief 'protec-tor' of Christians in the Empire. The position of Ottoman Christians was, true enough, less than ideal. Although each religious community was substantially autonomous in matters of worship, law, marriage, healthcare and education, and in this sense enjoyed privileges not extended to religious minorities, notably Jews, by western States, non-Muslims suffered from economic and social disabilities and occasional violence. From the mid-nineteenth cen-tury, a culture arose, among the increasingly nationalistic Christian subjects of the Sultan, of judicial and political recourse to the for-eign powers and their capitulatory jurisdictions. Predictably enough, this aggravated Turkish suspicions of Christian disloyalty, which exacerbated inter-communal hostilities, which, in completion of a self-perpetuating cycle, provided further grounds for western interventionism: most notoriously, in 1860 French troops occupied Syria in response to massacres of Syrian Christians. When I raised the subject in Mersin, nobody seemed to know about the massacres, even though they were extremely serious (25,000 Christians report-edly died in Damascus alone); had led to the creation of an autonomous Lebanon; and, it seemed to me, was possibly connected to their ancestors' decision to migrate: it was in around 1860, for example, that my grandmother's grandfather and his brother decided to leave Syria for Mersin.

The next major French action on behalf of Ottoman Christians came in 1895, when, as a result of 'atrocities' committed against Armenians, France and other European powers forced Abdul Hamid II, the Red Sultan, to introduce reforms. However, the reforms only led to further killings of Armenians: reported figures for the number of dead fluctuated between a few thousand to 200,000. This was a very wide spectrum, and all I could feel sure of, after I'd hesitantly dipped into the historical literature, was that the precise fate of the slaughtered lay at the bottom of a cold and profound sea of misconceptions into which, if I took my research further, fresh errors of my own would trickle. I took refuge in this problem, and also in a concrete thought: there were no reports of Armenian casualties in Adana or anywhere else close to my grandfather's world. This fortified my inclination to *skip* the Armenians, as if their history formed a disagreeable, non-vital college course. I was afraid, of course, of being sucked into the morass of the Armenian genocide, about which I only knew that it was hotly disputed, that it involved death-marches, and that it had taken place during the Great War. I couldn't see what Joseph Dakak had to do with the fate of the Armenians, which I had never had connected to Mersin. (Didn't the Armenians essentially come from north-east Turkey?) So I moved straight on to the next, most interesting, link between France and Turkey: the post-war French occupation of Cilicia, the name given by the occupiers to the boomerang of part-mountainous, part-fertile land comprising the eastern Taurus and the Amanus mountains and the maritime lowlands they enclosed.

And here I made a startling discovery. According to the French, Christians in Cilicia (215,000) outnumbered Muslims (185,000), and of the latter only a small minority were Turkish: in 1920, the French administration tallied 28,000 Greeks, 5000 Chaldaean and Assyrian Christians, 100,000 Ansarian Arabs, 30,000 Kurds, 15,000 Circassians, only 20,000 Turks, and finally 120,000 Armenians. These last were mainly shepherds and husbandmen living in small, prosperous settlements in the Taurus – the remnants of the old medieval kingdom – and maintained close contacts with Tarsus and Adana, where Armenians were an important commercial presence. Even allowing for gross imperialistic statistical manipulation – and the numbers given for the constituent ethnic groups fell around 80,000 short of the given total population of 400,000 – I was presented with a picture of ethnic and religious diversity completely at odds with my sense of a region I thought I knew reasonably well.

The first wave of French and British forces reached Iskenderun in November 1918, shortly after the signing of the Armistice. In February 1919, British troops arrived to reinforce the French and Armenian battalions. They made a magnificent impression. They organized tennis matches, played polo, put the finishing touches on the Taurus rail tunnels, and repaired the Mersin–Tarsus railway: every day, one French onlooker marvelled, six thousand Hindus, shepherded by sergeants carrying whips, went singing to work. In June, the permanent occupying force of French troops began to arrive. A Colonel Thibault received the following words of welcome from a schoolgirl:

> We salute you and acclaim France, whom we have
> summoned with our most fervent wishes. France, the object
> of our dreams; France, whose benevolent deeds in the world
> we have learned to bless; France, hitherto known only in the
> pale and cold reflections of history and the teachings of our
> schoolmasters, whom we at last see with our own eyes. She
> has set foot in our Cilician land, and our heart trembles with
> joy. . . . Flag of France, whose victory brings with it justice,
> peace, prosperity and liberty, flutter forever over this Cilician
> land.

I was again saddened by the reckless zeal of the schoolmasters who had placed this speech in the hands of a schoolgirl. But I wasn't surprised. Joseph de Maistre (1753–1821), the ideologue invoked in Oncle Georges' speech and obviously revered by the Capuchin brothers in Mersin, was an arch-conservative monarchist,

and his followers would not have hesitated to fit out their students –
the usual Levantine mix of Greeks, Syrians, and Armenians – in the
stiff, perilously enchanting garments of French nationalism. It must
have been a curiously improvised job of ideological costuming,
because surely not even the most francophile Cilician Christian
could have dreamt of living under the French flag alongside their
Kurdish, Circassians, Ansarian Arab and, yes, Turkish neighbours.
But it appeared that this was precisely what the Armenian Cilicians
were encouraged by the French to believe: that Cilicia, in some
form or other, would be a country they could call their own. In
1919, eight thousand repatriated Armenians landed at Mersin and
Iskenderun. Most of the Armenians resettled in Adana and the
Cilician highlands; two or three thousand went to Mersin.
Orphanages had to be build for hundreds, perhaps even thousands,
of Armenian children.

This information made me think of Joseph Dakak's spell as an
interpreter for the (presumably British or French) Red Cross. In his
capacity as a Red Cross worker, which he assumed at some point
after the termination of his employment on the railway construction
in February 1919, he would inevitably have been involved in local
relief efforts, which in Cilicia would have meant extensive contacts
with displaced and homeless Armenians.

For a while, the red, white and blue of France flew serenely over
Cilicia. On 14 July 1919, the anniversary of the storming of the
Bastille, the populace decked out the streets of Mersin and Adana in
French tricolours, Union Jacks, and Armenian and Greek flags; the
showing of Turkish colours remained unlawful. For the rest of the
year, Mersin was treated to a steady and glorious inflow of French
military dignitaries who would parade before the massed and cran-
ing townsfolk in superb cavalcades of carriages, motorcars and
chevaliers. The young Joseph Dakak certainly witnessed these
scenes and could only have been deeply excited. It was not hard to
imagine how scintillating these near-magical creatures, sprung from
the myths he'd consumed at school, must have appeared to an
alienated Syrian with no experience of a government that took an
active and apparently benevolent interest in his welfare. After the

British finally pulled out in October 1919, the French in Mersin (using Algerian and Senegalese labourers) paved streets, opened a hospital and public library, founded a literary society, and built a new port consisting of a customs house with a magazine, a concrete landing platform, and a wharf.

Militarily, however, things were not going well. Even as Oncle Georges welcomed General Gouraud in December 1919, French outposts in the Taurus mountains were under attack. Oncle Georges' comparison of General Gouraud with Bayard struck me, on further reflection, as more desperate than triumphant, because the salient point about Bayard was that he'd held at bay a besieging army of 35,000 with only a thousand men. And sure enough, by June 1920 Mersin and Tarsus and Adana were under siege and intermittent attack. Mersin was trapped – or, looking at it from the Turkish perspective, on the point of liberation.

While the fighting went on in Cilicia, the remnants of the Ottoman government were submitting to the terms of the Treaty of Sèvres, by which Turkey was dismembered and portioned out to the Allies with extraordinarily transparent rapacity: Istanbul was put under the jurisdiction of an international commission, Greece was given Thrace and the Izmir region, Italy the Antalya region, and France was authorized to occupy Cilicia and large tracts of south-east Anatolia; the cost of maintaining these foreign troops was, naturally, to be borne by Turkey, which in addition had to pay very high war reparations. The capitulations were restored and Turkish taxes, customs, loans and currency were put under the supervision of the Allied Financial Commission. The Treaty also provided – fantastically, it quickly became clear – for the establishment of an independent Armenia and an autonomous Kurdistan, whose projected territories respectively extended into vast parts of the north-east and south-east of modern Turkey.

In the year that followed, Atatürk's armies defeated the Greeks, the Italians, and the Armenians in north-east Anatolia. The French government lost interest in its Turkish adventure. Even though French troops had managed to regain control of the Cilician plain, in October 1921 the French government agreed to evacuate the occupied lands in return for an assurance that there would be no reprisals against Christians. The Christians, especially the Armenians, were not reassured. A panicked mass exodus began. By the end of November 1921, only 60,000 Christians were reportedly left in Cilicia, 20,000 of whom were sleeping in the port of Mersin, waiting for a ship out. On 4 January 1922, when the *Cassard* sailed from Mersin, the Cilician occupation, which had lasted for three years, was finally over; indeed, according to one French observer, 'The siren of the *Cassard* sounded the end of the glorious era that began with Charlemagne, in which the French flag swaddled in its folds whosoever raised his prayers to Jesus.'

Among the departed were my great-aunt Radié, who married a Frenchman stationed in Mersin, Lieutenant René Salendre. The couple left Mersin in 1920, going to Iskenderun and then to Aleppo, where Oncle René served until around 1930 as France's consul. Georges Dakak left for France when he was around sixteen or seventeen, in 1921 or 1922.

While thousands of Christians were fleeing from Mersin in terror at prospect of what the victorious Turks would do, Joseph Dakak stayed behind. It was an enormous gamble. The Dakak family had strong collaborationist links to the occupiers – Joseph had worked for the (admittedly neutral) Red Cross, his brother had given a welcoming speech to General Gouraud, his mother had taken English and French officers into her home as paying guests, and his sister had married a French officer – and Joseph had no property or family ties to Mersin. No doubt he stayed in the knowledge that his professional and social standing in Mersin was relatively certain; but there was also the complex matter of identity. My grandmother once told my mother that Joseph was 'too Oriental' to leave. He felt comfortable in Mersin. Thanks, perhaps, to counter-perspectives gained from his work alongside the Ottoman and German armies, he was not seduced by French promises of a homeland; and he reckoned he knew the Turks well enough to feel sure that they would not regard him, at least not to any hazardous degree, as a political threat. A Levantine of the Christian Syrian-displaced-to-Turkey variety, he did not belong to an ethnic group with nationalistic ambitions. He was not to be confused with an Armenian.

Although certain retaliatory measures were taken – Christian schools were closed, Christian shops were boycotted, and imports at Mersin were taxed very heavily – the fears of massacre turned out to be unfounded. Nevertheless, the exodus of Christians continued, and their numbers in Cilicia soon dwindled to next to nothing. The Greeks, for their part, were deported in accordance with the Turkish–Greek population exchange provided for by the Treaty of Lausanne 1923, by which, furthermore, the sovereignty of the Turkish Republic was recognized and all prospects of an independent Armenia or Kurdistan were extinguished.

I rang up my mother and discussed with her what I'd learned: that Cilicia used to be heavily Armenian and that the French occupation had ended with a massive regional depopulation of Christians. Joseph, in Mersin, and the young Georgette for that matter, must have witnessed unforgettable scenes as thousands of refugees poured in and out of the port. How come these events had not been perpetuated in the local folklore? Had she never been told about them?

'No,' my mother said.

'Did your father ever talk about the French occupation at all?' I asked.

'No, he didn't.'

'What about the Armenians?'

'Never. He never spoke about them. No one did.'

She paused as she reflected on her community's insulation from the fate of local Armenians. 'We didn't really mix with Armenians,' she finally observed. 'They were completely separate from us. They spoke Turkish, whereas we spoke French and Arabic. I think that in those days they were regarded as a lower class; I remember that when a Nader married an Armenian man it was regarded as something of a mismatch. Also,' she continued, 'they mainly lived in Adana. Even at the time I was growing up, the 1940s, Adana seemed very far away, almost another world. In my father's time it must have seemed even further away, because there were no real roads.' Then my mother mentioned something else. Now that she thought about it, she recalled that her father's family had migrated to Mersin from Iskenderun because of attacks on Armenians. The Dakaks fled to Cyprus first, and then sailed on to Mersin. Tante Radié, my mother said, used to relate that it was in Cyprus she first ate an ortolan – a finch so small and soft-boned that it could be popped into the mouth and eaten whole.

Thinking how typical it was of the Turkish side of the family to reduce a profoundly political episode to a gastronomic event, I decided to check this startling news with Pierre, who, like Brendan, was perceived to be the child who'd been closest to his father. My uncle lived in Paris for most of the year, only returning to Mersin for a few months at a time to do business, and I phoned him at the Montmartre apartment of his girlfriend, Katya, which had been Picasso's first Parisian studio. When I put the Cyprus story to him, Oncle Pierre muttered in assent. Then he said, 'You must be very careful about writing about such things. You shall show me what you've written, so that I can censor it. I'm being serious. And by the way, we are not Christians. We are Christian *Turks*.'

When I subsequently spoke to a few other Mersin Christians of Pierre's generation – women, mostly – about the Armenians in Cilicia, the general response was one of mystification and, in one or two cases, non-admission. More than once the phrase '*on ne les fréquentait pas*' was used: We didn't frequent them.

As with so much of Mersin's history, I had to resort to overseas documentary sources to fill in the huge voids in the city's oral account of its own regional past. In the case of the Adana massacres, the extraordinary testimony of an eye-witness was preserved in a Foreign Office file at the Public Records Office in London.

On the evening of Wednesday 14 April 1909, His Majesty's Vice-Consul at Mersin, Major C.H.M. Doughty Wylie, travelled from Mersin to Adana on the train. The consul had received a note that morning from the British dragoman at Adana, Mr Trypani, that there was a very dangerous feeling in the town, and he decided to investigate. About two stations distant from Adana, Doughty Wylie noticed a body by the track. A little further on, he saw people running in panic towards the train. More bodies began to appear near the railway track as the train approached Adana.

At Adana, the consul went quickly to Mr Trypani's house, witnessing en route the killing of two or three men in the street. Major Doughty Wylie put on his military uniform and, accompanied by an escort of four men, went by foot to the government offices. His route took him through the Armenian quarter and Armenian bazaar, and then the Turkish bazaar and the Muslim residential quarter. He found the town 'in undescribable tumult, with heavy fighting going on in the approaches to the Armenian quarter, and murder and fires everywhere.' A 'howling mob' was looting the shops, there was firing in all directions, and men were being killed in front of his eyes. At the government headquarters, the consul was met with scenes of panic and disorder and fear; the Vali, in whose very office two men had just been killed, did not dare send out troops to quell the violence.

The following morning, Doughty Wylie assembled a corps of some fifty Turkish troops. In an attempt to clear the streets, he led the men through the town with bugles blowing, but the house-to-house fighting and mayhem continued. The main bazaar was now on fire, and when Doughty Wylie was temporarily parted from his troops they became involved in an attack on an Armenian house in which all of its inhabitants were killed. The consul himself was shot in the arm by an Armenian. The violence continued until the evening of the following day, Friday 16 April, when *hojas* and Armenian priests finally kissed each other and made peace. Meanwhile, it was becoming clear from the inflow of Armenian refugees that terrible things were taking place in the surrounding country. In Antakya (or Antioch, where, tradition has it, the followers of Jesus Christ were first called 'Christians'), more than 100 Armenians had been killed. In Tarsus, around 200 armed men – Kurds, mostly – jumped out of the train from Adana and engaged in systematic pillaging and, according to one American missionary, the burning of 800 houses and killing of 500 Christians. Some Christians fled to the Tarsus American College (where seventy years later my cousins received their schooling). The Armenian

inhabitants of over 200 villages in the Cilician plain, mostly peasants and farmers and seasonal migrants down from the mountains,
were attacked. For example, every Armenian house in Inçirlik, the
village that nowadays hosts a base of the United States Air Force,
was burned to the ground.

Doughty Wylie eventually reckoned that 2000 corpses, of which
around 600 were Muslim dead, were buried in Adana; an inestimable number of bodies had been thrown into the river. Wylie put
the fatalities outside Adana at between 15,000 and 20,000, almost all
Armenian. The French consul arrived at the figure of 30,000 dead.
The Ottoman government reckoned casualties at 5400, including
418 Syrians and 62 Syrian Catholics.

Many Armenians avoided harm by fleeing to Mersin, where
some caught boats to Cyprus. That Mersin saw no violence was,
according to Doughty Wylie, largely due to the governor-general of
Mersin – 'the first Ottoman official there to refuse bribes and to
refuse to be entirely ruled by the Greek clique'. Mersin was also the
base of a flotilla of French and British warships that arrived soon
after news of massacres spread abroad. The surgeon aboard the
HMS *Swiftsure*, which sailed into Mersin on 21 April, went ashore
to treat patients in makeshift hospitals. 'The brutality and savagery
of the massacre are impossible to describe,' he later reported,
noting, in descending order of frequency, wounds caused by
Martini rifle bullets; swords and hatchets; clubs and sharp sticks;
Mauser and revolver bullets; and bayonets.

The international naval presence had a limited deterrent effect.
On the night of 25 April, there were further killings in Adana, and
the Armenian quarter was burned to rubble. The statistic emerged
that of the 4823 properties destroyed, 4437 belonged to Armenians.

Doughty Wylie was at a loss to explain the two massacres and by
what devilry, as he put it, the Turkish peasant, 'a kindly, honest and
hospitable man, can suddenly be changed into a cruel killer of
unarmed men and even in some cases of women and children'. On
further reflection, he identified a variety of factors. The constitution recently proclaimed by the Young Turk government, under
which Christians enjoyed equality with Muslims, was deeply

offensive to the Muslim Turks. This resentment was inflamed by the 'swaggering' behaviour of the Christians, who, 'with all the assertiveness of the newly emancipated, made equality to seem superiority'. This unseemly behaviour included the flaunting of weapons bought under a freshly acquired right to bear arms, and loud talk of what Doughty Wylie called 'Home Rule' – the establishment, with assistance of foreign powers, of an Armenian principality in Cilicia. The British consul, who regarded such talk as patently fantastical and ineffectual, commented that the 'incurably loquacious' Armenians 'never seem to have thought of the possible consequences of wild words. Natives of the country, they should have known its dangers, but with the word liberty they forgot them all.'

It was against this backdrop of communal hostility that, on Thursday 8 April, an Armenian shot dead two Turks. The funeral of the men, whose bodies were carried through the town, provoked strong feelings among the 'savage, ignorant, and fanatical' Turks, who misconstrued the incident as a seditious attack. The atmosphere in Adana worsened, and it was at this time that Armenians who could afford to do so began to flee by train to Mersin. On Wednesday 14 April, the uneasiness was so great that shops closed and groups of armed Muslims began to gather on the streets, saying the Armenians were going to revolt; some Armenians, in their turn, regrouped and assumed defensive positions. Then, shots were fired – who fired first was never established – and the killing began. Major Doughty Wylie concluded that the real fault lay with the local Ottoman authorities, whose response to the events was culpably feeble. He found that the Muslim violence, although inexcusable, had in the main been committed by persons gripped by a real fear for their Empire, their religion and their lives. The consul (who was to be killed by Turks in 1915, leading a charge on the Gallipoli peninsula) observed, 'Nothing is so cruel as fear.'

Meanwhile in Iskenderun, where the Dakak family lived, trouble started after rumours spread from Adana of violent Armenian insurrection. On 17 April, Muslims – Turks, Kurds, Circassians – armed with revolvers, long knives, and guns plundered from

272 JOSEPH O'NEILL

military stores, began to march about the town in white turbans and to terrorize the rural Christian populace; houses and hamlets in the hills surrounding Iskenderun could be seen in flames. That evening, the British Honorary Consul, Joseph Catoni, reported, 'A large number of families left Alexandretta by the Austrian mail steamer for Cyprus.' In the steamer, it could safely be inferred, travelled Caro and Basile Dakak and their three children – who included, of course, my nine-year-old grandfather.

On 30 June 1909, the representatives of the Christian communities – Gregorian, Armenian, Protestant, Roman Catholic, Syrian, Greek Catholic, and Chaldaean – made the following public declaration:

The Christians of the district and city of Adana desire to express their deep regret concerning the great misfortune which has befallen them, and the false imputation raised against them. They desire to make declaration as to their real position.

We, the Christians of Adana and adjacent districts, have been faithful to the constitution from the time of its proclamation, and we earnestly desire its continuance and success. As true Ottoman subjects, our desire and effort has been to protect the constitution and to be found on the side of those who love and serve it. We emphatically protest against all imputations of rebellion made against us. We have never rebelled, and the idea of rebellion has never entered our minds. We, although loyal subjects, have suffered and been persecuted, and we have been sacrificed to the envy and malevolence of bigoted and evil-minded persons. We are the victims of machinations and schemes which caused heaven and earth to weep and wonder. Our loyalty to the Government is proved by the fact that in the very beginning of the troubles we appealed for Government protection, and later, on the first possible opportunity, we renewed our appeal.

We again declare our loyalty to the constitution. We are

ready and eager to make any sacrifice for the true welfare of our beloved land, and we declare also that we cherish no spirit of revenge, notwithstanding the suffering which we have endured. Our earnest plea to our Muslim fellow countrymen is that they should work in harmony with the various other communities which compose the Ottoman Empire. May the goodwill and fellowship which appeared at the time of the proclamation of the constitution appear again!. . . . Let unity, fraternity, equality and justice prevail. . . .

As I read this pathetic announcement – all the more poignant if one looked back on it, as I later did, with knowledge of the apocalypse looming for the Armenians – I felt ashamed that I'd always held against my Turkish family and friends their aloofness from such issues as the oppression of Turkish Kurds. I'd had no real idea of the cost of political action in Turkey or of the abysmal hazards that faced a Christian Turk.

As for Joseph, I realized that, like Jim O'Neill, he had grown up in a malignant, dreadful world that had marked him in ways I had yet to evaluate.

A few days after returning from the north of Ireland with Brendan, I drove out to West Cork to take a stroll by the river. However, when I reached Manch, the scene of so many famous poaching adventures, I impulsively swung the car through the gates of the Manch estate. Somewhere in these woods, in some Big House I'd never seen, lived the Conner family, whose exclusive fishing rights over stretches of the Bandon had been persistently violated by generations of my own family. For all I knew, nobody in my family had laid eyes on the house, at least not from the perspective of a visitor winding his way up the drive to make a social call. I drove past a meadow and then slowly up a driveway that curved through rhododendron bushes and thick forest. Manch House appeared in a clearing in the woods. It stood at the far end of a small fairway, a large, graciously proportioned, pale-stoned building with a tower and a view of the valley that, by a trick of landscaping, was unreciprocated.

I had barely stopped the engine before a cat and three dogs, including an enormous Irish wolfhound, had surrounded the car. A white-haired, white-bearded fellow in his late fifties, who later introduced himself as Con (Cornelius) Conner, came out slowly with his hands in his pockets and asked if he could help me. I explained that I was a member of the O'Neill family, from Ardkitt, and that I was researching my grandfather's poaching antics on the river. Conner, a quiet-spoken, glumly humorous man with a soft English-Irish accent, did not know about any Ardkitt O'Neills, but he confirmed that his family owned about two miles of fishing rights. His father had given over a stretch of the river to the public in the hope of dissuading poachers, he said, but it was a crappy stretch and of course the ploy didn't work. A jeepload of bailiffs still wandered around the river now and again, Conner said gloomily. Their duties were diffuse these days, and they even went out to sea in a fast boat that came courtesy of the EC. There wasn't much poaching at all any more, Conner said, although needless to say there were still some idiots who took disproportionate risks, including some who engaged in an obscene competition to catch the most trout using a worm bait. There weren't the number of fish there used to be and the incentive to poach disappeared once salmon farming made the fish available to the masses. In the old days, things were different. He could remember selling an 18lb salmon for £5 in 1952, when land cost £50 an acre.

Con Conner mentioned that he was The O'Connor Kerry – the chief of the O'Connor Kerry clan. 'We have our own little world,' he volunteered with an air of faint dismay. 'We're West British, really; our cultural feelings would be closely tied to British culture. My father was on the English side to begin with,' he continued, seamlessly moving on to the subject of the Troubles, 'but then joined Fine Gael when the British failed to shoot de Valera after they'd captured him in 1916. The family hasn't always been union-ist or loyalist in sentiment,' he added. General O'Conner had fought against the Crown for Napoleon's army; Fergus O'Conner was an MP, Chartist and civil rights activist whose funeral was attended by 20,000 inside the cemetery and another 20,000 outside; and Roger and Arthur O'Conner were locked up in Cork Gaol in 1798.

He invited me into the house, which was built in 1826; the oldest Conner residence, the seventeenth century Carrigmore House, stood elsewhere on the estate. The ground floor living quarters had the chaotic, dustily charming ambience of a jumble sale. There was a clutter of old family portraits, old bits of furniture, and a giant old stove heater; and to complete the picture of decaying Ascendancy privilege, Oriana Conner, Con's wife, was seated in a corner of the kitchen totting up bills with the help of an associate. Over a cup of tea, I spoke a little about my family's years of theft on their stretch of the river. Oriana – an Irishwoman with an English accent – laughed, saying that families needed to be fed. We talked amiably for a while longer, and then the Conners showed me around the two self-contained apartments they had created for paying guests. As I left they placed a brochure and advertisement slips in my hand and urged me to tell my fishing friends at the English Bar to come over. Non-fishing guests would also find the Manch House Fishery to their liking, the brochure assured me. Riding, golf, sightseeing, gourmet restaurants and great pubs were all within easy reach. There was fresh organic produce available from the Manch organic farm, where a flock of milk sheep, poultry, and outdoor pigs lived pleasant, non-intensive lives. Over half of the estate was given over to organic farming; the rest of the estate was broadleaf woodland. A signed handwritten message appeared at the end of the brochure: *We enjoy sharing with our guests the beauty and tranquillity of Manch and the Bandon river. We want you to have a thoroughly enjoyable holiday and will do our best to make it so. Con and Oriana.*

I drove out of the Manch estate marvelling at the social reduction of these once-so-powerful families, whose way of life, which once turned on fastidious exclusiveness, now depended on the number of strangers they could persuade to stay in their homes. The change was, in its way, revolutionary. Moreover, by my unannounced visit the ancient, quasi-mystical distance that had separated the Conners and the O'Neills had suddenly shrunk to more normal proportions. They would no longer seem quite as powerful and strange and inhuman, and perhaps we, in the light of day, might no longer figure as purely anonymous shadows moving around the black river.

I stopped the car a couple of hundred yards away, by the Conner's West Farm, and parked on the verge of the road. I knew, from a recent visit here with my uncles Brendan and Jim, that the river flowed very close by, unseen behind hedges and greenery. I climbed over a locked gate (no entry was permitted without author-ization, a sign declared) and walked through uneven grassland, some of it thigh-high, toward the river. I stepped over the defunct track of the old railway line. I came to the river. A black concrete ridge had in recent years been built into the bank as a fortification against the erosive current. Waste paper and a plastic bottle dis-closed that someone had not long ago been fishing here. On the far side of the river were open fields; to the east, about half a mile away by the Curraghcrowley townland, was a wooded height. Kilcascan Castle, the only other Big House in the locality and the former home of the O'Neill Daunt family (no relation), was hidden by the magnificent hilltop trees, in the shelter of which my grandfather's getaway car had sometimes been parked.

I was standing by the pool known as the Key Hole, which even in daylight was like a still pool of ink. I tossed a stone into the pool; no salmon moved. I remembered that in the Skibbereen *Southern Star* of 4 February 1956, there had appeared a report about an action brought by Henry Conner, of Manch House, against Cork County Council in respect of loss suffered as a result of a poisoning of the Key Hole with bluestone by unknown poachers acting out of revenge. Six salmon – valued at £49 16s. 0d. – and 35 brown trout had been killed.

There was an irony about the poison used, because it was bluestone (a compound of copper sulphate) that finally eliminated the fungus which, in the second half of the 1840s, had repeatedly reduced the Irish potato crop to a black, rotting mess, a catastrophe that led to anything between 750,000 and 1.5 million excess deaths and a million or more emigrations. This part of Cork had not escaped the effects of the Great Famine. The Enniskean parish population fell by 46 per cent from 1841–51, the worst affected being the labourer-cottier class, whose dietary dependence on potatoes exposed them to starvation and whose living conditions – it was not unusual for a family to sleep with its pig on the mud floor of a turf-heated cabin – made them vulnerable to the cholera, dysentery and typhus epidemics that (as in the Mersin of those days) accounted for so many lives. The lack of decent shelter was exacerbated by opportunistic evictions and clearances undertaken by landlords (whose primary residence was often in England) to expand and consolidate their holdings. The townland of Ardkitt, which at that time was poorly drained and contained much more bog and rough pasture than today, saw its population drop by 35 per cent, and the village of Enniskean was depopulated by 53 per cent. The Great Famine was on my mind because, it so happened, its 150th anniversary had been marked earlier in the month by the Great Famine Event, in which President Mary Robinson and other notables had taken part. The Event took the form of musical concerts, readings and historical reconstructions, and the media reported it as a great success much enjoyed by young people.

It was unclear how the O'Neill family fitted into this scheme of devastation. There wasn't any family story about the Great Hunger, and I couldn't even be sure that my ancestors – Jim O'Neill's great-grandfather's generation – had lived in this area at the relevant time. At any rate, Jim O'Neill had surely been displeased about the blue-stone incident. However much he might have sympathized with the infliction of injury on Ascendancy landowners, he had a great respect for and, more importantly, a direct interest in the welfare of river and its stock; and the Key Hole was perhaps his favourite salmon holding pool.

I walked east along the bank. The trees grew thicker here and provided more cover than they did in the poaching days, when the railway company kept the branches in check. The bank, at this point a narrow ledge caught between the river and the railway embankment, rose six sheer feet above the water; dragging a net along here in the slippery darkness, from one pool to the next, could not have been an easy or safe business. The bank descended to water-level and I came to another bulge in the river. Here, among dripping alder trees, was the pool known as the Forge Hole. My grandfather used to reckon that if there was salmon in the Forge Hole there would be twice as many in the Key Hole.

There was something illicit about my solitary stroll, even though I was here with the consent of the Conners. But I would still have had to explain myself had a bailiff appeared and challenged me, and it was odd that I, an outsider with an English accent, might be less suspect in such a situation than a local like my grandfather. Which was not to say that Jim O'Neill was deterred by the laws of trespass or the people who enforced them. As a teenager (Grandma had told me), he was walking through the grounds of Kilbrittain Castle when a woman with a shotgun appeared and said to him, 'No tres-passing.' 'I'm not trespassing,' Jim said. 'I walked this land before you did and I'll come and go as I please.' On an other occasion, Jim returned from the river to his car to see his young son, Jim Junior, in the company of two men. He strolled up and asked peremptorily,

'Who are you?' 'I'm a guard, that's who I am,' replied one, stating the obvious. 'Did you identify yourself to my son?' Jim asked, noting that the men's uniforms were hidden under overcoats. 'I did not,' said the guard. 'Well then, what are you doing frightening my boy?' 'Dad,' Jim Junior piped up, 'he wouldn't believe me when I told him you were gone into the ditch for a call of nature.' My grandfather – who to the guards' knowledge had been gone for over half an hour – looked aggressively at the two men. 'How long I'm in there is my own business, do you understand?' Jim's antipathy for the authorities was such that, in the late 'fifties, he resisted 'out of principle' the attempts of John Scanlon, Chief Inspector, Cork Board of Fishery Conservators, to recruit him to the corps of Bandon bailiffs. Indeed, Jim actually succeeded (quite how was unclear) in securing the active assistance of two of the Chief Inspector's men, who would meet my grandfather in a pub in West Cork and tip him off about the whereabouts of the fish and the patrols. One of the two bailiffs, the story went, was a big bully of a man, but he was scared of Jim O'Neill.

The last time he went poaching was here, at Manch. It was in 1961, and with him were Jim Junior, Brendan, and Brendan's brother-in-law Seán O'Callaghan, who had just served seven and a half years in prison. The net was in the water when suddenly the bailiffs appeared. My grandfather and Seán ran for it in different directions, while Brendan – in accordance with precedent and practice and legislation, he told me dryly – assumed the responsibility, as the man on the opposite bank from the bailiffs, of trying to hang on to the net. There was a tug of war, which Brendan won by securing the net around a tree. He hid the net in Glenure farm, where the Kilmichael ambushers found billets, Brendan said. Everybody got away that night, even Seán O'Callaghan, who was picked up by the O'Neills near the Red Fort, outside Ballineen, in the early hours of the morning.

I stopped in at the Red Fort on my way back to Cork and ordered some lunch. On the wall above my table hung a framed newspaper clipping with a photograph taken of 'The Boys of Kilmichael' in 1938. The photo showed two rows of men in trenchcoats, smiling for the most part. All their names were set out, and below their names appeared the lyrics of the famous song about the ambush, 'The Boys of Kilmichael': 'We gathered our rifles and bayonets and soon left that glen so obscure,/And we never drew rein till we halted at the faraway camp of Glenure./Then here's to the boys of Kilmichael, those brave lads so gallant and true,/ Who fought 'neath the green flag of Erin and they conquered the red, white and blue.' The most famous Boy of Kilmichael of all was, of course, the man who authorized action against Admiral Somerville – Tom Barry.

It was quite a coincidence, seeing the photograph here. Only an hour or so beforehand I had learned from Oriana Conner that the Ballineen-Enniskean Historical Society, in which she was active, had produced a booklet detailing what eventually became of the men who carried out the Kilmichael ambush. What the Historical Society found, when it looked into the matter, was that the ambush seemed to have had an extraordinarily adverse effect on its partici-pants, many of whom went on to lead unusually difficult and saddening lives; and as I drove back to Cork city from the Red Fort, I wondered if there was any link between the Somerville shooting and my grandfather's hard life. I reflected that the time had come to take a trip to Castletownshend.

And so, the next day, my grandmother and I drove into West Cork. It surprised me a little that Grandma, who had never in her eighty-five years in county Cork been to Castletownshend, should have so cheerfully assumed the role of my accomplice in the histor-ical disturbance I was intent on committing. She knew about the Ardkitt gun and the abandonment of the getaway car near her aunt's house in Rathduff, and it must have been apparent that somebody she knew very well had been involved in the killing.

We drove to Bandon and from there headed south-west to Clonakilty. It was a June day of breezes and sunshine, and we trav-elled, as if through cathedrals, under brilliant and shadowy vaults of leaves. Nettles, ferns, brambles, furze, and flowers – fuchsia, blazing yellow dandelions, gigantic daisies – grew densely on the road bor-ders. West of Clonakilty, the air became briny and the country open and rough and boggy. The road narrowed further. Blue bodies of water appeared in fields, and violet rhododendron blooms leaned out of gardens. In places the road revealed a rocky and peninsular shoreline, where the Atlantic showed in patches that were as blue as the Cilician Mediterranean. Eventually, after negotiating a succession of disorienting crossroads, we came to a remote village that adhered to a hillside at the mouth of a fjord. Its remoteness was not a question of absolute isolation. Skibbereen, where Jim O'Neill used to poach for autumn salmon, was only five and half miles away, and there were many places further to the west – Baltimore, Schull, Ahakista, for example – that were more distant from Cork city. The faraway quality of Castletownshend lay in the fact that, unlike these other places, it was not the terminus of any particular route or a point on the way to anywhere else. Of the net of lanes and alleys in which West Cork is caught, only a straggly, circuitous and otherwise fruitless loop makes it out to Castletownshend, with the result that only a purposeful traveller – a person with a specific reason for veering off the small main road that continues on to Bantry and, many miles later, Killarney – is likely to wind up there.

Castletownshend was as pretty and prosperous as any village I'd seen in West Cork. At its entrance, on the crest of the hill down which the village neatly tumbled, was Drishane House, of which only high walls, huge gates and a drive that curved into a wooded distance could be seen. This was the home of Christopher Somerville, who I'd phoned a couple of days earlier; he declined to meet me, but he did confirm, in a sonorous English voice, that the Admiral was a relation – his great-uncle, to be exact. Past Drishane House was the plunging main street, lined with unusually handsome houses and brick and stone cottages. About halfway down the hill, two sycamore trees stood in the middle of the road, surrounded by a retaining wall; and nearby was a pub. We stopped there for lunch. I asked a lady where we might find Point House, explaining that I was interested in Admiral Somerville. After giving us directions, the woman suggested that we call in at the Castle and speak, if we could, to Mrs Salter-Townshend; she was an elderly lady and would probably well remember the incident of sixty-one years ago. So Grandma and I walked down to the Castle, whose high walls and large open gate could be seen at the bottom of the hill. It was a short stroll from the gate to the Castle itself, a three-storey building of dark stone, crenellations and square towers overlooking the haven, where small fishing and sailing boats were moored. Immediately to the rear of the building was a thickly forested hill and the Protestant church of the village, St Barrahane, where Admiral Somerville was buried. At the front of the Castle were a level gravel forecourt, on which a few cars were parked, and a lawn where Germans were trying to play croquet; the place was evidently now in use as a guest house or hotel. The sea was held at bay by a stone wall, at the foot of which becalmed ocean water washed onto a tiny pebbled strand.

We rang at the door of the Castle. A woman of around forty, dressed in jeans and a sweatshirt, greeted us. She told us that Mrs Salter-Townshend lived in the bungalow these days. She added, not unkindly, 'Whether she'll be prepared to speak to you or not will depend on the mood she's in. I can't say what she'll be like.' Passing two grazing white goats, we headed up to the bungalow, which was located, I later learned, on the site of the original house built by the Townshend family shortly after its arrival in Cork, in 1648, as part of the English Parliamentary army. It was Richard Townsend [*sic*] who personally delivered the keys of Cork to Oliver Cromwell.

The bungalow was built in the eyesore style characteristic of many of the hacienda-like constructions that were materializing in rural West Cork. The door was answered by a woman dressed in a down-to-earth, utilitarian way who was, I guessed, in her late seventies. I explained that I was looking for Mrs Salter-Townshend and wished to discuss the shooting of Admiral Somerville with her. The lady answered, in that slightly mumbling voice used by the ascendancy class to take the edge off an English accent, 'Well, I remember that; he was my cousin. It caused great pain to the family. I don't think it would be right to go over it again, do you?' As she looked at me, a man, red-faced, heroically dishevelled, whom for moment I took to be the gardener, poked his head around the door: Mr Salter-Townshend, I later learned. Mrs Salter-Townshend regarded me grimly. 'We still don't know who did it,' she said.

Speaking in my most English accent, I mentioned another former resident of Castletownshend, the Admiral's nephew Sir Patrick Coghill – the SIME agent and subsequent captor of Joseph Dakak. Mrs Salter-Townshend said that, yes, she remembered him; he spoke Arabic and Turkish. The Coghill family still lived here, she added. Sir Toby Coghill, Patrick's nephew, had two properties in the village and he spent part of the year here. She looked at us again, probably taking in for the first time the unlikely character of the couple standing before her. 'Well, you can't keep your grandmother outside. Please come in.'

We sat down in the front room, which had an unsurpassable view of the bay and a carpet that featured the same furiously swirling colours I'd seen in the farmhouses at Graunriagh and Ardkitt. Modest heirlooms furnished the room, and a painting by Sir Patrick's father, Sir Egerton Coghill, Bt., hung on a wall. We continued chatting about the Coghills. Mrs Salter-Townshend said that the Coghill family home, Glenbarrahane, had been destroyed, which led to Grandma to chip in about the shameful neglect of old homes generally, which led to a discussion of the Georgian Society and, finally, of the unfortunate disappearance of Bowen's Court, the ancestral home of the writer Elizabeth Bowen. One would never have guessed Grandma's close connection to those who had so assiduously burned down Big Houses during the Anglo-Irish War. When Mrs Salter-Townshend momentarily turned away to pour tea, my grandmother gave me a conspiratorial wink that said, 'You see, we've got her talking now.'

At this point it occurred to me that the conversation between the two old ladies – Mrs Salter-Townshend impatient, assertive and very kind, Grandma effusive and warm as ever – had a decidedly strange, even eerie, aspect: it was entirely possible that the cousin of the person serving the tea had been shot dead by the husband of the person drinking it. Feeling slightly compromised, I thought that the time had perhaps come to return to the subject of Admiral Somerville and disclose my interest in him. However, just as I was pondering precisely what the nature of that interest might be, our hostess rose and said that she'd an appointment and regrettably had to go. As we were accompanied to the door, Mrs Salter-Townshend handed me some brochures about properties in Castletownshend which she handled as agent for the owners. She said warmly to my grandmother, 'Come by whenever you're next here.'

We left the grounds of the Castle and started to walk back to the car, Grandma stepping tirelessly up the hill with the slightly rolling gait that practically all her sons have inherited. We got into the car and moved off. As we reached the two trees about a third of the way up the hill, I turned left down a lane called the Mall, which headed down towards the ocean. Immediately to our right, as we slowly descended, was the sizeable lodge house which was all that remained of the Coghill family property, Glenbarrahane, and which, one of Mrs Salter-Townshend's brochures informed me, hosted in its roof space the largest known nursery of bats in Europe.

After the war, Sir Patrick Coghill, a little lost, spent a few years at this property with his elderly mother and aunt. In 1952, he left to set up the Special Branch of the Police of Jordan, from where he was expelled in 1956. He returned to Castletownshend and, he wrote in his autobiography, 'to futility, to a bogus 18th century civilisation which was quite moribund, if not mummified, and what was worse, to boredom'. Furthermore, 'having spent most of my life in England or serving the Crown, I intensely disliked living under the Irish Republican flag and government'. In the 'sixties, he finally decided to move across the water. Sir Patrick Somerville Coghill died in England in 1981, at the age of 84.

We reached the bottom of the lane. To our right was the entrance to Point House or, to be precise, The Point, as the property had been renamed by Admiral Somerville when he retired there after the Great War. 'Do Not Enter' notices were plastered everywhere.

Driving in, we found ourselves traversing an extraordinarily beautiful, tilted garden which ran down the landscaped contours of the hill by way of lawns, spectacular rock formations and exotic shrubbery; and looking out to the sunlit west, there was a dumb-foundingly beautiful view of a wild headland and the ocean. Then we came to the house. I recognized it from the newspaper photographs I'd seen. A late Victorian mansion of great simplicity, its charm was reduced only marginally by incongruous new window frames and a new entrance porch that stood in the place of the old porch where the Admiral's corpse had lain for days pending the arrival of the pathologist. It was my intention to ring the bell and talk to whoever lived in the building – an Austrian countess, a villager had told me – about the terrible moment in the house's past, and to try to find out if and how it still haunted the house. But I lost my nerve. It seemed a shame to mar the achieved quietness of this place with an old and unpleasant matter, and I allowed myself to conclude, without ringing the bell or even stopping the car, that no one was in. As we drove back to gate, gravel crunched under the car's tyres just as, no doubt, it had crunched under the shoes of the men sprinting away from the house that night in March 1936. It was not a short driveway, a hundred yards or so, and the men, already breathless with terror and excitement, must have been gasping by the time they reached the car waiting at the gate. It wasn't difficult, as we left Castletownshend, to imagine the country darkness into which the killers had sped, a shapeless obscurity of heaths and boglands and hills yielding only to the dull gaslight flare of an isolated cottage and the short track of light spewed out by the car.

We took an especially roundabout route back to Cork, heading north to Dunmanway, which, though she has not lived there for nearly seventy years, is my grandmother's everlasting home town. Dunmanway marks the western extremity of the fertile Bandon valley, which constitutes an exception to the relatively poor land of which most of West Cork is composed. We drove along Main Street and arrived at a picturesque octagonal square. Grandma pointed out the location of the first home she remembered, which was now a vacant lot just off the square. The next Lynch home, in Railway Street, was still intact. The nearest thing to trees on the street were the tall wooden poles that strung cables over the rooftops and the road. My grandmother pointed out her old home, where she'd lived in terror of the British forces, a grey, two-storey terraced house that was part of a long, sullenly unadorned terrace of houses that ran the length of Railway Street under black roofs and gave abruptly on to the pavement without so much as a doorstep.

As we headed out of Dunmanway, Grandma pointed to a
substantial townhouse. 'That one,' she said, 'used to belong to
Fitzmaurice, a solicitor, who fled Ireland after two men, Gray and
Buttimer, were shot dead in Dunmanway square in 1921 during the
Black and Tan War. After Fitzmaurice,' Grandma said, 'the house
belonged to Henry Smith, a Protestant from the North with twenty-
four children, who once gave shelter to your great-uncle Jack Lynch
when he was on the run; and after the Smiths it was occupied by the
Duffys, famous all over the country for their circus.'

I made a note of Grandma's story that evening and did not give
it any further thought; I vaguely assumed that Gray and Buttimer,
in common with the other dead from those times mentioned by my
grandmother, were the victims of yet another British atrocity.

We drove east along the Bandon valley and soon came to
Ballineen and Enniskean, whose gradual physical merger over the
years was acknowledged by a signboard announcing the Ballineen–
Enniskean Development Area. We drove through Bandon town and
then Inishannon, where the road, an unsightly and pot-holed strip
of tarmac in my grandfather's time, had been widened and
smartened by EC money. Skimming along the new highway, we
passed an ancient railway viaduct that hovered over a valley, and
soon after crossed the boundary of Cork city, population 136,000,
which declared itself a Nuclear Free Zone and a special friend of
Cologne, Rennes, and Coventry. As we turned onto the new ring
road that sped traffic efficiently into south-east Cork, I would not
have been surprised to see, in this wave of up-beat redesignation, a
sign announcing our presence in Emerald Tiger Country. Whereas
uncle Brendan saw persistent poverty and social injustice and class
struggle, it was possible to gain the impression from the mainstream media that the chief economic problem in Cork, in these
unprecedented times of high growth and low inflation and net
immigration and soaring property values, was finding sufficient
numbers of takers for the vacancies (in high-technology work,
especially) that were opening up in their hundreds. The old political and religious obsessions seemed further away than ever, and I
asked my grandmother what she made of the changes taking place.

It turned out that although she was proud of what had been achieved, Grandma was troubled by the emerging national character. She was worried, and a little amazed, by the sudden loss of authority of the Catholic church, which had become the source of a seemingly ever-flowing stream of sexual scandals and the butt of nihilistic TV comedies. 'There *is* a God,' Grandma said with an uncharacteristically anxious vehemence that made me glance over at her small, seat-belted figure, 'as one day those that think there isn't will find out to their cost.' Grandma also didn't understand the apathy amongst young people towards politics – 'They say that they're not "interested" in the elections. Sure, if you're not interested in your country, what are you interested in?' – and history: 'A country is nothing without its history,' my grandmother declared.

We arrived home. While Grandma went upstairs, I waited in the kitchen, the hub of the house and its point of entry, through the back door, for family and friends. Small pictures hung on the wall: reproduction paintings of a basket of peaches and a basket of strawberries, a photograph of a sunset at sea seen through reeds, and two watercolours of birds. Pope John Paul II appeared in a white frame, and a porcelain wall-figurine of the Virgin Mary kissing the baby Jesus. Also displayed were postcards from children and grandchildren mailed from Aqaba, New York, Santander, Youghal, Lanzarote, Portugal, Bretagne, Majorca. The family horizons were expanding. Above the table hung the text of a house blessing:

> God bless the corners of this house,
> And be the lintel blest;
> And bless the hearth and bless the board
> And bless each door that opens wide
> To stranger as to kin;
> And bless each crystal window pane
> That lets the starlight in;
> And bless the roof tree overhead
> And every sturdy wall.
>
> The peace of man, the peace of God,
> The peace of love on all.

This was what a republican safe house looked like: it was here that Grandma, on a couple of occasions after her husband's death, gave refuge, without the family's knowledge, to republicans – 'proper gentlemen', in her recollection – wanted by the authorities in connection with acts of extreme political violence.

When Grandma returned to the kitchen, we drank a cup of tea and ate bread and butter and ham. We talked about various things, and gradually we came back to the topic of my grandfather. Grandma said that in the 'sixties, when they were living here, the two would go off to Bodenstown and other republican commemorations and marches together. In about 1970, they went to the North with a party from the south. Jim and Eileen and the others crossed the border at Monaghan on foot with a tricolour held before them and repaired a road that had been cratered in an attempt to close down the border crossing. A British army helicopter flew overhead as they worked. It fell to Jim O'Neill, the senior republican present, to address some remarks to the volunteer road-gang; and he did so. The party headed back that evening on the bus, singing songs. When she got home, Grandma removed her boots and hung them in the shed with the Northern mud still sticking to them. The boots hung untouched for years, a monument to the unvanquishable urge for freedom and, it turned out, to the only time my grandfather set foot north of the border.

Grandma told me this story and then, going into a declamatory trance, she looked me in the eye and said, without hesitation:

> Who is Ireland's enemy?
> Not Germany nor Austria,
> Nor Russia, France nor Spain
> That robbed and reaved this land of ours,
> That forged her rusty chain
> But England of the wily words
> A crafty, treacherous foe.
> 'Twas England scourged our motherland,
> 'Twas England laid her low.

I thought that she had finished, but there was more to come:

Rise up, O dead of Ireland
And rouse her living men,
The chance will come to us at last
To win our own again;
To sweep the English enemy
From hill and glen and bay,
And in your name, O holy dead
Our secret debt to pay!

There was a silence, and eventually I asked Grandma whether Jim, if he could have his time again, would do anything differently. 'No,' my grandmother said, 'I don't think so.' She gave the question a moment's further reflection and then, in a twist I hadn't at all expected, added, 'Like his father, he was a very intelligent man. If he were alive today, with all the education and opportunities that you now have. . . . ' My grandmother wrinkled her mouth pensively.

I was slightly taken aback. For all of her political passion and her doubts about the country's new money culture and her stories of the Black and Tans and her photographs of her husband's IRA

Grandma

burial, for all of her investment in her husband's configuration as an
IRA hero, my grandmother, in what seemed to be the final analysis,
was dwelling on Jim O'Neill's life in economic terms and contem-
plating, somewhat wistfully, the affluent and fulfilling life that, in
more opportune times, he might have led. Was she tacitly acknowl-
edging that in different circumstances her husband might have left
the business of revolution to others? After all, if Jim had stood to
inherit Ardkitt, would he have risked years of imprisonment and
separation from his farm? Or would he, like the vast majority of the
Cork farming class, have been diverted from active service in the
IRA by the demands and preoccupations of country life – a life of
ploughing championships, carts and harnesses, colts, hens, heifers,
horses, cows, potatoes, wheat seeds, whist drives, of dropping in on
Enniskean Hall for a party thrown by the Newcestown, Ballineen
and Enniskean Coursing Club (music by the Heatherbell Band,
dancing 9 to 2) and attending the meetings and dances of the West
Cork Branch of the Irish Creamery Managers' Association, the
Clonakilty Agricultural Society, and the Co. Cork Farmers'
Assocation (Ballineen Branch)? This was the lost world that Jim
O'Neill dreamed of inhabiting, a world in which a rebel might in
good conscience limit his involvement to the cause to making contributions to the Republican Prisoners' Dependants Fund or
turning a blind eye to the dumping of arms on his land.

If Jim's political involvement might have been contingent on his
social and economic situation, the question arose as to the degree to
which his internment at the Curragh, and perhaps even his convictions on the issue of national freedom, were manifestations of a
deeper captivity. But what kind of captivity? Poverty was a cage of
sorts, certainly; but it was not exclusive to Jim and did not affect
him in his last years; and it didn't fully account for an image of my
grandfather that had crept into my mind and would not go away,
that of a man who gripped life's every stick and pole with the white-
knuckled rage of a man gripping the bars of a cell.

A day or two after our visit to Castletownshend, Grandma
arranged a visit to Peig Lynch. I'd never met Peig, and fixing

up the meeting had not been an entirely straightforward business, because there was a sense that over the years Peig had held herself – and her late husband Jack, an easy-going, convivial man if left to his own devices – at a distance from the O'Neill/Lynch axis of the family. (Jack had died in 1990, aged 83. His Mass card read, 'All I ask of you is that wherever you may be you will always remember me at the altar of God.') Nonetheless, Grandma and I received a very cordial welcome from Peig, an irreverent, sharp, slightly dramatic woman who refused to disclose her age and hobbled along with the help of a black cane and shot out crafty, knowing glances as she spoke; it interested her that I was a lawyer and that I was writing a book. Peig was an amateur painter, and numerous examples of her work hung on the walls of the living-room where we sat.

Peig came from Crossbarry, the West Cork village best known as the scene of another famous ambush by Tom Barry and his men. Her father, a teacher, and mother died young, and Peig was brought up by an aunt and grandmother. Although not from a republican family – 'They were interested in the price of cows and eggs,' Peig said – she grew up in a highly politicized world. 'There was nothing else spoken of in Crossbarry but politics. I thought Easter was to celebrate the Rising; I knew nothing about the resurrection.' At any rate, she was 'very much aware of the political situation' when she met Jack Lynch, in Clonakilty, in around 1941, just over a year or so after he'd returned from active service in the English bombing campaign. The young couple, who were not to marry until 1949, had different ideological positions. 'I was more of a trade unionist, or socialist, than a nationalist, whereas Jack was very military in his outlook,' Peig said, before adding, as a mischievous concession, ' – although he did think *a bit*.' Jack was on the run when he and Peig started going together, and it wasn't long before he was arrested and locked up – first at Mountjoy, then at Arbour Hill, then at the Curragh. 'He was a grand subject for jail,' Peig said. 'He didn't think of the outside until he got out.'

Grandma said, 'Jim was very suspicious when he came out. He wouldn't give anything away until he knew you. But then he was always a careful man.'

Shortly after Jack's arrest, Peig was herself picked up. She was remanded in custody in Limerick for a time and then, after her trial and conviction, imprisoned for two and a half years at Mountjoy Prison. She was both proud and blasé about the episode. 'I never did an awful lot, only talk,' she said. 'They found me in possession of a broken-up gun. I didn't know the front from the back.'

The subject of guns having been raised, I mentioned the Ardkitt gun, and then I mentioned Admiral Somerville. I told Peig that it had been suggested I ask her about it. Peig glanced at Grandma, her eyes and glasses gleaming. 'What does it matter,' she said slyly. 'They're all dead now.' Then she mentioned three names, and it seemed to me that for a moment Grandma's face was covered in confusion.

I was surprised, too. Jim O'Neill did not kill Henry Boyle Somerville. Neither did Peig's husband, the man of action, Jack Lynch. Somerville's killers, according to Peig, were my great-uncle Tadhg Lynch; Angela Lynch; and a man called Joe Collins.

'Joe Collins?' I said.

'Joe was from Dunmanway,' Peig said. 'He used to come to us on Tuesday nights. He was a grand character. He would never tell a lie.'

Grandma spoke up: 'Joe was a true blue. You could trust him with your life.'

Peig said, 'Tadhg was an aggressive person, but very clever. One time he and a great friend of mine, Mrs O'Hagan, who was real racy, burned huts on the border and then went to the races together dressed to kill. Tadhg never changed over the years,' Peig said. 'He was a colourful character.'

'Tadhg was one,' Grandma agreed. She was fully composed once more.

There was a pause as Peig Lynch shifted in her chair, making herself more comfortable. Then she said, with an odd emphasis, 'Angela was a *true* republican.'

I asked Grandma about Angela. 'Angela was my sister,' Grandma said. 'She was perhaps four or five years younger than me. She was a great camogie player. She died at the age of 22, from septicaemia she got in England, where she worked as a nurse. When her body was returned to Ireland it was buried with full military honours by Cumann na mBan. It was the last funeral attended by Mrs Tomás MacCurtain Senior,' Grandma said.

My grandmother and her sister-in-law began to chat about this and that.

When I spoke to Brendan afterwards, he confirmed that Tadhg and Angela and Joe Collins were the names he'd been given. Angela, he added, had taken part in the 1939 English bombing campaign, probably in the reconnaissance and/or decoy role that had no doubt been hers at Castletownshend.

Brendan also told me that his father knew that the Somerville gun had been dumped somewhere at Ardkitt. In fact, Jim O'Neill often searched for the revolver, paying particular attention to the thick walls of the farmhouse, in which he suspected the weapon had been buried. But he never found anything. In the end, the Colt .45 only surfaced by accident, when the current owner, Pat O'Neill, passed a metal detector over a hedge near the farmhouse.

When I flew back to London, I could find no mention in the historical literature of Angela Lynch, which was perhaps not surprising in view of the chauvinist slant of Irish republican self-history. There were numerous references, by contrast, to Joe Collins.

Like Angela and her brother Jack, Joe Collins served in the English campaign. Years afterwards, he went on record with a description of the near-fatal moment when his home-made bomb, packed in a suitcase and ready to be delivered to its target, exploded in his room: unlike the Hezbollah guerrilla who blew himself to bits at the Lawrence Hotel, Collins was saved by answering the door at the moment of the explosion. Not long afterwards, Collins was arrested in Manchester and sentenced to twenty years of prison. In Parkhurst Prison, he procured his official file with the help of a professional safe-cracker. The file contained a report by his prison priest, in which it was stated that Joseph Collins was a 'very difficult case, and a confirmed Rebel – both here and in Ireland. . . . There's no change in this prisoner's political ideas. . . . [He] is apparently unmoved by getting 20 years P.S. . . . It's most doubtful whether this man will ever lead a law-abiding life.' Joe Collins served a total of nine years in England, but afterwards still cut an impressively confident and likeable figure. My father enthusiastically recalled 'A tall, slim, very distinguished-looking guy, very well-dressed. He went to the States in the end, I think. I can see him standing in front of me now, standing there with a broad smile on his face.'

Finally, there was Tadhg, the senior member and almost certainly the commander of the unit – whom Grandma had once described to me as a strategist and not one to go out and do the shooting. In addition to what I already knew about him – it seemed significant, in retrospect, that he became adjutant-general of the IRA, and Tom Barry's right-hand-man, only months after the Somerville shooting – I learned that Tadhg was great footballer, that he'd won a gold medal for excellence in his school leaving certificate, that he never drank, that he managed greyhound tracks at Shelbourne Park and Harold's Cross in Dublin, and that he died suddenly of a heart attack, at the age of 55, while watching the harecoursing. To my father, Tadhg figured as an emblem of academic prowess. Kevin found his uncle a thoughtful and kindly man. Kevin liked and respected his uncle so much that my full name is Tadhg Joseph O'Neill.

I didn't really know what to make of this strange link – except, perhaps, that it gave me a peculiar justification for grappling with what my namesake Tadhg had done. This was emboldening, because once the main facts of the shooting were known to me, I was assailed by self-doubt. What had I ever done to earn the right to pronounce, favourably or unfavourably, on the actions of my elders? Who was I to sit in a judicial capacity? My misgivings were exacerbated by the paradoxical fact that Peig Lynch's act of disclosure, which had been actively facilitated by my grandmother and uncle, effectively constituted my family's authority to reveal its role in the Somerville killing. Such authorization was unlikely to mean that the family now wished to disassociate itself from the killing; if it signified anything, it was that the passage of years had finally made it possible for us to publicly lay claim to it. It was relevant, here, that even though my grandfather played no active part in the shooting, it was difficult to disentangle him from it. He was the only connection between the killers and Ardkitt, and there was no reason to doubt that, if called on, my grandfather would have used on Admiral Somerville the gun dumped at Ardkitt.

The Colt .45 used to shoot Admiral Somerville

As I chewed on what to do, it occurred to me that in any event I should contact the deceased's family and offer to disclose to them the identities of his killers before I made them public. Christopher Somerville responded promptly to my letter. He wrote back, 'I have no wish to know who shot my great-uncle, and those who were really affected by his death (his widow and children) are all dead and I could not speak for them. Sorry!' And Mrs Salter-Townshend wrote, 'I am not interested in knowing the names of the murderers of Admiral Somerville, who you say are now dead. It serves no useful purpose, being "water under the bridge" now.' In a slight undermining of this last assertion, she combatively added, 'I am sure that anyone who knows anything about it, or who knew Admiral Somerville would agree that it was a most cowardly act to shoot an unarmed and much loved and respected man for no apparent reason. He was a second cousin and friend of my Father's, they had been at school together as small children. The whole village and parish were profoundly shocked and upset by the murder as both he and his family were very popular and on good terms with everyone.' Mrs Salter-Townshend continued:

> This is a quiet and peaceful village, interested in fishing and tourism, both in the 1930s and today, with a sea-going tradition like all the coast of West Cork.

Although slightly puzzled by this last remark, which seemed to veer off the point, I put her reaction, and that of Christopher Somerville, down to a perfectly natural reluctance to re-open a painful and long-gone episode. And as the summer of 1997 wore on, a sudden flow of events in Ireland led me to wonder whether the rights and wrongs of a night in 1936 were not, as Mrs Salter-Townshend had said, simply water under the bridge. On 20 July 1997, the IRA declared a new ceasefire and entered into negotiations for a new political dispensation. The negotiations, mediated by the former United States senator George Mitchell, dragged on for months against a backdrop of sectarian killings of Catholics, bombings carried out by furiously disaffected republicans, and gruesome IRA 'punishment shootings' of suspected drug-dealers and other unpopular elements of the nationalist community. But on Good Friday, 10 April 1998, the parties signed an accord that provided, in effect, for the creation of a Northern Irish assembly; a cross-border ministerial council linking Belfast and Dublin on issues of mutual interest, such as tourism and agriculture; the abandonment of the Republic of Ireland constitutional claim to the Six Counties; an amnesty for all political prisoners; and the use by all parties of 'any influence they may have' to persuade paramilitary groups to disarm by June 2000. Like almost everybody else, I was jubilant. The Good Friday Agreement addressed (though of course did not fully meet) the central grievance of northern nationalists by giving Dublin a say in the government of their affairs, yet did so without diminishing the unionist capacity for self-government. The Agreement did not end the dispute as to the proper government of all Ireland, but it did promise to limit the dispute to the non-violent realm of constitutional politics; in other words, it promised peace. In May 1998, island-wide referendums resulted in 94.5 per cent of voters in the Republic and 71.1 per cent in Northern Ireland approving the measures proposed by the Good Friday Agreement. Even Grandma voted Yes. 'My head said no, but my heart said yes,' she told me on the phone with a slightly apologetic laugh.

I was very happy for my grandmother, glad that she could take pleasure in the thought that her years of political effort had reached a fruitful conclusion. It had required an ideological leap on her part to launch her into the political mainstream, a leap which, moreover, took her further away from her late husband. Jim O'Neill, said everyone whose views I canvassed, would have voted No. He would have regarded the Agreement as having set at naught a lifetime of republican toil.

I couldn't really understand this viewpoint, because it seemed obvious to me that republican violence had achieved all that it was ever going to achieve. That said, it was also now obvious to me that the violence had, in fact, been efficacious. The inter-party negotiations, during which the Ulster Unionist leader, David Trimble, experienced the greatest difficulty in persuading his party members to accept the slightest measure of political change, had clarified that it was only the prospect of a return to war of the last thirty years that had spurred London to act and persevere and induced unionists to loosen their supremacist attachment to the Northern Irish status quo. The modern IRA campaign therefore passed Yitzhak Shamir's test for the validity of an act of lethal political violence: it changed the course of history. Shamir's extremely consequentialist test was obviously flawed as an ethical proposition, because it sanctioned the use of any effective means for any purpose. But if the 3,200 killings in the recent Troubles – up to two-thirds of which had been by republicans – had brought about a substantial amelioration in the lot of nationalists that would not otherwise have been achieved, suddenly it became very difficult for me to affirm that the price of change had been excessive – even if I felt that the principle merit of the Agreement may have been to bring to an end the very violence that had produced it. This line of thought led to another: if the apparently fruitless IRA activities of old had, by keeping the battered vehicle of republicanism on the road, substantially contributed to the IRA's modern campaign, could those activities also be said, in retrospect, to have served a positive purpose? If yes, could the same be said about the Somerville killing, which jump-started the republican motor in 1936?

A justification of this kind entailed rationalizing the assassination as a form of *notice*. The purpose of such violence was not to bring about direct or immediate change or to make a measurable military gain but, rather, to alert the world to the existence of a wrongful political injury – in this case, the continuing trespass of the English in the north of Ireland – with a view to preserving, and enabling the eventual enforcement of, the rights of the injured party. Just as, in an ordinary case of trespass, signs of continuing ownership were required to defeat the claim of a long-term trespasser, so the title of the Irish nation in the land occupied by the English, if it was not to fall by the wayside, had to be asserted. More basically, after years of republican inactivity, a national revival of the IRA and its cause was required in 1936. Simply warning Admiral Somerville to stop helping would-be recruits to the Royal Navy would not have accomplished this; shooting him undoubtedly did. The fact that the Admiral had not been warned, and therefore might be said not to have 'deserved' his fate, was in this context (rather than in the context of a just war) an ethical irrelevance. It was not necessary to identify a 'deserving' target of violence, because in many ways the less deserving and more shocking the target, the greater the notice that would be taken of the existence and seriousness of the injury complained of and, as a consequence, the less gratuitous – and the more effective and morally coherent – would be the act of violence. Violence of this kind also gave rise to this assessment of the killers: that, in their readiness to assume the guilt and risks that came with the killing, they were to be applauded for assuming a moral burden on behalf of society; for, as the Good Friday Agreement illustrated, it was a well-recognized phenomenon that the apparently pacific majority in Ireland furtively but gratefully adopted the outcomes produced by the violent actions of republicans.

Having constructed this cold-hearted polemic, I recoiled from it. Although its final proposition rang true, taken as a whole it was clearly specious, not least because it appeared to sanction, say, the massacre of a classroom of schoolchildren as a mechanism of political complaint; and every moral intuition I possessed told me that was surely wrong. In any event, the polemic was a red herring: for Admiral Somerville was almost certainly killed by people who thought he deserved to die. What I still didn't fully understand was *why* they thought this – or why they thought that killing *him* would be politically productive.

However, to return to Mrs Salter-Townshend's point, did any of this matter any more? A palpable change in the political culture in Ireland suggested that it did not. Irish nationalism had entered a phase in which even the republican wing of the movement increasingly recognized the distinction between improving the lot of northern nationalists and unifying the island. It was more noticeable than ever that, with the progress of the peace process – i.e., the 1994 and 1997 ceasefires, the IRA's agreement to the 'Mitchell principles' of non-violence, the all-party talks, and finally the Good Friday agreement – people in the Republic felt increasingly able to take an interest in the bloodshed of Irish history as a kind of entertainment, and anguished and bitter scrutiny of this or that unpleasant incident suddenly seemed misplaced and old hat. As old tensions disappeared, I wondered if it wasn't a hard reality of certain kinds of political change that, after a point, certain victims and injustices were best forgotten about; and if, perhaps, the healthiest thing might not simply be to let Admiral Somerville rest.

8

The storm-blown, starving travellers landed, their mouths watering at the sight of all this wealth of food, but directly they seized a bread-fruit from the nearest tree, it passed from their hands into a shadow, and everything they met with had the same evanescent quality. . . . At length they met with some of the inhabitants. Like everything else in this strange country, though they appeared to be solid, they, too, were shades, and the living men passed through their forms as if there was nothing there. The shades spoke, however, and told them that this was Bulotu, the Place of Departed Souls, and they were the Tangaloa of old time, and the Souls of Eiki, their departed Chiefs. They said that no solid food, such as they needed, could be got here, for all that grew was shadow-food, the Food of the Gods, for their shadowy sustenance. . . .

But Bulotu is a bourne from which no traveller may ever return for long. It is the Land of the Dead, and its air, however deliciously scented, is the air of Death, not fitted for mortal lungs. In the course of a few days after reaching Tonga, all these travellers died, and being Chiefs, went permanently to Bulotu; not as a punishment for their temerity, but as the natural consequence of once breathing that fatal atmosphere.

– Admiral Boyle Townshend Somerville, *Will Mariner*

Adana, the fourth biggest city in Turkey, sits on the inland rim of a sweltering delta largely given over to the cultivation of cotton. In 1942, the counter-espionage agent Sir Patrick Coghill found Adana 'a deadly, absolutely one-horse town for all of its 80,000 inhabitants', and forty years afterwards, with its population approaching one million, Adana was still looked on – at least, from the maritime, relatively cosmopolitan vantage-point of Mersin – as tedious, insular, and provincial; which was perhaps why my own interaction with the place was limited to flying into and out of its small, stifling airport. In recent times, these adverse perceptions have been challenged. Although to drive into the city is still to penetrate a spattering of industrial buildings and dreary, dimly-lit blocks of housing, with its theatre and its resident orchestra and its archaeological and ethnographical museums and its university hospital and its increasingly cherished antiquity – Hittites, Persians, Greeks and Romans were settled here, the last-mentioned building a twenty-one-arch bridge that still carries traffic across the river Seyhan – Adana is developing another image. We are now invited to see a vigorous and self-confident city that, although devout as ever – a new mosque has the tallest minaret in Turkey and a capacity close to 30,000 – is not afraid to look the west in the eye or, even, to glance at the face of its pre-Kemalist past. One aspect of this modified vision, I discovered one night in late August 1998 was the restoration of Adana's rather magnificent three-storey station-house to its original glory. Its stones and brick had been cleaned and its red roof tiles renewed, and in the tree-lined plaza at the front of the station a shiny, vividly painted steam engine was marooned on a length of track. The installation functioned as spectacle and technological homage – who does not admire steam engines? – but, like any relic, it also gave off a spray of history which for most people no doubt fell as fine, inconsequential vapour.

A railroad first arrived in Adana back in 1886, on the completion of the short but valuable Mersin–Adana line, which, like most of the few disjointed railways then in existence in Turkey, was wholly owned by British capitalists. In 1908, the Mersin–Adana line officially became a branch line of the Deutsche Bank-financed

Baghdad Railway, which was seen by Germany's rival powers, themselves engaged since the Crimean War in the exploitation and manipulation of the disintegrating, systemically out-dated and finally debt-crippled Ottoman Empire, as one of the most sinister features of German expansionism: for the BBB (Berlin–Byzantium–Baghdad) promised German-controlled railways from the Baltic to the Persian Gulf and German growth in Mesopotamia, Syria and Arabia. For the German public, the appeal of the *drang nach Osten* was entrancing. German traders ranging from travelling salesmen to infrastructural contractors followed the banking syndicates into the Ottoman Empire, and by 1898, when the Kaiser visited Istanbul, the finance and trade of the Empire, which previously had been practically exclusive to France and Great Britain, was predominantly in German hands. In order to fund the Railway – regarded by Sultan Abdul Hamid II as a crucial military transport link between the great cities of Istanbul, Izmir, Aleppo, Damascus, Beirut, Mosul and Baghdad – the Ottoman government issued guarantees which committed it to paying investors huge sums; the result was German control over the Ottoman treasury and powerful political influence over the Sultan and, after his removal from power in 1908, the Young Turk government.

Although British influence in the Near East went back a long way – in *Macbeth*, Act I Scene iii, there is a reference to a sailor who's 'to Aleppo gone' – it was France, as the dominant regional power, that had the most to lose from the growth of German influence. In imitation of the French imperial method, German missions and schools sprang up in the Near East to promote knowledge and appreciation of *das Deutschum* – the values and character of German civilization, German history and, most importantly, the German language. In the words of one Dr Rohrbach, an influential commentator of the time,

> No lasting and secure cultural influences are possible
> without the connecting link of language. The intelligent and
> progressive young men of Turkey should have an abundant
> opportunity to learn German. . . . We can give the Turks an

impression of our civilisation and a desire to become familiar
with it only when we teach them our language and thus open
the door for them to all of our cultural possessions.

The epitome of the intelligent and progressive young man of
Turkey was, of course, the linguistically gifted sixteen-year-old
who, in September 1916, presented himself to his German superiors for work in the construction of the Berlin–Baghdad Railway,
Joseph Dakak.

The station-house at Adana gave way to two relatively humble
platforms. In the rafters of the platform roofs, hundreds of swallows had established a colony. The birds fidgeted and cleaned their
feathers and looked out of nest-holes and darted around in the
warm air, while below them sprawling families played out scenes of
good-tempered restlessness. The women, every one wearing a headscarf, kept an eye on the children, often grabbing them and giving
them ferocious and unselfconscious kisses. The men, cigarettes constantly ablaze, sat with their legs daintily crossed, the toe of the
dangling foot pointed towards the ground so as not impolitely to
expose the sole of the shoe. They wore pyjama-like trousers, knitted hats, cloth caps, baggy short-sleeved shirts (the buttons undone
to reveal a white vest and an undergrowth of chest hair), faded blue
or grey or brown suits. I was the only westernized traveller, Turkish
or foreign, to be seen.

At four in the morning, a blinding, otherworldly light, accompanied by a terrible blast of a horn, advanced out of the western
darkness. The Taurus Express had arrived. There was a brief crush
as passengers with cases and packages descended from the carriages.
Then I boarded the train. It was packed with overnight travellers
struggling for sleep, and the odour of feet was distinctive. There
was no restaurant car, and First Class consisted of claustrophobic
six-seat compartments that appeared marginally less comfortable
than the open seating in the Second Class carriages.

Inexplicably delayed, the train remained immobile for an hour.
Then, at daybreak, we finally dawdled out of the station, the diesel
engine roaring like a bus. We crossed the river Seyhan and

sluggishly traversed the northern part of city, where nomads had made camp in a wasteland of cement structures ruined by an earth-quake a couple of months before. The train continued to emit monstrous hoots, scattering wild dogs roaming around the track and awakening people in the ramshackle sleeping platforms built on the houses' flat rooftops. A flock of storks hovered on air currents high in the pale sky. Ahead, the railway line made a frail curve towards the east.

When I first conceived of this outing, my thought was simply to follow in my grandfather's footsteps on the Taurus Express. But the Taurus Express was no longer an international spy-train. It was merely bound for Gaziantep, a couple of hundred kilometres to the east, and not, as in the old days, across the frontier to Aleppo and beyond. The luxurious wagon-lits had been replaced by tired car-riages, and the cosmopolitan gentlemen and shady diplomats and pulp-fiction blondes of the war years had disappeared. Nowadays the train only carried families who could not afford to travel by bus and who in the old days would have sat crushed into hard-seated, sweaty third-class coaches armed with bags of dates, grapes, white cheese and salted nuts. This was not Joseph Dakak's scene at all. He would never had travelled, for example, in the company of the group of men seated next to me. Dressed in old-fashioned rustic attire, they spoke in an extremely expressive and intent manner, their serious looks and emphatic gestures and low, urgent tones suggesting important and telling confabulations; but I had no idea what any of them was saying, and even if my Turkish had allowed me to eavesdrop I would have been little the wiser, because I had no real idea who these people were or what kind of existence they led. Although, in westernized Mersin, the public lives and values of Christians and Muslims had merged to such an extent as to be superficially indistinguishable, my fellow travellers came from a world I knew little about – and actually feared. They belonged to the Anatolian hinterland into which the train was headed, a region that, on the dozen or so nights I'd crossed it by bus from Istanbul or Izmir to Mersin, had always filled me with a dread of my impending annihilation. I knew it as a black, unfathomable zone of flickering petrol stations, senseless land formations and barely lit villages, a place in which humanity, almost entirely rubbed out by the vast dark erasers of the plains and mountains and sky, was exposed at its most nugatory. What I was really feeling, during these journeys, was the solipsistic anxiety that can result from being plunged among people with whom I stood in a relation of near-total mutual ignorance. To be among such strangers was a form of eradication; for which of them could bear witness to who I was? And the converse was also true: unable meaningfully to incorporate these Anatolians into my narratives about the world, I lacked the ability to do them justice. They were literally insignificant.

I was confronting this disagreeable truth, as the train pulled slowly clear of Adana and trundled through the dull, industrialized flatlands of the Çukurova delta, because I was thinking of the hundreds of thousands of Armenians who had passed this way in the autumn of 1915. The Armenians had been forcibly evacuated from places as distant and diverse as Erzerum and Van in the far northeast, and Sivas and Istanbul and Izmir in the west, and Adana and Mersin. They were sent, without proper sustenance, on a journey which took most of them through hundreds of kilometres of mountains and deserts before they reached the Taurus Mountains, where they funnelled through Pozanti and the Cilician Gates before struggling on across Çukurova. Much of their ghastly voyage followed the railroad on which I was travelling. Almost all major stations on the line were the site of lethally unsanitary accumulations of deportees. In November, 20,000 were reported at Tarsus, another 20,000 at Adana, 150,000 more scattered between Adana and the Amanus Mountains. They were on their way to Aleppo and, from there, bound for the Mesopotamian and Syrian deserts. As they marched across Turkey and Syria, the Armenians were subjected to robbery, butchery, starvation, thirst, sexual attacks, and disease. Estimates of the final number of fatalities ranged from 300,000 to over 1.3 million. To put it another way, before the Great War around one and a half million Armenians lived in the territory occupied by modern-day Turkey; by 1923, only 100,000 remained.

In September 1915, Joseph Dakak also headed for Aleppo, where he was about to start his last year of school. It was practically certain that he saw the Armenians trekking east, and since as a schoolboy in Aleppo he was not confined to the grounds of the school and was at liberty to walk around town, he would have seen thousands of Armenians in transit in Aleppo. They formed, by all accounts, a terrifying and heart-rending spectacle. And yet my grandfather never spoke of the death-marches, just as he never spoke about the massacres of 1909 or the Armenian exodus in 1921. At first I'd thought that his was a terrorized dumbness; but I came to realize that it reflected the kind of benighted gulf that divided me from my fellow train passengers.

Just how many Armenians were killed, and in what circumstances, and due to what causes, were questions that continued to cause great controversy. Over eighty years later, Armenians were haunted by an awful sense that a terrible and clear crime against their nation, which had been witnessed and contemporaneously documented in detail by missionaries, consuls, medical workers and other western bystanders resident in Turkey, had gone unacknowledged. Groups like the Armenian National Institute in Washington DC conducted a passionate and relentless campaign to perpetuate the memory of the victims and to gain international recognition of the genocidal character of their deaths and losses: in other words, that what happened was a premeditated effort by the Ottoman government to exterminate the Armenian people. Orthodox Turkish history maintained that the Ottoman government undertook drastic but essentially defensive wartime evacuation measures designed to eliminate a real threat to the security of the State: for example, the Armenian population in Van, in the far east of Anatolia, sided with the Russian forces in a campaign in which tens of thousands of Turkish soldiers died. Insofar as mass deaths and brutalities did occur – and doubt was cast in this regard on 'pro-Armenian' accounts – it was said that these were, in essence, the unauthorized work of independent third parties, Kurds, bandits, rogue gendarmes and war-crazed military personnel, whose dreadful actions, calmly considered, were not proof of a State intention of racial annihilation.

Earlier that summer, the French national assembly had voted to declare its recognition of what it expressly called the Armenian genocide. Although the vote was unlikely to be ratified by the Senate, it represented a significant triumph for the Armenian campaign, which had only met with full official success in Russia and Canada. The United States, for example, limited itself to expressing sympathy for the 'tragedy', since its relationship with Turkey, a key NATO ally, precluded any further acknowledgement. There was also the wider hazard of setting a precedent. If the Armenians were accommodated, what would there be to stop an even more influential political grouping – the Irish-Americans, for example – from pressing for similar recognition, and historical crystallization, of the moral and legal character of events in their national past? Current Irish historical grievances went at least as far back as 1649, the year Oliver Cromwell re-established the English Parliament's control of Ireland. Ireland had been unruly since October 1641, when perhaps 4,000 Protestant Ulster settlers were killed by their Catholic neighbours. The massacre – never forgotten by the settlers or their unionist descendants, for whom it served as an example of what would happen to them in Ireland without the protection of the Crown – inspired a widespread Irish rebellion headed, most notably, by Owen Roe O'Neill (no relation); Cromwell's response was to authorize the killing of thousands of non-combatants at the towns of Drogheda and Wexford. Three and a half centuries later, these slaughters still resonated in certain Irish (and Irish-American) minds as examples not of military barbarity but of a genocidal tendency in the British treatment of the Irish. This tendency was also to be glimpsed in Cromwell's shipment as slaves to the West Indies of thousands of captured Irish soldiers, and in the ethnic cleansing of the Irish propertied classes in the 1650s, when land in the ownership of indigenous Roman Catholics was turned over to British Protestant settlers while the natives were deported to the wilds of Connacht; but its fullest manifestation occurred with the Great Potato Famine. In terms of the number of dead and deported – the Irish emigrants had, arguably, been subject to a species of expulsion – and also in terms of the catastrophic testimonies of squalor and mass starvation and disease they generated, the victims of the Famine were comparable to the victims of the Armenian holocaust; and from there it was only a short step to another comparison, namely of the nature of the English government's responsibility for the Famine with that of the Young Turk government's responsibility for the fate of the Armenians.

I had always doubted that many Irish people subscribed to this kind of analysis with any vehemence or, if they did, gave it much contemporary significance. Most of us felt that the injustice and oppression suffered by our ancestors had been adequately ventilated over the past century and that our duties to them were sufficiently performed by the moderate forms of remembrance that were now in place: classroom history lessons, the occasional film or book, and ceremonies like the Great Famine Event in 1997. We were ready for fresh stories about ourselves, and this had apparently been con- firmed by the famous referendums of 22 May 1998. But on 15 August 1998, which was only a week before I boarded the Taurus Express at Adana, a huge bomb exploded in the centre of Omagh, a market town in Co. Tyrone, killing 29 civilians. The massacre – the worst in the last 30 years of violence – was said to be the work of the Real IRA, a group associated by the press with Bernadette Sands, the sister of the hunger striker Bobby Sands. Bernadette Sands had come to my notice a few months before Omagh, when I'd heard her bitterly pronouncing on the failure of the Good Friday Agreement to make definite provision for a united Ireland. What had interested me wasn't the fact of her opposition to the peace process – inevitably, some republicans would be incapable of compromise – but the grounds she relied on: that the Agreement rendered vain the sacrifices and exertions of bygone republicans – republicans like her dead brother and, of course, Jim O'Neill. Was it for a devolved assembly, she rhetorically asked, that so many volunteers died and sacrificed years of freedom? For Sands, it seemed, the resolution of present-day political grievances turned, on some fundamental level, on the discharge of assumed obligations to the wronged dead, whose shadowy needs were to be added to those of the living and unborn.

At what point were we released from participation in the

injustices of the past? The Armenian nation still craved our attention and made demands on our pity and outrage, and as I sat on the
Taurus Express, I felt under a blurry duty to fight off my tiredness,
to remember those who passed through this unremarkable landscape eighty years before. But I fell asleep.

When I awoke, we were moving along the edge of a cool valley in
a corridor of pine trees. Clusters of poplars signalled the course of
a small river, and, in the hills, villages thick with fruit trees appeared
among the pine woods. Every five minutes, it seemed, we stopped at
a tiny, beautiful old station.

We climbed higher and the train began pleasantly to pass in and
out of tunnels. We had reached the Amanus Mountains, which were
the scene in the Great War of frantic efforts by the Baghdad
Railway Company to complete the construction of the railway.
Nevertheless, the Armenians working here were rounded up and
marched off in June 1916 and replaced by 1,600 British and Indian
prisoners of war. Just over a month later, Joseph Dakak started
work at the construction camp at Belemedik, where the Taurus
tunnels, the longest on the Baghdad railway, were being built.
There, the Armenian workforce was still in place: the military
imperative of completing the work and the lack of readily available
skilled replacements had contrived to exempt them from deportation. The luck of these railway workers and their families held out
for the rest of the war. They formed one of the very few cadres of
Armenians to escape deportation.

After a lengthy stop in a hill-station, the train descended from the
Amanus into typical Anatolian territory: flat farmland and marshy
scrubland stretching out for miles up to a blur of distant hills. The
train continued to crab towards Gaziantep, which lay directly to the
east, along a maddeningly indirect loop of track. I fell asleep again
and awoke again. Still the same scenes: cottonfields, cornfields and
inconsequential stony fields. When I next opened my eyes, the
train, escorted by a cloud of butterflies, was thundering by groves of
pistachio trees. We entered the sprawling, dusty industrial city of
Gaziantep, the source of so many summer visitors to Mersin's
coastline.

I didn't linger. I went straight from the train station to the *otogar* and caught a mini-bus back towards the coast, to Iskenderun. My thoughts went back to a character in my grandfather's testimony, Aram Hachadourian, the Armenian native of Gaziantep who'd lived in Iskenderun until he was forced out in 1939, when France conceded Hatay – that fertile strip of East Mediterranean shoreline to which Syria still laid claim – to Turkey.

It was mid-afternoon when I arrived in Hatay. The mini-bus stopped at Dörtyol, which used to be a mainly Armenian village, and then continued south. On the left, the Amanus loomed as vaporous and cloud-smudged as the Wicklow Mountains viewed from the Curragh. Passing through lemon and orange groves that over-whelmed me with memories – or fantasies – of a time when Mersin was ringed by just such gardens, we reached the coast at the small port of Payas. During the 1909 massacres, 272 Armenian deaths were reported in Payas, Dörtyol and other villages around Iskenderun.

After going through a heavily industrialized area of factories and container yards, we came to Iskenderun, picturesquely wedged between steaming, spectacularly proximate wooded mountains, and a Mediterranean Sea that seemed greyer and choppier than the one that lapped against the shore at Mersin. I checked into the Hitit Hotel, a half-gutted 'seventies construction that either had never been completed or was already ruined. The balcony of my room overlooked the sea and the post office, a grand limestone building built by the French. I took a shower and then strolled out into the humid early evening. I wasn't sure what to expect. This was my first visit to my grandfather's birthplace.

The waterfront was a less polished, more intimate version of the one at Mersin. There was a boulevard, palm trees, sparse traffic, and a congenial little park where, after dinner and dark, children would play on swings and seesaws until late in the warm night. A couple of horse-drawn carriages made their way decoratively up and down the boulevard, where a very few degenerating examples remained of the row of Ottoman villas that had, during the Second World War, housed the residence of the Turkish general com-manding the region, and the Italian and German and British and

United States consulates. Behind the waterfront was a neighbourhood of narrow streets and small, rickety houses. It was
wonderfully quiet, and the odour of jasmine and the echoing calls of
turtle doves stirred in me a sharp, bittersweet ache. My nostalgia
intensified when I was surprised by the chatter of Arabic drifting
from the small gardens; how comforting was the sound of a language I first heard spoken by elderly ladies who loved me! It was in
this quarter, just behind the waterfront, that I came across the
Greek consulate, housed in an old building that retained a crumbling, slightly ludicrous grandeur. Next door to it, in the only
carefully restored Ottoman structure I'd seen, was the British consulate: it had returned to its 1909 location, the offices of Catoni,
maritime agents and agent of Lloyd's underwriters. I sensed, as I
wandered back to the waterfront to the sound of Arabic mingled
with Turkish and the smell of horse-dung, that something was left
of the Ottoman Syrian town in which Joseph Dakak had passed his
first ten years. There still stood in Iskenderun a Catholic church,
two Orthodox churches and even an Armenian church. It was also
easy to imagine, as the Amanus Mountains darkened in the east
and I rejoined the locals in strolling along the boulevard, the
intrigue and espionage that had taken place in this small, intense
port during the last war. C.T.C. Taylor, the British SIME agent,
wrote that German intelligence had approached a certain Y, a
prominent resident of Hatay, to use his position to obtain intelligence about Allied troop movements in Syria and Palestine, but Y
notified the British of the approach and offered his services as a
double agent. On one occasion, Taylor met Y at Antakya under the
surveillance of intensely suspicious Turkish plainclothes detectives;
another time, they met at the open air restaurant of Joseph
Ayvazian, the Axis informer, where Taylor dropped a parcel in the
darkness for collection by Y. Taylor's greatest coup was bribing the
cleaner at the Italian consulate to place the contents of the
consul's – the Marquis di San Felice's – waste-paper baskets into
bags and pass them on to the British.

I simply could not imagine Joseph Dakak taking part in such
capers. Given what I now knew of his circumstances and

background, I doubted that the thought of acting as a partisan would have even entered his mind.

When, in 1922, Joseph Dakak entrusted his fortunes to the nascent Turkish nation-state, he also assumed the responsibility, as a member of a minority with a history of disloyalty, of winning the trust of his new country. He was, in effect, committing himself to the politics of good citizenship – of ingratiation and submission and compliance. Such an outlook involved complete withdrawal from the risks of the political fray and a profound aversion to trouble, and it seemed to me that neither money nor an infatuation with Franz von Papen or German culture would have been likely to disturb this stance. Besides, Joseph's 'Germanophilia', such as it was, ante-dated the rise of National Socialism by fifteen years and, in the absence of any evidence that he was pro-Hitler, could not fairly be equated with support for Germany in its war aims. As Denis Wright observed, 'Allegations that many of these people were pro-Axis in the early days of the war should not be taken too seriously'. Nor was there evidence to substantiate Salvator Avigdor's suspicion that Joseph Dakak had been pressured into anything.

I'd also concluded that my grandfather at all times *believed* that he was acting correctly. This didn't get him off the hook, because the state of a man's conscience might be little more than an index of his capacity for self-reproach; but it was something. It seemed to me that the very flagrancy of Joseph's dealings with Papen, Hilmi and the Husseinis could only betoken an artless conviction on his part that he had nothing to hide. A spy, unless he was playing a crazily risky hand of double-bluff – not at all Joseph's style at the card-table – would certainly have acted more discreetly than Joseph and, almost by definition, would not have been so brazen. Nor, it seemed to me, would Joseph have been bold enough to bring his thorny case to the attention of the Turkish authorities – who, in his paranoia, loomed all-powerful and all-seeing – if he had not truly believed that there was no real basis for his guilt; and his testimony would certainly not have culminated, as had finally become clear to me, in an elaborately indirect, but very real, accusation against the Turkish Republic of a breach of the trust he'd reposed in it.

I found a seat in a café looking across the boulevard to the park, ordered baklava, and took pleasure, as I always do, in the solicitous yet democratic atmosphere of Turkish restaurants. The baklava, my grandfather's favourite sweet, arrived. It was strangely moving to think that he loved these flavours of millefeuille pastry and sugar and pistachios and had precisely known the delight I took in these mouthfuls.

By 1939, Joseph Dakak must have thought that his decision to stay in Turkey had worked out nicely. Atatürk's famously radical reforms – the declaration of a secular republic oblivious to all religious and ethnic affiliations; the introduction of a Gregorian calendar and 24-hour day; the emancipation of women; the introduction of the Latin alphabet; the purification of Turkish language from all foreign (especially Arabic and Persian) words; the centralized overhaul of the economy; the scrapping of the oriental fez and turban – largely corresponded to Joseph's own notion of progress, and he must have felt that, as a literate, modern, westernized, economically productive man, he embodied key virtues demanded of the new Turk. In other respects, admittedly, his citizenship was less certain. A true Turk was someone who 'habitually speaks Turkish and has assimilated Turkish culture' this being a prerequisite for membership of the Republican People's Party, essential for any public position of importance, and my grandfather continued to speak French and Arabic with his friends and family and to embrace European cultural preferences. In 1939, he even changed his name from Dakak to Dakad to make it sound more French. The attitude that ethnic and religious minorities were not proper Turks – evident from Atatürk's outburst in March 1923, when, annoyed by the number of large properties owned by Syrians and Greeks, he urged the 'people of Mersin' to take possession of their town – was still widespread. But Joseph felt that he had handled these difficulties well. Unlike many Syrians, he didn't hold himself completely aloof from the Turks or voice complaints about his lot as a Christian. He was on good terms with the well-connected Muslim figures of Mersin, with whom he played cards at the Club and did business. The Günes Cinema, for example, was launched in

partnership with a war hero in Atatürk's army and with a prominent
Muslim landowner. Yet even his association with these figures did
not prevent criticism of the cinema's lighting scheme: the red, white
and blue bulbs, somebody complained to the Ankara authorities,
signalled the French tricolour. The cinema owners naturally
protested the absurdity of the allegations but, anxious not to cause
offence, removed the blue bulbs and left only the red and white, the
colours of Turkey.

This semi-comic episode no doubt reminded Joseph, in case
he'd forgotten, of the fragile and antagonistic sensitivities of the
State. But he no doubt felt that he'd acted, as always, as an impec-
cably loyal citizen of Turkey. This sense of himself lay beneath the
heated assertion with which he ended the testimony: *'What most
enraged me were the insinuations directed at making me believe that
my own government had delivered me to the English.'* Although ostensibly rejecting these insinuations, my grandfather was in fact
bitterly adopting them: Nazim Gandour's allegation that Desmond
Doran had Turkish policemen in his pocket, and Captain
Sylvester's sly advice that Dakak look to his own government for
compensation.

This was cloudy, roundabout stuff – a way of pointing a finger
while keeping his hands in his pockets – but my grandfather's conviction of Turkish involvement in his arrest was almost certainly
well-founded. The Turkish security services co-operated closely
with their British counterparts and, as Denis Wright had said and
Norman Mayers had hinted, were quite capable of acting against
people they didn't like; and they didn't like rich 'Syrians'. Joseph
felt, though, that he had done nothing to deserve such treatment.
He was a solid Turkish citizen and a neutral. Was he not entitled,
like Bogart's avowedly non-partisan Rick in *Casablanca*, to declare
'I'm just an innkeeper'? Why shouldn't he entertain Franz von
Papen and treat him with the courtesy to be extended to all guests?
And why shouldn't he take advantage of the fluctuations in the
lemon market? Unlike his own government, which was selling
highly profitable quantities of chrome and magnesium to both the
Axis and the Allies, it wasn't as though he was dealing in goods of

military value. Why not, in short, carry on with business as usual? Why not apply for visas to travel to Egypt in the autumn of 1941, when the Mediterranean islands and waters were the scenes of carnage, and ferocious battles were being fought in Libya, and a German advance on the Suez Canal was on the cards? Why not travel to and from Allied-occupied territories of critical military importance – Syria and Palestine – and combine the trip with a fortnight of close contacts with Arab nationalist extremists with plenty of intelligence to communicate to their Axis allies in Turkey? Why not quiz the chief of Mersin's political police about Olga Caton and Togo Makzoumé's links with British intelligence?

Put in this way, my grandfather's position was inescapably, absurdly, vulnerable. And yet it seemed that he could not see, even in retrospect, that he may have left the British and their Turkish collaborators with little choice other than to arrest him. It was, of course, possible that had the intelligence services been more competent and less prejudiced towards Levantines and Christians, Joseph would have been released after interrogation. But of course they were prejudiced, because racial and religious stereotypes are never more reductive than in times of war. My grandfather, a well-informed, watchful man who prided himself on his knowledge of the ways of the world, must have appreciated this; and yet he was blind to the appearance of his actions and the impressions they would make in the minds of unsympathetic authorities and the opportunity they presented to certain people – people like Osman Emre Bey – to denounce him. How could this have happened?

I could only think that a clue lay in the humble, agreeable scenes that surrounded me. Although an ancient port and perhaps busier than at any time in its history, Iskenderun remained an unimportant place for anyone other than the small class of people who lived or made money here; but even a local might sometimes feel marooned in such a place. My grandfather was, it seemed to me, in this kind of situation. Although happily rooted in Mersin, he was enthralled by the spectacle of the wider world, which he monitored by reading four newspapers a day and with which he stayed in touch through his work and languages. The documents that he'd chosen to preserve in his safe told a story of sorts. The letter of claim to the British embassy (in English) that was never mailed, the letter of appointment from Lenz & Co. (in German), the letter of commendation from the Baghdad Railway Company (in French) – these papers had no lasting function, yet Joseph Dakak kept them as he might keep land deeds or contracts or promissory notes: as the most valuable documents he possessed. The mystique of foreigners must have been particularly great during the isolated and introspective years Turkey went through from 1923 to 1940, when severe travel restrictions meant that visitors to the country were rare and Mersin was more cut off than ever. Then the war changed everything. There was an influx of European newcomers – diplomats, construction workers, sailors, business people – and it seemed to Joseph that the exciting streams of history on which they arrived were safely navigable by a man like himself. His craft, for this purpose, was neutrality; and his object was to succeed as never before in his central ambition: to be a *gentleman of importance.* Important meant rich, of course, hence the tin and lemon ventures, but it also meant being connected and knowledgeable – about world affairs, languages, one's horse, legal matters, archaeology, Turkish politics, important personalities; and, perhaps just as importantly, it meant being *seen to be in the know.* In wartime, there were hazards attached to such a profile, particularly if (as Oncle Pierre had once remarked to me) the guiding political precept for Mersin Christians was that *il ne faillait pas se mouiller*: it wouldn't do to get wet. My grandfather, intoxicated by the success of the hotel and restaurant and the new opportunities, lost sight of this precept, or of its meaning. The fortnight with the Husseini crowd at the Modern Hotel, when he simply could not drag himself away from the action, was a case in point. In his mind, playing cards with the Arabs and listening to their fervent chatter no more rendered him, a Turkish neutral, a political protagonist than a ringside seat turned a spectator into a boxer. He was mesmerized by the idea of himself as a man at the centre of things, a man of accomplishments, a *chevalier*; and it was this that led to his incarceration in the house at Emmaus-Latrun, *la tour des chevaliers*: the tower of the cavaliers.

The egotism at the root of my grandfather's undoing was not purely spontaneous. Its manifestation, in his cultivated persona of polyglot, gallant, man-about-town, equestrian, revealed the deep impression made by his youthful exposure to the glamorous types from France and England and Germany; but more fundamentally, his self-centredness was in many ways the outcome of the compact he'd made with the Turkish Republic in the early 'twenties. Perhaps because all his life he'd been the object of self-seeking imperialist attention (by 1922, the young Syrian had been educated by the French and employed by the Germans and ruled by the Ottomans, the British, the French and the Turks), Joseph had little sense of the State as an instrument of personal autonomy. If he had cherished the possibility of full-blown freedom, or believed in it, he could have emigrated to France with his brother and sister and reinvented himself. Instead, he settled for modest liberties: a liberty to prosper economically, a liberty to develop his personal qualities, a liberty to mind his own business. It didn't trouble him that as a Christian Turk he would be excluded from jobs in public service because these exclusions complemented the detachment he felt from Turkey and its powerful nationalist narratives and, in a way, exempted him from anything more than a formal engagement in the country's affairs. By a tacit agreement, his role was limited to acquiescing in the new order and keeping quiet; in particular, colluding in the national silence about the discrepancy between the Kemalist doctrine of equal citizenship of all Turks and the actual treatment of minority groups – notably the Armenians. It was a sad fact that Joseph and the rest of the Syrian community could be counted on in this regard. The social and religious and racial divisions that had immemorially separated the Syrians and the Armenians were so deep, it seemed, that the groups barely existed for each other. This was evinced, in Joseph's case, by his total failure to perpetuate the fact of their obliteration, which he'd seen with his own eyes, and also by the express words of his testimony. In order to establish his credentials as a staunch Turkish citizen, Joseph portrayed all Armenians mentioned in the testimony in an unflattering, threatening light: Hachadourian was a British spy who spouted anti-Turkish rubbish; the hotelier Ayvazian was a pro-German troublemaker; the Armenian who formerly occupied the condemned men's cell in the Prison des Sables was a multiple murderer; and, in a conflation of every Turkish fear imaginable, the Armenian prison sergeant in Beirut was an ominous figure who intimated that he'd worked, during the French occupation, as a butcher in Adana.

I knew that my grandfather wrote his testimony at a desperate time, that he had good reason to distance himself from Armenians, and even that he may well have encountered a succession of unpleasant Armenian nationals; but I couldn't help feeling that these portraits reflected an incapacity to attach significance to the vivid ordeals of his fellow Cilicians or, indeed, to the political passions that lay behind their disastrous fate. True, this incapacity was perhaps necessitated by the demands of survival in Turkey. But my grandfather chose to stay in Turkey and in a sense, therefore, chose to incapacitate himself. He paid a very high price for his choice. When the Second World War came to Mersin, he was unable to appreciate quite how much the issues at stake mattered to its participants, who were being killed in their millions, and what this might mean to their perception of him and his formally neutral actions.

This misconception about the responsibilities of neutrality may have had other consequences. An intelligence agent did not have to be a spy. He could also be a party, acting neither for reward nor out of ideological conviction, who simply offered information openly, gratuitously, unsystematically and therefore, he might feel, innocuously. Joseph Dakak, with no sense that he was taking sides in the conflict, might have given foreigners at the Toros Hotel the benefit of his opinions on current affairs in Turkey, or on the personalities of Mersin society, or on anything he could reasonably help them with. Few things would have been more pleasant or have come more naturally: after all, his function as a hotelier was precisely to be of service to his guests. Joseph Dakak may have been innocent, but innocent of what? It pained me to acknowledge it, but this was a question I would never be able to answer with certainty.

When I returned to the Hitit Hotel later that evening, the

receptionist at the hotel, Ali, invited me to join him and a man from Lebanon, who described himself as a Phalangist and was dressed in a vest and pair of stripy underpants, for a glass of tea. The three of us sat outside attempting conversation, Ali and I in pidgin Turkish, the Phalangist gentleman and I in pidgin French, and Ali and the Phalangist gentleman in fluent-sounding Arabic. It was a situation of the old Levant that my grandfather, as a speaker of French, Turkish, Arabic and English, would have enjoyed and mastered. There was something else that he would have liked: the Phalangist (who mysteriously wouldn't reveal what his business was) was on his way to Mersin, where he had a room booked at the Toros Hotel.

It only occurred to me afterwards, as I stood on the balcony of my room looking out towards the lights of the port of Iskenderun, that the hotel I'd chosen at random was named after the Hittites. This made me think of John Garstang. In 1957, the archaeologist returned to Mersin after an interval of ten years. He was met off the boat by Joseph Dakak, who was delighted to see his extremely old and very frail friend and accompanied him to the hotel. After a rest, Professor Garstang and others drove out to the Hittite site at Karatepe, where the Englishman drew himself up and gave a speech to the assembly of onlookers. On his return to Mersin, John Garstang was again met by Joseph and rested one last time at the hotel. Then he returned to his ship, where he died.

It gave me pleasure that my grandfather's friend had lived long enough to return to the scene of his life's greatest work, just as it pleased me that Denis Wright had prospered and that Norman Mayers, after serving in a variety of posts in El Salvador, Costa Rica, and Brazil, finally retired as the ambassador to Ecuador; Mayers died in 1986, at the age of ninety. On the subject of after-lives, I could not help smiling at the thought of what happened to Nazim Gandour. The Lebanese merchant returned to Mersin after his release from internment and carried on doing business there until the late 'sixties, when he skipped town and returned to the Lebanon owing the Turkish Republic a fortune in taxes. He thus revealed himself to be a levanter in the secondary sense of the noun, too: one who absconds, especially with bets unpaid. What happened to Osman Emre Bey and Hilmi Bey I never found out. I hoped they lived more happily, and longer, than the other people apparently involved in Joseph Dakak's apprehension. These fared badly; so badly, indeed, that superstition might lead one to attribute their fates to nemesis. Williams, the SIME man in Mersin, was accidentally shot dead in Athens in 1944. Desmond Doran died in a bomb explosion in Tel Aviv in 1947. His boss in Istanbul, Thomson, was killed by EOKA in Cyprus in the early 'fifties; and Harold Gibson, Arthur Maltass' boss, committed suicide in Rome over enormous debts run up by the Rumanian dancing girl he'd married.

Thankfully, the jinx was not uniformly fatal. Arthur Maltass, as far as I knew, merely fell into professional disgrace. Towards the end of 1943, it came to Denis Wright's notice that a local importer had given Maltass a brand new Japanese or German bicycle, and, armed with this evidence of unpatriotic corruption, the consul was able to arrange for Maltass' recall home – much to his distress, Wright said, as he was in his element in Mersin, where he used his position in Economic Warfare to threaten Mersin merchants with the Black List.

Denis Wright also put an end to the activities of William Rickards. On the consul's advice, the British embassy concluded that 'It is scandalous that Lloyd's should allow Rickards to act for them' and terminated his Lloyd's agency in Mersin on 8 May 1944. On 6 June 1944, Rickards wrote to the British ambassador:

I beg to mention that since the beginning of this year I have noticed a difference in the attitude of the Mersin consulate towards me. A few months back I heard that some of our people of influence, for reasons of their own, were planning to relieve me of my post as Lloyd's Agent. One of them openly boasted to Syrian friends of hers that she was going to take Lloyd's agency from Rickards. Though I disregarded this information at the time I regret to say it has now come true.

After conscientiously and faithfully serving my Country

and Lloyd's during the past four difficult years – I refused several offers of partnership in important firms to devote my time exclusively to Lloyd's work – I find I have not had a fair deal and therefore have a right to know the reason for this change which has affected my position in town and is likely to have harmful effects on my business in the future.

The embassy never replied. On 10 November 1944, a diplomat there recorded that 'the notorious Rickards had completely faded into the background and was giving no trouble'.

But perhaps the most telling fate was reserved for Franz von Papen, my grandfather's alter ego. The German ambassador, who quit Ankara in August 1944, went on the run after the Allied invasion of Germany and was captured in April 1945. He was moved from place to place for interrogations until, finally, in August, he was taken to Nuremberg and imprisoned in a cell of the Palace of Justice. The cell was furnished with a collapsible bed, a grey blanket, a small table and a stool. The light fixture had been removed from the ceiling and thick iron bars secured the window. As a precaution against suicide, the hatch in the door was permanently open to enable observation by guards. Like Joseph Dakak – and Nazim Gandour and William Rickards – Papen experienced the torment of not knowing what crime he was supposed to have committed. Under interrogation, he was persistently pressed on why he'd continued to serve Hitler in the face of the Anschluss and the Nazis' acts of political terror and persecution, particularly of Jews. Papen, who pointed out that in Turkey he'd helped 1,500 Rumanian Jewish children escape to Israel, said he had acted out of patriotism rather than for the good of the Nazi party. In October 1945, he was charged with conspiring to prepare for a war of aggression. In October 1946, he was acquitted of war crimes, although the Nuremberg court found that he'd engaged in 'bullying and intrigue'. Papen's ordeal was not over. As soon as he left the Palace of Justice he was taken into the custody of the Bavarian police for denazification. In January 1947, a denazification court found Papen guilty of aiding and abetting Hitler in his rise to power and conspiring to overcome President Hindenberg's objections to Hitler becoming Chancellor. He was sentenced to eight years in a labour camp, his personal assets were confiscated, and he was deprived of his civil rights. From April 1947 to February 1949, Papen was moved from one camp to another. Like Joseph Dakak, his imprisonment led to heart trouble and, in May 1948, hospitalization. On appeal, the Court of Appeal classified Papen as 'incriminated in Category II' and assessed his contribution to the *Wiedergutmachung* at DM30,000. He was also deprived of the right to vote, receive a state pension, hold political office, drive a car, or perform any work except ordinary labour. The former Chancellor and ambassador devoted the years that followed to the defence of his reputation, writing a memoir and articles. As a result, the highest court in Bavaria reviewed his case in May 1965 and downgraded his incrimination to Category III, which restored his civil rights. He died in 1969. Why Papen, a deeply reactionary Catholic monarchist but not a Nazi, allowed himself to be used by Hitler was a question that detained historians. The emerging consensus was that his doubts about Nazism, such as they were, were exceeded by the desire, which Joseph Dakak knew well, to be in the mix of things, to be a player. The two men were also linked by a weird symbolic detail. Immediately after his acquittal of war crimes, Papen went to the refectory for lunch. In order to distinguish him from those defendants found guilty, his place at the table was marked by the presence on his plate of Joseph Dakak's beloved fruit, an orange.

In May 1999, my attention was caught by two news items from Ireland. I read, first of all, that in the preliminary proceedings of the Bloody Sunday Inquiry, convened in response to an intense campaign by nationalists, the (Catholic) families of the victims were resisting the grant of anonymity to British soldiers present at the scene of the shootings. Next, I read that an effort was underway to locate and exhume the remains of Catholics alleged to have been informers who had been killed by the IRA over twenty years previously. It was an awful, inconclusive business, with the families of the dead waiting in suspense as Gardai, acting on information received from republican sources, dug around bogs and beaches with no success; evidently, it was far from easy, after so many years, for anybody, even the deceased's executioners, to remember exactly where the graves were situated. The silting up and erosion of the coast, the dying and cutting and growth of trees and shrubs, the disappearance and appearance of buildings, all of these alterations had removed the landscape beyond the scope of recollection or recognition. But the urge to uncover the past, when it is a component of the inextinguishable and tormenting urge for justice, is extremely powerful, and the search for skeletons continued.

Even allowing for the fact that the 'seventies were much more recent than a night in March 1936, I was struck by the difference between the vociferously retrospective attitude of Catholic families to the political violence they'd suffered and that of Admiral Somerville's Protestant descendants, who didn't want to know the names of the killers and displayed a reticence about the past that almost amounted to a denial of their victimhood. It was a curious state of affairs, since the ascendancy class, with its preoccupation with the glamour of its own pedigree, characteristically took a lively interest in matters of family history.

At around that time, May 1999, I came across a book, published the year before in England, by a historian named Peter Hart – a Protestant name, I couldn't help thinking – called *The IRA and Its Enemies*. Flicking through the index, my eye was drawn to a cluster of references to my grandfather's cousins, the murdered Coffey brothers. Then I was surprised to encounter, on the relevant chapter's first page, three names mentioned by my grandmother on our visit to Dunmanway the previous summer: Buttimer, Gray and Fitzmaurice.

It turned out that Grandma's account of what had happened to these men was slightly inaccurate. It was true that Gray and Buttimer had been shot dead; however, they were shot dead at their homes on Main Street, Dunmanway and not, as Grandma recalled, in Dunmanway Square. David Gray, a chemist, died from multiple gunshot wounds inflicted by a gang of men who burst open his door. The same gang hammered on the door of James Buttimer, an eighty-two-year-old retired draper who was Gray's neighbour; when Buttimer, who answered the door, failed to step outside, he was shot in the face and died at once, his brains and teeth blown out. And although Grandma may have been right to say that a man called Fitzmaurice left the country and sold his house to Henry Smith as a result of these killings, it was more likely that Fitzmaurice fled because he had barely escaped death himself that night and because his brother, a seventy-year-old solicitor called Francis Fitzmaurice, had been shot twelve times in his doorway while his wife looked on. These incidents did not take place during the Black and Tan War, as Grandma believed, but in the peacetime of April 1922, four months after the making of the Treaty with the British. To be exact, Buttimer and Gray and Fitzmaurice were all killed on the night of 26/27 April, a night that also saw attempts on the lives of a shopkeeper, George Applebe Bryan; a teacher, William Morrison; and a draper called William Jagoe. (I'd come across this name before: Mrs Salter-Townshend's husband, according to *Burke's Irish Family Records*, was the son of one William Jagoe Salter.) The following night saw further homicides: the farmers and neighbours Robert Howe and John Chinnery were killed at their homes in Ballaghanure; slightly further east, in Ballineen, a sixteen-year-old called Alexander Mackinley was shot three times in the back of the head as he lay in bed; a curate, Ralph Habord, was shot on the steps of the rectory at Murragh; a farmer, John Buttimer, and a farm servant, Jim Greenfield, were shot in Caher, a townland to the west of Ballineen: Buttimer in the head and stomach and Greenfield, lying in bed, in the back of the head. All of the above-named victims of violence lived in the Dunmanway-Ballineen- Enniskean stretch of the Bandon valley: Lynch–O'Neill territory, you might say. On the night that followed, another fatal shooting occurred ten or so miles south of Enniskean, in Clonakilty: there, a sixteen-year-old called Robert Nagle was killed at his home on MacCurtain Hill. Finally, on the night of 28/29 April, two nights after the Dunmanway killings, John Bradfield, a farmer from Killowen, near Murragh, was roused from his bed, told to stand up, and shot in the back of the neck; his cousin and neighbour, Henry

Bradfield would also have been killed had he not fled earlier. The name Bradfield rang a bell; and it turned out that John and Henry were cousins of Thomas Bradfield, whose shooting the previous year the *Cork Examiner* had connected, geographically at least, with that of the Coffey brothers.

All told, ten men had been killed and one wounded in the space of three days. They were all Protestants. No Catholic – not one pro-Treaty 'Free Stater' or landlord or perceived informer – was even shot at.

Viewed broadly, the massacre was the vengeful expression of a sense of grievance arising from recent lethal attacks on Catholics in Belfast, outrages such as the killing of Canon Magner in the Anglo-Irish War, and agrarian discontent with the landlord class (to which, incidentally, few of the dead belonged). Its actual spark, though, was the death on the night of 25/26 April of Michael O'Neill (no relation), who was shot while leading a break-in by the IRA Bandon battalion into a house in Ballygroman, between Bandon and Cork. At daybreak, the three male occupants of the house – the well-known unionists Thomas and Samuel Hornibrook (father and son) and Captain Herbert Woods (son-in-law of Thomas Hornibrook) – were taken captive by the IRA. Woods, the man who'd shot Michael O'Neill, was killed that day and the two Hornibrooks the next day. Ballygroman House was burned to the ground. Judging from the subsequent massacre, these killings were evidently not deemed to be a sufficient reprisal.

In April 1922, Jim O'Neill was twelve and a half years old and living in Kilbrittain. He would have learned of the killings from tense adult mutterings and coded kitchen discussions. What he may not have picked up was that the deadly events were deeply rooted in his own family. The IRA had broken into Ballygroman House in the first place because Woods and the Hornibrooks were suspected of involvement in a shadowy counter-revolutionary loyalist under-ground, the Protestant Action Group. The most notable of the killings attributed to the Protestant Action Group, the ones that cried most loudly for vengeance, were the unrequited deaths, in February 1921, of Jim O'Neill's first cousins, James and Timothy Coffey.

But there was a twist: the Coffeys' killers were not the Protestant Action Group, an entity that was very probably mythic rather than real. The brothers were killed by members of a Royal Irish Constabulary undercover 'special squad' disguised as farmers; not, in other words, by Captain Woods or the Hornibrooks.

These three dead Protestants were multiply entombed. Their violent deaths were not reported in the Irish newspapers; their bodies were buried in secret somewhere in West Cork; and their remains, unlike those of northern Catholics shot dead as informers, were never officially missed.

Although a few prominent republicans voiced disapproval of the April massacre, its perpetrators, who were almost certainly active members of the IRA, were never identified or 'brought to justice': not by the IRA, which at the time was effectively responsible for law and order in Cork, nor by history. The April massacre, as Peter Hart observed, was as unknown as the Kilmichael ambush was celebrated. Grandma, with her phenomenal memory and longevity, represented a near-exception to the general non-remembrance; but in her mind the sectarian slaughter had survived only as a story of the curious succession of families to occupy a town house in Dunmanway. In this sense, the April massacre was comparable to the Adana massacre of 1909, which lived on in the Dakad family as a tale of eating ortolans in Cyprus.

But there were further and deeper parallels between events in Cork and Cilicia. The April shootings in the Bandon valley were accompanied by a wave of death threats against Protestants, and the combination caused a panicked exodus from the county, with trains and boats out of Cork packed with refugees for a fortnight. Only six months before, in November 1921, just such scenes had taken place on the jetties of Mersin, as Cilicia's terrified Armenians and other Christians fled the country en masse. The migrant groups in Ireland and Turkey were remarkably similar. Both were minorities regarded as a fifth column of the foreign enemy; both suffered a demographic cataclysm unmentioned by dominant nationalist histories; and finally, both left a vestigial population in the new nation-state whose members instinctively understood that, whatever the political and constitutional affirmations to the contrary, their citizenship was a matter of indulgence and not of right. I'd always suspected that Admiral Somerville's descendants' lack of interest in knowing the identity of his killers reflected their belief that it didn't really matter which meaningless Ryan or Murphy – or O'Neill – had pulled the trigger. Now I sensed that their disdain may also have been due to an inherited, self-preservative knowledge that to lay claim to certain kinds of justice, historical or political, was to overstep the mark; and I understood why Mrs Salter-Townshend had gone out of her way to characterize Castletownshend as sleepy fishing village of no political importance.

I found myself in a state of shocked, almost angry clarity, as if these revelations of Cork's past, which were so tangled with my family's past, formed a recovered memory of something I'd concealed from myself. I'd always known, of course, that families and nations have self-serving editions of their pasts, and would have freely admitted that Ireland was no exception. But I hadn't been asked to think hard about it in relation to the Protestants, and therefore I didn't: because, for all my objectivity and outsider's perspective, I was as susceptible as any Catholic Irishman to dazzling by the national myths.

In the brilliant assertion of the Proclamation of Independence, the Irish Republic guarantees religious and civil liberty, equal rights and the equal opportunities to all its citizens, cherishing all the children of the nation equally, no matter their religion. And so it is a great cause of pride to the overwhelmingly Catholic nationalist movement, and vital to the credibility of its vision of an inclusive united Ireland, that so many of its greatest soldiers and apologists and martyrs have been Protestants: Theobald Wolfe Tone, Charles Stuart Parnell, Roger Casement, Erskine Childers, Countess Markiewicz. These admirable figures invest the idea of the Irish nation-state with an extraordinary moral pedigree, and in my mind they stacked up in a kind of totem pole symbolic of nationalism's unseen, ecstatic intimacy with the forces of justice. This didn't prevent me from taking a critical view of republican activities or even of the aspiration to a united Ireland; but it did equip me with the conviction that the nationalist *impulse*, even in its most misguided and violent manifestations, was essentially high-minded.

As a consequence, I had always viewed sectarian killings – in which the victim is marked for death because of his religion – as essentially the preserve of loyalists, who seemed to specialize in shooting Catholic taxi-drivers and (as happened in July 1998) burning to death young Catholic children. Republican political violence, by contrast, was – shockingly but nevertheless sincerely – directed at targets designated by their functions: soldiers, police officers, judges, politicians, and contractors who supplied these instruments of British government with goods and services. Occasionally, a particularly horrifying or inexplicable killing would shake this dichotomy, but not for long. As time passed, the outrage would assume a maverick character and the totemic figures, unyielding in their virtue, would hover again into view. I wasn't immune to the appeal of the modern icons, either: the deaths in 1981 of Bobby Sands and nine others in Long Kesh Prison, hunger striking in protest at the treatment of IRA prisoners as ordinary criminal inmates, attested to the idealism with which even the most violent nationalists acted. And finally, of course, there was my own family: my knowledge of their good faith extinguished any real doubt in my mind about the essential purity of the nationalist enterprise. Which explains why I felt guilty and anguished not only about the Cork pogrom but about another terrible thing that had, at last, become apparent to me: that Admiral Somerville had been killed because he was a Protestant.

There was no way around it. Somerville wasn't the only Irishman in Cork to give references to local men seeking to enlist in the Crown's forces. What distinguished him from the other referees – priests, councillors and other men of standing, a significant number of whom, like Somerville and indeed Tom Barry, had at some point served in the British army – was his religion.

How could this be? How could my great-uncle Tadhg, the man I was named after, who'd earned the respect and warm remembrance of my father and other decent people for his humanity and intelligence, who considered sectarianism anathematical to his strongly held nationalist principles, have reconciled himself to a sectarian killing?

Answer: because the onus of reconciliation only arises on the appearance of two mutually inconsistent facts. Tadhg didn't for a moment see that he was committing a sectarian act, and so there was nothing for him to reconcile. And why didn't he see? Once again, because only a single set of facts was visible to him: that Somerville's actions made him a British agent who had forfeited life. A second, irreconcilable set of facts – that Somerville's actions were no different from those of scores of others – was nowhere in sight. In this way, my great-uncle's principles and conscience stayed intact. There were no double standards because there were no double facts.

This structure of ethical thinking had a wider application. I had often wondered how so many republicans could be highly sensitive to injustice and suffering and yet highly adept at living with the consequences of their bombings and shootings. I'd put it down to an unusually rigorous self-belief that helped them to overcome internal conflict. Now I suspected that there was little or no internal conflict to overcome, because only the strategic consequences of violence were internalized. The human consequences – the consequences to the victims – were externalized into a moral outer space.

I knew, of course, that this kind of morally self-sparing compartmentalization is common to military organizations everywhere. All armed forces narrate the world in terms that will enable their combatants, who are ordinary men and women, to kill and inflict damage effectively. Most basically, the humanity of the prospective victims is effaced in wartime by blankly characterizing them as the enemy. But most wars and their brutalizing narratives are temporary and, crucially, coterminous; the war ends, its lethal editions of the world dry up like floodwaters, and the former adversaries fall back on a residual pool of humane, or at least non-martial, narratives about themselves and each other. But what if there is no healthful reservoir? The conflict in which Somerville was killed was well over three centuries old by the time of his death, and I began to ask myself whether this miserable perpetuity was the sign of a country saturated from top to bottom with deadly narratives. The surface currents of Protestant bigotry were clearly visible; but there also had to be less perceptible flows, deeper down. It was obvious, once I thought about it, that these could only come from one source. The only narratives that pervaded to the very bed of Ireland's political culture were those of Irish nationalism, which are treasured to this day.

The stated principles of nationalism – equality, freedom, brotherhood, etc. – were as noble and unimpeachable as its dead, and they shed a beautiful light on the dim and perilous moral terrain that had to be crossed to achieve our nation's autonomy. In a fundamental sense, though, this luminosity led us astray; unlike the Old Masters who slipped a skull or some other token of human fallibility into their paintings' darknesses, in our self-righteousness we lost sight of what lay in the shade.

The human significance of Protestants in Ireland, like that of any other ethnic minority, depended on the visibility in the culture of their complex narratives about themselves. Not surprisingly, these narratives, which included contrarian unionist narratives, were overshadowed by the nationalist revolution. This was not solely the result of the nationalist doctrine that all the people of Ireland were Irish and equally so, but also of a set of secondary wartime doctrines that derived their logic and virtue from the primary doctrine: and so Protestant opponents of the revolution, actual or perceived, were cast as informers or Orangemen or British agents and were liable to be 'executed' and, in death, to be literally labelled as such. The April massacre, however, occurred during the truce after the Anglo-Irish War. None of the military epithets could be applied to the victims, and their deaths therefore could not be explained in the usual nationalist terms. What was startling was that, in the absence of a conventional nationalist explanation, the Catholic community was struck dumb; it possessed no *alternative* vocabulary with which to speak of the dead. It seemed that the only significance Protestants were capable of enjoying was nationalist significance; which meant that most of them, including the April massacre victims, had no real significance at all.

Evidently, just as centuries of hostile interrelations had done little or nothing to humanize Syrians and Armenians and Turks in each other's eyes, so it was with the Protestants and Catholics of West Cork, who, in Con Conner's euphemistic phrase, lived in their own little worlds. I had always known that the Bandon valley Protestants, tainted by a reputation for extreme bigotry, formed one of the most resented of the seventeenth-century plantation settlements, but I'd never really contemplated the political effects of the animosity and had roughly assumed that, somehow or other, nationalism's uplifting tenets elevated its adherents from sectarian emotions. In fact, the April massacre and the Catholic community's response to it – silence and more violence – suggested that the opposite was true: that nationalism simultaneously nurtured and concealed a capacity in ourselves for a hatred as powerful as that which led to the oblivion of the Armenians.

All of which explained how Tadhg Lynch could commit a sectarian killing without him – or, decades later, me – seeing it for what it was; and why Tadhg and Angela and Joe Collins were prompted to pick out a Protestant for death: because, at some level, they must have sensed that the killing of a prominent Protestant would sound, after the IRA's years of military inactivity, like a tribal siren.

It was precisely this primitivism that so disturbed the Catholic public at the time. Had Somerville ignored a warning, the killing could have been shaped into a story of hard but fair play; but the absence of warning left the community face to face with its sectarian demons – a prospect so haunting that even Tom Barry disassociated himself from an action he himself had sanctioned. In the event, a communal exorcism was performed by a deft act of narrative. By repeated references to anti-unionist episodes in his ancestry and to the fact that he never engaged in *active* recruitment, the Admiral was cast as a quasi-nationalist good old boy. There was, of course, no direct mention of his religion. The actual, nuanced identities of this Protestant, unionist Anglo-Irishman were blotted out like the shadows of a man under floodlights.

Naturally, public outrage over Admiral Somerville quickly died out. There were no songs written about him or bars named after him or annual commemorations instigated. His ghost, unlike the ghosts of the patriot dead, did not make demands on the consciences of the living.

As it happened, Boyle Somerville was a great enthusiast of ghosts and paranormal phenomena. His interest was shared by his sister Edith, who believed that during the Civil War, when republicans posed a grave threat to the family and its properties, her late uncle Kendal Coghill had organized the spirits of bygone Somervilles and Coghills into a squadron that protected their living kin. After his retirement from the Royal Navy, the Admiral decided to specialize in the field of psychometry, a method of communication with the dead in which the medium makes use of some object or place closely associated with a deceased person. Boyle agreed to put his particular skill at the disposition of Edith, who planned to write a family history, and to contact their deceased ancestors on her behalf; but he was shot before he was able to help her in this way. Edith Somerville was undeterred. She invoked Boyle's co-operation from beyond the grave and incorporated into her book information about the family that her brother's spirit had been able to convey to her. In acknowledgement of his ghostly input, she credited him as co-author of *Records of the Somerville Family* (1940).

A glance at this book informed me that the Somervilles came to Ireland in 1692, in the aftermath of the final defeat of the Catholic rebel army of James Stuart by the forces of the Protestant King William of Orange. This was the time of the introduction of the Penal Laws, which prohibited Catholics from voting, holding office, practising law, teaching, owning a horse worth more than five pounds, receiving an education at a Catholic school, or leaving land to a single son. The Somervilles themselves arrived as refugees from religious persecution by Catholics in Scotland, and it occurred to me that Admiral Somerville in this sense resembled Joseph Dakak, whose family had likewise come to Mersin in response to religious oppression. Admiral Somerville, like Joseph, belonged to a rich and profoundly self-sufficient religious minority with a tradition of looking on the national majority as an unfrequentable, undifferentiated and largely negligible mass. Like Joseph, Somerville made gestures of goodwill to the majority group (for example, making donations to St Vincent de Paul Society) but insisted on retaining his ethnic and cultural distinctiveness including his military title, which, like Joseph's adopted surname of Dakad, had the effect of associating him very closely with recent imperial oppressors. Both men were self-cultivating types with an interest in history. Both relied on unreliable nationalist assurances of their equal citizenship. And finally, both failed to appreciate the appearance of their actions in the eyes of men who saw the world through nationalist eyes, men like Tadhg Lynch and, of course, Jim O'Neill. An unsettling scenario of shadows presented itself: if one substituted Joseph Dakak for his double, Somerville, and Jim O'Neill for Tadhg Lynch, one was left with the scenario of Jim shooting Joseph dead.

I had never really invested the image of my moonlighting grandfather with political significance. But now, when I imagined him walking through the black fields of West Cork, net in hand, or tracking the dark water with his sons, I associated his hand-me-down knowledge of river currents, mudbanks, copses, and salmon pools with another West Cork inheritance. Included in the birthright and estate of my grandfather, who never came into Ardkitt or Graunriagh, was a tutelary hatred that imprisoned him long before, and long after, the Curragh. I now understood what had frightened my father on those nights when Jim O'Neill took him out to the river; it was his patrimony.

Epilogue

Freedom, a new life, resurrection from the dead. . . . What a glorious moment!

— Fyodor Dostoevsky, *The House of the Dead*

One evening in the last December of the twentieth century, I pulled down an old, blood-red Cassell's French–English dictionary from a bookcase in my mother's house. It was a battered volume, and the hardback cover, which had come loose at some point, was raggedly taped together. I looked up the word I was after and then, as I was shutting the book, noticed the following written (in English) in Joseph's handwriting on the inside of the back cover:

J. Dakak, Mersin, Turkey
No matter what we have suffered and what we have
undergone, we must try to forgive those who injured us and
only remember the lessons gained thereby.
Mrs Chiang Kay-Shek.

To my surprise, it was my father who was able to tell me something about this inscription: nearly forty years ago, in the course of a solemn discussion about Roger Casement and Terence MacSwiney, Joseph Dakak retrieved the Cassell's dictionary and pointed out the quotation to him. He was, my father said, suggesting a connection between himself and Casement and MacSwiney.

This suggestion – incidentally, Joseph wasn't aware that Kevin O'Neill's father was also an ex-internee – was intriguing but unconvincing. I couldn't see how his internment – the result of a misconceived business trip – bore comparison with the ideology-driven self-sacrifice of the two Irishmen except in the very broad sense of an undeserved personal calamity suffered at the hands of the British. That Joseph had constructed a heroic, blameless version of his past was not surprising, but it did leave me wondering about the lessons he claimed to have learned from his experiences. The fact was, neither Joseph nor Jim significantly changed their outlook and approach to life after the war. Joseph remained culturally assertive – assertive enough to complain to young Christians whom he overheard speaking Turkish that they were wasting their education at French-speaking schools – and socially conspicuous and entangled with the powers-that-be. He became the secretary of the Mersin Tourist Association, served as an honorary interpreter for two provincial governors, who were very good friends of his, and embarked on the ambitious modernization of the hotel. And he continued to keep silent on the subject of the Armenians. Back in Cork, meanwhile, Jim went back to his old life: providing for his family, poaching, working hard. His raging republican animus remained intact, and although he never rejoined or took part in active service, Jim regained his faith in the Irish Republican Army. Likewise, Joseph regained his faith in the possibilities of Turkish citizenship and, for that matter, life in Mersin – to which, I belatedly realized, he was as attached as Jim was to West Cork. In short, my grandfathers consigned their internments to the past and to silence.

Of course, pained taciturnity is typical of many survivors of the Second World War, but my grandfathers' case is complicated by the fact that, unlike the prisoner of war or the wounded combatant or the displaced civilian or even the interned enemy alien, Jim and

Joseph did not have the benefit of having suffered a universally creditable and understood misfortune of war; and the fall-out of the Curragh infighting meant that for a long time Jim was even deprived of recognition within republican circles. Denied conventional acknowledgement of what they'd been through, my grandfathers can only have been shaken in their faith in the narratives that conventionally explained the world. The effect of this disillusionment was not to radicalize them – Joseph remained a conservative bourgeois, Jim an orthodox republican – but, rather, to make them wary of unseen, undeclared forces of the State: paranoid, it might be said. This shared trait was one of the very few things the two men, who were opposites in almost every respect expect their authoritarianism, had in common.

But in one sense, their paranoia – evident from Joseph's testimony and Jim's perennial suspiciousness – was well-founded. I don't mean that after their release from internment they continued to be under the surveillance of the Special Branch or the Turkish secret police, although for all I know this was in fact the case; I mean that historical dark matter surrounded and manoeuvred my grandfathers more than they ever knew or, perhaps, could have known.

This is one way of saying that they were, of course, unlucky. They lived in extraordinarily hateful and hazardous places and times, in which men with powerful egos were especially exposed. I don't have any confidence that, in their shoes, I would have fared any better than they did, or indeed that a descendant of mine, looking back with the benefit of fifty years of hindsight and a comfortable chair, won't be able to point to defects in my apprehension of the world and make a case that I culpably failed to notice, or act or speak about, something that is perfectly clear to him; and no doubt my ghost will exclaim, 'No! You don't understand! That's not how it was at all!'

However scrupulous I have tried to be, I have unavoidably subjected my grandfathers, defenceless in their graves, to an unfair trial; and sometimes, thinking back to the hostility I felt towards them at the outset, I have even worried if I haven't been driven by a desire to lock them up in words as a punishment for the hurt silence which, I rightly or wrongly sensed, they'd bequeathed my parents. In the end, though, I like to think differently. Joseph and Jim may well be my prisoners, interned in death behind the bars of these paragraphs, but they are also escapees from the hush in which they were held by my family. And, no longer absent, they are, in spite of everything, and a little miraculously, no longer in the wrong. I now understand something about them, and understanding, as everybody knows, is the better part of forgiveness.

Which brings me to a story my aunt Amy once told me. Walking down the street one day, years after the war, her father caught sight a man with whom, because of some disagreement in the past, he was no longer on speaking terms. Joseph crossed the road and said to the man, 'Would you go to my funeral?' 'I would,' said the other. 'And I would go to your funeral, too,' Joseph replied, 'so why don't we talk now, before it's too late?' In his lack of rancour, Amy said, Papa was like Mandela.

It was an extravagant comparison, but I caught Amy's drift: for it was Nelson Mandela who pronounced that if he'd been bitter and angry about his imprisonment of 27 years, he would not have been a free man. It had been a puzzle to me how my grandfather was able to enjoy agreeable post-war relations with Olga Caton and William Rickards when he knew that they'd almost certainly informed on him to the British; but now I understand that Joseph knew, and by his notation in his dictionary sought to transmit, something important about the need to forgive and – here I am thinking of his death-bed request for absolution from his wife – to receive and stimulate forgiveness. Of course, a capacity for amnesty may be indistinguishable from a capacity for forgetfulness.

Amy's story is connected in my mind to something that happened on the last Sunday of Jim O'Neill's life. My grandfather was lying in his hospital bed when he was stunned to receive a visit from his brother Paddy. An All-Ireland hurling final was being played that day, and the two brothers, who had been bitterly estranged since their fight at Ardkitt all those years before, watched the game on television together in near-silence. However awkward, the fraternization was powerful. The following day, Jim rescinded his instruction to Terry that Paddy be barred from his funeral. 'Forget about that thing I told you,' he told his son. 'I'm sure,' Terry said, 'that he waited for his brother before he died.'

I claim the privilege, as a grandson, to dwell on my grandfathers in a way of my choosing. I could think of their lives as tragedies, as others have done, noting with sadness that the Toros Hotel, Joseph Dakak's monument, was finally sold on 30 December 1999 and as I write is being gutted to accommodate a multi-storey shopping mall. I could linger on the continuing hatred and violence in Turkey and Ireland, and link my grandfathers' shortcomings to the lethal infirmities in those countries' political cultures. But I would rather release Jim and Joseph from such gloominess and think of them at ease and home free. I want to see Joseph dancing with my grandmother in the mountains, she with her rectangular forehead and deep-set eyes and good cheekbones and sturdy ankles, he with a flower in his lapel, holding her neatly, moving her sure-footedly to the tunes of the Club orchestra, giving her his exclusive attention. I want to see Jim in his hat and suit walking in the country on an early, preternaturally hot summer's Sunday. The children are nowhere to be seen, Cora the greyhound is off chasing a bird, and my grandmother is holding her husband's hand. The couple are walking by the river when, to Eileen's horror and delight, Jim suddenly tears off his clothes and wades quickly into a freezing swimming pool and calls for her to join him. This is how I would like to think of my grandfathers, at liberty from mortal emotions.